ISBN 978-0-260-86329-4
PIBN 11193459

1 MONTH OF
FREE
READING

at

www.ForgottenBooks.com

By purchasing this book you are
eligible for one month membership to
ForgottenBooks.com, giving you
unlimited access to our entire
collection of over 1,000,000 titles via
our web site and mobile apps.

To claim your free month visit:
www.forgottenbooks.com/free1193459

English
Français
Deutsche
Italiano
Español
Português

www.forgottenbooks.com

Mythology Photography **Fiction**
Fishing Christianity **Art** Cooking
Essays Buddhism Freemasonry
Medicine **Biology** Music **Ancient
Egypt** Evolution Carpentry Physics
Dance Geology **Mathematics** Fitness
Shakespeare **Folklore** Yoga Marketing
Confidence Immortality Biographies
Poetry **Psychology** Witchcraft
Electronics Chemistry History **Law**
Accounting **Philosophy** Anthropology
Alchemy Drama Quantum Mechanics
Atheism Sexual Health **Ancient History**
Entrepreneurship Languages Sport
Paleontology Needlework Islam
Metaphysics Investment Archaeology
Parenting Statistics Criminology
Motivational

IERS WHAT NEXT!

BY

KATHERINE MAYO

BOSTON AND NEW YORK
HOUGHTON MIFFLIN COMPANY
The Riverside Press Cambridge
1934

The Riverside Press
CAMBRIDGE · MASSACHUSETTS
PRINTED IN THE U.S.A.

TO AMERICA'S DEAD AND HER HEAVILY DISABLED
IN THE WORLD WAR
IN COMBAT ON SEA AND LAND
MAY THEIR HONOUR ARISE AND SHINE
TO THEIR WIDOWS AND THEIR ORPHANS
MAY THE NATION TRULY ASSUME THEIR CARE

ERRATA

Page 108 — Number of men on compensation payroll, 1924 —
For 190,737 read 179,037

Page 167 — Total Expenditure, 1931–32 (France) — For $277,-
015,071 read $297,842,031

Total Expenditure, 1931–32 (France, Germany, and
United Kingdom) — For $803,115,795 read $823,-
942,755

Line 3 from bottom of page — For $57,500,000
read $36,692,245

Page 194 — Germany — Number of men pensioned in 1932 —
For 900,000 read 820,403

FOREWORD

IN PRESENTING the following studies, it is the pleasantest of privileges to acknowledge those courtesies and that helpfulness that on the part of each Government concerned has forwarded my work.

To Monsieur de Fleuriau, Ambassador of France to Great Britain, to Monsieur A. Berthod, French Minister of Pensions, and to Monsieur Bernard d'Été, Directeur du Contrôle, my debt is great.

The ready responsiveness that at the French Ministry of Pensions met my first requests for information with a fullness that one would scarcely have ventured to ask has been continued in careful and swift replies to the many questions that, in the interest of accuracy, I have since put. Such co-operation is beyond praise.

As to Germany, the initial material was gathered there before the accession of the present Government and was then much facilitated by the Ministry of Labour, in whose province it lies.

In Italy, the generosity of His Excellency the Premier, and after him of Signor Guido Jung, Minister of Finance, opened wide all doors to an enquiry so persistent that it must have overtaxed the endurance of any ordinary patience. Every advantage was put freely at my disposal, and the spirit of the many departmental heads and departmental officials whose assistance was involved was such as to tempt one to forget the burden one was laying upon their shoulders. This excellent and understanding

aid has been steadily continued since and with all liberality.

Turning to England, it is not easy to express the gratitude that is due to the Minister of Pensions, Major the
Honourable George Tryon, M.P., and to Sir George
Chrystal, Secretary to the Ministry since its beginning.
Their kindness has been limitless. To Sir Adair Hore,
and to Colonel Sir Lisle Webb, Director-General of Medical Services of the Ministry, warm appreciation also
must be expressed. Field Marshal Sir Claud Jacob, and
Colonel G. R. Crosfield, long identified with ex-service
men's interests, Major-General Sir Frederick Maurice,
Chairman of the British Legion, the Honourable Sir
Arthur Stanley, Chairman of the British Red Cross, and
Captain Ian Fraser, Chairman of St. Dunstan's, have all
and most kindly aided my search for facts in their several
fields; the latter three have been so good as to ensure the
accuracy of the passages relating to their work.

Cordial thanks are due, too, to the Duchess of Atholl
and to Viscount and Viscountess Astor for truly friendly
offices of great value. And to Mr. Lint-Smith, of the London *Times*, as well as to Mr. Douglas Crawford, of the
London *Daily Mail*, I owe a lasting debt for important
help.

Of the English section of this book, in its dealings with
the work of the Ministry of Pensions, I am glad to be able
to say that, in respect of statement of fact and figures,
although not in respect of statement of opinion, it has
had, as it stands, the advantage of revision by the Ministry of Pensions.

The same is true regarding the Italian and the French

sections. As they appear here, so, for facts and for figures, they have passed examination by official authority, although in matters of opinion all responsibility is mine.

With respect to Germany, the manuscript, as it now is, was checked by the Ministry of Labour in August, 1933. But the delays occasioned by Germany's internal changes during the past year have made co-operation and amplification difficult, and leave, small as this section is, a possibility of the creeping-in of error which, in the sections dealing with the three other countries, scarcely exists.

Turning to America: As to my third and fourth chapters, I am under obligation to Dr. William H. Glasson for his leave to make full use, as I have done, of his book, *Federal Military Pensions in the United States* (Oxford University Press, 1918). As to the American section beyond that stage, a helpfulness as liberal as that of the European countries has on all sides met my enquiry after facts. But there the parallel ends. I have diligently tried to attain correctness of statement, and official revision, if requested, would not be refused. But since in America and America alone the matter of ex-service men's benefits is a political issue, I have, though with regret, refrained from asking an official check of the manuscript, in order that no other person may be charged with any measure of responsibility for so plain a story as is here set down.

Finally, I thankfully emphasize my constant debt to my friend and collaborator of many years, Miss M. Moyca Newell, who has shared equally in this task and whose wisdom, skill, acute judgment and tireless energy have doubled my power.

K. M.

CONTENTS

CONTENTS

CONTENTS

xiii

CONTENTS

CONTENTS

CONTENTS

SOLDIERS WHAT NEXT!
UNITED STATES OF AMERICA

SOLDIERS WHAT NEXT!

UNITED STATES OF AMERICA

CHAPTER I

THE FLAME WE QUENCHED

ONCE there was a young king called Solomon, to whom
his Maker appeared in a dream by night, saying: 'Ask
what I shall give thee.' And Solomon replied:

'O Lord my God... I am but a little child... in the
midst of thy people... that cannot be numbered nor
counted for multitude. Give therefore thy servant an
understanding heart.'

Then came the answer: 'Because thou hast asked this
thing and hast not asked... riches for thyself... I have
given thee a wise and an understanding heart.... And I
have also given thee that which thou hast not asked, both
riches and honour.'

Once there was a people great in number, great in
riches, and by reason of its riches great in honour amongst
nations. But, because that people had not an understanding heart, both its riches and its honour that rested
on riches vanished in a day, like a wraith of smoke.

Now, of all the precious secrets hidden from this people,
none was more precious nor more deeply hidden than
this: The spiritual essence of its young men. So that

when of a sudden it chose to uproot its young men by millions, to fling them across an ocean into a strange land to fight a war, and thence, after many months of life and death, to snatch them home again, it expected them to snap from the ships' gangplanks straight into their old sockets, there to start revolving their old round, as if nothing whatever had intervened.

And when the impossible failed to occur, this people bleated, in simplicity as sincere as its disappointment: 'What *can* be the matter with our Overseas boys!'

Nothing was the matter with the Overseas boys. They came home finer than they went, bringing with them that which, had it been fittingly received, would have swept the nation to a level above its dreams. And just because of that — just because the nation's dreams reached no such height — the nation turned their gifts away.

If, then, there is blame to be born for the monstrous desert of spiritual loss that lies between the American Army in France and the Bonus Army in Washington, that blame lies at the door of the American people. For they, when their home-coming sons would have blessed them, changed blessing into bitterness, riches into poverty, honour into degradation, and all by their lack of the understanding heart.

Many books have been written about the squalor and the baseness of war — written by men who speak with the authority of experience. But theirs was not the only insight that the War produced. There was also the insight acquired by those women to whom was granted the privilege of serving with troops Overseas. And of this perhaps a woman may speak without undue presumption.

4

America declared war on the sixth of April, 1917. Two months later came the first registration of the draft. Out of three drafts, we selected and inducted into our Army over 2,800,000 men. Our total number of inductions reached 4,000,000. So, although the Navy was a volunteer force, almost three quarters of our entire World War Army consisted, not of volunteers, but of men who were drafted.

And a draft is a dragnet that sweeps up the fish, willing or not, to be picked according to physical fitness, with little enough regard to any other distinction.

All conditions of men, therefore, made up the enlisted ranks — a cross-section of our social structure; and since that structure is broadest at the base, the Army reflected the characteristic.

Moreover, the cross-section was nation-wide. It spoke in the accents of Texas, Wisconsin, Nevada, of Alabama, New Jersey, Maine. Men who at home were almost foreigners, each to each, since the width of a continent separated their habitats, now mingled, equally adrift in a world strange to all alike. All alike were subjected to abnormal conditions and unheard-of strains. All alike were deprived of — or freed from — whatever compulsion or support they normally drew from surrounding society.

In other words, they were stripped so close to the core of their souls that one saw, not seldom, the stuff those souls were made of. And hundreds of American women who knew them Overseas affirm that the stuff was good — good.

No wonder the women loved their work, rough as it was, often dangerous and always taxing their strength as

never it was taxed before. Every effort they put forth
brought its quick and amazing reward. They discovered
in themselves, if ever they had time to think of themselves, reserves and resources till then unguessed and
endurance equal to all demands. With power and with
satisfaction they *lived*.

And the base of it all was the innate decency of that
dragnetted draft army that they served.

Some sculpins came in the catch and an occasional
shark. Our police said that we brought the Old World a
present of the finest extant professionals in crime; and
our police had reason to know whereof they spoke. But
the women saw little, almost nothing, of that; and the
fact in itself is of prime significance. For the distance between a people whose men of all classes by instinct respect
their women and a people without that trait is a long
road to go.

This seems, perhaps, a small thing, but was it really
small? In eight months spent Overseas in the company
of our private soldiers, not once did I hear from an American doughboy a phrase coarse in spirit, or an oath. And
such, from American women, was the general report. 'Cut
it out! There's a lady inside' — one did hear things like
that, but never the speech to be hushed.

It was amazing how thoughtful they were of all women
— of any woman who had come to their help. Their
deference, their respect, their welcome, their unquestion-
ing faith and confidence, for middle-aged and young alike.
I have seen young Kansan farmers, the roar of the guns
of the Saint Mihiel drive heavy in the air, working like
mad to 'rig up a room for Mother' in a house whose roof

6

they had just blown off. Our advance had pushed on beyond, leaving Kansas to hold this village it had wrecked. Wrecked indeed! But here was a fragment of upstanding wall — an angle that, with the aid of stretched blankets, could make a shelter. Somehow, in the hour they had been there, they had stirred up a species of whitewash. Now with feverish haste they were daubing those splinters of walls. They had snatched together a bunch of flowers from the wreck of a garden. And the flowers and the whitewash and the blankets were to 'make things nice for Mother, for she'll sure soon be here now.'

Nor was she long — their beloved Mother Fitzgerald — who always managed, in some felonious way, to receive no contrary orders and to surmount all physical obstacles between her and 'her boys' on the war-path whenever they paused. Before the whitewash was dried, up she came, with her chocolate-boiler and her biscuit tins and her cartons of cigarettes and her triumphant smile, perched beside the driver of an ammunition truck, who stopped its rolling long enough to drop her and her belongings into Kansas's outstretched arms.

Those prairie farmer boys were weary to the point of exhaustion. They had been marching and fighting for three days. Once they lay down they would sleep like wooden idols. But the moment the stop came, to 'rig up a nice place for Mother' was their first thought.

It would be as easy as pleasant to heap up remembered incidents illustrating in variety the sheer good-heartedness of our rank and file as known to the women of the A.E.F.[1] But the women knew things other than that; for

[1] American Expeditionary Force — the official name of the Overseas Army.

example, the physical explosions, the explosions of
nerves, with all their phenomena, that war can induce.
Yet, if confidences of sorry secrets were brought to them,
it was all for one reason: the boy who so bared his heart
was sick at heart because, having emerged from his
tempest, he felt suddenly miserable in his own company —
cut off from his inner anchorage, having offended against
the faith of a mother or a sweetheart in the far-away
home. He took out their pictures, as he talked — snap-
shots, mostly, cracked and dulled with much handling —
and soon, perhaps, to be blotted out with his blood.

'The best woman in the world,' he called his mother,
and that mother, even more than 'the truest, bravest,
girl in the world,' dwelt in his mind. Always he knew that
both mother and girl were following him hourly with their
thoughts, surrounding him with their prayers.

The idea of death had changed from a vague abstraction belonging to the far and unconsidered future to the
master reality of the hour. Whether he had gone through
actual battle — had been wounded — had seen men close
beside him die; whether he awaited in replacement camp
the killing of that unknown comrade whose place he must
fill; or whether he was loading trucks in S.O.S., just
watching the khaki push past on its way to its fate,
whatever his mental calibre, whatever his old-time level,
now he caught flashes of light that, had they been continuous, had they been more than flashes, he probably
could not have borne.

But nothing in all his previous existence had been of
such moment to his spiritual nature or had approached
their transfiguring power.

THE FLAME WE QUENCHED

'If I live to get home there are some things I want to do different' — this he said with painful reserve, yet with endless repetition that made clear the universality of the thought. 'If ever I get home I want to live a little different than I used to. Guess I didn't do much thinking in those days. But after this — I'd like to *do* something for the country, if I can.'

'God's Own Country,' he called America then, speaking shyly, under his breath — and the words so spoken meant no foolish brag.

After Armistice one might have expected a change. But such change as came was only an intensification. Homesickness set in with violence; impatience of what now seemed useless detention in exile. Yet not the schoolboy homesickness bred of mere absence; not impatience for mere resumption of old pleasures. Rather it was a deep longing for the country they had come to revere, and for those few out of all the world who, they felt, would understand.

Mother would understand. 'The bravest girl' would understand. Both would be angels of welcoming help — for did not both already live in that higher air that their boy now longed to breathe?

Not everyone — not even the majority, perhaps — actually formed such phrases, even to himself. But the substance was there, and the greater part of them needed only a touch to release the power of their new manhood.

They ached, now, to give, not to get. They were young, they were generous-hearted. They had seen divine flame.

A new and more glorious America — an America done with cheap ideals, with shams and ignoble values — an

9

America exalting, not money and show, not material things, but honour, generosity, cleanness, courage — an America growing always more worthy of the deaths of those who had died for her, in France.

Such was the America toward which the crowded transports ploughed their homeward way across the ocean.

With hearts big in their throats they saw the land line rise in the West. However they had forecast it, the sight itself brought an emotion that nothing in their former lives could match — an emotion past either power or desire to put into speech.

'God's Own Country!' *Their* Country!

If, in that hour, they could have heard a good marching tune and the voice of one real leader — if they had found awaiting them a People with an Understanding Heart — those two millions of home-coming men, spread broadcast through every community in the land, would have taken their country on their strong young shoulders and carried it to unimagined heights.

CHAPTER II

E CASE AGAINST THE PEOPLE

what did happen?

lization over, the men scattered to their homes.
' Home at last! How big you've grown! You
had *such* interesting experiences! We're crazy
ow many Bosches did you kill? You'll have
ll about everything. The Joneses are coming in
this evening. He plays a very good game.
much. Pity we can't have him without her!
urse... How many Bosches did you say you
Oh, yes, that's true — you said you didn't
d you get my letter about our trip to Atlantic
was very interesting — all so different — the
ilk and all! And Mrs. Bennett was there with
stopping at the same hotel. Wasn't that strange
:e are so many hotels in Atlantic City! You
sister married your cousin Joseph's stepson.
quite pleasant. I never met him before. Well —
' will be waiting to see you, Jimmy. How many
- oh, yes, of course — I remember! Well —
to have you back! So *interesting* to hear how
lly were in France! You see, I had to give up
:ead the papers about it. It took so much time,
:tails were so hard to understand, and I've been
:h my committees and my social duties and all —
"Now I'll just leave it alone till Jimmy comes
imy'll tell us everything." '

As for Jimmy's wife, Jimmy's little, pretty new wife who couldn't bear a draught across her bedroom at night — she *so* wanted a big new motor, *so* hoped Jimmy would get down quickly into business, now, and make up for lost time. She *so* hated to think how far ahead of him men had got who stayed at home! And now, it would be *so* nice having Jimmy back. There was really such a lot going on, dinners and bridge and movies and all! And as for the things Jimmy said to her, in the once or twice he tried to speak, she couldn't imagine what he meant. The home town, surely, was good enough for anyone. Why, a clever man like Jimmy could get rich here by the time he was forty, if he'd only keep his wits alive, and *work.*

'Jimmy won't talk about the War!' 'No, none of the boys will. You see, it was all so very disagreeable, of course. They want to forget it as quickly as they can,' said God's Own People, one to the other.

How could Jimmy talk about the War? Should he first write a glossary, a history, a geography, a psychology to define his terms and subject? If he did, they wouldn't read it, or, reading, would not understand. They assured him that We Won the War, to be sure, and they took his affronted intelligence and his outraged sportsmanship for embarrassed gratification and pride.

To them, even as they spoke, the War itself was last year's game and khaki out of fashion. Their well-meant questions were so perfunctory that their attention could scarcely survive one serious answer. The winds of war had swept over them, but so briefly as to stir only their surface. The centre of the storm was at once so remote and so strange that their imaginations collapsed. Nor was it, perhaps, in human power to realize the truth except by means of sight and touch. For all the pictures of shell-craters and tree-stumps and shattered cities that had filled the press, the scene itself seemed utterly new to those who first saw the front after the guns were stilled.

And one recalls the reported refusal of Mr. Wilson to visit the battle-fields during his sojourn in Paris lest his mind be stirred from its calm by a sight of the facts of war.

The War is over! Let's do the next thing now. Life is practical. Business is practical. Politics are practical. Compromise is practical. Money talks. 'Ideals?' 'Public duty?' 'World brotherhood?' Well enough, dear boy, as recruiting patter! *But*, the War is over! Charity begins at home. Get down to brass tacks, or you'll be left behind the procession, to swallow other folks' dust.

'What *is* the matter with this Overseas lot!' groaned employers, for a year to come. 'Why can't they settle into harness and carry on? Why are their minds forty per cent on the job and the other sixty God knows where? They aren't worth their salt!'

But said Jimmy — and it was curious how often he chose just this phrase — said Jimmy, to such as could understand, 'What is the matter with our people? *Their eyes are so dead!*'

And he hid things away in his own heart — sacred things, precious things that he could not bear the daws to peck at.

If America had been longer in the War, perhaps it

13

would not have happened. The Angel of Death, passing from door to door, hovering always near, would have wrought a change. 'Sacrifices' of sugar and gasoline and the purchase of Liberty bonds might have ceased to seem the sort of thing to which that word applies. Our people might have begun to think beyond the day, beyond their own span of earth's life, even as the peoples of other lands were driven to think, who lived for years within the glare of the central flames.

Nor did our Overseas men themselves know the pull and strain of the War as the veteran armies knew it. Else, perhaps, their dreams might have taken deeper root — might have gathered strength to withstand the shock of awakening.

As it was, coming home from a distance long in leagues, but infinitely longer in spiritual experience, they looked at Home with eyes holding a new question and a new wistfulness.

What did they see? God help us all, we *are* a people amongst His peoples. We *do* love Right and Justice, Honour, Courage, Grace. But let us face the truth. What did they see?

They saw their own dearest untouched at heart by events that, for them, had changed the world; eager only to 'reabsorb' their returning sons in the daily round of the old life; eager only to see them 'make up for lost time,' on the road to the thing they still call 'Success.'

They saw the nation at large passionately 'success'-hunting — hunting under its own hoofs, waxing fat and grunting, 'Big, big, big!'

'Quick, quick, quick! This is the job worth doing! Big,

14

big, big!' squealed the nation, its snout in the rich black mess. 'Come help us grub!'

'Why should we?' they asked, sick at the sight.

Squealed the nation, annoyed by their dull delay: 'Money, money, money! Shoulders all together! Quick, quick, quick! Keep the others out of the trough!'

Then came the presidential campaign. God's Own Country would appoint a new High Priest. It called its sons to do their part in the solemn task. And it offered them a choice — a choice between Harding and Cox.

It all hurt — Heavens! how it hurt! How lost they felt — how dazed, bleak, solitary!

And still, 'They won't work!' the nation repeated, marvelling.

But if, in those days, one strong leader had arisen to call out to them:

'Come work twenty-five hours a day, with no pay, no thanks, plenty of hardships and no renown — come work yourselves to an unknown death, not for yourselves, but for the sake of the true America and the Light that Shone Over the Top' — they would have rushed to enlist.

Not every one of them, of course. Some were born without much means for thought, a few were born slackers, more were born sluggards, and more again soon lost the divine glow under the grey cynicism born of disillusionment. But a great army remained.

Nine years passed.

At the end thereof, without one creak of warning audible to the general ear, over went the trough, upside-down and empty, with a Crash that echoed around the world.

Riches vanished. Honours vanished. In the space of a single day Ruin and Fear took their place. Surely this was the moment, at last, for the great army that had dreamed dreams! ....

Time passed. The dark sky blackened. The nation staggered under blow after blow, faint from weakness and exhaustion — but her army of dreamers never appeared. For she the nation had broken their dream, mocked their vision, refused their gift. And now, in their place, named by their name, prowled a pack of ravening wolves, snarling at her heels to pull her down.

The A.E.F. had become the Bonus Army! The American Legion howled for the nation's blood!

This was the tale we heard.

Could it possibly be true? No one who knew our boys in France could or would accept it as true without proof, and proof to the hilt.

If so foul a miracle had indeed occurred, then what had brought it about? Was it one of the automatic sequels of War? Did the other belligerent nations exhibit the same phenomenon? Or must we confess our rank and file the poorest moral stuff in the civilized world?

On the spiritual side we had indeed and bitterly failed them when they came home to us. But that failure was not of intention. How could we offer them what we had not — an understanding heart?

But on the other, the material side, did we do for them less than we should? Were we niggardly in providing for their physical needs? Ungenerous in recognizing their compensatory dues? Did we give them, on that score too, a right to accuse us? The answer seemed well worth

16

seeking, whether for love of the good days gone, or for hope of amends to-come.

So I who now write went forth to seek that answer, beginning first abroad, the better to focus the picture of home.

I went to France, to Germany, to Italy and England, in each capital addressing myself first to the Government, then to the ex-service organizations, enquiring as to the outline of the pension system applying to the ex-service men of the World War, its methods and standards; as to the ex-service organizations and their relation to Government; and as to the part played by such bodies in the life of the nation.

Greater courtesy could not be imagined, more liberal help, facilities, co-operation, could not be desired than that with which each Government met the appeal for light.

On my return to America, after digesting the material gathered abroad, I went to the original sources in Washington for information about our own work for ex-service men. What I found there is presented in the first section of this book. The story of the European countries follows it.

CHAPTER III

THE BED WE MADE

IN ORDER, however, to understand America's present War-pension system, it is necessary, first, to dig down a bit and uncover its roots in the past. The nature of that growth, prior to the World War, gives food for thought rather than for pride. It was the gradual work of tricksters playing upon ignorance to evoke and organize the meaner mind.

No element of comparable diligence fought on the other side. Of the men of the Northern Army who served in the Civil War, the majority, it is alleged, had neither part nor interest in its outgrowth, the war upon the Treasury. But the fact remains that they allowed that war to be waged in the name of their famous ex-service organization, the Grand Army of the Republic. And if they protested, their protest was too faint, too half-hearted, too theoretical to make its mark. Such few champions of decency as now and again stood forth found no public support behind them. To fight till they built that support was, in general, beyond their calibre.

Meantime, the old Haitian maxim, *L'État, c'est voler* ('Statecraft is the art of stealing'), seemed good enough doctrine for a large and complaisant section of our people.

One shining example we had of the opposite type of citizenship — of the fearless patriot militant who fights

18

alone when conscience drives. Grover Cleveland, first Democratic President since the Civil War, in his first term as President (1885–89) vigorously employed both his veto power and his gift of trenchant speech against the hordes of pension racketeers then working the country. He vetoed, in that period, 228 private pension bills introduced by Congressmen on behalf of their constituents — vetoed them with biting comment, exposing some as proposals to subsidize for life men who were deserters from the army, subjects less for pension than for prison. In particular he vetoed the Dependant Pension Bill.

This measure proposed an annuity for all men who had served ninety days in the Northern Army, who had been honourably discharged, and who now, twenty-two years after the close of the war, found themselves short of money and 'suffering from mental or physical disability, not the result of their own vicious habits or gross carelessness,' to a degree rendering them unable to earn a living. Whether or not the disability in question was in any way connected with war service was in no wise to affect the claim.

In other words, every man who had worn the Northern uniform for three months and who had quitted it without disgrace was to acquire thereby a health and accident insurance policy payable by the rest of the Nation, and good for the rest of his life if he could show a need for the money.

Certain Democratic Senators and Congressmen — men of his own party — upheld Mr. Cleveland's hands when he refused to sanction this bill. But it was a Democratic House Committee that recommended its passage over the President's veto. And the vote by which that course was rejected [1] — 175 yeas to 125 nays — was too close to warrant the confidence of the Administration.

The *New York Times*, the New York *Nation* and many other journals supported Mr. Cleveland's action. But the *National Tribune*, unofficial organ of the Grand Army of the Republic, attacked him with venom. And prominent members of the G.A.R., discarding respect for the Presidential office, publicly warned Mr. Cleveland to keep his distance from the city of St. Louis during the impending Annual Convention of the G.A.R., lest that body of ex-soldier patriots battering at the doors of the Treasury offer open affront to the Head of the Nation.

And when, in June of the following year, the Republican Convention met to lay out its course for the coming Presidential campaign, it hastened, in its platform, to capitalize the situation. Pointing to the presence of 'an overflowing treasury,' 'We denounce,' it declared, 'the hostile spirit shown by President Cleveland in his numerous vetoes of measures for pension relief.'

Throughout the political battles of the year, Republican policy held that torch steadily aloft until the taking of the ballot that denied Mr. Cleveland re-election. If his defeat was not due to the Civil War ex-service vote, it was certainly no fault either of the Republican campaign managers or of those of the Grand Army of the Republic.

With the inauguration of Mr. Cleveland's successor, a new day dawned. Whether or not President Harrison literally instructed Corporal Tanner, his first Commissioner of Pensions and a former pensions claims agent, to

[1] February 24, 1887. A two-thirds affirmative vote is necessary for passage over the President's veto.

'be liberal with the boys'; whether or not Corporal Tanner jubilantly responded with a pledge to 'drive a six-mule team through the Treasury,' these words commonly credited to President and to Corporal, chimed with the deeds that followed. Before he had been four months in office, Corporal Tanner, disbursing retroactive favours, was raising pension awards in individual favoured cases to the number of from seven to eight thousand a week — until the Secretary of the Interior remonstrated that a continuance meant swift ruin to Government resources.

Congress, meantime, not to be outdone, had also laboured to acquire merit. On June 27, 1890, it had the satisfaction of witnessing President Harrison's blessing on a new-born offspring of its brain — a pension bill so much more 'liberal' than that which President Cleveland had vetoed because of its extravagance that the G.A.R. lobbyists may have found it embarrassing. What if, in its sudden broad leap, it had robbed them of their job, leaving them nothing to lobby for? Did their hearts misgive them when the G.A.R. officials reported of it, to their organization's next annual convention: 'It is the most liberal pension measure ever passed by any legislative body in the world and will place upon the rolls all of the survivors of the war whose conditions of health are not practically perfect'?[1]

The number of men who served in the Northern Army and Navy during the Civil War is estimated as approxi-

[1] It was this enactment of June 27, 1890, that, for example, put military pensions within the lawful right of any woman who at any time should marry an ex-service man of the Civil War and survive him, no matter what occasioned his demise. The Civil War was then a quarter-century past. But another quarter-century would go by before the last girl-child was born who would qualify for the Civil War-widow's pension under that 'liberality.'

mately 2,400,000 — about one to every ten inhabitants
of the Northern States. The dead from wounds, disease,
and accidents were officially given as 359,528. This seems
to suggest that a total of slightly over 2,000,000 ex-service
men of the Northern Army, less such mortality as the
intervening quarter-century may have brought, were
presented on June 27, 1890, with paid-up accident and
sickness insurance policies good for the rest of their days
on earth and all the vicissitudes thereof.

No longer were they required to show need of largess.
The new 'liberalizations' had killed that clause. No
longer were they asked to show disability 'to a degree
rendering them unable to earn a living.' If they could
show disability to earn an entire livelihood by *manual
labour*, that sufficed. And, save for the vicious-habits
clause, it mattered not at all when or how the disability
was incurred.

To examine President Harrison's measure farther would
be to uncover no offset of quality finer than that of a politicians' bargain struck with the leaders of a supposedly
deliverable vote, at the cost of the ever-unorganized and
therefore ever politically friendless majority of the American people.

Mr. Cleveland, succeeding Mr. Harrison in the Presidency and aided by a staunch Pension Commissioner,
resumed his old and unpopular course, administering the
law with whatever decency could be educed under it.
President McKinley, in 1898 following Mr. Cleveland,
appointed one of the best Pension Commissioners who
had ever held office, Mr. Henry Clay Evans of Tennessee,
a just man and fearless. This administration was detested

by the element that, gathered in the G.A.R. Convention of 1901, applauded the speech of their fellow-member, General Daniel E. Sickles.

General Sickles, knowing his audience well, arose before it to denounce Commissioner Evans's policy as 'conceived in a desire to turn money back into the Treasury that belongs to you and me, my comrades, a policy born of a cringing desire to serve taxpayers and earn newspaper applause by reducing expenditures, a mean, stingy, grinding policy, and unworthy of a great and generous government and a noble and grateful people.' [1]

Resentment, so evoked and fanned, grew in volume and bitterness as Mr. Evans pursued his unflinching course. But it beat in vain against President McKinley's loyalty to his subordinate. Then came President McKinley's assassination; whereupon G.A.R. officials, freed from their strong observer, assembled in Washington, there to set up on their own initiative and authority an 'investigation' of the murdered President's administration of pension affairs. Their investigation completed, they drafted a report condemnatory of the record; condemnatory, also, of Commissioner Evans, signifying their desire for his head. These findings, this fiat — for such it practically was — they handed to President Theodore Roosevelt, who from the Vice-Presidency had succeeded to the Executive Chair.

Mr. Evans forthwith laid his resignation at the President's disposal. President Roosevelt accepted the resignation.

Exhilarated by success so spectacular, the G.A.R. leaders now planned fresh advances. By 1904 so much ground

[1] *Journal of the Thirty-Fifth National Encampment*, G.A.R., 1901, p. 198.

had been gained that at word of command they could concentrate upon Washington a well-synchronized fire of many calibres and ranges. What they now demanded — for they no longer asked — was more than even the new Commissioner of Pensions dared advocate. But the year was again the year of a presidential campaign — an ill time to defy organizations. Therefore came compromise. By means of Executive Order Number 78, issued by President Roosevelt, 'the most liberal pension measure in the world' was now enriched with still wider liberality, conceding to the most-favoured class this further benefit:

All Civil War ex-service men, upon reaching their sixty-second year, regardless of physical condition, whether robust or ailing, regardless of financial condition, whether rich or poor, were accounted eligible to pension. At the ages of sixty-five, sixty-eight, and seventy, the rate progressively increased. Only two conditions attached; ninety days' service, no matter how spent; and an honourable discharge from the Federal Army. This new executive order operated as such until 1907, when, still in Mr. Roosevelt's administration, it became full statutory law.

Thus the measure approved by President Harrison on June 27, 1890, curb-bitted by President Cleveland in the next administration, corn-fed by amendments pledged in the Republican campaign of 1900, curbed again by Commissioner Evans under President McKinley, and finally by President Roosevelt turned loose in the pasture with a slap on the haunch — that Act of June 27, 1890, became the most costly single military pension law known to any country in pre-World War history. Up to the end of the fiscal year of 1907 it alone had cost America $3,389,-

000,000, of which amount a heavy percentage was due to President Roosevelt's Executive Order Number 78.

In the fiscal years 1866 to 1917, inclusive, the country paid more than $4,917,000,000 to Civil War pensioners and their dependants without condition of disablement or death connected with war service.

Our total War-pension expenditure during that period, aside from administration costs, and reckoning only benefits disbursed to ex-service men and their dependants, was over $5,250,000,000. It included payments of over $200,000,000 on account of wars other than the Civil War. It came to birth in an ever-spawning hodge-podge of laws and amendments of laws flung together without thought, system, or cause other than the sporadic impulses of miscellaneous individuals to lay hold on the Nation's property for their own private ends.

For the purpose of this writing it has seemed sufficient not to catalogue that illogical chaos, but, instead, to follow one specimen measure through some years of its career, since the larger may be judged from the less.

It may, however, be useful to bestow a second glance on the special industry in private pension bills, remembering that each one of these undertakings represents a Congressman's favour to some single beneficiary who is thereby granted advantages in excess of those open to other citizens in the same circumstances and with the same rights but without Congressional friends.

In the course of Mr. Cleveland's second tenure of the Presidency (1893–97), despite his vigilance, 497 private bills were enacted. In President McKinley's time (1897–1901) the number rose to 2085. Then came Mr. Roose-

velt's Presidency, 1901–09, during which the number of
these extra-legal benefits conferred upon protégés of
Senators and Representatives increased to 18,156. Mr.
Roosevelt's successor, Mr. Taft, in his single term in the
Presidency, signed 15,999 such bills. President Wilson
took office in 1913. Thence until 1917, the year of America's entry into the World War, 10,946 private pension
measures became law.

The passage of private pension measures has become an
undisputed perquisite of the members of both Houses,
attained by reciprocal courtesy, like the giving out of
local patronage. It has had, as a rule, nothing to do with
the merits of any given case, nor has it involved any examination of the adequacy or inadequacy of those provisions with which pensioners in general must be content.
An hour with the *Congressional Record* will show that at
any period during the present century, the main visible
activity of not a few of our law-makers has been the
presentation of private pension bills. Such business, however, has devoured less Congressional time than might
be supposed. Shied through some sessions, thousands in
a single day, at a speed of two to three a minute, at other
times these friendship's tokens, clotted together in lumps,
have been heaped on omnibus bills and so carted off by
wholesale.

Taking all together — all our types of War-pension
legislation and the wire-works behind them, up to the
opening of the World War — little or nothing can honestly
be said in defence of their wide excursions away from the
field of war-disablement to create a parasitic, specially
privileged civilian class within our supposed democracy.

26

Now, where shall the blame be laid? Scarcely upon the country as a whole, for, with few exceptions, Northerners alone profited by these excesses; and, however sportsmanlike the South in accepting the fate of the vanquished, it could hardly be suspected of originating measures, through the whole post-rebellion half-century, to strip its own meagre purse for further fattening of the victors.

Was it the fault of the victors themselves, the ex-service men of the North? To suggest such a matter would be terribly to arraign the whole Northern people; for one out of every ten had entered the armed service, and a proportion so heavy must implicate the remainder.

Was it, then, the fault of that purely American product, the pension claims agents, they who, from frail beginnings soon after the War of 1812, had by 1867 so built up their trade that a law-book could be hurled at their heads like Saint Dunstan's inkpot at the Devil — in a hope to force them 'to earn some portion of their bread by honest toil, where honest men will not be insulted by their presence nor public virtue further interfered with by their running at large.' [1]

---

[1] Henry Clay Harmon, *A Manual of the Pension Laws of the United States of America*, W. H. and O. H. Morrison, Washington, 1862, p. x. Mr. Harmon was Chief of the bureau for investigation of frauds, in the United States Treasury.

CHAPTER IV

LEMON

Pensions claims agents 'running at large' had certainly much to answer for in the breakdown of 'public virtue' that made possible the story just outlined — so much that, in order to understand both that story and the story to come, it is necessary to pause here and give the claims agent his due.

Pension claims agents were private adventurers. Their habit was to seek out persons in whose name, by hook or by crook — no matter how crooked — application might be made for pensions on grounds of war service. They combed and swept and sifted the country to find such persons. They crooned to them, when found, the old incantation of the quack-medicine vendor — 'no cure no pay.' 'It will cost you nothing if we don't get your money for you, and only ten dollars if we do. Come on, Comrade, you can't lose.'

The law of the land had established their right to that ten dollars — an 'attorney's fee.' On so firm a foundation well might they build.

Many an ex-service man who knew his 'claim' ridiculous, yet who somewhat shamefacedly allowed it to be made, was presently amazed to find it granted. Half-eagles, flocking into the pockets of the agents, spurred them to further effort on larger scales. And ever as they worked the law of the moment, the provident creatures fanned sentiment for fresh legislation of wider reach that should open new game for their hunting.

28

Year by year, as the industry grew, it developed its technique and its masters. Some of these, to speed their chase, set up newspapers of sorts in whose pages appeared such harrowing expositions of the ex-soldiers' claims upon the substantial gratitude of the Nation, such blasting denunciation of the Nation's failure to respond, such luscious suggestions of golden hoards bursting the vaults of the Treasury, that, bit by bit, the rank and file of the G.A.R. came to believe themselves a band of martyrs in a cruel and apostate world.

The most effective organ of this propaganda, the *National Tribune*, first appeared in October, 1877.[1] Printed in Washington, it represented the most successful of all the claims agents — George E. Lemon. Among its earliest specific enterprises was advocacy of new legislation in connection with the War of 1812. In this advocacy the other claims agents joined, with the result that in the following year, by heavy majorities, Congress passed a law admitting to pension any man who had served for two weeks, or even in a single engagement, in a war now sixty-three years past. The new law[2] required in proof of claim neither record of that service nor of honourable discharge. Widows of such men were also pensioned without limit as to the date of their marriage — by which bounty many a one was to profit whose mother was a baby when the war of 1812 finished its course. In less than eight months after the taking-effect of the measure, 25,000 new claims were presented under it, only one-

[1] The *National Tribune*, still published, now gives special voice to the lobby of the Spanish War ex-service men's organization.
[2] Act of March 9, 1878.

seventh of which were lodged on behalf of alleged ex-
service survivors. These claims represented the thrift of
the agents in squeezing last drops from a sponge already
wrung nearly dry.[1]

A synchronous scheme of Mr. Lemon and his fellow-
operators, he in his *National Tribune*, they in their respective organs, was the creation of pressure for an Arrears of
Pension Act. And now that the pasturage of 1812, long
growing thin, was finally gnawed into the ground, they
could move in force for further feeding. Great numbers
of men, they reflected, who had served in the Civil War
had never yet asked for pensions. If a law could be put
through, making all Civil War pensions payable as from
the date of the pensioner's discharge from service, or from
his death, rather than from his or his heirs' application; and
if by that law all time-limit could be removed with regard
to the filing and acceptance of claims, a great new feast
would thereby open. Under such a law, properly worked,
arrears checks running into real figures would rain over
the face of the wide North country; and the size and fame
thereof would stimulate new business for claims agents
among the wide ranks of those comfortable folk whom
small annuities had failed to interest.

Energy and skill did the rest. Congress as usual came
to heel. On January 25, 1879, President Hayes signed the
Arrears Pensions law.

The new enactment imposed no time-limit whatever
upon the filing of fresh applications. It relaxed the al-

[1] The United States Pension Rolls carried, in 1878, 10,407 War of 1812 ex-
service men, and 3725 widows. Under the stimulus of the law of 1878, the number of men rose in the year following to 11,621, and by 1880 the number of
widows had increased to 24,750.

ready lax requirements of proof, although, according to the then Commissioner of Pensions, Mr. James Bentley, at least $2,000,000 a year was already being disbursed on fraudulent pensions claims. It provided, (*a*) that each claim thereafter granted should produce back-pay from the date of the claimant's discharge from the Army; or from the date of his death if the claim was advanced on behalf of heirs; and, (*b*) that all claims already established should draw a sort of extra dividend representing the difference between the date of the service-man's death or discharge and the date when payment of pension on his behalf had begun, under former law.

Commissioner Bentley, on February 4, 1879, ten days after the enactment of the new legislation, produced his estimate of the amount of money that it would consume before June 30, 1880, the end of the next fiscal year. According to this latest law, said he, $34,000,000 was due at once in back pay to people already on the pay-rolls; $2,500,000 would be spent for arrears on claims allowed and to be allowed before July, 1879; and $5,000,000 must be reckoned for arrears on new claims that would be accepted before June 30, 1880. That made a total of $41,500,000, increased expenditure, to meet eighteen months' operation of this one measure.

Congress, confronted with the estimate, was dismayed. Lemon, in his *National Tribune*, that month frankly remarked: 'It begins to look very much as if Congress intended to back down and fail to appropriate at all. They seem frightened by the magnitude of their own previous action and alarmed by the results of the measure so unanimously passed.'

31

John Sherman, United States Treasurer, estimated that this expenditure would produce, for the National Budget of 1880, a deficit of over $27,000,000. He advocated raising the money by an issue of 4 per cent Government bonds.

But the *National Tribune* had a better expedient. Fifty million dollars should be witched into existence by the issue of legal-tender notes. 'Undoubtedly the right thing to do,' said Lemon, turned financier; and, it 'will not cost the Government anything.' Nor was Lemon the man to forget that the Greenback doctrine had polled a million votes in the Congressional elections of the previous year.

Between fright and necessity, Congress now executed a few backward staggers: it modified some of the provisions of the Arrears Act. Nevertheless, during the fiscal year 1880 that Act alone sent 138,195 new claims through the hands of the jubilant claims agent. And in 1880, the total cost of pensions rose to $56,689,220,[1] as against $26,786,-000,[1] the total for the year before the Arrears Act began to operate. In 1881, the average arrears check paid to an ex-service pensioner under the new law was $953.62; that to army widows and dependants, $1021.25. In that year, too, Commissioner Bentley somewhat raised his estimate of the volume of current frauds. Commenting on the superior opportunities afforded to many by this new licence, he expressed the belief that in 1881 not less than 10 per cent — over $5,000,000 — of all pension appropriation being paid out of the Treasury was paid on false and illegal claims.

In the year previous, 1880, Lemon was already boast-

[1] *Annual Report of the Administrator of Veterans' Affairs*, 1932, p. 158.

ing that he alone represented 30,000 cases pending in the Pensions Office. 'These accumulations,' drily commented Commissioner Bentley,[1] 'make a great and very profitable business to these gentlemen under the present system.'

But a Pensions Commissioner so watchful and so outspoken could not long survive. The next year President Garfield removed him from office, appointing in his stead a man of another type.

In the Arrears Act a feint had been made to disguise its nature as a claims agent's measure, by the insertion of a clause disallowing agents' fees for service in presenting arrears applications of already-enrolled pensioners.[2] Congress saw fit to let that feint save the Congressional face, turning its blind eye toward the fact that the agent's real harvest lay, not in arrears, but in the rush of new business now released, upon all of which he remained undisturbed in his title to collect tribute.

In the following year (1882) in public recognition of the usefulness of the *National Tribune* to the Grand Army of the Republic, the G.A.R. Commander-in-Chief appointed Lemon to be his official aide-de-camp. This connection publicly established, Lemon adopted a still more threatening attitude toward opponents in his path. While bending his skill to the multiplication of G.A.R. posts, he exhorted every ex-soldier to vote against all candidates for political office save such as were committed to the cause of pensions increase, and to boycott every newspaper that dared oppose the cause.

[1] June 12, 1880, before a House Committee.
[2] *Congressional Record*, 45th Congress, 2nd Session, Part 5, pp. 4874–75.

From this time forward the *National Tribune* waged open war upon any Government official who in respect to pensions tried to discharge his duties as a faithful public servant. With each good-bye to an honest and plucky Commissioner wrested from a tactful President, with each Congressional crawl for favours, Lemon's paper gained strength and fame. By Mr. Cleveland's time, as we have seen, it had discarded even the pretence of respect for the dignity of the Presidential office.

Casting itself into general politics, it drummed up enthusiasm for high tariffs. High tariffs meant full treasuries; full treasuries must be emptied in order not to impair the argument for high tariffs; and how better or faster to empty full treasuries than by grinding the pension mill?

The G.A.R., so tutored, learned to shout for high tariffs. The G.A.R. learned other things, under Lemon and his like — learned, too, from the orations of Lemon's marionettes in Congress. They learned, for example, that the country truly owed them more than the utmost outpouring of pension money could ever hope to repay; that only the greed of the selfish urban rich stood between them and their rights; that their claims rested, not upon national gratitude and grace, but upon a definite contract which, though it had been implied rather than stated, could none the less be repudiated only at the expense of the Nation's good name. To all of which the G.A.R. saw convincing proof of the Nation's tacit agreement. How else should it interpret this continued yielding to all its demands?

General Hawley, Senator from Connecticut, speaking

in the Senate in the year of Lemon's apotheosis as Friend
of the G.A.R., came warmly to the defence of Civil War
ex-service men. The majority of them are not pensioners,
and hope never to become so, he declared. They desire
to see needy comrades relieved and liberally relieved, but,
as taxpayers themselves, they object to be mulcted, by
excessive taxation, to pay pensions that are excessive
and unnecessary. They know that, according to the law
of averages, among two million ex-soldiers there must be
a 'proportion of unworthy men who are the natural prey
of the creatures that always fly from afar to the disbursement of great treasures.' To which tribute to Lemon and
his political trainband, General Hawley adds his own
belief that if the majority of ex-service men had framed
and controlled pension legislation it would not have
shown the features that now disfigure it.

Unfortunately, this better element left its identity too
much a matter of surmise, its honour too much at the
mercy of 'unworthy men.' Elsewhere lay its major interests in life; and no desultory and intermittent effort
could prevail against the attack of fighters who, whatever their sins, fought full-time and in earnest.

Congress, too, had its other element. Not Senator
Hawley alone, but Senators Sherman, Morrill, Edmunds,
Slater, Saulsbury, sometimes kicked against the pricks.
Said Senator Saulsbury in 1884, addressing the Upper
House:

> The pension agents who sit around this Capitol issue their
> circulars and decrees, and petitions come up for pension, and
> the Senators of the United States, great and mighty as they
> may be, bow to the behests of the pension agents and vote the

money they require, and they are afraid not to do it for fear that they would lose political status at home. We all know it, and the country knows it.[1]

Senator Beck, in the previous session, had denounced the Arrears Act as 'a standing monument to the ignorance selfishness, and cowardice of the American Congress.' But Senator Beck, as a Kentuckian and a Democrat, was answered in advance.

Neither in the House of Representatives did the claims agent find an always open road. A Northern Democrat, Brigadier-General Bragg of Wisconsin, on February 24, 1887, spoke plain words in connection with the Dependant Pensions Bill vetoed by President Cleveland a few days earlier. As to the *National Tribune*, its publishers, said General Bragg,[2]

receive from $25,000 to $45,000 a month as fees from pensioners,... in every column of that paper [appears] some squib, some abuse of the President of the United States and of those who dare to think differently from those men upon the propriety of the passage of this bill.... These newspapers that pretend to be 'friends of soldiers' are the friend of soldiers as vultures are the friends of dead bodies — because they feed and fatten on them.

And again:

The men who advocate this bill... [do so] simply because the men whom they expect to buy by the bill can vote.... If [a proposed pensioner under the bill] were to call upon them individually for aid, they would say, 'You lazy, good-for-nothing scoundrel, you are as competent to work as I am.'

Representative Warner of Ohio, in the same discussion, speaks of the *National Tribune* as

[1] *Congressional Record*, 48th Congress, 1st Session, 1884, Part 5, pp. 5045–46.
[2] *Congressional Record*, 49th Congress, 2nd Session, 1884, Part 3, pp. 2202–26.

LEMON

...edited by that scoundrel who in the last Congress admitted,
on oath,[1] that he had paid thousands of dollars to attorneys
to lobby through a conference committee a bill which increased his fees from $10 to $25 and gave him, it has been
estimated, a million and a half of dollars —. taking it out of
the pensions of the soldiers and their widows. Where the
soldier gets $1 a month pension, that act gave two years'
pension to this scoundrel, and he is one of the men that claim
to be the special 'friends of the soldier.'

This 'lemon-squeezer and blood-sucker of soldiers,'
Lemon, with his fellow-claims agents, said Mr. Warner,
'dominate the Grand Army posts in a great measure.
They do. They dictate the appointments of the chief
officers.'

If they did, they had worked for it; and they stuck to
their work night and day, in season and out. In any
dispute over the prey, they had no poor case against their
critics.

Senator John Sherman, for example, in 1884, opposed a
liberalizing amendment to the Arrears Act of 1879. But
before the next Congress sat he had turned his coat. In
explanation, he told his fellow-Senators that in the interval he had heard from his constituents. Thereafter
he abode by his revised status. Senator Sherman's
original stand had been taken, so he said at the time, on
principle.[2] It was probably also his principle that, as an
elected representative, he should advocate the pleasure of
his people.

If, then, the great majority of those constituents from

[1] *House Report*, no. 2683, 48th Congress, 2nd Session, January 15, 1885. Mr.
Lemon admitted that he had employed Robert G. Ingersoll and others for
service in this connection.

[2] *Congressional Record*, 48th Congress, 1st Session, Part 5, pp. 5049-50.

37

whom he heard were unanimous in demanding one definite course, that course, barring the existence of some over-ruling and perhaps less visible control, he would adopt. And to be told, as by Senator Hawley he was told, that the greater part of the Civil War ex-service men were not pensioners, not members of the G.A.R., and not friends of Treasury raiding, would scarcely move him. Because, whatever its numbers, that element showed, to the eye of the professional politician, little intelligent signs of life.

The better press of the country, it is important to remember, had, as a whole, faithfully decried pension excesses. In January, 1883, the *National Tribune,* under the caption 'The Hue and Cry Which the Newspaper Bloodhounds are Raising Against our Ex-Soldiers,' re-printed editorials from nine major newspapers such as the *New York Sun,* the *Chicago Tribune,* the *St. Louis Globe-Democrat.* But the load was too heavy to be lifted by the press alone, for all its good-will. The Nation's press, definitely, was little to blame for the situation. It fought well, but lacked that militant popular support essential to victory.

Returning, then, to the original question, 'Whose was the blame?' Only a whine as abject as Adam's own — 'the woman tempted me' — could lay it wholly at the door of the claims agents. Such are always with us, in one guise or many; their marks stare like potato-bugs' stripes; they live according to their nature; they have only that power that their neighbours give them; and they could have done little, indeed, against a higher element intelligent and energetic enough to possess, man by man, a civic conscience and a civic value.

38

Where, then, will the guilt stick? Upon the heads of Senators and Congressmen? But why should these be expected to mount the funeral pyre alone, to commit political suicide for the sake of scruples either non-existent or inert in the public mind?

The public mind. What does that mean?

The story just outlined makes no pretence of completeness. Rather, it attempts, by glimpses, to show the general quality and direction of a trend. Congress, as we have seen, shied and broke after its first spurt with the Arrears Act. But the steady hand on whip and rein soon brought it back to its stride, and from that point on it travelled kindly. No need to record the incidents of the road, nor the few faint cries of 'Stop, thief!' raised by onlookers left behind in the whirling dust. The only real limit was that of the inventiveness of the claims agent. Wider and wider grew the field, lower and lower the bars, higher and higher the prize, with each Congress.

General Isaac R. Sherwood (Democrat), Representative from Ohio in the Congress of 1911-13, introduced a bill to give a dollar a day for life to every man, regardless of physical or financial condition, who had served a year or more in the Northern Army during the Civil War, with graded awards for lesser terms of service. Over seventy per cent of the Civil War survivors would qualify for that dollar and the sum total would be formidable, but, 'You can get anyone to vote for any pension bill... in any legislature in the North,' so Sherwood, advocating his proposal on the floor of the House, mocked his colleagues — 'because the members do not dare to vote against it.'[1]

One at least of such as listened would have liked to fling back the taunt and call it false. Martin Dies was a Texan Democrat and the hands of Southern Democrats were clean of Civil War pension plunder. Yet the party had its Northern contingent. 'I want my party to win,' declared Martin Dies, 'but the naked truth is that the Democratic Party is just as cowardly on this pension question as ever the Republican Party dared to be.'

The measure evolved from this beginning was signed by President Taft on May 11, 1912 — again a Presidential campaign year. In the course of the next fiscal year it alone added to the draft on the Treasury by over twenty-one million dollars.

Each succeeding Presidential or Congressional campaign rolled up its crest of opportunities. Each new enactment increased the number of pensioned voters in each Northern legislator's constituency; increased, also, the prestige of the claims agent. No more Congressional tremors were indulged, no more backward steps permitted. The original Lemon dropped in time from the branch. But his work was done. His guild was established. His virus had entered the Nation's blood. Pension grafting was 'politics,' pension grafting was a trade. And so our sleepy public let it go.

[1] *Congressional Record*, 62nd Congress, 2nd Session, Part 1, p. 127.

CHAPTER V

DEMOCRACY AND THE DRAGON

THEN came a day, an hour, a moment when the sleeper sprang awake. Something had crashed through the dream. War. On April 6, 1917, America entered a conflict-at-arms for which, before its end, she was to assemble strength of over 4,700,000 men.[1]

Preparation for hostilities had found no welcome in President Wilson's mind. But war was now a fact, and Mr. Wilson, historian of America, Southerner, Democrat, character of great moral pride, was only the second of his party since the Rebellion to reach the Presidency. Mr. Cleveland, his forerunner, had left a record unapproached as Saint George to the Pension Dragon. The renaissance of the Democracy, long delayed, must equal that example. Nay, more: this Administration should raze the whole infamous fabric, start afresh on fair

---

[1] As of March 31, 1917, the entire Federal Army numbered 199,705 men, of whom 127,588 were Regulars, 66,594 were National Guardsmen in Federal Service, and 5523 were Philippine Scouts. Four thousand members of the Reserve Corps were also in active service at that time, and there were 117,539 men in State Military Service.

On May 18, 1917, the Selective Service or Draft Act became law, in accordance with which the President, by proclamation, set June 5 for the first registration, calling up all male persons between the ages of 21 and 30, inclusive. Voluntary enlistments of men so registered were discontinued in the Army after December 15, 1917, although non-registered volunteers were still accepted until August 8, 1918. War Department Statistics as of July, 1933, show the total strength of the United States World War Army to have been 4,057,101, of whom 1,274,007 entered the service voluntarily, 545,773 coming through the Regular Army. The first draft took about 2,400,000 men, out of about 10,500,000 called up for examination. The Navy strength, all volunteer, was 596,073; that of the Marine Corps was 104,066. Army, Navy, and Marine Corps total, 4,757,240.

ground, and build honourably. The power, the opportunity, now given it were such as only an emergency
equal to war puts into the hands of a President. The end
of this giant struggle, whenever it came, would con-
front the Nation with a problem in ex-service adjustment
greater than any she had known. The country must
prepare to handle it.

To Judge Julian W. Mack, of the United States Circuit
Court, fell the privilege of planning the effort. Judge
Mack was requested to frame a scheme that, while providing liberally for all soldiers' just claims, should shield
the Nation from a continuance of the old ugly smirchings.

Through the early summer of 1917, Judge Mack and his
assistants, outstanding men all, worked out the problem.
In August a Congressional Committee listened to their
exposition of the system evolved.[1]

Mr. Samuel Gompers, President of the American
Federation of Labour and Member of the Advisory
Commission of the Committee of National Defence,
spoke thus warmly in its praise:

> I have not yet seen a measure prepared for introduction in
> the Congress of the United States that seemed to be so per-
> fect a piece of legislation as this prepared by Judge Mack and
> his associates.... The purpose of the bill is to make [the War-
> pension system] a permanent institution... to take it out of
> the realm of controversial political discussion, and to estab-
> lish it as a system not dependent upon the whim or fancy
> of one or the other political party.... I am under the impres-
> sion that when this bill shall have been enacted into law you
> will hear very little about claims for pensions.... The whole

[1] *Hearings before the Committee on Interstate and Foreign Commerce of the
House of Representatives, 65th Congress,* 1st Session, on H.R. 5723, August 11,
1917, pp. 42-43.

42

scheme is very comprehensive and very just and very practical.

Judge Mack himself upon the same occasion[1] assured the Committee that the passage of the proposed measure would 'make it a moral outrage' for any subsequent Congress to return to service pension legislation,[2] 'bane of the pension system.' Further, he said, it would 'deprive of any moral standing ex-service men who should ask for service pension thereafter.'

The Honourable W. G. McAdoo, Secretary of the Treasury, recorded his judgment as follows:[3]

This scientific, well-balanced, equitable and comprehensive insurance and compensation measure will be a substitute, or should be a substitute, for the pension system as applied to the present war, and ought to make impossible, as it certainly will make unnecessary, future pension legislation, with all its inequalities and favouritism.

Finally, President Wilson himself, having examined the scheme, thus pronounced upon it:[4]

... it takes into consideration the whole obligation... of the Government — the obligation of justice and humanity, both to the soldier and to his family. It is one of the most admirable pieces of legislation that has been proposed in connection with the war and I cannot too earnestly urge its adoption.

[1] *Hearings before the Committee on Interstate and Foreign Commerce of the House of Representatives, 65th Congress,* 1st Session, H.R. 5723, August 11, 1917, pp. 77–78.

[2] The term 'Service Pension' signifies a pension paid merely for having served, no injury having been suffered. Such pensions had been set up in 1818 for ex-service men of the Revolution (1775–83), in 1871 for the men of the War of 1812, in 1887 for those of the Mexican War (1846–48), and in 1890, by the claims agents' diligence, for the Civil War (1861–65).

[3] The Honourable W. G. McAdoo to the Honourable W. C. Adamson, Chairman of the Committee on Interstate and Foreign Commerce, August 24, 1917.

[4] Letter to the Honourable W. C. Adamson, House of Representatives, dated September 1, 1917.

The measure so highly commended took form under four heads. It provided:

1st. Compulsory monthly allotment, up to half their pay, by men below commissioned rank, for the support of dependants, if such they had, within certain specified degrees of relationship. To this allotment, Government itself would, on application, add a family allowance not to exceed $50 a month, the amount being determined by the number of the man's dependants.

2d. Compensation for injuries sustained in active military service, the amount of compensation to be fixed by the degree of injury incurred and by the number and relationship of the man's dependants. This provision applied to all ranks, without distinction, and to Army and Navy nurses.

3d. In addition to compensation the injured person was given medical, surgical, and hospital treatment, free supply of artificial limbs and other prosthetics.[1] Also, re-education and vocational training of men war-injured in ways generally accepted as entailing permanent disability.[2] Such re-education was made compulsory in the sense that if or while it was refused, payment of compensation stopped.

4th. And this fourth feature was the bright particular star of the whole scheme — insurance protection at peace-time rates, available for every man in the service, against

[1] Heretofore no medical treatment had been provided for the ex-soldier save that given in National or State Soldiers' Homes. Pensioned men who had lost a limb had been, however, entitled to a new limb every three years, or to money in lieu thereof. The money was usually chosen.

[2] This provision underwent radical changes in the Amending Act of June 27, 1918.

44

permanent total disablement through any disease or injury, and to provide for his dependants in case of his death. Service origin, whether of death or of disability, was not in this case a factor.

Under this last provision, Government itself assumed the expense arising from excess mortality and disablements involved in the war hazard, together with all costs of administration — which were large. It accepted each and every applicant, officer and man alike, premium rates being net rates based on the American Experience Table of Mortality and interest at 3½ per cent per annum, on the yearly renewable term basis, computed for premium payment monthly — the premium to be deducted at source from the man's monthly pay.

Insurance could be taken out for from $1000, by any multiple of $500, up to $10,000. For a man twenty-five years old, the monthly premium on $10,000 insurance was $6.60. Benefits were payable in 240 equal monthly instalments of $5.75 for each $1000 of insurance. Further, under the deferred payment plan, an additional sum of $380 per $1000, representing interest at 3½ per cent, raised the actual payment made by Government to $1380 for each $1000 of insurance.

On the death of the injured man, payment went to the wife, child, grandchild, parent, brother, sister, one or all.

For the further protection of the man and his dependants, insurance, like disability compensation, was made both non-assignable and non-taxable. Neither was it open to the claim of any creditor, whether of the insured or of his heirs. In case of total disability, benefits were payable as above to the injured man, but without limit as to number. They continued not merely for 240 instalments, but for life, if his total disability so long endured.

No compulsion was exerted to force men to insure, but it was stipulated that application for insurance, if made, should be made within one hundred and twenty days after entering the service or after the publication of the new measure. Yet the bill also provided as follows: If a man who had not applied for insurance became permanently and totally disabled before the one hundred and twenty days had expired, he was to be considered as 'automatically insured' and entitled thereby for the remainder of his life to monthly instalments of $25; these instalments, in the event of his death before 240 payments had been made, to be continued to his widow while not remarried, or to his minor children or widowed mother — not more than 240 instalments being paid in all.

Further, the measure provided that not later than five years after the end of the War,[1] this term insurance must be converted, without medical examination, into any of the usual forms of policy that the insured might select, payments of premiums not to be required for periods of more than one month in advance. Unless so converted the insurance would lapse.

Disability compensation was in no wise to diminish on account of enjoyment of insurance benefits. Thus, a totally disabled man who held a $10,000 insurance policy would receive $57.50 in insurance, monthly, plus his disability compensation.

[1] This time limit was later extended by law to July 2, 1927, inclusive.

Congress in due course debated the whole measure. Congress, part-author of the past, recognized clearly enough the effort to cleave past from future with one mortal blow. Some legislators applauded the hope. Others openly laughed it to scorn as an impossibility under the American system of government.

On October 6, 1917, the bill, since generally known as the War Risk Insurance Act,[1] became law. Ten days later, Government assembled in Washington a conference of selected officers and enlisted men of the Army and Navy to hear the new law explained, in order that they, in turn, might explain it among the armed Forces. The conference sat for three days — October 16, 17, 18 — threshing out the subject in statement, question, and answer.

Judge Mack, from the chair, delivered expositions both luminous and simple. Appealing straight to the self-respect as well as to the patriotism of his hearers, he reiterated the fact[2] that one of the major objects of Government was to save its own good name and that of the citizen soldier from the odium cast by the pre-1917 War pension system. The man injured in service, or the family left in need by his service-incurred death, must have good care. But the idea of claiming lifelong tribute, as hale and hearty Mexican and Civil War ex-service men had been misled to claim it, simply for having responded to the country's call to arms, although their

[1] C. 105, 40 Stat. 398. The Bureau of War Risk Insurance had been established as part of the Treasury Department, by the Act of September 2, 1914, to cover ships against War risks.

[2] *Regulations and Procedure*, U.S. Veterans' Bureau, Government Printing Office, 1930, Part 2, p. 1260.

47

service in arms had cost them no harm whatsoever —
that idea, Judge Mack believed, could hardly be recon-
ciled with the pride of normal American manhood.

As for the disability compensation rates appertaining
to the Act, they in themselves, so Judge Mack made
clear, were not intended to provide full support to any
save the totally disabled. Further and better help lay
in forwarding self-help. With this in view, vocational
training would be given to restore disabled men to their
best earning status. Also, by insuring himself a man can,
through his proper forethought and care, protect himself
financially against disability and secure his family in the
event of his death.

But insurance for men going to war was by some
private companies refused at any price. Other such
companies were ready to insure at from $37.50 to $100
per thousand above the ordinary rate. 'This would mean,
for you,' Judge Mack showed his audience, 'from $375
to $1000 a year, extra, on $10,000, over and above the
ordinary premium that we civilians would pay, just because you are in the service.' Government, he continued,
desired to restore to the citizen in arms an insurability
as good as that of the civilian. And this Government
could the better accomplish, since it had no taxes to
meet, no medical, advertising, and commission fees to
pay, and none of the other loading that private companies add for expenses and emergencies — loading that
raises by 25 to 35 per cent the premiums that would
otherwise be ample for their business.

To show that the new law was democratic, in that, by
its terms, any enlisted man could meet out of his service

pay the premiums on the maximum insurance offer, Judge Mack adduced a recently received appeal from General Pershing:[1]

As Commander-in-Chief of the American Expeditionary Force in France, General Pershing was already urging upon Government a reduction of the overseas soldiers' spending money. 'In his [General Pershing's] judgment, expressed and brought over here with his sanction, $10 a month is more spending money than a man ought to have in the trenches under the circumstances.'

'The French and the English get very little pay,'[2] continued the speaker, 'and your spending money... is going to be a great deal more than their entire pay, and that may be demoralizing. For a French peasant in ordinary times a franc is as big as a dollar; in these times it is a great deal more than a dollar. But for the American boy going over there with comparatively plenty of money in his pocket, a dollar does not seem large.... When he throws away that dollar, he is throwing away nearly six francs.... Through that extravagance we are raising the price of all supplies in France.'

Nor did the chairman conclude without repeating his efforts to drive home to his hearers the root-purpose of the new law — to save both men and country from the creeping rot of the old system.

'Whether or not service pension legislation will be averted,' he concluded, 'of course no man can foretell.

[1] *Regulations and Procedure*, p. 1251.

[2] The base-pay of the American Regular Army private, first-class, before the War was $18 a month. This, in the beginning of the War, was raised to $30, home pay, and $33 for overseas. The pay of non-commissioned officers was raised accordingly.

49

No Congress can tie the hands of any subsequent Congress. But this Congress has erected a moral barrier on the firm American basis of self-reliance and self-protection.'

'A moral barrier,' erected by Congress, 'on a firm American basis of self-reliance and self-protection.' [1] How much stability did those three elements suggest, in the light of the previous half-century's performance?

That the War Risk Insurance Act was soundly drawn and carefully balanced, few questioned. That its provisions exceeded in liberality those of any other of the belligerent nations was conspicuously true, even when allowance was made for America's more luxurious scale of living.

But it was also conspicuously true that this costly burden had been laid upon America alone, at the outset of a costly war, for the reason that America alone, of all civilized nations, had trained her sons, for one hundred and one years,[2] to set a price upon filial loyalty — had taught them through decades of cheap trading to raise that price with each new extortion won. Here, now, was a fresh generation of youngsters, in the main high-hearted, surely clean of greed, going forth to a new war; and those whose love and pride for them was truest would keep them so.

[1] *Regulations and Procedure*, p. 1260.
[2] Cf. Note 2 of this chapter, page 43.

CHAPTER VI

WELCOME HOME!

CONGRESS as a whole, however, was built neither of generous youth nor of idealists. Beneath its festoons of new bunting, Congress remained exactly the same old Congress that Lemon knew as soul's brother. Whereof immediate signs appeared in an emphatic dislike of the new word 'Compensation,' as used in the War Risk Insurance measure. Debating the bill, certain members candidly expressed their alarm. 'Compensation' bore to their nostrils a fearsome smell as of finality — as an end to business; whereas 'pension' betokened the ever-juiceful, the incapable of exhaustion, the continuously valid tender of election trades. Almost they wept tears over future heroes whose sacrifices they might be unable to reward.

But such tremors wearied the stouter brethren. Millions of heroes — and voters, so these comforters pointed out in debate — must eventually emerge from the current war. Congress-of-the-untieable-hands could be relied upon to remember those voters. Pension or compensation, call it what you like, the principle remained the same. The good old trade could never die.

Meantime, sentiment thick as January molasses dripped from legislative lips into the pages of the *Congressional Record*; every draftee in training camp was already a martyr and the honourable speaker his moonstruck aunt.

51

As for the War Risk Insurance Act, just eight months
and nineteen days did it survive inviolate. Then, on
June 25, 1918, before half the American Expeditionary
Force had been shipped to France, Congress passed an
amending law whereby twenty-two sections and sub-
sections of the War Risk Insurance Act were altered.
Fourteen of these changes, to use the ominous old label,
were 'liberalizations.'

The pregnant feature in the Amending Act was, however, its provision that all men be 'held and taken to
have been in sound condition when examined, accepted,
and enrolled for service.'

In support of this step, the following argument was
adduced: The army was hurriedly recruited. Physical
examinations were hasty, incomplete, less rigorous in
standard than established military practice requires, and
sometimes imperfectly recorded. Consequently, large
numbers of weaker types were swept into the service.

Such types, even though subjected to no strain more
severe than the ordinary life of the home training camps,
might be seriously affected by the novelty of camp experience and perhaps by dread of what lay ahead. Therefore, even though they never crossed the water, they
might some day, in consequence of their enrolment, need
both financial and medical aid. Yet the War Risk Insurance Act provided financial and medical aid only on
account of War-incurred or War-aggravated injury. Obviously, then, here was a chasm that could be bridged
only by fiat.

Congress therefore issued the fiat, retroactively legis-
lating all men into sound mental and physical condition

when taken into the service. Any ailment, any deficiency later discovered, must, consequently, be service-incurred, and so must constitute title to War Risk Insurance Act benefits.[1]

At this point, pension legislation paused, while the World War continued.

So, at last, came the Armistice; after which our Army in France started toward home.

From the latter part of November, 1918, through the following June, the A.E.F., two million strong, was rolling home as fast as ships could be found to bring it. But Home, somehow, seemed not to have foreseen this amazing contingency. Home seemed almost as unprepared to come out of the War as she had been to go into it. 'Go back to work!' she told the debarking regiments. Rather petulantly, rather resentfully, soon she repeated it. For they somehow bothered her pride, nettled her self-esteem, standing there trustful, expectant, looking her square between the eyes. Small thought had she taken of what work they should do tomorrow or what bread they should eat today. Small thought, indeed, for body or soul. Nor did she want to think now.

Men who had left jobs to go to the War now found those jobs well and firmly grasped in others' hands. Employers, as a rule, saw no point in displacing satisfactory men or women closely familiar with the current affairs of their business to take back old personnel that,

[1] War Risk Insurance Act, Section 300, as amended June 25, 1918; amendment retroactive to October 6, 1917. Again amended, December 24, 1919, to apply to all World-War service men.

at best, would need time to rub off its rust. If it came back, let it fall in behind the newcomer, take the pre-War wage, or go to the bottom of the queue. And the day itself, with its problems of quick descent from abnormal production to production for normal needs, was unpropitious for the immediate absorption into industry of extra millions of men.

Also, there was, as in every belligerent country, the difficult element of disorganized youth. Ninety per cent of the American Armed Forces were, at the time of recruitment, under twenty-five years of age. Many boys who had left school, college, or university, their courses unfinished, to join the colours, now felt small desire to return to books. Few, before entering the service, had determined their future trade or calling, or acquired skill in any earning capacity. They had been too young.

And rare were those demobilized Americans, whatever their age or pre-War walk in life, who could now face with inner calm the idea of condemnation to a life led for the little old objects on the dull old lines. To run an elevator up and down a shaft, with one's best hope an occasional stolen glance into the pages of a book by an eye-killing light; or to sit all day behind an Italian walnut desk in a furnace-broiled room issuing orders and signing checks — one was as unbearable as the other to the man from overseas. 'I can't stand an indoor job!' gasped the man in the lift. 'I can't stand this idiot treadmill,' gasped the man at the desk — to equal effect.

Excepting for the casualties, relatively so few, most men came out of the service better than they went in —

54

broader of chest, thicker of blood, harder of muscle, sounder of nerve, wider-visioned, maturer and abler of mind. To tell such men to go back to the old, stuffy, pallor-breeding, imagination-killing round was like telling new-hatched eaglets to cram themselves back into their shells. Man or eaglet, the finer the creature, the higher the power, the deadlier the notion. A year or two, at least, would elapse before they could commit the necessary suicide and decently shroud its signs.

Meantime, did Home do nothing for them? She gave them popular mass welcomes, at first effusive, then — and quickly — more and more perfunctory as more and more ships came in; until the grand old First Division of Regulars, earliest overseas, longest in combat, late returning, could leave its transports and march down Fifth Avenue without eliciting as much enthusiasm as would greet a Tammany picnic.

Khaki was already out of fashion. Which indisputable fact rather piteously affected the value of the full new uniform, army boots and army greatcoat included, to which every soldier was entitled on his discharge from service.

As for Congress, three months after the homeward tide began to flow, Congress voted, besides the uniform, a 'bonus' of sixty dollars — two months' minimum pay to each demobilized man — regardless of whether or not he had seen Overseas service.[1]

That bonus was tossed with indifferent hand, alike to the draft-evader brought in by the police on the day before the Armistice and to the man who, volunteering

[1] Public 254, 65th Congress, February 24, 1919.

55

the moment the Shadow of War rose above America's horizon, served in combat commands till the end.

Congress, it may safely be said, never did a stupider or a grosser thing. For no palliative accompanied it. There it glared, in its cheap, solitary, imbecile nakedness. To the Overseas men it was at once so chilling, so affronting, and in every sense so ungenerous, that, save for the actual want in which many thousands now found themselves, there had better have been no gift at all. But the want was there, for Government had made no adequate provision either to assist those in need of work and fit to work to find work, nor to enable them to live while they sought work themselves.

Any inclination to excuse these facts may find its sufficient reply in the course adopted by England, the only other country which, in respect of the circumstances involved in this particular issue, may fairly be compared with our own.

Meanwhile, many people at home in America — people heretofore unused to the possession of money — had made much money with an ease and a suddenness that went to their heads. Wages and profits had been high. Luxuries had become necessities, spending had soared in common life. Clothing, food, rents had reached figures that, to an ordinary jobless ex-service man just come home from France, where for a year the Army had fed, clothed, and lodged him, were nothing short of appalling. His wife, if he had that kind of a wife, might point across the street to the wife of the small draft-escaped profiteer, their neighbour: 'Look at her fine clothes, look at her new fur coat, while I had to wear old duds and scrape along on your little allotment! Next time there's a war, I'll see you know what to do about it!' Uneasiness, half-formed resentments, and bruised disillusion choked the air. All sorts of things were lacking — the Best Things most of all.

CHAPTER VII

ALL ALONG O' MESS

'All along o' dirtiness, all along o' mess,
All along o' doin' things rather-more-or-less.'

KIPLING

COMPARED with the effort of the four European nations,
America's participation in the World War was small, both
in time and in men. Her casualties, consequently, were
few. Yet, even so, and for all her resources, all her efficiency, she found herself curiously embarrassed, at first,
to meet the needs, not only of her unemployed, who at
whatever cost could be pushed away, but of her sick and
disabled from whom she had no escape. Here again the
same unpreparedness that had plagued her start in the
War survived to haunt her beyond its end. Confusion
resulted. In the first post-War period, all medical work
for demobilized men fell into the hands of the United
States Public Health Service. But questions of awards of
medical benefits and of compensation for disablement
belonged to the Bureau of War Risk Insurance. Yet
matters relating to Rehabilitation, although, like medical
care, originally part and parcel of the War Risk Insurance
Act, must be referred to a Federal Board for Vocational
Education.[1] As to disbursement of pensions, that was
the business of still another office, the Bureau of Pensions.[2]

---

[1] Established by 'An Act to provide for vocational rehabilitation and return
to civil employment of disabled persons discharged from the military or naval
forces of the United States, and for other purposes.' (June 27,. 1918, c. 107,
40 Stat. 617.)

[2] Pensions were paid quarterly, following precedent, until the Act of May
3, 1922, instituted monthly payments.

All four of these agencies were housed, in Washington, under separate roofs, at a distance each from each. Under separate heads responsible to separate superiors, uncoordinated, often overlapping, sometimes diametrically disagreeing, the first three not seldom trod on each other's toes or tripped each other's heels, while documents wore weak and dingy wandering back and forth from bureau to bureau, desk to desk, or dribbled over the continent, hither and yon, awaiting the attention of an overworked, harassed, and badly muddled personnel. The local offices of the first-named three services, scattered about the land, laboured under the same handicap. Ailing ex-service men, short of cash, out of work, applicants for benefits to which the law entitled them, grew heartsick and hungry under delays, denials, mystifications, and incomprehensible futilities.

Also, there was much hard talk about hospitals — talk that still survives for occasional use, but which is somewhat less easy to justify.

America had built no hospitals during the War for the special reception of the sick and wounded to be returned from France. After the Armistice the sick, as they arrived, were placed in United States Public Health Hospitals, in Regular Army and Navy hospitals, in civilian hospitals on a contract basis, and in the numerous base hospitals that in each of the great training camps scattered over the country had served sick recruits.

These latter buildings — Adrian barracks types — could not have been accepted, without alteration, for permanent use. But the oldest had scarcely stood two years when the rush of returning troops began. And nowhere save in America would they have been thought unfit to serve the temporary needs of cases not so serious as to require the ultra-facilities of modern equipment.

These resources, combined, produced room enough for all the invalided men who came back from France. Some of the barracks hospitals were draughty and inconvenient; some of the contract places were definitely bad. But on the whole, such real trouble as arose came, not from lack of room, not from makeshifting, not from private hospitals' shortcomings and sins, but rather from two other main causes: First, the already indicated confusion resulting from unsystematized and unco-ordinated controls. And, second, the heavy percentage of mental cases found among the sick. These last, if let slip down the cracks between the various relief agencies, might indeed be slow to unearth themselves, and might suffer considerably while lost.

In hope of minimizing the number of the mentally infirm imposed upon the Army, the Surgeon General, at the beginning of the War, set up a neuropsychiatric service to identify and weed out such cases before their enrolment as soldiers.[1] The name of Dr. Pearce Bailey, at the head of that service, is enough to attest its quality.

Alas, the hope! Other 'orders from Washington instructed examiners to consider no man unfit for military service who should grade up to or over ten years' mental rating.'[2] To which decree was added the ruling that men

[1] See Report of the Surgeon General, U.S. Army, *Medical History of the War*, 1919, Vol. II.

[2] *The Medical Department of the U.S. Army in the World War*, 'Neuropsychiatry in the United States,' U.S. Government Printing Office, Washington, 1929, Vol. X, p. 82.

must 'grade eight years or lower' before they could be excused from home service because of their feeble wits.

Thus, in spite of the Surgeon General's care, great numbers of mental defectives were put into uniform, so many of whom were shipped overseas as eventually to elicit from the Commander-in-Chief in France the following protest: [1]

> Prevalence of mental disorders in replacement troops recently received suggests urgent importance of intensive efforts in eliminating mentally unfit from organization new draft prior to departure from the U.S. Psychiatric forces and accommodations here inadequate to handle a greater proportion of mental cases than heretofore arriving, and if less time is taken to organize and train new divisions. elimination work should be speeded.

In later years the psychiatric specialists who, with too little success, had urged the rejection of such material, thus reviewed the position that ensued: [2]

> Many [mental deficients and defectives], while unable to adjust themselves to the military environment, might be useful citizens if permitted to remain in their accustomed surroundings. Left on the farm or in the factory or store, where their associates were accustomed to their peculiarities, they might prove of material service to the country in time of war.
>
> [But] if men of this type became soldiers, they were almost certain in the future to present a serious economic problem to the country.... If after a short period in the Army, a soldier was necessarily discharged by reason of mental or nervous disability, he became a beneficiary of the Bureau of War Risk Insurance... and thus was entitled to Governmental compensation and hospital care. Many of the former sol-

---

[1] Cable from General Pershing, G.H.Q. in France, July 15, 1918, to the Chief of Staff in Washington, *Medical Department of the United States Army in the World War*, Vol. X, p. 58.

[2] *Medical Department of the U.S. Army in the World War*, Vol. X, pp. 57–58.

diers discharged by reason of nervous or mental diseases are drawing compensation from the Federal Government, some with a rating of total permanent disability. A large proportion of these men rendered practically no service to the country, their time in the Army having been spent in base or general hospitals, or under observation for the defect which in a short period after induction or enlistment [1] resulted in discharge.

How serious was the economic burden on the public, aside from the physical distress to individuals and to families incurred by neglect of this warning, may to some degree be gathered from the fact that by February, 1927, ex-service men with neuropsychiatric disabilities — 'shell-shock,' dementia præcox, and others — constituted 49.48 per cent of all patients receiving hospital treatment as beneficiaries of the United States Veterans' Bureau.

Now for another topic of the early post-War period — that of Rehabilitation, or Vocational Training:

The War Risk Insurance Act, in its Vocational Training section, aimed at preserving and building up the War-injured man's remaining ability. It meant to open his way to an interesting and productive future attainable by his own exertion, rather than to tempt him to destructive idleness by gifts of money sufficient to meet his needs. To reach that end, it decreed that the man seriously disabled and thereby unfitted for his pre-War calling should be retrained to a type of work that would develop his best powers.

The dream was fair. But awakening followed on swift, dark wings. The original law provided that the student whose injury or whose hours of training prevented his

[1] The term 'enlisted' designated the volunteer, 'inducted' the drafted man.

earning a living while under tuition could be required to enlist in the Army or Navy for his training period. He would then be entitled to subsistence, in the form of full pay to the amount he had received during his last month of active service. Also, and more important, he would work under reasonable control, insuring his good conduct and diligence.

Congress, however, intervened with sentimental objections to military control of trainees, thereby doing much to reduce the value of the whole Rehabilitation effort and the number of those who really profited by its great opportunities.

Congress, well within the year, embarked here also on the usual series of 'liberalizing' amendments. Under what we see fit to call 'political' pressure, the requirement of serious disability was soon wiped out. Any man drawing any compensation, down to the point rated as 'temporary partial' of the slightest degree, might now have free placement, free tuition, free books and apparatus, in any sort of schooling that he chose. Any draftee who had spent a day in training camp and thence had been sent home rejected, if he established claim to disability incurred or aggravated in that brief interval, could demand free vocational training on grounds as good as if he had served two years overseas. A four-year arts course at Harvard or Yale, or a post-graduate course in law or medicine or science, tuition, books, and full maintenance provided, was as much within the reach of one as of the other. And no questions, in any case, could be asked as to private means.

Training pay, at first sixty, then eighty dollars a month,

was provided for men who for any cause could not earn money while studying. The American Legion demanded that the pay be raised to one hundred dollars monthly. The Director of the Federal Board of Vocational Training earnestly protested that so large a sum would work against the man's best interest. The Legion countered with a gathering and demonstration by disabled ex-service men in the gallery of the House of Representatives, while appropriate eloquence streamed up from the floor.

The usual result followed. Congress voted a monthly allowance of $80 for single men, and $100 for married men, with additional allowances for dependants.

The sequel justified the Director's prophecy. Having too much money to spend, many men played when they should have been studying. Many others, taking advantage of the privilege to test their aptitude by plural trial, after pursuing one course of study for some months would choose another and then another; in the intervals so created not seldom feigning sickness — so the doctors say — and successfully demanding periods in hospital 'for observation.' Thus did they long protract a comfortable interval of loafing.

Great numbers, again, whose brains were never built to soar above the pick-and-shovel grade demanded vocational training simply because training pay would quadruple their disablement compensation. And under the law, however plain the fact, they could not be denied. Yet again hundreds of men with badly jangled brains were forced upon schools wherein their chief activity lay in producing grave problems of discipline.

On the other hand stands the record of a considerable

number of men of better minds and better mental and physical condition. One such group was sent to institutions of college grade. There, being more mature, more experienced, and of greater independence and intelligence of thought than their civilian co-students, they often handsomely outstripped the remainder of the student body. In the agricultural and engineering colleges, such men often overcame lack of previous education beyond grammar-school grade. And in the vocational schools for industry and commerce their record was also excellent. The real question, as developed, was always the question of the man's personal character.

No general survey, to determine the lasting value of the work, has as yet been made. But the following summary, in questionnaire form, comes from a source of the highest authority — a former official of Government who was intimately connected with the Rehabilitation Service for Disabled Soldiers in its early days. Its date is 1933.

1. Have the results in improved vocational efficiency of the group trained, taken as a whole, justified the cost of the rehabilitation program? No.

2. Has the training of disabled men at Government expense decreased the past outlay for other forms of soldier compensation and relief? No.

3. Will it, in years to come, cause a decrease in pensions, including service pension? No.

4. Would the results of the work for disabled men have justified the cost if this service had been confined to competent and ambitious trainees? Yes.

5. Would it have been possible, politically, to provide a programme of retraining for a selected group of handicapped men? No.

6. Would such a policy be constitutional? I doubt it very much.

7. If we had another war, would it be advisable to provide a retraining programme for disabled men? No, if it were like the last one. Yes, if the selective principle were set up or the law fearlessly and intelligently applied.

To which a second special authority of indisputable competence adds:

If political influence could have been kept out, the job could have been done at one-half the cost almost from the beginning.

'Political' influence, however, was not kept out. As a result, where about thirty-five thousand men, it is estimated, would have received re-training under the War Risk Insurance Act as it stood before it was done to death, over one hundred thousand actually broke through the lines. And the quality of the administrative staff, at one time the ablest the country could produce, was, it is attested, forced down and downward by the same smirched hand of 'politics.'

The total sum spent on this project was $644,900,000. Yet the cost that counts is not the cost in dollars, but the immeasurable cost in lost opportunity faithfully to serve our young men.

CHAPTER VIII

MAJOR-GENERAL LEONARD WOOD

THE opportunity to serve our young men, as it came to us at the end of the World War, was the most glorious opportunity for self-service that America ever faced. Had we seized it, it would have put us ahead beyond the power of reckoning. But we missed it completely, pitifully — missed it essentially; for we had neither eyes to see nor desire to grasp nor means to fill it. For all our supposed material strength and riches, for all our goodwill, we were a People Without an Understanding Heart.

We pushed the sacramental cup from their young hands with an impatient laugh. We chilled their newborn, unworded, infinitely potential idealism with our thin blank stare. Our answer to their hunger for the Bread of Life was to call them to join the herd grubbing husks in the trough, and to wonder at their lack of eagerness to answer that call.

Blurred and weakened of moral conviction, without strong abstract purpose, generally superficial in thought, generally devoid of sense of individual responsibility toward public affairs, we abounded in good and generous impulses. But our impulses and enthusiasms flashed up, burned hot, and were gone in an hour while we ran off after new excitements. Under heavy disaster we could show unselfishness, patriotism, and sticking power as good as the best. But our moral development had yet not reached the stage that produces individual and mass steadiness of standard — character, self-discipline, as the constant factor in everyday life.

Into this atmosphere of careless, good-humoured materialism, our boys came home from the War. They had fought our battles for us abroad. God knows we needed them to fight our battles at home. But abroad they fought in an atmosphere of life and of reality. Here our atmosphere was dead and stale with the smudge of unreal things. Abroad they had fought under leaders; here were no leaders such as living souls could follow. As for their officers that brought them home from France, these, swallowed up in the same thick fog that enveloped us all, sank away into it like the rest, and soon, to all outward seeming, lost their identity in the great civilian swarm.

Also, the A.E.F. as a whole, except for the Regular Army, had cordially disliked their officers. The discipline under which they lived overseas had been mentally, morally, and physically severe. And discipline of any sort was then strange to them. The average young American could not understand its meaning, still less conceive its necessity in his own case.[1] When his company officer drilled him till his tongue hung out, forcing him for the first time in his life to obey orders — smartly, too, and without benefit of current explanation — he loathed

[1] A curious interest now attaches to the inscription on the statue erected in Washington, by Congress, in 1910, to Frederick William Augustus Henry Ferdinand, Baron von Steuben, 'in grateful Recognition of his Service to the American People in their Struggle for Liberty.... After serving as Aide-de-Camp to Frederick the Great of Prussia, he offered his Service to the American Colonies and was appointed Major-General and Inspector-General in the Continental Army. He gave Military Training and Discipline to the Citizen Soldiers who achieved the Independence of the United States.'

that company officer. And although he sometimes learned that discipline not only squared the sum of his own value as a fighting man, but also could save his life in battle, he still hugged his grudge against the man that had taught him that truth.

Had the War lasted longer, or had America entered it earlier, all this might gradually have changed. As it was, the rank and file of the A.E.F. carried home in its heart no small resentment toward the men whose orders it had obeyed. Many a challenge of this statement must arise on behalf of many a born officer taken practically unprepared from civilian life, yet well and justly respected and beloved. But too great a prevalence of another attitude may be read in the desire of a considerable element in the American Legion, in its early days, to bar officers from membership.

The American Legion was first foreshadowed in a meeting convened in Paris in March, 1919. Officers and enlisted men there together discussed plans for a future organization to keep alive the best spirit of the War and to carry it forward in a brotherhood sworn to remembrance, mutual help, and public service. But by the time the Legion's First National Convention was held, eight months later,[1] in Minneapolis, few of the outstanding persons associated with the start of the movement remained prominent in it; nor had figures of mark come to the helm. Proven men from whom powerful, inspiring, and disinterested guidance might fairly have been hoped had perhaps failed to offer their services. Men of high character and ability, here and there over the

[1] November 11, 1919.

country, were heading local Legion posts, but they were relatively few, most of their sort having, unfortunately, already turned their whole minds to personal and business affairs. The places so left open had been assumed by other types, and these had already affected the tone of the new organization. Many a man who might have done great service had he remained in the Legion's ranks to fight for its honour, once catching the dread familiar scent in the Minneapolis air, then and there turned his back on the Legion forever.

'If this is to be nothing but the old pre-War game — political machine-building and gang-raiding for money,' such said to each other, 'I'd rather hunt my own kill like a decent private jackal than run with a pack snarling, "For God and Country." ' [1]

So, not being quite stout enough to stick — and therefore, perhaps, the less loss — they threw in their hands. Thus the story began.

As to how the story was to continue no one need long have doubted. By the terms of its Constitution the American Legion had pledged itself to abstain utterly from political activities.[2] But so slight was the weight or so loose the interpretation attaching to its pledge that this same First National Convention set up a Legislative Committee authorized 'to establish a Washington bureau, rent offices and employ such personnel as it deems necessary for the furtherance of the legislative programs of the

[1] Opening words of the Preamble to the Constitution of the American Legion.

[2] Article II, Sec. 2: 'The American Legion shall be absolutely non-political, and shall not be used for the dissemination of partisan principles nor for the promotion of the candidacy of any person seeking public office or preferment....'

70

American Legion.' [1] This program included the 'demanding of Congress the enactment of certain specified legislation.'

In other words, one of the first steps of the newborn
American Legion was to provide for the establishment
of its salaried Washington Lobby.

As to the methods, the quick uptake, the vigour of the
infant Lobby's procedure, we have an early self-portrait,
rendered to the Convention of the following year: [2]

> The Second Session of the Sixty-Sixth Congress came into
> existence on December 2, 1919, and adjourned June 5, 1920.
> ... Your Committee has carried out the instructions of the
> [Legion's] First National Convention and has had bills intro-
> duced in the Senate and the House specifically covering every
> resolution adopted at that Convention.[3] ... At all hearings
> upon bills affecting ex-service men and covered by your reso-
> lutions, the National Legislative Committee has appeared
> and presented the views and opinions of the American Legion.
> ... Since the existence of your National Legislative Commit-
> tee in Washington, D.C., the appropriations for [disabled
> ex-service men's] benefit... have increased over 100 per
> cent — $385,545,000 having been appropriated for that pur-
> pose. This, together with the other beneficial legislation
> enacted for the ex-service men, we are informed equals the
> thirty years' efforts of the veterans of the Civil War.

[1] *Report of the National Legislative Committee*, Second National Convention
of the American Legion, Cleveland, Ohio, September 27, 28, 29, 1920, p. 4.

[2] *Ibid.*, pp. 4–7.

[3] The text of the *Report* at this point thus explains the course of procedure:
'Legislation can originate either in the Senate or in the House, with the exception that all legislation requiring an appropriation of money must originate in
the House. When bills are introduced in either branch of Congress, they are
referred to the proper committee for consideration, which committee holds
hearings and reports its findings to that branch in which the bill has been
introduced. If there is any disagreement between the Senate and the House
upon legislation, it is referred to a joint committee of both bodies for a conference, and upon an agreement being reached and a conference report submitted,
it is again passed by both branches and sent to the President for signature.'

SOLDIERS WHAT NEXT!

A vital feature of this Lobby's work is to form, instruct, and train the machine behind it — most of it built of green material — to function with speed and force at the word of command. To this end it issues clear instructions and dins them in. Organized bombardment of Congress by post in the interest of specific measures is carefully explained for the benefit of those as yet unfamiliar with the technique; and attention is called to the wisdom of acting promptly on Lobby signals to 'write to your Congressman.'

Assistance can be rendered, it is indicated, not only by letters and telegrams shot in at the Lobby's word, but also by pressure exerted upon the Congressman at home. For convenience in this matter, this and other *Annual Reports* print the full list of Congressional votes on main bills touching Legion interests. The name of each Senator and Representative is recorded with his vote, yea or nay, his presence without voting, his absence or his pairing.

Dealing with its main objective for the coming year, the Lobby, in its *Report* of 1920, steps back into the past to exhibit the root of that effort. Their First Convention, so legionnaires are reminded, had adopted this resolution:[1]

> That while the American Legion was not founded for the purpose of promoting legislation in its selfish interest, yet it recognizes that our Government has an obligation to all service men and women to relieve the financial disadvantages incident to their military service... an obligation second only to that of caring for the disabled and for the widows and orphans of those who sacrificed their lives.... But the American Legion feels that it cannot ask for legislation in its selfish interest and leaves with confidence to Congress the discharge of this obligation.

[1] *Report of the National Legislative Committee*, 1920, pp. 27–28.

72

Congress, however, had failed to appreciate the refinement of that suggestion. Congressmen, instead of seeking guidance at the fountain head, had taken matters into their own hands — had, so the Lobby laments, 'proceeded to construe the resolution in every possible manner in order to have [it] coincide with their own personal point of view.' [1]

Thus three sterile months had worn by. Then the policy of the Legion's National Executive Committee [2] forbade further patience. On February 9, 1920, it adopted a resolution interpreting the over-delicate language of its earlier statement, and in words of one syllable 'demanding of Congress the passage of a bill giving to each ex-service man a $50.00 bond for each month of his service.' [3]

A fortnight later, on March 2, 1920, the National Commander of the Legion, accompanied by the Lobby, appeared before the Ways and Means Committee of the House of Representatives in Washington to lay down their dictum. With chill suggestion they added that 'a War-service adjustment will not detract from that high sense of patriotism which the ex-service man will ever hold as a heritage.' [4]

The Second National Convention, held in Cleveland in September, 1920, passed many resolutions. Some of these were incontestably good, some were trifling, some were as definitely political as any that could be produced by a

---

[1] *Report of the National Legislative Committee*, 1920, p. 28.

[2] The National Executive Committee of the American Legion is understood to formulate policies, which the National Legislative Committee (the Washington Lobby) then handles in Congress. The Legion's National Commander is elected, annually, for a one-year term of office.

[3] *Report of the National Legislative Committee*, 1920, p. 28.　　[4] *Ibid.*, p. 34.

party caucus. Yet throughout it was clear that the average delegate present — they may have numbered two thousand, more or less — was thinking on points of local or personal interest, or, scarcely troubling to think at all, was merely swapping memories and enjoying a holiday.

Meantime, what happened on the platform of the Convention was concerning them but little — was passing mainly unnoticed, as the routine business of their responsible employés.

One thing that happened on that platform, on the last day of the Convention, under all eyes, was a prolonged exhibition of flagrant disrespect aimed at a foreign officer of high rank, the Legion's invited guest.

The assembly hall, floor and galleries alike, was packed with khaki-clad men. The stage, reserved for Legion officials, was filled with ordered rows of chairs divided into two sections by one longitudinal aisle.

All the officials had seated themselves on the left side of the aisle, leaving the right half empty, and were so sitting when a sudden stir in the house signalled the arrival of distinguished personages — Major-General Leonard Wood, then commanding that Army Area, accompanied by Admiral Grant of the British Navy and by a French general, each of the two foreign officers having come in response to the Legion's invitation addressed to his Government, as official bearer of his Government's greetings.

At the request of the chairman, the British admiral presently left the distinguished guest's box, mounted the stage and addressed the audience. A moment after he had begun speaking, a conspicuous and popular national

74

officer of the Legion, wearing his khaki, suddenly appeared at the back of the stage and, accompanied by a single 'doughboy,' walked slowly down the central aisle to the front, seating himself with his companion, on the right, in the otherwise empty space and just behind the speaker. In this conspicuous position he embarked on a parade of unmistakably intentional discourtesy, talking, shifting, sneering, laughing, and in every way demonstrating to the audience before him the attitude that he, as a leader, would have them assume toward their British guest.

The admiral, who could not but be aware of the scene in progress at his elbow, showed no signs of such knowledge, but, unruffled, brought his brief speech to its natural close. He was succeeded by the French general, toward whom the volunteer conductor of sentiment now snapped to attention with a sudden deference so faultless as finally to emphasize his earlier disorder.

The lesson was too plain to be escaped. The Irish propaganda was then at its height. Anti-British feeling was then strong in the land. Its doctrine was being taught from that platform in that incident. The young legionnaires on the floor and in the galleries, consciously or not, would absorb it.

From his seat in the stage box General Wood had witnessed the affront — witnessed also the disastrous failure of the responsible and presiding Legion officials to intervene with any sort of reparation. The General bided his time — his own time to address the Convention, following the speeches of the foreign guests.

Then, a sturdy, soldierly figure in full uniform, he advanced down the stage. Spontaneously and as one man,

75

the whole house rose to him. 'Our — General! Our — General!' they shouted, with all the power of their young lungs, on and on and on, until, as the cry took rhythm and thrill and cadence, the building itself seemed to sway. '*Our* — General! *Our* — General!' — for many of them had belonged to that Division that he himself had trained for France. And the great love that men who served under Leonard Wood always bore him was given, for these, lasting poignancy by their grief and sheer rage, when, at the very gangplank, Washington forbade him to sail with his command.

And if they loved him, so did he love them — too truly to stand by in silence while they, in their innocent carelessness, were betrayed into sharing in an unworthy act. He accepted, acknowledged, and at last quieted their welcome (dear it was to him!). Then, in the straightest, manliest language that friend could use to friend — yet without one word in direct mention of the scene just enacted — he brought them back to their true selves. Speaking slowly, with intense earnestness:

'Before I tell you what I came to tell,' he began, 'there is something else I must say at once: Some of us have a way of asking, "Who won the War?" Not very soldierly, is it, that question asked that way! Before any one of you utters it again, I want him to ask himself two other questions. These:

'If you were so lucky as to get to France, by what means did you get there?

'Do you know the answer? I'll tell you: By means, half of you, of the British Merchant Marine. That splendid service with its great War-record of steady bravery and sacrifice of life — gave you the honour of carrying the Flag to France.

'Now the second question: "If the War was not over and lost long before we ever came into it, why was that?" Do you know? That, too, I will tell you:

'It was because of the British Navy.'

And there he paused — standing quiet in the tense, eager silence, looking down at them all with a great and visible yearning in his eyes.

Again he spoke — as if to himself, almost as if in prayer — and obviously his mind was beholding not the incident just witnessed but the long years to come.

'Ninety-two per cent of you would be *good* boys if *only* you had decent leadership!'

It was General Wood's most cherished hope, when his task as Governor-General of the Philippines should end, to offer his services to the American Legion. Had that hope been realized, a new day would have dawned for America.

CHAPTER IX

EX-LIEUTENANT LEWIS DOUGLAS

To MANY subdivisions of the Legion, to great numbers of individual legionnaires, news of their central organization's demand for cash tribute came as a shock. Even those who had served overseas had now been at home a year, more or less. For the great able-bodied majority that recognition and governmental assistance, that might well have been more liberally rendered in the first unsettled period of demobilization and unemployment, was now no longer more necessary than it was to their average civilian compatriots. To a large percentage, happily, it was not necessary at all. Furthermore, America was entering upon a period of financial and industrial depression. Widespread unemployment pinched the land. The prospect looked grim. As one speaker put it, 'We are all in the same boat, and it is a pretty leaky boat, a long way from shore right now.... It is a good thing not to rock it [or]... overload it.' [1]

Generally speaking, everyone felt poor, whatever his walk in life. Both President Wilson's Secretary of the Treasury and the President of the Federal Reserve Board had already appeared before Congress urgently to plead

[1] *Congressional Record*, July 15, 1921, p. 3862. The speaker, Senator New of Indiana, further said: 'Since those fat [war] years the price of wool, for instance, has gone down, so that you could not sell the whole clip from the biggest ram... for enough to make a mitten for a one-armed doll.... That state of affairs extends to nearly every man in the United States who is doing business today.... The fact is that if the banks today were to try to close in on business and collect, this country would be in the hands of a receiver before sunset.'

for the whole country's sake against the burden of new loans and taxes implied in the Legion's demand. Profits and wages of war-time had taken wing together. Man and man alike now viewed the present with heaviness and the future with fear-filled eyes.

At which hour of common distress, behold a great drove of citizen ex-soldiers, vowed 'to God and Country,' pushing forward, horns down, fighting for its own advantage to the hurt of all the people; and on grounds that amounted to capitalizing a 'patriotism' that seemed given the lie direct by that gross assault.

Yet all over the country were hosts of ex-service men whom such seeming did injustice. Men absorbed in their daily work, not given to thinking of things in the large, neither asking nor wanting any latter-day 'bonus' for themselves, yet aware of no duty to roll out as stumbling-blocks into the path of those otherwise minded. Not even a quarter of the late Army belonged to the Legion. And even within the organization hundreds of thousands of men were as innocently unconscious of the light in which they were exhibited as were the legionnaires of the Cleveland Convention until General Leonard Wood, in his chivalry, came to their defence. Yet, leaderless as they were — for where was their Haig, their young Mussolini, their Franz Seldte? — they did not all take it lying down.

In South Carolina — which proud little State, by the way, had captured, in the World War, six Congressional Medals of Honour for gallantry in action [1]—in South Caro-

---

[1] Only 93 Congressional Medals of Honour were awarded for service in the World War. Fifteen were won by the men of the State of New York, which state produced 9.79 per cent of the American National Army for the World War. Authority of the Adjutant General, as of July 22, 1933.

lina the Executive Committee of the State Legion, ablaze with wrath, called a special meeting to clear the State's good name. In a session attended by every member resolutions were adopted as follows: [1]

Whereas the American Legion was formed with the express purpose of furthering all patriotic causes and not for selfish or political reasons; and

Whereas the granting of a cash bonus to able-bodied veterans of the Great War would be admittedly harmful to the welfare of the American public; and

Whereas a request from the American Legion for a cash bonus rightly renders that organization liable to suspicions as to its sincerity... and is debasing and inconsistent with the high ideals on which the American Legion was founded;

[Now, therefore, be it Resolved]... That we disapprove of the action of the said national executive committee and that we view their motives with suspicion; and

Resolved, That in our opinion the action... tarnishes the honor and glory which the American soldier and sailor won on the field of battle, and its action, if ratified by the next national convention, renders the further affiliation of the South Carolina department with the national organization harmful to the future of the said department.

Nor was South Carolina alone in her resentment. Other Legion Posts and individual members of posts, here and there, arose in angry protest; and many, whose sense of responsibility forbade their awaiting the next National Convention to apply whatever corrective lay in their power, wrote strong letters to Cabinet members, to Senators and to Congressmen, disowning and condemning an action which they felt as an affront to American manhood.

Out in a certain Arizona mining town, for example,

[1] From the Columbia (S.C.) *State*, May 30, 1920.

the Legion meeting was plunging for the Bonus until one solitary young ex-lieutenant captured the floor — no titular soldier he, but one who had 'paid with his body for his soul's desire' — one who in France had been cited by our Commander-in-Chief for gallantry in action.

Thus spoke the ex-lieutenant:

'Look here: Why did all we fellows go into that War? Wasn't it for the honour of serving our country? Are we going, now, to sell out our own record? Haven't we got our youth and our lives, and our country, still, and the right to go on serving? Isn't America worth fighting for, always and forever? Do we climb down today, down off the honour-roll, and ask to be *paid* for doing it?'

The Post came over with a rush — gladly, wholeheartedly, as our people always come when by special mercy there is found a man to stir them.

That man's name was Lewis Douglas.

But the watchful Legion heads saw clearly enough their danger from such revolts. So much is proved by the sharp clang of the alarm-bell rung by the Legion Lobby toward the end of the year:[1]

> The slogan of the Legion is 'Let's stick together,' and upon matters of national legislation this should be particularly true. It has not been so during the past year.... Direct correspondence by Posts or members of Posts with executives of Government or Members of Congress upon national legislation should not be had except upon instructions or request from the National Legislative Committee, and under no circumstances should opposing views or resolutions be forwarded to such persons once the National Executive Committee has expressed itself on the subject. This was done in a

[1] *Report*, to the National Convention of the American Legion, September 27–29, 1920, p. 7.

great number of instances during the past session of Congress, to the embarrassment of your Committee and with detrimental effect upon the results which we set out to accomplish.

Thus was announced the 'steam-roller' policy, the gag-rule, which, thenceforward consistently and rigorously enforced, was soon to weld the Legion into a powerful political engine, while fundamentally affecting the quality both of its influence and of its membership.

Meanwhile, hard times continued. By March, 1921, when President Harding was inaugurated, the national budget had become a subject of the gravest anxiety to those few men who could not evade its gaunt and basilisk glare.

The number so impaled, however, by no means included the United States Senate's Committee on Finance. A sub-committee of this body, sitting in consultation with the Legion's Lobby, was soon to learn from the lips of the latter's chairman that the Legion as a whole spoke single-voiced in demanding cash settlement. 'Of course,' this authority hastened to concede, 'one cannot say there is no one who dissents... but whenever the thing comes up for formal action, such as post action or departmental action or national convention action, the approval is unanimous.' [1]

He had no need, in that well-instructed company, to allude to the Legion's votes; but he did, however, take occasion to remark that the *American Legion Weekly*, the organization's official sheet, 'which has a circulation of al-

[1] *Soldiers' Adjusted Compensation.* Hearings before a Sub-Committee of the Committee on Finance, United States Senate, 67th Congress, on S. 506, June 2, 1921, pp. 10 and 13. Cf. the statement of the National Legislative Committee of the Legion covering the period.

most 1,000,000, has pledged itself to propagandize among the soldiers.'

Given co-operation so sound,[1] the Senate Committee was shortly able to report out and recommend for passage a Legion-born measure formally christened the 'Veterans' Adjusted Compensation Bill,' though doomed to be branded the 'Bonus Bill,' in spite of diligent efforts to popularize the finer name. Said the Senate Finance Committee,[2] introducing its godchild:

> ... In simple, plain English, the purpose of this bill is to give to the soldier who offered his life with his services a compensation that will more nearly approach that of the laborers who remained at home secure from danger, and whose compensation increased from 200 to 300 per cent.... We cannot deny that by allowing the man who fought for his country, who placed his life in pawn for his country, the increase in his compensation provided for in this bill, we are still giving him for his services with all their risks and hardships [a recompense far below his deserts].

It may be questioned how many ordinary citizens who saw those words or who caught their distant echoes escaped the impression that the benefits concerned were meant definitely for men who had fought in France, or who, at least, had crossed the water. For at that early stage the word 'war-veteran' still retained in America something of the meaning attached thereto in other parts of the world.

'Two out of every three American soldiers who reached

[1] 'This bill has the unanimous indorsement of the National Legislative Committee of the American Legion, who assisted the Finance Committee in framing and reporting it.' Senator Fletcher, *Congressional Record*, July 15, 1921, p. 3872.

[2] 67th Congress, 1st Session, Senate *Report* to accompany S. 506, June, 1921, pp. 1-2.

France, it is stated, 'took part in battle,' [1] but some two million men taken into the American Army, and destined for France had the War continued, never entrained for the docks; and of these over half a million were drafted during the last two months of war.

Yet each man of the whole 4,700,000 was equally entitled to the Senatorial tribute.

The Bonus Bill so recommended for passage offered all ex-service men four options. Of these one only need detain us here. This was the first offering — a gift of money payable, either cash down, or, augmented by accumulated interest, after twenty years' time. As to the costs involved in this provision the Senate Committee hazarded the guess that its total would reach about $4,396,000,000, scattered through the twenty years, and that 'the greatest amount due in any one year prior to 1943 will not exceed $200,000,000.' [2]

As to whence those costs are to come, the bill itself is silent. But, using a hard-driven Legion doctrine, 'the Committee begs to remind the Senate' that Great Britain owes the United States, War-debt and interest together, about five billions of dollars; that France and Italy together owe about four and a half billions; that other nations owe other sums, and that the interest on these combined debts 'will, in our opinion, more than care for the payments necessary each year to meet the requirements of the proposed legislation.' [3]

---

[1] *The War with Germany*, A Statistical Survey, Col. Leonard P. Ayres, Chief of the Statistical Branch of the General Staff, Government Printing Office, Washington, 1919, p. 101.

[2] Senate *Report*, to accompany S. 506, June, 1921, on Veterans Adjusted Compensation Bill, p. 5.   [3] *Ibid.*, p. 4.

EX-LIEUTENANT LEWIS DOUGLAS

It was at this point that the urgent warning of an unhappy man, the Secretary of the Treasury, Mr. Andrew W. Mellon, was laid before the Senate.[1] Like his Democratic forerunner in office, Secretary Houston of Mr. Wilson's Cabinet, Mr. Mellon, a Republican, felt it his duty to defend the threatened solvency of the Nation against such attack. Analyzing the bill recommended for passage by the Senate Finance Committee, the Secretary declared:

> It would greatly swell the cost of Government and virtually defeat the Administration's program of economy and retrenchment. It could be financed only by adding to the burden of debt and taxes under which the country is now staggering. However financed no such sum could be taken out of the Public Treasury without throwing a corresponding load upon the whole people.... This burden, moreover, would be in addition to that already imposed in most of the States, which have provided bonuses in varying degrees of liberality to veterans of the late war.[2]

'Cash payments to able-bodied soldiers and sailors,' in this period and in this volume, would, the Secretary declared, produce general disaster in which the ex-service men themselves, as inseparable from the general citizenry, must be involved.

> In these circumstances [he concluded], I believe that the best interests of the country demand that action be deferred upon the soldiers' bonus.

But the Senate's ear was bent to other voices. And the well-driven machine behind the bill was whirling

[1] Letter to Senator Frelinghuysen, June 2, 1921. *Congressional Record*, July 6, 1921, pp. 3375–76.

[2] Sixteen States have provided such bonuses running from $10 to $30 a month, without relation to the Federal provision. A seventeenth, New Hampshire, gives a bonus determined by the Federal provision.

85

those voices into maddening *crescendo*, as an orchestra leader lifts and spurs his instruments to their climax of sound. In spite of the warning from the Treasury, in spite of the protests of graver Senators, there was every prospect that the bill would pass.

At this juncture, and at the very moment when the final step impended, occurred an event that, some Senators indignantly declared, had no precedent in American history. The President of the United States in person entered the upper chamber, during debate, to ask the Senate, in the whole people's name, to abstain from the deed it was about to commit. And he deliberately chose this dramatic method in order that the situation in all its dangers might be illumined to the whole Nation, as by a lightning flash before the storm.

In President Harding's speech the following passages occurred:[1]

> Our Government must undertake no obligation which it does not intend to meet. No Government fiat will pay our bills. The exchanges of the world testify today to that erroneous theory.
>
> It has been my privilege to speak to Congress on our obligations to the disabled and dependent soldiers,... I should be ashamed of the Republic if it failed in its duty to them.... Contemplating this tremendous liability, which the Government will never shirk, I would be remiss in my duty if I failed to ask Congress to pause at this particular time, rather than break down our Treasury, from which so much is later on to be expected....
>
> I know the feelings of my own breast, and that of yours and the grateful people of this Republic. But no thoughtful person, possessed with all the facts, is ready for added compensation for the healthful, self-reliant masses of our great

[1] *Congressional Record*, July 12, 1921, pp. 3597-98.

armies at the cost of a Treasury breakdown which will bring its hardships to all citizens of the Republic.

Next day, in the same place, Senator Watson of Georgia, not alone in his action and tone, heatedly denounced the President as having 'by his personal interposition evidently sought to overawe the Senators in the discharge of their duties.'[1] 'The time has been, Senators,' continued the speaker, 'when a King of France, booted and spurred for the hunt, with a whip in his hand, could come before the Parliament of Paris and order a certain edict registered, and have it registered and go on to his hunt. It was not long before his great-grandson died in the Powder House.... That kind of personal rule is absolutely antagonistic to our democratic form of government.'

Then the Senator from Georgia brought forth his own expedients.[2] The Bonus Bill, undeniably, looked somewhat anæmic in its lack of any appropriation clause. To cure this lack, the Senator offered, in preliminary outline, two 'practical amendments.'

'The laws now on the statute books passed during the Civil War,' said he, 'allow the Secretary of the Treasury to issue right now $102,000,000 of greenbacks. I would issue that money, and I would distribute it among the soldiers on the miller's rule of "First come, first served!" and next I would give them the billion dollars of free gold in the Treasury.'

Hot debate followed. But the Senate vote, taken on July 15, stood 47 to 29 to shelve the bill for the present by recommitting it to the Committee on Finance.

[1] *Congressional Record*, July 13, 1921, p. 3654.

[2] *Congressional Record*, July 13, 1921, p. 3658. Cf. Lemon's advocacy of greenback issue. *See ante*, p. 32.

CHAPTER X ·

WE ABANDON OUR THEORY OF PATRIOTISM

THE regulations under which America's World-War Army was built up permitted the recruitment of aliens, illiterates, and non-English-speaking citizens. Of the men examined by the draft boards 24.9 per cent could read or write little or no English.[1] The American Legion, while not requiring citizenship of its members,[2] never missed the significance of these facts, and from the first placed Americanization work high on its program of activities.

This service it was physically well equipped to render. Its many posts were scattered over town and country. To use its own words, it had early 'developed a highly specialized and effective means for carrying its message to the people,' having its film section for pictorial teaching; its corps of ready speakers, to an intended strength of 4000; its *American Legion Weekly*, which it both owned and edited; its news service, spreading copy among 10,000 newspapers said to be read by 40,000,000 persons — the whole effort controlled by one director of publicity.[3]

[1] *Official Report* of the Division of Psychology, Medical Department of the Army. In Senate Document No. 421. 66th Congress, 3rd Session.

[2] Excepting in the case of men whose claim rests on having served in the forces of one of the Allies. Otherwise, assignment to active duty with any branch of the Armed Forces of the United States at any time between April 6, 1917, and November 11, 1918, with honourable discharge, constitutes eligibility, whether or not active service was rendered.

[3] *Proceedings of the Third National Convention of the American Legion*, 1921. Statement by the National Commander. See *Congressional Record*, Nov. 9, 1921, pp. 7578, 7581.

'Education in citizenship,' declared the Legion's Americanism committee, 'is the keynote of Americanism. ... There are in this country many foreign-born residents who are not being assimilated, due largely to the fact that the opportunity has not been afforded them to acquaint themselves with the American language, customs and laws.... This ignorance on their part has a tendency to promote radicalism in our midst,... and we... deem it our duty to assist them in acquiring... some knowledge of our language and institutions.' [1]

Beyond any doubt, not only a part of the foreign element but also a larger number of native-born Americans were now forming their first active ideas of America's governmental institutions and of their own proper attitude thereto and participation therein, under the guidance of Legion mentors. It is therefore of value to see how 'radicalism' has been combated, how respect for the dignity and authority of the American Government has been inculcated in the wide publicity directed by Legion control.

The letter of the Secretary of the Treasury, explaining the financial distress of the Nation and declaring that 'the best interests of the country demand that action be deferred upon the soldiers' bonus,' was made public on July 6, 1921. On July 11 the Legion's Lobby released a press announcement of which the following is part: [2]

---

[1] *Proceedings of the Third National Convention of the American Legion*, 1921. *The United States Census of 1920*, p. 1153, Table 4, showed a male population 21 years old and over, numbering 2,005,697, who could neither read nor write in any language. Of these, 770,592 were foreign-born whites.

[2] Reprinted in the *Report of the National Legislative Committee*, Third National Convention, October 31, 1921, p. 47.

SOLDIERS WHAT NEXT!

The American Legion have weighed the matter with the utmost care as to whether or not the Legion should, in view of Secretary Mellon's statement, consent without protest to further delay in the passage of the Adjusted Compensation Bill by Congress.

The American Legion can do no such thing. [The Statement of the Secretary] is intellectually dishonest, economically unwarranted, and politically ludicrous.... Secretary Mellon's diatribe against the Adjusted Compensation Bill is nothing more than a mere re-hash of the objections long ago interposed by his predecessor in office, former Secretary of the Treasury Houston.

Nor did the office of the Secretary of War command more respect at these hands. Having dared to render an adverse opinion on another of the Legion's measures, the Secretary of War is held up to public contempt for the edification of pupils in 'Americanism.' A letter is broadcast before them as addressed by their Washington Lobby to the Secretary of War. With such a rattling of the sabre, such a stamping of jackboots as to prove that the gallery rather than the Secretary is really addressed, the latter is nailed in his place. He is informed that 'The American Legion cannot acquiesce in the ill-founded objections of the War Department,' and that it will 'undertake to secure the passage through the House' of the measure he has ventured to dislike.[1]

But these object-lessons were shortly to be outstripped, and that by the Legion's own supreme authority, its National Commander.

Addressing the Legion's Third Annual Convention, and speaking through that audience to the wider field

[1] *Ibid.*, p. 223. Letter to Secretary Weeks, September 14, 1921, on Emergency Officers' Retirement Bill, and comment.

unseen, this official first proclaimed anew 'the Legion's task to maintain in the hearts of our people allegiance to those basically American institutions and ideals of Government which have made the name "America" the hope of the world.' This done, he proceeded, still in his capacity as Chief of the American Legion, not only to attack the honesty and competence of a distinguished Cabinet member, but also, and under the thinnest of veils, to threaten both Congress and the President of the United States.

Scornfully referring to 'the sensational letter of the Secretary of the Treasury,' in which letter, he affirms, 'the cost of the [Bonus] bill was grossly exaggerated,' the speaker told how 'Mr. Mellon's intemperate statements failed of their purpose'; and how the bill was on the point of passing the Senate, when the President, 'decided on his extraordinary course,' made his sudden entry and personal appeal.

'In my opinion,' continued the Commander of the Legion, 'when the Senate yielded to the President's dictation it bowed to the will of the Executive and not to fact or reason.... In connection with our attitude toward Congress and others in legislative matters, *your Commander has felt that we should act as fearlessly toward them as did our brothers who lie in Flanders Field when they dealt with our enemies.'* [1]

Look again at those words. Then think of the fate of Lincoln, of Garfield, of McKinley — three Chief Executives of the Nation dead by the assassin's hand — and of

---

[1] Italics the author's. This speech was printed in full in the *Congressional Record* of November 9, 1921, p. 7578.

the bullet that took Mayor Cermak's life. Remember the suggestibility of unbalanced minds. Remember the many thousands of unbalanced men released from our World-War Army after their thoughts and hands had been well familiarized with the use of deadly weapons. Now they are scattered about the country, everywhere uprooted, a prey to brooding, to obsession, to extreme impulse, fostered, often, by the pinch of want. Think of the American Legion Commander's words, falling upon such ground. Rarely, perhaps, is the guiltiest man he who actually throws the bomb or fires the shot.

Nor is that inflammable tinder left without showers of sparks, deliberately scattered, persistently fanned. Mr. Mellon, Legionnaires are told again and again, is the enemy of the poor and suffering soldier; in which connection, Mr. Mellon, they are to mark and well remember, 'has been rated the second richest man in America.'

'Big Business,' also, and always, is the enemy of the poor and suffering soldier, who made its riches possible. 'Who is it,' they are asked, 'that opposes the Bonus?' Who but 'those who profited most from the War?' and who now 'fear that they might have to disgorge a pittance of the vast wealth they accumulated while the veteran was serving at a dollar a day.'[1]

Such doctrines the Legion's leaders have hammered in with ceaseless repetition through the years. Let them be a thousand times true, they are, as these men have handled them, both cowardly and traitorous. Not as to

[1] *Report of the National Legislative Committee*, Fourth National American Legion Convention, 1922, p. 35. Printed for circulation. See also Bulletins distributed to the posts.

92

the men against whom they are ostensibly aimed — for such may be able to protect themselves; but as to the poor, honest crack-witted devil who has no protection within or without and who must go to the electric chair if, in his simplicity, he lends his hand to give action to the words of his 'friend.'

Both Houses of Congress, coming to heel, passed the Bonus Bill as ordered. But President Harding, be it recorded, added his name to the succession of Presidents of the United States who, beginning with President Cleveland, have tried, at whatever cost to themselves, to protect the people of the United States from the War-pension raider. President Harding, on September 19, 1922, vetoed the Bonus Bill.[1]

The President's veto evoked from the Senate both foam and sparks. The sympathies of Senator Ashurst of Arizona welled up and softly overflowed for 'the soldier who remained at home and who prepared himself physically and spiritually to go.' That man, the Senator from Arizona was convinced, had faced 'intangible fires' as hot as the fire of the Hun, for whose blisters applications of cash, he felt, were now distinctly indicated.[2]

[1] Message of the President of the United States, dated September 19, 1922. House Document 396, 67th Congress, 2nd Session, September 20, 1922, p. 4. The President said, in brief and in part, that with a budget showing a deficit for the current fiscal year of over $650,000,000; and facing a further deficit for the coming year, over and above all probable receipts of interest on foreign debts; and in view of the liberal provision already made for all the war-disabled, he could not sanction the pledging of a minimum of over $4,000,000,000 to able-bodied ex-service men.

The Legion Lobby, at this time, took to itself much credit for the fact that in the year 1922 appropriations from the United States Treasury for the benefit of ex-service men more than doubled those of the year previous, reaching the sum of $582,381,954. See *Annual Report* for 1922, p.11.

[2] *Congressional Record*, September 20, 1922, p. 12983.

But Senator John Sharp Williams of Mississippi was otherwise affected.[1]

> This is a bill to give a bonus to something like 4,000,000 men over one-half of whom never faced a shot, over one-half of whom never went across the seas, about one-fourth of whom never served outside of a military camp, about one-fourth of whom, men and women, were serving with shoulder straps in Washington... and never got anywhere to illustrate their courage.... You put them all in because you know you could not carry off the steal without putting them all in. You knew that if you confined it to the... men who went to France ... you would not have gotten much consideration from the politicians of America. You wanted to take in the... millions serving in the training camps, some of them serving in the departments at Washington, wearing spurs, as old Joe Cannon said, for fear their heels might slip off the desks.... Let us get rid of this pretense of eloquence and oratory and heroism about the bill. If you will confine it to the men who actually entered action in France or in Belgium in American uniforms, you will get my approbation; but if you dare do that you know you cannot pass the bill.

The Senate refused to follow the example of the House, which passed the Bonus Bill over the veto.

The course of events henceforward is easily traced. Sure of the lower House, the Lobby had concentrated, 'ever since the failure of the Senate to override the Presidential veto in 1922,'[2] on improving the Senate's complexion. So well did it succeed that nineteen new Senators, elected during the ensuing year to fill vacancies, came into office pledged to vote for the Bonus Bill. Outside objectors, though rather amateurishly, now began to exhibit signs of life — a phenomenon so rare that 'a seri-

---

[1] *Congressional Record*, September 20, 1922, pp. 12978–79.

[2] *Proceedings of the Sixth National Convention of the American Legion*, 1924, pp. 220–21.

ous reversal of sentiment' became evident among weather-
cocks always lightly poised to the winds. That was the
Lobby's moment. Not amateurishly, it used its moment,
and with an eye to the long run. It dealt with each Congressional backslider on grounds of his personal fortune —
dealt firmly, often terrifyingly, but with no unnecessary
noise. Meantime, to preserve his face and to earn from
him a species of gratitude, it was 'directed that mass
meetings be held throughout the United States, led by
legionnaires, but participated in by the general public, to
demonstrate to the Congress the national desire' that
the Bonus be granted.[1]

'The result of these mass meetings,' continues the
Lobby solemnly, 'was immediate in its effect upon Congress.' On May 5, 1924, the Bonus Bill, having passed
both Houses, went to the President for signature.

The 'World War Adjusted Compensation' measure —
to give it for once its full official name — had, in the course
of its vicissitudes, been stripped of much plumage and
substance. At this stage only its backbone remained.
All 'options' had dropped away, including that which
offered cash down and which, be it noted, the Legion
Lobby now opposed, for reasons later to be developed.[2]
Nothing survived but the twenty-year insurance provision,
and that in a modified form.

As the measure now stood, it gave 'adjusted service
credit' to every person whose rank did not exceed that of
captain in the Army or lieutenant in the Navy, who had
been a member of any branch of the military or naval

---

[1] *Proceedings of Sixth Annual Convention of the American Legion*, p. 221.
[2] *Ibid.*, p. 225.

95

forces during the World War, and who had not been dishonourably discharged.

The amount of the credit was to be computed at the
rate of $1 a day for each day of home service, in excess of
sixty days after April 5, 1917, and before July 1, 1919; and
$1.25 for each day of overseas' service during that period.
Home service credit was limited to a total of $500, that
of overseas to $625.

If the credit of John Doe, so computed, did not exceed
$50, it would be paid to him or to his heir in lump cash.
If it exceeded $50, John Doe was to receive a certificate
for a certain amount of money payable to him at the end
of twenty years or to his designated beneficiary if his
death occurred before that time. The recipe for determining the exact amount that John was then to get ran
as follows:

Take the credit due as calculated by the scheme above
stated. Increase it by 25 per cent. Apply the total in a
lump as a single net premium to buy John a twenty-year
endowment insurance, according to the regular rates and
conditions established in commercial insurance usage,
with interest at four per cent compounded annually. If
John is thirty years old when he takes out his certificate
and if his credit amounts to $625, the face value of that
certificate will be $1577.50.[1]

If he lives twenty years, he will get that money, minus
whatever he may have borrowed on it in the interval;
for, beginning two years from the date of his certificate,

---

[1] 'The average amount being at least $962.' (Message of the President, May
15, 1924. House Document, 281, p. 1.) The 25 per cent addition is understood to have been in consideration of deferment of payment.

he may borrow from the Government or from banks, under fixed and favourable conditions. If he fails to repay the banks, Government must do so in his stead. If he dies before the end of the twentieth year, his heir will receive the face value of the certificate, in one lump sum, less the amount of whatever loan he may have had with interest at 4½ per cent compounded annually.

In order to remove it from the realm of abstraction, the proposal was stiffened with an appropriation clause.[1]

And yet, in spite of all the years of labour and worry, all the eloquence and terror and shaking of gory locks that had combined to bring forth this product and place it upon the Presidential desk, Calvin Coolidge, like Warren Harding, refused to turn it loose upon the land. Here are some of the reasons, beginning with prophecy, that, so refusing, he laid down:[2]

> ... *No one supposes the effort will stop here. Already suggestions are made for a cash bonus, in addition, to be paid at once. Such action logically would be encouraged if this bill becomes law.*[3] Neither the rich nor the profiteers will meet this expense. All of this enormous sum has to be earned by the people of this country through their toil.... The people of this country ought not to be required by their Government to bear any such additional burden. They are not deserving any such treatment....

[1] Title V, Section 505. 'There is hereby authorized to be appropriated for each calendar year [beginning with the year 1925, and ending with the calendar year 1946] an amount sufficient as an annual premium to provide for the payment of the face value of each adjusted service certificate in twenty years from its date or on the prior death of the veteran.... The amounts so appropriated shall be set aside in the fund on the first day of the calendar year for which appropriated. The appropriation for the calendar year 1925 shall not be in excess of $100,000,000.'

[2] Message from the President of the United States returning without approval the bill H.R. 7959, May 15, 1924. House Document 281.

[3] Italics the author's.

If this bill be considered as insurance, the opportunity... has already been provided. Nearly $3,000,000,000 of war risk and Government life insurance is now outstanding, and over $500,000,000 has been paid on such policies. When the provision was made in 1917... this opportunity was afforded to all those who entered the service. The intent of this bill now to provide free insurance lacks both a legal or moral requirement....

Considering this bill from the standpoint of its intrinsic merit, I see no justification for its enactment into law. We owe no bonus to able-bodied veterans of the World War. The first duty of every citizen is to the Nation. The veterans of the World War performed this first duty. To confer upon them a cash consideration or its equivalent for performing their first duty is unjustified.

I am not unmindful that this bill also embraces... the disabled of our veterans.... The nation stands ready to expend any amount needed for their proper care. *But that is not the object of this bill....* Our country cannot afford it. The veterans as a whole do not want it. All our American principles are opposed to it. There is no moral justification for it.

And —

We must either abandon our theory of patriotism or abandon this bill....

Congress leapt to its choice. Next day the lower House repassed the measure, by a vote of 331 to 87; the Senate followed 61 to 27; and on May 19, four days from the date of President Coolidge's veto message, the Bonus Act became law of the land.

CHAPTER XI

BEADS AND JACK-KNIVES

WE HAVE just seen the rotund Bonus Bill seat itself on the prostrate body of the War Risk Insurance Act, that once-proud 'scientific, well-balanced, equitable' creature that 'ought to make impossible as it will certainly make unnecessary, future pension legislation.'[1] But the War Risk Insurance Act was now inured to violence and to shame. Since its birth in late 1917 it had suffered no fewer than ninety-two assaults-at-law, some of them fundamental changes of far-reaching and serious effect, the greater part 'liberalizations.'

Yet not until June 7, 1924, did Congress, weary at last of teasing its no-longer-recognizable victim, knock the poor thing on the head once for all and put it out of its misery. In its stead on that day it propped up a new victim.

The World-War Veterans' Act, as this object was called, sprang, it appears, mainly from anxiety on the part of those few men who had built up the Legion as a trading company. For three years, now, Legion paid-up membership had been falling. In 1920 it had totalled 845,186. By 1923, through steady leakage, it had dwindled within the limits of continental United States, to 640,478. By 1924 it had further dropped to 606,490, as against a list of eligibles estimated at 5,276,331.[2]

If Congress was still to be cowed and dazzled with fist-

[1] The words are the Honourable W. G. McAdoo's.

[2] *Proceedings, Sixth National Convention of the American Legion*, 1924, p. 308. The membership as of Sept. 25, 1933, as given by the National Commander to the National Convention in Chicago five days later was 758,430.

banging assertions of the Legion's deliverable vote — one million — two million — two and a half million ballots — the actual figure of membership should not be allowed to shrink much lower than its present ebb.

Yet, what to do about it?

Certain radical strokes lay ahead in the realm of schemes; but time and the men were not ripe for those now. Some sort of lesser bait must be found to attract and hold new members while the whole body of organized ex-service men were being trained out of their troublesome War-time obsessions of patriotism and altruism, and, by patient drilling, were being moulded for practical use as a buccaneer crew to board the Ship of State.

Such, in the main, was the influence that gave the new Act its special form as an emergency device, a time-gainer, a grab-bag of odds and ends, out of which miscellaneous thousands might pluck unexpected prizes and be drawn to the ranks thereby.

But to War-disabled men, the Legion control saw little now to offer. If plain truth be told, the votes of the War-disabled were too few to repay attention.[1] The ex-service man industry, if it was to push forward as a major Big Business, must eventually be cut free from connection with War-disablement. But in view of the remaining resistance in the minds of the men themselves, such a thing were better done by soft degrees, insensibly.

It might, perhaps, be led up to through 'borderland cases.' Tuberculosis, a disease widespread in the land, suggested such a path of approach; a certain vagueness

---

For actual numbers of World-War ex-service men on compensation rolls for amputations, wounds, etc., see United States Appendix IV.

often enshrouds its origin. So the Law of 1924 exempted all tuberculous affections of whatever sort from medical judgment as to their occasion. Diagnosis by statute replaced diagnosis by science, decreeing that if any ex-service man should show an active tuberculous development of any type, to a ten per cent degree, between the date of his enlistment and January 1, 1925, his malady [1] lay beyond the pale of medical judgment and he must therefore, without attempt at rebuttal, be dealt with as a War-pensions beneficiary.

Neuropsychiatric diseases, with special specification of *paralysis agitans* and *encephalitis lethargica* (sleeping sickness), as well as amœbic dysentery, if appearing to a degree of ten per cent before January 1, 1925, were also now legislated into War-service connection unless Government could prove to the contrary. But the burden of proof lay entirely upon Government, and the claimant was freed from any requirement to furnish medical evidence.

These two provisions of the Act of 1924 led the great invasion of the main principle of the Act of 1917 — War-service-incurred injury the basis of War pensions. Bracketed in the famous 'Presumption Clause,' and thenceforth known as 'Presumptive Cases,' they immediately added to the pension rolls thousands of men who could not connect their ailments with War service; because no service record showed such connection and also because good medical judgment not infrequently denied the likelihood, or even the possibility of War-service connection with onset so tardy.

Incidentally, they transferred from War experience to

[1] World-War Veterans' Act, Section 200.

the accidents and attritions of common life no small part of the responsibility for the fact that forty per cent of the men who by 1932 were drawing American World-War pensions were doing so on claims of tuberculous or neuropsychiatric maladies.[1]

Another provision of the same Act [2] further attacked the intention of the older law without actually violating its letter. It gave, not the War pension itself, but the perquisites of the War pensioner to all persons who had served in 'any war, military occupation, or military expedition,' and who had not been dishonourably discharged from the service. Thenceforth, it decreed, all these, when at any future time they fell ill, 'without regard to the nature or origin of their disabilities,' should be provided with free hospitalization and incidental traveling expenses, 'so far as ... existing Government facilities permit.'

'Preference,' it was added — preference in admission to hospital — should be granted to the financially unable. But, obeying the Legion Lobby's continuous interdict of what it shrewdly damns 'the pauper clause,' the law omitted any requirement that the person asking hospitalization at public expense should be unable to bear his own charges.

This half-hearted precaution proved as well justified as it was inadequate and vain. From all over the country well-to-do persons in need of operations for appendicitis, of rest cures for too merry a life, of medical or surgical attention for a thousand ills unrelated to war, stepped quickly forward to seize the opening.

[1] *Annual Report of the Administrator of Veterans' Affairs*, 1932, p. 31.
[2] Section 202 (10).

Among them appeared, it is said, not a few Congress-men whose private means were as ample as their War service was problematic, yet who did not hesitate to bring their civilian aches and pains of advancing years to be salved luxuriously at the expense of the Nation.

For Veterans' Administration hospitals are indeed luxurious — enriched with every comfort and advantage. The best science, whether diagnostic, medical, or surgical, the best scientific equipment in the country, are there placed free of any cost at the disposal of the highly priv-ileged class. Rooms, nursing, diet, entertainment, leave. nothing to be desired by any reasonable man, and all are his without price. Furthermore, and not to be overlooked, the opportunity is given, while thus lying in drydock for chronic alcoholism or gout, to even scores with your pri-vate dentist. For now, while your cure is in progress, you may have your teeth put completely in order; or, if you like, an entire new set made, all at Government cost by a good Government dentist.

The complaint for which you are hospitalized need not, for practical purposes, be even remotely associated with your teeth; and if any hospital chief too pressingly raises a question thereof, you have but to speak to your Congress-man or, perhaps, to the Legion, and all will be well.

Another feature of the Act of 1924 began, somewhat gingerly, to undermine the 'Misconduct Clause' as signi-fying social diseases; but it confined this initial step to certain specific conditions.

This amendment provided [1] that the man blinded or

---

[1] World-War Veterans' Act, June 7, 1924, Section 200, amending the War Risk Insurance Act, Section 300.

paralyzed by the progress of a venereal disease, whether he acquired that disease before or after joining the service, should enjoy free maintenance and medical care in United States Veterans' hospitals, and, while there, should be paid a monthly pension of from $100 to $150, subject to no deductions. Approximately two thousand ex-service men hitherto barred from War pension by the 'Misconduct Clause' now cleared the barrier, at a cost to the Nation of about $2,000,000 a year.

But the Legion Lobby, reporting on the matter to the National Legion Convention, admitted a partial defeat. Its own provision as drafted for enactment had been more generous, imposing no condition of hospitalization as prerequisite to the drawing of high pension by the man disabled by venereal disease. Congressmen and Senators, timorously changing the wording, had so curtailed the benefits intended that, said the Lobby in its first flush of annoyance, 'as passed into the law, the proviso is not thought to be of great value.' [1]

Yet, in view of the opinion of a considerable part of the American public, and the consequent delicacy of the ground, the gain was not meagre. Moreover, as the law now stood, it set no limit as to time or source. Any ex-service man who, at any future period, however remote, should develop a venereal disease, no matter when contracted, was now sure of the best of domicile and hospital care for the remainder of his life in a place made specially beautiful and luxurious to honour our War-disabled.

The Legion's National executives, however, were on this

---

[1] *Proceedings of the Sixth National Convention of the American Legion*, 1924, p. 168.

point still far from satisfied. Obeying orders, the Lobby, therefore, continued pressure upon an unusually obstinate Congress. Nine months later the next gains showed: men blind or in any way helpless through venereal diseases need no longer stay in hospital in order to draw their pay.[1] They might live where they chose, drawing, in addition to their $100 or $150 a month, an extra $50 for attendance.[2] At which point, for the moment, Congress appears completely to have balked, leaving the matter in the Lobby's category of unfinished business.

A further provision of the new law upset completely the former system of disability rating, by which a man's assessment depended on the degree of physical damage actually sustained, reckoned on an average basis alike for all men. Henceforth, said the Law of 1924, it must rest on —

> the average impairments of earning capacity resulting from such injuries in civil occupations similar to the occupation of the injured man at the time of enlistment and not upon impairment in earning capacity in each individual case, so that there shall be no reduction in the rate of compensation for individual success in overcoming the handicap of an injury.[3]

The rating schedule worked out under this demand was exceedingly complex. It undertook to identify a man's precise disability, in terms of single degrees up to one hundred per cent, i.e., to determine whether his earning power was reduced thirty-seven per cent or only thirty-six per cent — fifty-five per cent or fifty-four. To make this process possible, a separate table was set up showing

---

[1] Act of March 4, 1925, amendment of Section 200 of the Law of 1924.
[2] World-War Veterans' Act, 1924, Section 202 (3) and (5).
[3] Section 202 (4).

approximately one thousand representative occupations. In relation to each of the thousand callings, Table I set forth all parts of the body — eye, ear, leg, chest, etc., assigned to each part its value as to the occupation in question, and recognizing nine variants or differentiations as to a given occupation. The degree of disability then must be assessed as to the importance to the specific calling of the part affected. Some fifteen hundred diseases and injuries were thus listed in a second table, each subdivided into its possible relations to a thousand occupational aspects. Every disability being given nine rates, except in comparatively few instances, wherein one rate was assigned for all occupations; or wherein one rate was provided for certain groups of variants.[1]

Great administrative difficulties, an enormous volume of work, and many strange inequalities were created by this device. Men who had been trained for new occupations under the Vocational Rehabilitation Act were now paid on the basis of their pre-War occupation. Thus a bricklayer who lost a hand and who had been trained by Government to be a salesman was compensated at a higher rate than a man who had been a salesman before the War and who, having lost a hand, did not need vocational retraining, because his injury did not prevent his resuming his pre-War calling.

Or again, a farmer's leg, by the new rating, was valued at $60 a month; but a man who had been a bookkeeper before the War would draw $29 a month for the same injury. Yet when the one-legged farmer, accepting vocational training, had become a bookkeeper, the two might

[1] For an example of the rating schedule see United States Appendix II.

sit in the same office, at neighbouring desks, and for the same injury draw, the one $60, the other $29.

In most cases the new scheme of rating raised the compensation — at a combined cost of many millions yearly.

And so the World-War Veterans' Act of 1924, in itself a nonpareil of no mean oddity, was launched upon the fate of all its predecessors in American War-pension legislation. It had become, within a year of its birth, the beads and jack-knives, the rum-and-wampum, the common trading-stock, of 'politics.'

The structure that so continued to develop cannot properly be called a code or system of any sort, nor is it worth the attempt so to deal with it. Rather it was a formless, haphazard conglomeration of unrelated lumps, flung together one by one, swelling with fungus-like speed. For the major part, it represented, on the one hand, spasms of zeal not of political parties, but of individual Congressmen to further their personal fortunes; and on the other hand, progressive strategies of able and daring racketeers to mould their public and build up their gang.

In 1926, twenty-two sections of the World-War Veterans' Act were thus amended (its amendments were to grow to eighty-two, in the following six years) and practically always to lower bars and increase the number of beneficiaries. Cerebrospinal meningitis was added to the group of 'presumptively' War-occasioned diseases now exempted from medical judgment and, by the strong hand of statute, made conclusively of War origin, if showing a ten per cent degree of development prior to January 1, 1925.[1]

[1] Act of July 2, 1926, amendment of Section 200. The law, sloppily phrased

Now, cerebrospinal meningitis, an infectious, communicable and essentially acute disease, ordinarily shows itself in three weeks from the occurrence of the infection. 'Six weeks,' says medical science, 'would cover the most prolonged incubation.'

'Hold thy peace,' retorts the Act; 'if cerebrospinal meningitis shows up before January, 1925, in any man who ever served in America's World-War forces, that man contracted that disease in the World War. And the fact that the war ended six years earlier has no place in the picture.'

The few random items just touched upon show the quality, rather than the content of the World-War Veterans' Act and its early amendments. By 1928, these sources had borne fruit as shown, in part, in the following figures:

	NUMBER OF MEN ON COMPENSATION PAY-ROLL	AMOUNT OF COMPENSATION PAID
1924	190,737	$96,089,557
1928	257,536	$150,980,629

Thus, almost wholly from 'borderland cases' of, at best, extremely dubious War connection, we had added 78,499 men to our War-pension roster, at a cost, aside from administrative, medical and hospital expenses, of nearly fifty-five million dollars.[1] Both numbers and costs were to mount rapidly.

by laymen, named 'spinal meningitis,' leaving the exact malady to be identified by administrative surmise.

[1] *Annual Report of the Administrator of Veterans' Affairs*, 1932, pp. 114 and 160.

CHAPTER XII

LEAP-FROG

'RANK does not exist in the Legion; no member shall be addressed by his military or naval title in any conversations or meeting of the Legion' — so decrees the American Legion's Constitution.[1]

We have seen the marked dislike that, in the early days, threatened to exclude all ex-officers from this organization. We have seen, too, the deliberate barring of all ex-service men above the degree of captain from the benefits of the Legion's victorious Bonus Bill. Taken together with the just-quoted article in its Constitution these points serve to make more striking the fact that, from the day of its earliest national meeting,[2] the American Legion first asked and then roundly demanded of Congress legislation conferring unparalleled advantages upon disabled ex-service officers.

The main advantage thus demanded by the Legion was that all disabled ex-service officers be transferred from the compensation pay-roll common to all disabled ex-service men alike, and be endowed for life with three-quarters of the pay that they drew as officers in the World-War Army.

No officer of the Regular Army of the United States can be retired as disabled, drawing his three-quarters pay,

[1] Article II, Section 1.
[2] In St. Louis, 1919. Cf. *Proceedings of Tenth National Convention of American Legion*, 1928, p. 145.

unless he is totally disabled for further commissioned service. But these 'disabled Emergency Officers' were now asking, on the strength of their disablement, full re-tired officers' annuities for disabilities so slight as barely to be recognized as compensable at all, in such countries as, for example, Italy and Germany.

Special perquisites of considerable money value accom-panied this dispensation, but the fact just mentioned will suffice to identify its basic character.

Congress, however, persistently shied. Year after year, led up to the hurdle by its trainers, it reared and wheeled, refusing the jump. The word 'rank' seemed somehow to frighten it. At last, in May, 1928, suddenly picking up courage, over it sailed. All ex-service officers who, within a year from that date, could by any means get themselves certified for an injury of a thirty per cent degree incurred in a service then ten years past, were bidden to the party.

President Calvin Coolidge vetoed [1] the Bill. In doing so, he said:

> What this bill proposes is to compensate a limited number of emergency officers not according to their disability but ac-cording to the rank which they held in the World War. It breaches the fundamental principles of our Government.... The most sacred duty of our citizenry is to enroll in the de-fense of their Country in time of need.... Both the commis-sioned officer and the enlisted man who entered the service for this emergency were serving in the same duty.... [This bill] is a gross discrimination against the enlisted men.

Two days later — May 24, 1928 — Congress enacted the Bill over the President's head.

This means that some 6500 men who drew, before the

[1] Senate Document no. 153, 70th Congress, 1st Session, May 22, 1928.

110

passage of the measure, an average disability compensation of $51 a month, drew, after its enactment an average of $140 a month. And that a sergeant whose right hand had been torn off in Flanders got $75, while a second lieutenant who, fighting the War in a Washington office, there complained of bronchitis and was prescribed a dose of cough-medicine, now received $106.25 a month to console him for his War-injury.

Also, it cost the country in pensions alone about $7,000,000 yearly.

The Legion Lobby viewed the outcome with peculiar relief. It had felt its credit somewhat imperilled by the slow progress of this undertaking. The project in itself was of minor interest, but an unbroken record of success in capturing every objective for which it had once started — such a record was, to the Lobby, of transcendent value in handling both Congress and its own clientèle.

Its annual report thus reflected satisfaction in yet another victory won by the Legion Lobby against a President of the United States.[1]

> This, of course, was the most spectacular fight your national legislative committee has ever had on its hands, because it was an attempt to defeat a specific piece of legislation which would mean the destruction of the growing influence and prestige which your national legislative committee enjoys at the National Capitol. As a result, however, of the victory, the American Legion today occupies a stronger position than it has ever held in its entire history.

An infinitude of curious results have arisen from this measure, which the Legion had successfully defended from any condition as to the beneficiary's private means.

---

[1] *Proceedings of Tenth National Convention of the American Legion*, 1928, p. 145.

And it is, by the way, worthy of note that most if not all the Legion's fights against the inclusion, in any law, of a needs clause, steadily stigmatized by the Legion Lobby as 'the pauper clause,' in effect fights to put money into the pockets of the well-to-do. There seems something curiously hard, cruel, and unchivalrous in this tacit branding of decent poverty, unmerited misfortune, and natural dependency with the epithet 'pauper.' One of the less forgivable tricks of the 'racket,' it seems to have done its work on its face value, through the years, seldom analyzed or challenged.

As for the situations sometimes produced by the Disabled Emergency Officers' Retirement Act, take this:

The mayor of a certain Northern Atlantic seaboard city, a warm citizen with a good personal income, and for a number of years past in the enjoyment, besides, of his mayoralty salary, has drawn, since the passage of the Act, a retired officer's pay of $2800. The ground on which he retired is mental disability.

The argument in support of the Disabled Emergency Officers' Retirement Act urged that the ex-emergency officer deserved as much of his country as did the retired officer of the Regular Establishment. What seems left out of account is the fact that the professional officer gives the major part of his life to the Army as a career, at a pay much lower than he might reasonably expect to earn in civil life, and too low, if he has a family, or if life makes many demands on him, to enable him to save for his old age. This he dares do because of a contract with his Government that assures him, in consideration of long service, subsistence in his declining years. On the other hand, the 'emergency officer,' unless he was an unplaced boy when he entered the service, had then some calling. If, when demobilized, he was suffering from an injury that handicapped him for return to that pre-War calling, he was offered liberal education in any other line he chose, at Government expense. In any case, he had, in general, been ten years established in some paying job, or had been living on his own or other's means, or had been ten years in receipt of a good total disablement pension, when the 'Disabled Emergency Officers' Retirement Act' was passed. The Regular Army officer, when his hour strikes, retires from the Army — at an age at which the average man can find no new paid position. But from what, in the year 1929, did the ex-emergency officer of our War of 1917–18 retire, and by virtue of a disability allowed at least eleven years time in which to discover and develop itself since his service was rendered? [1]

Whatever question may be raised, however, as to the rights and wrongs of this measure vainly vetoed by President Coolidge, it is difficult to defend President Coolidge's capitulation less than ten months later to attack upon the quality of the Civil Service.

According to Civil Service rules, applicants must earn, in eligibility examinations, a rating of 70 per cent. By early efforts of the Legion Lobby, all World-War ex-service men were given an advantage of five points, and all who

[1] The Disabled Emergency Officers' Retirement Law reads: '... all persons who have served as officers... during the World War, other than as officers of the Regular Army, Navy, or Marine Corps, who during such service have incurred physical disability in the line of duty, and who have been, *or may hereafter, within one year*, be rated in accordance with law at not less than 30 per centum permanent disability, shall be placed on the special officers' list above described.'

were drawing any disablement pay, however slight, were given five additional points, applicable to such examinations.

Therefore, all able-bodied ex-service men who earn 65 per cent, and all pensioned ex-service men who earn 60 per cent, pass their examinations by virtue of their handicap and are entered on the list of eligibles. Once there, their names, automatically, leap straight to the top; on which the Lobby comments, with a happy consciousness of successful effort, 'as under the civil service laws it is necessary for the appointing officer to select the appointee from the three highest names on the list, the veterans were achieving a very substantial preference.'[1]

In awarding an appointment demanding expert scientific knowledge, the brilliant and able non-World-War man who scores 99 per cent in his examinations and could give superlative value to the public must thus be set aside for the ex-service man who, having earned 60 or 65 per cent, has entered the list of the eligibles only by the skin of his teeth plus his automatic advantage. Though his World-War service had been as brief and as slight as are his training and ability, neither matters. Against all competitors he wins the appointment.

A specific instance, cited by a Congressional Committee in 1931, will illustrate the natural result.[2]

Leading the list for junior chemists, out of a total of 172 candidates, appears only one disabled veteran. He had ob-

[1] *Proceedings* of the Tenth National Convention of the American Legion, 1928, p. 156.
[2] Cf. *Veterans' Legislation and its Relations to Health. Report* of the Committee on Public Health Relations of the New York Academy of Medicine, 1932, p. 9.

tained the lowest mark in the examination, 69.04, a rating that would normally disqualify him. But under the Executive Order, he, though unqualified, is entitled to certification for appointment to the position, which may involve the health of the American people, before even the highest person on the list, whose earned rate was 97.5.

The course of civil service preference legislation and regulations... [continues the report just quoted], shows that once a special privilege is granted to a favoured class, the flood-gates are opened for further and further favours to larger and larger classes, regardless of the disadvantage... to the unprivileged majority and of its serious detriment to the efficiency of the public service.

President Harding, by Executive Order of March 3, 1923, five months before his death, repealed the provision that shot World-War men to the top of the list the moment they cleared its bottom. Instead, said his Order, all persons, ex-service and non-service alike, must now stand in the order of their earned ratings, after ex-service men had received their original percentage of preference.

But the Legion, at this — so its Lobby reported — had complained loudly concerning the difficulty of obtaining Civil Service appointments. That complaint the Lobby worked hard to satisfy. And it is something of a testimony to the survival of scruples, in the mind of Congress, that the Lobby's endeavours were slow of fruition. In the event, it was not Congress but President Coolidge who wiped out his predecessor's effort in behalf of the country.

President Coolidge's Executive Order, issued two days before Mr. Hoover succeeded him in office, further contained the following passage:

... When reductions are being made in the force, in any part of the classified service, no employee entitled to military preference in appointment shall be discharged or dropped or reduced in rank or salary if his record is good, or if his efficiency rating is equal to that of any employee in competition with him who is retained in the service.

The word 'good,' in this connection, is a technical term signifying an efficiency rating of 80 per cent, which is accounted low.

As to the effect on the Civil Service as a whole, one has but to picture the eventual status of any public service from which every withdrawal is subject to the necessity of retaining the possibly least efficient — and he, moreover, taken from an aggressive organized class representing less than four per cent of the population.

CHAPTER XIII

THE SPANISH MAIN

MEANTIME, out on the broad blue piratical sea, one little black-flagged tub heavy with last-century barnacles was rolling its wonted way, undisturbed by time and changes. This was the Special Pension Act — the bill brought in by one legislator to benefit a single client — the little favour wangled by exchange of Congressional courtesy. The war waged upon this industry by President Cleveland [1] had dealt it no lasting discouragement. President Coolidge, in the Seventieth Congress, saw 7569 such bills become law. On their general merits an unusually outspoken Congressional Committee report declared, in language like Mr. Cleveland's own:

> ... the special [pension] act is in the nature of a political plum, and, apportioned to the Representatives and Senators as such, it is ordinarily awarded where it will do the most good for its sponsors.... There seems to be a prevalent opinion that it is proper to bring every sort of claim to the attention of Congress, and in many instances the Bureau of Pensions and the general laws are wholly ignored.... Thus there has been an allowance of pensions to widows of men who had no part in the war in the remotest degree... to [men] whose military service was nominal; to those whose contracts of service were dishonourably terminated; to those who were never entered for military service; to women who had not been the soldiers' lawful wives; to women who have several times remarried since the soldiers' death.... The tendency is to go beyond the law (not simply to waive some slight technicality) and to create an entirely new class of pensioners. [2]

[1] See *ante*, pp. 18–19.

[2] The pension rolls now carry 14,522 special act cases at monthly rates ranging from $6 to $416.66.

Thus, farther and wider reached the clutch of the privileged class. Deeper and deeper struck its roots into the common resources of the country, appetite growing as it fed, till nothing was too small to seek or too great to swallow.

Then, one fine day, tardy as Rip Van Winkle, the men of the War with Spain started from their sleep. Witnessing the spectacle in full career before them — the simplicity of the game and the richness of its stakes — they cursed their own moss-grown stupidity. Their little war, with its two pendants, the Philippine Insurrection and the China Relief Expedition, had begun and ended between April 21, 1898, and October 1, 1900. Their whole mobilized force had numbered only 392,000 men, of whom but 5000 were wounded. Yet a good deal of sickness had occurred, both in the home camps and in Cuba, largely due to lack of camp sanitation among non-Regular Army contingents; so that in 1919, 23,382 of them were on the pension rolls as War-disabled.[1]

That they might have been War-pensioned without War-disablement seems not to have entered their simple heads until, twenty years after their war was over, in 1920, they caught sight of the American Legion's objective. Whereat, unlimbering their stiffened joints, they gallantly leap-frogged to the head of the column.

For why should they, who stood ready to save the country in case the Spanish fleet shelled Atlantic City, not be perpetually rewarded for that willingness, as well as World-War 'Veterans' who enlisted after the Armistice and who, six years later, picked up an infection in civil life?

[1] *Annual Report of Administrator, Veterans' Affairs*, 1931, p. 126.

118

Why, indeed!

So they got them a first-rate lobby. That lobby dealt with Congress in the good old way, and Congress performed as by precedent. Every Spanish Warrior who had seen ninety days' service and who had escaped scatheless, so only that he could show an honourable discharge, was now entitled to pension running from $12 to $30 monthly, for any and all ailments, not due to vicious habits, that might hereafter befall him through the years. Or, if no ailment came his way, then mere age should bring him gifts, beginning with his sixty-second year and rising by stages.[1]

Through subsequent lobbying, the rates and terms of this law were bettered in successive enactments, so that by 1929, the 1919 roster of 23,382 pensioned men had been submerged in a list over seven-fold longer, comprising 58 per cent of the entire Spanish-War body, and consisting mostly of non-service connected cases.

Its cost to the National Treasury in 1931 was about $100,000,000, including payments to widows.

The Spanish-War pension law, like those of the Mexican, Indian, and Civil Wars, has stood by itself, unconnected with World-War pension legislation. It finds place

---

[1] Act of June 5, 1920. Its age benefits were thus determined:

For 90 days' service		For 70 days' service (by Amendment of 1926)
62 years of age......	$30 monthly	$12 monthly
68 years of age......	40 monthly	18 monthly
72 years of age......	50 monthly	24 monthly
75 years of age......	60 monthly	30 monthly
75 years and needing attendant......	72 monthly	50 monthly

here only on grounds of moral relationship, in that one gave birth to the other, while both illustrate the spirit determining our national performance.

For this reason, and because we shall not return to the subject of Spanish-War pensions, it may be well here to pursue it a step farther in advance of our period. From their 1919 roster of 23,382, through steady climbing, the number of men pensioned as Spanish-War Veterans had reached, by 1932, 196,541. These men and the widows drew in that year $113,463,154. In the Act of June 2, 1930, their Lobby had won them substantial advantages, visible now both in awards and in numbers. By the first of these, their pensions, both for disability and for age, were practically doubled, being raised respectively to $20–$60, and $30–$72 for the ninety-day men; or to $12–$30, and $12–$50 for those who served seventy days.

Another and a unique distinction fell to the Spanish-War Lobby's arms. Overriding a Presidential veto that specifically denounced the step, Congress freed all Spanish-War Veterans from the burden of that 'vicious-habits' clause that apparently had hitherto embarrassed their progress. 'This bill,' President Hoover had pointed out,[1] 'opens the door for claims of disability incurred at any time in the life of the pensioner, arising from venereal disease, alcoholism, drug habit, etc. Certainly such claims for public help cannot be fairly based upon sacrifice to the Nation in war and must be opposed to national policy.'

But Congress's generous sympathies were now ignited. Cried Senator Ashurst, all ablaze:[2]

[1] Message from the President of the United States, May 28, 1930. Senate Document, No. 155, 71st Congress, 2d Session.
[2] *Congressional Record*, June 2, 1930, p. 9869.

... We are inclined to forget the historical significance of
the Spanish-American War. It was the Spanish-American
War that made America a world power.... I have always felt,
and now feel that the veterans of the Spanish-American War
have never received that complete and true meed of justice
and recognition, at the hands of their opulent and grateful
Government, to which they are entitled.

With which words of exhortation, the Senator proceeded
to lay at their feet the Perfect Tribute — his vote for
their exemption from the misconduct clause.

Sixty-one against eighteen, two hundred and twenty-
nine against fourteen, Senate and House agreed, and the
tribute became law.

In this the Spanish-War Lobby scored a distinct triumph
over its World-War colleagues. At the Legion's urgent
behest, both Houses of Congress, almost synchronously
with their action as to the Spanish-War Veterans, passed
an amendment on behalf of World-War men, abolishing
the 'wilful misconduct' clause entirely and admitting to
full benefit of World-War pensions persons suffering from
venereal diseases, not only in advanced stages, as already
granted, but in all degrees of progress. That also, President Hoover had vetoed, as an idea 'the whole conception of which must be repugnant to family life.' [1]

But in this instance Congress sustained the veto. The
project, therefore, returned to its old place on the Legion
program of unfinished business — to its old place beside
a companion project — that to remove the United States
Comptroller from the Veterans' Bureau. Both of these
steps were announced by the Legion as of major im-

[1] Message from the President of the United States, June 26, 1930. House
Document No. 495, 71st Congress, 2d Session.

portance to the further relief of distressed veterans. [1]

It is here of interest to state the practice of other nations in the same matter.

Neither France nor Italy, for pension purposes, dissociates venereal diseases from other maladies contracted during or aggravated by War-service, basing their attitude largely on bad hygienic conditions or on lack of prophylactic facilities available to their troops during war.

The English position is, broadly, this:

In the case of men below officers' rank, venereal diseases and their after-effects have not been handled under the misconduct rule. Where infection was contracted before the War, and where, in the opinion of Ministry doctors, definite conditions of the man's service aggravated and hastened the otherwise slow working of the poison, producing paresis, paralysis, blindness, etc., the Ministry has conceded aggravation by service and has granted pension according to the man's condition. If, on the other hand, the infection was contracted while in service, the Ministry, when advanced consequences have eventually become manifest, has taken the line that the trouble was neither due to nor aggravated by War-service and is therefore not War-pensionable.

With regard to officers, however, the position is otherwise. Following the practice of the Navy and the Army, the Ministry of Pensions takes the stand that, both because of the officer's educational standard and because of his position, infection contracted in service is misconduct. The Ministry has accepted liability only in cases where

[1] See *Proceedings of Twelfth National Convention American Legion*, 1930, pp. 199–200, and other *Annual Reports* of the Legion.

conditions of War-service were shown to be such as to 'light up' a pre-War infection; otherwise the officer's case is held non-pensionable.

Appeal tribunals [1] have occasionally allowed claims that had been rejected by the Ministry. But the above statement shows the principle governing the English procedure.

[1] See *post*, pp. 434–35.

CHAPTER XIV

COMPARISONS

HAVING now tested the general quality of our performance from 1917 to 1929, let us stop for a moment to take account of stock.

What, roughly, had we done, during this period?

We had utilized our bright and shining effort, the War Risk Insurance Act, as foundation of a junk-heap. On it we had piled any rubbish that came along, until no part of the original fabric remained in sight and until the lump itself smelled to Heaven.

We had witnessed the birth and growth of an organization vowed, 'For God and Country,' 'to inculcate a sense of individual obligation to the community, state and nation.' [1] We had consented to see that organization tear down barrier after barrier erected in the interests of our War-disabled men, shamelessly trading on their merit and good name, letting loose upon their sacred precincts ever-increasing hordes devoid of just title. We had seen that same organization, in periods of the Nation's grave economic distress, mock her danger, openly jeer at each succeeding Secretary of the Treasury, and set itself up as our Supreme Court of Finance. More, we had seen it with truculence defy each President of the United States when these, in turn, came forward, in ominous helplessness, to plead for the whole people against the voracity of

[1] Preamble to the Constitution of the American Legion, and Section 2 of that Constitution.

124

the racketeer. And we had seen Congress after Congress rush to override both Secretarial warnings and Presidential vetoes, like a herd of stampeded cattle scared senseless by the drivers' shouts.

All this we had seen done under cover of a sleight-of-hand man's din — a hocus-pocus about 'the disabled buddy' too palpable, too thin, too cheap to have deceived the slightest study by an honest eye — a trick as false and cruel and harmful to the War-disabled man as it was shameless toward the Nation. Yet, ourselves not less guilty in our soft indifference, we did nothing. We, the public, went our easy way.

For the rest, we had brought home from France 192,369 [1] wounded men, of whom the Chief of the Statistics Branch of the General Staff recorded that 'about half... were reported as slightly wounded and many of them would not have been recorded as casualties in previous wars.' [2]

However, by fixing our minimum degree of compensable disablement low, by fixing our disability ratings high, and by adding the product of 'presumptive.' clauses, guinea-pigs in fertility, we had built up by 1929 a pension roll of allegedly World-War-disabled men totalling 262,138.[3] Of these 74,481 were listed as less than 20 per cent disabled.

As to costs: In the year 1920, we spent in payment of compensation to World-War-disabled men $82,012,777 [4]

[1] War Department figures.

[2] War with Germany, p. 122.

[3] Annual Report of the Administrator of Veterans' Affairs, 1932, p. 106. For table of Disability Compensation beneficiaries, by degrees of disability, with amounts received monthly, as of 1932. See United States Appendix III.

[4] Annual Report of the Administrator of Veterans' Affairs, 1932, p. 106.

aside from payments to dependants of the dead and from administration charges and War Risk Insurance. By 1929 that sum had increased to $153,090,387.

We had built, or otherwise created or acquired, many grand new hospitals, not one of which was needed to care for our actually service-disabled men. We had flung six hundred and forty-five millions of dollars into a rehabilitation scheme of dubious value. We had misty memories of a Government Land Settlement scheme that came to little or naught but noise and gesture. And we had assumed, in the Bonus Act, the burden of building up, by annual appropriations, a testimonial bouquet of some two and a quarter billion dollars, to be presented in the year 1945 to all those who, willingly or unwillingly, early or late, had put on America's World-War uniform. This over and above War Risk Insurance policies still extant in excess of one and a half billion dollars — those War Risk Insurance policies that, in the year of innocence 1917, we fondly thought would, in addition to true War-disablement compensation, cover the whole matter.

Such are a few of the high points in our record — touched at random here and there to recall its general tenour.

How does that record compare with those of the four great European nations that shared in the World War? Did they, too, profane the name of their War-disabled, using it as a mask for racketeers? Did they, too, bestow the title of 'veteran' on men who saw no service beyond a training camp or a draft board office? Did they class with battle casualties persons kicked by a mule or frightened by a tree-toad ten years after the War was over?

COMPARISONS

The story of what they did, and of why they did it, each in her own way, forms the second part of this book. But it is pertinent here to compare some main results of their systems, as shown by a decade of their work, with the results of our own methods at that period.

Let us, however, begin with this prefatory table of 1919:

	Killed in Battle or Died of Wounds or Sickness	Disabled by Wounds or Service-Incurred Sickness
United States...	130,128 [1]	192,369 [2]
France	1,393,388 [3]	2,052,984 [4]
Germany	2,050,466 [5]	4,202,028 [5]
Italy	700,000 [6]	1,000,000 [6]
United Kingdom	812,317 [7]	1,869,567 [8]

Thus it appears that our losses by death, like our disablements, not only come lowest on the list, but fall, roughly, 500 per cent beneath the next minimum.

Now for the number of men pensioned by the several countries, on account of World-War service, at the beginning and at the end of the decade:

	Disabled Men Pensioned in Fiscal Year, 1919	Disabled Men Pensioned in Fiscal Year, 1929
United States...	27,128 [9]	262,138 [10]
France	1,200,000 [11]	1,030,000 [12]
Italy	275,000 [13]	210,000 [13]
United Kingdom	610,812 [14]	503,250 [14]

From the two tables above, the two below follow — and attention must be called to the italicized words:

[1] War Department figures of 1933. This estimate includes 35,000 deaths in home training camps, largely in the influenza world-epidemic.

[2] War Department figures, 1933.

[3] *Les Dommages*, p. 497. For full title, see *post*, p. 224, note 1.

[4] *Ibid.*, p. 501.   [5] *Whitaker's Almanack*

[6] Authority of the Italian Government. See *post*, p. 301.

[7] *Whitaker's Almanack*, 1933, p. 381.

[8] House of Commons *Report*, May 5, 1921.

[9] *Annual Report of the Administrator of Veterans' Affairs*, 1932, p. 104.

[10] *Ibid.*, p. 106.   [11] *Les Dommages*, p. 505.   [12] See *post*, p. 247.

[13] See *post*, p. 336.   [14] See British Appendix IX.

SOLDIERS WHAT NEXT!

NUMERICAL COMPARISON OF WORLD-WAR DISABLED MEN, AS OF
1919, WITH WORLD-WAR PENSIONERS AS OF 1929

United States.	36 per cent	*increase*
France.	49.8	decrease
Italy.	79.	decrease
England.	73.08	decrease

NUMERICAL COMPARISON OF WORLD-WAR PENSIONERS AS OF 1929,
WITH WORLD-WAR PENSIONERS OF 1919

United States.	866 per cent	*increase*
France.	14.1	decrease
Italy.	23.6	decrease
England.	17.4	decrease

During this general period — from 1919 to 1932 —
expenditure on ex-service měn's benefits compare as below. All the figures are as supplied by the respective Governments concerned, and include, save in Italy's case,
hospital and administrative costs and those benefits extended to the dependants of the dead. The American
figures do not, however, include insurance, the Bonus, or
hospital and domiciliary construction.

	U.S.A.	France	Germany	Italy[3]	United Kingdom
1919.	$33,083,883[1]			$14,171,724	$226,300,224
1920.	125,579,632			43,345,741	480,749,562
1921.	184,570,687			61,125,379	516,941,190
1922.	208,422,056			74,066,928	463,181,119
1923.	220,611,606			74,447,033	389,415,733
1924.	198,379,019			62,878,338	350,453,093
1925.	217,032,592			70,873,290	337,413,548
1926.	246,066,084	$151,758,828		70,195,203	324,626,072
1927.	249,647,462	162,857,780		69,068,753	306,750,865
1928.	258,605,473	172,544,680	$404,940,000[2]	66,545,293	290,357,356
1929.	268,177,952	176,217,720		65,317,411	275,515,101
1930.	284,550,265			63,464,624	262,759,628
1931.	348,714,973		285,840,000	62,168,201	251,395,548
1932.	417,738,652	297,842,031		60,758,885	240,260,724

[1] *Report of Administrator of Veterans' Affairs*, 1932, p. 157.   [2] Peak year.
[3] Italy's figures do not include expenditures in her three Institutes, for the
disabled, the orphans, and ex-service men. See *post*, pp. 316–17 and Italian
Appendix II.

COMPARISONS

This table shows that between 1920 and 1932 the American World-War budget rose 233 per cent, while the budgets of Italy and the United Kingdom began to diminish, as they logically should, from a period shortly after the War. Furthermore, our American official estimate, based on continuance of the laws in effect in 1932 without additional 'liberalizations,' indicated a continuous increase of the budget up to and including the year 1958.[1] Two years later, in 1960, the English World-War pension budget,[2] by orderly decline, will be extinguished.

In these four countries here discussed, four nations radically differing in character and circumstance, sought out their several ways.

In France a people passionately devoted to their soil, by age-long experience keyed to constant danger, took the World War with philosophy. Fought on their ground, it brought them wholesale destruction. But when it was done, it left no 'heroes'; for the reason that defence of country is one of the simple duties to which every Frenchman conceives himself born and about which he does not strut, neither does he whine nor threaten.

French law at all times compels children to provide shelter, food, and clothing, when required, for their parents and their parents-in-law. Parents, by the same token, must so care for their children's needs. For the rest, there are the hospitals and the asylums provided to mend all the people's hurts or shelter their distress, whencesoever derived. No hospitals were or are provided for soldiers as

[1] Administrator of Veterans' Affairs. Article in *New York Times*, July 30, 1933.

[2] See *post*, pp. 257-58.

such, because no logical or sympathetic line could be drawn separating the citizen when a soldier from himself in civil life.

The number of persons pensioned and the sums set down on the national budget to meet those pensions decreased annually until the year 1930; because, up to that year France fundamentally adhered to the principle that war pensions can be based only upon disability or death incurred by a man fighting in his country's service.

In 1930, however, our sister Republic — although in a degree incomparably slighter than our own — submitted to major political tinkering of her World-War pension rolls. Both the number of her pensioners and the sum-total of costs from that point rose faster than, before, they fell. Yet as this book goes to press, the day's news indicates that France may be about to retrace her steps and reduce her Great-War pensions, in order to balance her budget and save the national currency.[1]

And always the Frenchman's most cherished reward of valour is a row of faded ribbons pinned on a faded coat — and the distinguished care of the children of the dead.

To turn to Germany is to find a people like a fine, strong, high-spirited animal dazed with terrible blows, imprisoned behind bars, bruising itself ever afresh in its maddened efforts at escape — and yet, untamed within its untamable heart, burning with a fiery devotion to its own traditions and pride of race.

To speak to a German of 'service pensions' — cash

[1] Also, following the Act of March 31, 1933, all cases pensioned by virtue of legal presumption of War origin or aggravation (cf. *post*, p. 233), are due for review and probable reduction in number.

rewards paid out by a Government to the citizen for having borne arms in his country's behalf without injury sustained — is to evoke the last word in almost incredulous contempt. But the American who names to a German gentleman the American Legion and its Bonus will as a rule evoke no word at all, because no word that courtesy can employ eases the German's scorn.

The numbers of Germany's killed in the World War and the numbers of America's entire Overseas Army were practically identical. The number of Germany's War-disabled — 4,202,028 — was, again, practically identical with the number of America's whole recruited force, both overseas and at home. But the number of men who, in January, 1933, were drawing American pensions for War-disablements, of a degree too slight to be recognized as pensionable at all under the German law,[1] was 182,261 and the amount of money they were drawing was $55,-313,000 a year.

As to the attitude of the German ex-service men's organizations, the condition of that tormented country has been too confused, since 1918, to support a general statement. But whatever any German Government has done or may do, his would be a dull mind who could deny to the Stahlhelm, while yet it was directing its own work of civic devotion, both respect and sympathy.

In Italy, the theme again changes. Here is a nation not static, like France; not confused and storm-driven like Germany, but superbly happy, confident, and hard at work, superbly clear and single of purpose, going forward,

[1] The German War-Pension Law, like that of Italy, considers no injury of less than 30 per cent disablement sufficiently serious to warrant pension.

not by guesswork and experiment, not by hullabaloo and
tentative jerks, but by cool, far-seeing, intelligent design
justified by a decade of logically unfolding success. One
man's mind has guided all — but the mind is a mind of
the first calibre and sagacity; the character a character of
immense original strength.

Italy's roster of World-War disabled exceeds America's
nearly five times over. Her war pension is given only to
men disabled above 30 per cent in active fighting service.
She takes extremely good care of her injured soldiers.
Upon the heavily crippled she confers, besides that care,
such distinguished honour as proves the Nation's respect.
To the children of the soldier dead she is a tender, wise,
and solicitous foster mother.

But for the able-bodied ex-service man she has honour
too — and a privilege! The honour of giving himself for
his country's service in peace as in war — the privilege of
being the first and the most diligent to build up the whole
Nation's resources for the whole Nation's aggrandisement.

Of Italy's ex-service men as a body — 'Our old soldiers
are a strong moral force in the Nation,' says Il Duce,
with stern pride.

As to England, hers is a record, not of guidance by a
great man or by great men, but of guidance by the inborn
character of a homogeneous and intensely civic-minded
people; guidance by a self-disciplined and responsible
common conscience that makes of each average citizen a
working custodian of the common weal. When England's
soldiers came home from the War, it was every man's job,
every woman's job, to do his or her bit in looking after
their needs. And it was the soldier's job to take up at

once, and equally, his citizen's duty toward the country. Neither side has tired nor failed in sober loyalty to their commitment.

England faced her full case at the start. She established her War-pension entitlement as adamant: to draw a war pension a man must have been disabled in War. That man she pensioned and cared for to the best of her powers, the whole people helping, leaving nothing to chance. With all the grinding hardships of the last decade, in which every other pay has been cut, England has never cut war pensions. Nor has the Nation, though burdened by taxation almost beyond endurance, desired it done; because it has known to a certainty that War pensions go only to or for actually War-crippled men.

England's thesis is that a sound war-pension system must, in any country, produce its maximum number of pensioners and its maximum costs, a few years after the War. England's World-War pension system produced that peak in 1921, since which year her figures have been steadily falling. Meantime administrative costs have been worked down and down until now they are less than two per cent of the budget, all the remainder of each shilling expended going straight to the pensioner.

As for the British Legion, they, like the *Combattenti* of Italy, are 'a strong moral force in the Nation,' leaving political matters wholly to Government, attempting no raiding in their own behalf, but serving in the civic field as an army of active labourers at their Government's right hand.

Taken all together, on this side of the Atlantic and on that, the contrast just indicated seems too wholesale to be true. Unfortunately, the more closely the details are studied, the more extreme the contrast revealed. But, for those who, wisely, choose to form their own judgment from the facts rather than to take another's opinion, the detailed stories provide the means.

CHAPTER XV

PULL DOWN THE FLAG

The spectacle of the Government practising subterfuge in order to say that what did not happen in the War did happen in the War, impairs the integrity of Government; reduces the respect for Government, and undermines the morale of all the people. —HERBERT HOOVER, President of the United States. Veto Message, June 26, 1930.[1]

THE year 1930 found us branded with the record just summarized. The French, whose War-disabled were over ten times more numerous than ours, had pensioned about four times as many men as we. The Italians, whose disabled exceeded ours by over 500 per cent, had pensioned less than four-fifths of our number. The United Kingdom whose disabled, without counting those of the rest of the Empire, were more than nine-fold as many as America's, carried a World-War pension roll less than twice our length.

And yet, in all three countries, the War-disabled were honoured and suitably cared for and the ex-service organizations as nearly content as human nature allows.

The difference was, that our chief ex-service organization, working as a dominant political machine and only 'politically' interested in our few War-disabled, had stuffed the pension rolls with cases whose War-connection, more and more tenuous, was rapidly nearing the vanishing point.

[1] See *post*, p. 139.

Were our American racketeers now content with their winnings? Certainly not.

Furthermore, their period of preparation was about accomplished. They had patiently and skilfully ploughed and harrowed, planted and cultivated. Their day of harvest was nigh. Meantime, amendments fed into the Congressional mill had rolled out with routine certainty, all signed, addressed, and franked for delivery. But the process was too slow, the production too small, to utilize that mill's magnificent capacity. Mass production for mass consumption — there's your doctrine!

It had, indeed, taken time to prepare the way — yet little enough in view of the step involved. For first the flag of America must come down from its honourable place beside those of England and Italy and Germany on their common Gibraltar of War-pension entitlement. That altitude, it seemed, was too bleak for our moral physique to endure.

Briefly, the thing we did was this: we stripped off our last rag of pretence that War injury was the basis of our War pensions; we acknowledged before all the world that we had set up, by law, in the midst of our democracy, a favoured class. To govern World-War procedure, we enacted a new measure [1] whereby every man enrolled before Armistice Day, 1918, who served for ninety days before June 2, 1921, and who was honourably discharged, became entitled to tribute. This tribute, called 'disability allowance,' was payable for any permanent disability *not* acquired in War service. The disability must rate at or above 25 per cent; but it could come through any accident,

[1] Act of July 3, 1930, Public 522, 71st Congress.

any injury, any sickness, any normal effect of advancing years.

It was, in fact, a free sickness-insurance policy.

Such governmental help may be the due of every industrious citizen whose power to earn his daily bread is reduced by age, accident, sickness, or unemployment, below the reasonable minimum, and who has no other means of support. Other countries, in various ways and degrees, recognize justice in that claim. But by what logic shall we justify bestowing such aid upon one selected and circumscribed section of our citizenry to the exclusion and at the expense of all the rest?

The Disability Allowance statute fixed the scale of monthly awards thus:

25 per centum permanent disability	$12
50	18
75	24
Total disability	40

To look ahead to December, 1932,[1] is to find 438,618 new 'veteran' pensioners drawing pay under this law. To such pensioners, in the fiscal year 1932, was disbursed $75,458,233. Of this sum over 63 per cent, or $37,000,000, went to persons in the lowest class of disablement, and only 13 per cent to those in the two upper grades.

Yet, large as the figures are, it is well to realize that under the Act in question, practically every one of the 4,263,000 World-War ex-service men today living would, as time goes on, draw a monthly award for ordinary physical wear and tear such as is the common mortal lot — un-

[1] Hearings before Joint Congressional Committee on Veterans' Affairs, December, 1932, Vol. I, p. 16. Testimony of the Administrator of Veterans' Affairs.

less he were ashamed to take it and then look his neighbour in the face.

In view of the size of the totals involved and of the fact
that the law giving them birth was enacted in the first
year of the Depression, it may seem strange to find the
Legion insistently disclaiming authorship of a feat of
which, ordinarily, it would be proud. This 'enactment
was not sponsored by the Legion.' 'These pensions...
had not been requested by the Legion' — so the Lobby
persists, in its annual reports.[1] And Senator Bronson
Cutting, its ally in the Upper House, arises to express
amazement that no attention is directed upon the fact
that President Hoover and his councillors, not the Legion,
sponsored the new Act with its enormous draught upon
the Treasury.

Those repudiations, those decoys were thoroughly dishonest — gamesters' bluffs staked on the likelihood —
always great — that a careless public would not trouble
itself to search out the fact.

The fact repays examination: President Hoover produced the Disability Allowance Bill as a desperate last-
moment effort to save the country from a more monstrous
and all-but-accomplished hold-up.

The story, in brief, runs as follows: At its Annual Convention in the autumn of 1929, the Legion adopted its
usual 'legislative relief' program. Conspicuous on the list
was the proposal arbitrarily to assign full 'presumptive'
status, carrying World-War-disability compensation bene-

[1] *Report of National Legislative Committee*, Fourteenth Annual National Convention of the American Legion, 1932, p. 175. *Proceedings of Thirteenth National
Convention of the American Legion*, 1931, p. 206.

fits to all ex-service men suffering from any constitutional and chronic disease developed prior to January 1, 1925.

Congressional allies enriched this conception, and on April 25, 1930, the House of Representatives passed, by a vote of 325 to 49, a bill declaring War-service origin for any disability whatsoever developed by any ex-service man whatsoever, to the degree of 10 per cent, prior to January 1, 1930.

As to how pronounced a development must be in order to be rated at 10 per cent, a member of the Medical Service of the Veterans' Administration thus testifies, at about this period:[1] 'I am frank to say, when a man has any evidence of disability, the practice is to call it ten per cent; at least, that is the practice in my experience.'

The Senate followed suit, with a vote of 66 to 6. This move evoked a Presidential protest, a Presidential veto, a White House conference, and the substitution and enactment of the Disability Allowance measure, bad as it was, to avert the even more fantastic disaster about to be inflicted upon the Nation. Such, said the Lobby, is 'the Administration's reply to the Legion's request for presumptive service connection for the chronic and constitutional diseases, from which thousands of veterans were suffering and *which the Legion considered as much due to service as many of the disabilities for which the presumption has been granted.'*[2]

[1] Dr. Martin Cooley. Hearings before Committee on World-War Veterans' Legislation, House of Representatives, 71st Congress, 2nd Session, January 21, 1930, p. 109.

[2] *Proceedings of the Thirteenth National Convention of the American Legion,* 1931, *Report of the National Legislative Committee,* p. 206. Italics the author's. The Legion's account of the whole incident will be found in the *Proceedings of the Twelfth National Convention,* 1930, pp. 200 *et seq.*

This final phrase should be marked and digested, embodying as it does the Legion's franker estimate of the validity of the 'presumptive cases' that, in the summer and autumn of 1933, were to be objects of a general review by order of President Roosevelt.

The measure with which we have just been dealing, the Disability Allowance, was so called in distinction from the older Disability Compensation, which latter term still clung to the pension paid for War-incurred injury real or presumed. The man in receipt of Disability Compensation is, at least in theory, a man who sustained some hurt in or in consequence of War service. The man in receipt of Disability Allowance is shown, by token of the term itself, to have sustained, in whatever War service he may have rendered, no hurt at all. He is merely capitalizing the fact that he once wore World-War uniform to arrogate to himself privileges which, if they belong to him, equally belong to every citizen of the State.[1]

Entitlements to Disability Allowance were subject to two conditions not heretofore mentioned. The first of these conditions was, that the claimant must have been exempt from Federal income tax in the year previous to the filing of application. The second condition lay in the 'wilful-misconduct' clause; no claim could yet be based on an ailment contracted by wilful misconduct.

Neither condition, however, could be regarded as other than short-lived, for the Legion, always eventually victorious, had underscored both for the guillotine. Indeed, in the following year, it caused to be introduced in Con-

[1] For number of Disability Allowance men, their degrees of disability, and pay as of 1932, see United States Appendix III.

140

gress an amendment to remove the 'needs' clause from the Disability Allowance provision, and to provide that the term 'wilful misconduct' shall be deemed to apply only to such injuries as a man inflicts upon himself in order to escape service or to draw pay.[1]

The latter provision echoed a question that had caused some worriment in the previous year. The matter may best be shown in concrete example: On Christmas Day, 1919, a certain ex-service man sat down to celebrate the holiday with his uncle. The means at hand was called whiskey; and such was its effect, says the official report, that 'after taking eight or nine drinks he was temporarily blinded and a few days later, lost sight in both eyes.' His blindness remained complete. But not until the Disability Allowance amendment came into effect, eleven years later, could this unfortunate claim a war pension. When the good day dawned, he reached out gladly to grasp his luck.

The question then arose: does drinking wood alcohol called whiskey until you put your own eyes out constitute wilful misconduct; and does it, therefore, bar the law's relief? The Attorney General of the United States, being inquired of, responded as follows, on January 20, 1931:

... there is no ground for supposing that the veteran intended by drinking the whiskey in question to do himself harm....

There being no law prohibiting the drinking of intoxicating liquor, no evidence that the veteran knew that the liquor might blind him, in short, no evil intent of any kind, I am of opinion that the veteran is eligible to receive a disability allowance.

[1] House Bill 5850, introduced December 15, 1931, by Representative John E. Rankin.

141

How, indeed, could any other decision have been rendered, under the Act? So that long-blighted merry-maker was set down upon the War-pension rolls of the United States to receive $40 monthly for the rest of his life. But one distressful point is still unclear: What becomes of his uncle, who, poor soul, can draw no comfort at all until Congress, made alive to its duty, repairs the gap by pensioning all uncles who gave their nephews to the defence of a grateful country! In any case, so was begun a special category of World-War pensioners soon to swell to respectable proportions.[1]

Meantime a second major stimulus of the industry had been gradually evolving. The original War Risk Insurance Act of 1917 had provided free hospitalization and medical care for all War-disabled soldiers, thus far keeping to the practice of the other nations. Upon that position, the first attack was delivered in the World-War Veterans' Act of 1924. Again 'liberalized' by amendments of 1925, 1926, and 1930, the law as it stood in 1930 [2] 'authorized' the Director of the Veterans' Administration, 'so far as... existing Governmental facilities permit, to furnish hospitalization and necessary traveling expenses incident to hospitalization to veterans of any war, military occupation or military expedition... not dishonourably discharged, *without regard to the nature or origin of their disabilities.*'

The National Executive Committee of the Legion, meeting in the autumn of 1930, just prior to the convening of

---

[1] The later vogue of alleged Jamaica ginger, as a beverage, producing what became known as the ' Jaic Ginger Cases,' ran the pay-roll up with a dash.

[2] World-War Veterans' Act, 1924, Section 202 (10) as amended, July 3, 1930. Italics the author's.

142

Congress, had, however, come out flatly for a law that, cutting wholly loose from War-incurred or War-aggravated physical troubles, should no longer merely 'authorize,' but should definitely compel, free Government hospitalization for all ex-service men, irrespective of when, how, or where they had acquired or should acquire their ailments.

Senate Committee hearings were later held, witnesses to the number of 253 testifying, nearly all Legionnaires.

'From the very beginning of the hearings,' runs the Legion Lobby's report on the matter, 'it was conceded... that sufficient Government hospital beds existed to care for all service-connected cases in the event that the beds occupied by non-service-connected cases should be vacated.'[1]

The only question then was, Would Congress obey the Legion's goad and build for the uniform?

'Congress,' concluded the Lobby report, 'did not meet this question through the formal enunciation of a policy, nor did it go on record as declining to declare such a policy — *it simply went ahead and authorized hospital construction for non-service cases.*'[2]

The result as of the year 1932 was officially stated as follows:[3]

At an annual maintenance expense of $41,739,618.32, the Veterans' Administration, besides operating 59 hospitals of its own, was using a part of the facilities of 49 other governmental hospitals and 255 civilian hospitals. As of September 30, 1932, it was carrying a total patient load numbering 43,949. Of these 65 per cent were non-service-

[1] *Proceedings of Thirteenth National Convention of the American Legion*, 1931, p. 209.
[2] Italics the author's.
[3] *Annual Report of the Administrator of Veterans' Affairs*, 1932, p. 24.

connected cases.[1] Also, 44,772 Veterans' Administration Hospital beds, exclusive of beds in other Government hospitals and in contract hospitals, were promised by June 30, 1934.[2]

'If we only had the service-connected problem... we could close 15 hospitals,' the Director of the Administration had already stated.[3]

Notwithstanding this undisputed fact, and notwithstanding the disastrous condition of the Nation's finances, the Legion in 1932 still persisted in its demand for more and yet more buildings. Again, to quote its own report, 'the Legion asked for $52,000,000 for sixty-one new hospital projects, notwithstanding the previous session [of Congress] had adopted a program calculated to take care of the needs to 1933, and appropriated $25,165,180 therefore.'[4]

In the unlikely event that no further 'liberalizations' should be exacted, and by the automatic working of existent laws, it was estimated in 1931 that by the year 1965 our 'disabled veterans' would require 81,459 hospital beds, aside from those provided in Soldiers' Homes.[5]

In this connection it is interesting to reflect that Ger-

[1] Statement of General Frank T. Hines, Administrator of Veterans' Affairs before the Joint Congressional Committee on Veterans' Affairs, December 9, and 10, 1932.

[2] *Annual Report of the Administrator of Veterans' Affairs*, 1932, pp. 166–67.

[3] Hearing before the Committee on Finance, United States Senate, February 5, 1931, p. 48.

[4] *Reports of Legislative Committee*, Fourteenth Annual National Convention of the American Legion, September, 1932, p. 139.

[5] Testimony of General Hines, Director of the Veterans' Administration before the Senate Finance Committee, February 5, 1931, p. 6.

many, whose disabled soldiers of the World War out-numbered ours by over four million, in 1932 found 1400 beds sufficient for their needs. And England, with her keen regard for her ex-service disabled, her generous and advanced ideas of medical and surgical care for all their necessities, and her roster of World-War invalids exceed-ing ours by nearly a million men, today finds 3500 beds sufficient to care for them all, and reports the number, year by year, steadily diminishing.

Without attempting a detailed statement, it may be said that this multiplication of great Federally main-tained hospitals for the exclusive and free benefit of a privileged class is reported a curse to some communities. If our American Government, as is largely the practice of other Governments, maintained a heavy percentage of its ex-service patients on a capitation basis in approved hospitals that serve the whole community, those hospitals, and therefore the communities, would, it is held, be strengthened and bettered thereby. Instead of which, our Government spends large sums of money in building, equipping and running fine establishments that deflect from the general hospitals a considerable revenue, and which, although built with tax payers' money, receive only those persons who once wore uniform; this regardless alike of their financial competence and of the source of their maladies.

Essential as hospitals are to the welfare of local life, they are essentials so costly that it is often difficult for their communities to sustain them. The effect of the erec-tion of a great veterans' hospital in a given district has, it is said, sometimes been exceedingly harmful or even fatal

to struggling institutions that serve all the people and
that have always their load of free patients to carry.

Between March, 1919, and the end of 1932, Congress
authorized the expenditure of just under $150,000,000
for new hospital buildings and extension of existing
facilities. Of this sum, $11,550,000 was devoted to the
expansion of National Homes for Disabled Volunteer
Soldiers.[1] As of February, 1931, over sixty per cent of the
men established in Federal Soldiers' Homes were World-
War Veterans, ex-service men averaging about thirty-
eight years of age. Said General Hines, whose duty it is
not to reason why, but to execute laws as Congress makes
them, 'unless there is a real disability I do not think it is
a good policy for them to start life in a soldiers' home so
young.' To which he adds, mildly, that unless some
change sets in 'we are going to convert the old soldiers'
homes into young soldiers' homes.'[2]

Nor is the idea a jest. Our Federal Soldiers' Homes
and many of our Veterans' Administration Hospitals are
like handsome country clubs. The man with a pension for
a missing finger-joint who can muster an ailment that
some doctor will certify as unfitting him, temporarily,
for work, can live in a Soldiers' Home, be outfitted with
all good new clothes that he seems to want,[3] from overcoat
to spats, get his dentistry done for nothing, and be freely
given his excellent board, lodging, medical care, and en-

[1] Testimony of the Director of the Veterans' Administration before the Joint
Congressional Committee on Veterans' Affairs, December 9, 1932.

[2] Testimony of the Director of the Veterans' Administration before the
Senate Finance Committee, February 5, 1931, pp. 26-27.

[3] The statement is not figurative. Veterans' Administration expenditure for
clothing, under this head, in the fiscal year 1932 was over one-half million
dollars. See Administrator's *Report*, 1932, p. 152.

146

tertainment. He may be, and often is, a 'sleepout,' going away for the night and returning to the Home for his medical treatment, rest, meals, and daytime diversions. Also, with the monthly 'temporary total disability' allowance due him as a hospitalized man, he is soon able to get himself a car, as many do. And the authorities are slow to dislodge him from a pleasant life into a world of hard times and general unemployment. By no means few, it is credibly reported, are the men of that type, snugly riding at anchorage and in no haste at all to recover from their enabling disabilities.

The same thing is admittedly true as to the hospitals, where the surgeons in charge would, as a rule, be easier in their minds if their patients had not so much money to spend, and if some of them were not such shrewd masters of the law and art of securing extended residence.

CHAPTER XVI

LEMON RE-BORN

MEANTIME, while the infant industries of Young Soldiers' Homes, of World-War pensions for post-War recruits, and of life annuities for men unscratched in the War by whose name they profit — while all these promising yet tender industries are protected and furthered, a mature concern of goodly proportions is left to take its course without remark.

This is because the less one knows about it, the more easily one believes that which is told.

In an earlier chapter that Government insurance scheme which was the major feature of the original War Risk Insurance Act, has been described. The Legion's publicity on the subject, clothed in shrewd monotony, has run as follows:

> ...Insurance... was paid for by the veterans themselves and therefore should not be a proper charge against expenditures in their behalf, the Government having collected hundreds of millions of dollars in premiums from the veterans to afford them this insurance protection.[1]
>
> The War Risk Insurance... the veterans bought and paid for out of their meager Army and Navy pay while they were in the service.[2]
>
> It must be remembered the soldiers paid the Government the premiums on this insurance out of their own pockets.[3]

---

[1] *Proceedings of Thirteenth National Convention of the American Legion*, September, 1931, p. 193.

[2] National Legislative Committee of the American Legion, *Special Bulletin No. 1*, October 8, 1932, p. 8.

[3] *Ibid.*, *Preliminary Bulletin*, December 3, 1932, p. 21.

This doctrine, by dint of steady, long-continued repetition, has come to stand as knowledge in uncritical minds. 'If any poor devil got anything back out of Government, it was no more than belonged to him. Most of 'em couldn't afford to carry insurance after the Army pay stopped. So they let it go. Uncle Sam pocketed the premium and made a damn good thing out of the whole deal.' Such is the impression now rooted in the heads of the Legion's pupils in Americanism.

The dominant facts need only a glance:

The entire fund created by insurance premiums drawn from soldiers' and sailors' pay was $453,845,000, while over $1,600,000,000 has already been paid out in benefits.

This fund, never charged with administration costs, which were heavy, was entirely exhausted by the payment of claims before the end of 1922. Beginning in 1922, each succeeding Congress has therefore been obliged to appropriate public money to meet the Federal liabilities on these same War Risk Insurance policies. The appropriations have been:

Initial	$23,000,000
1923	13,235,000
1924	90,000,000
1925	88,000,000
1926	116,080,000
1927	123,000,000
1928	114,000,000
1929	115,250,000
1930	123,849,104
1931	120,000,000
1932	125,733,000
1933	127,850,000
	$1,179,997,104

Every one of the men who bought War Risk Insurance, as the Legion Lobby says, 'out of their meager Army and

Navy pay while they were in the service,' got all that they paid for — insurance protection, and at extraordinarily low rates, for themselves and their dependants while exposed to the dangers of War. That protection, after the War, was convertible without medical examination into other regular forms of insurance offered by Government, and must be so converted within a given period. The period was repeatedly extended until, on July 2, 1927, it finally expired.

Congress, however, met the difficulty through the dovetailing of two amendments. First, the Presumption laws,[1] admitting to compensation great numbers of persons whose ailments owed their War connection to statute, independent of fact. Second, the decree [2] dealing with the man who, while suffering from a compensable disability for which he had not collected compensation, allowed his insurance to lapse; that man, said the decree, if he dies or becomes permanently totally disabled while his compensation is still uncollected, is automatically reinstated in as much of his insurance as his uncollected compensation would have covered had this been applied in premiums when premium fell due.

The theory there was that Government ought not to be permitted to escape from its contract with a disabled man at a time when it owed him money which, had it been paid him, he might have used to maintain his insurance. As far as really service-connected cases were concerned, the theory was perhaps sound, but its conse-

[1] See *ante*, p. 101.
[2] Act of June 7, 1924, Section 305, amending Section 408 of the Act of March 4, 1923.

quences spread beyond all reason through the ever-increasing number of retroactive compensation awards produced by the statutory presumptions.

This device, never contemplated in the original plan of 1917, added heavily to the number of the insured and heaped up the burden upon the Treasury. But the Legion still fanned its ill-will-breeding fable — a course that at last drove one Congressman, long the Legion's ally, to this brusque outbreak, addressed to his colleagues of the Lower Chamber:[1]

> I am tired of all this bunk about Government Insurance that has been used on the floor of the House for the last five or six years. The war risk insurance has cost the Government about $1,350,000,000 more than the soldiers paid for it, and yet they say, 'Oh, they took the money away from us.' It has come back to them a thousand-fold.

The original War Risk Insurance Act provided that the United States Government, as party to a contract, might be sued in the courts on War Risk Insurance claims — provided, also, for attorneys' fees deductible at source. From this seed sprang a new crop of Lemons bigger even than the pre-War yield, dealing largely in cases alleged to have been prevented from lapse through uncollected compensation as above explained.

One attorney declared, in December, 1932, that he had at that moment in his office about 1200 such suits pending against the Government.[2] Others are credited with having

[1] The Honourable Royal C. Johnson of South Dakota. Speech in the House of Representatives, May 3, 1932.

[2] Hearing before the Joint Congressional Committee on Veterans' Affairs, December, 1932, vol. 1, p. 212.

gathered considerably greater numbers by their diligence and skill. And the Administration's estimate, at the end of 1932, gave 53,900 as the number of potential lawsuits then hanging over its head.[1]

The claims attorney's method, typically, is to hunt up a man whose insurance lapsed immediately after the War and to present his name to the Veterans' Administration as that of one totally and permanently disabled before the lapse of his insurance, which, therefore, had matured.[2] The attorney, however, is careful to offer little or no evidence in support of the allegation. The Veterans' Administration, consequently and perforce, rejects it. The attorney then takes his case to court, produces his client in as dilapidated a physical condition as possible — on crutches, choking with asthma, or what not — and tells his tale. Court and jury cast an eye on the suitor. 'Once he fought for our country. Now look at him, poor soul! What if his evidence *is* fishy? He needs help anyway, and Uncle Sam is rich.' They give him his claim.

A typical and actual instance is that of a man brought into court as having been totally and permanently disabled long years ago while yet his insurance was in force, yet denied his rightful award by a flinty-hearted Administration. The Administration produced positive proof that the plaintiff had worked for years as a railway brakeman during the period of his 'total and permanent disability,' earning good pay and often working overtime. The court,

[1] Hearing before the Joint Congressional Committee on Veterans' Affairs, December, 1932, vol. I, pp. 11–12. Testimony of the Administrator of Veterans' Affairs.

[2] See *ante*, p. 150. The time-limit for the filing of suits on insurance claims was advanced, by successive Congressional amendments, to July 3, 1931.

nevertheless, rendered judgment for the plaintiff and a higher court sustained that judgment.[1]

The testimony of the plaintiff himself, supported, if at all, by that of his immediate family, has frequently been enough to cost Government its case — even when, as often occurs, the claim is grossly and palpably fraudulent. On charge of fraud it is exceedingly difficult to get indictments, and more difficult still to secure convictions. Even in those rare instances when conviction is secured, involving, as it does, loss of pension, a Presidential pardon has not. seldom followed.

'The business of suing the Government on War risk insurance is bound to grow,' says the Administrator of Veterans' Affairs,[2] 'it is good business for the legal profession.' And he places the possible cost to the country at many hundreds of millions of dollars.

It was Congressman Royal C. Johnson who asked, in his speech above quoted,

> Just how long would the Prudential or Equitable or the New York Life... last if every time somebody dropped a policy and did not pay the premium, he could come in 12 years after he had paid a cent, and revive it on a pretext such as is being [used] here?

Commercial insurance companies, obviously, must feel the inroads of their great competitor; and one cannot but wonder how they view the rivalry of a Government that lets itself be fleeced to the tune of multi-millions by its own courts, and with its eyes open.

As to the ordinary citizen who has not the luck to be a

[1] Hearing before the Joint Congressional Committee on Veterans' Affairs, December, 1932, p. 13. Testimony of the Administrator of Veterans' Affairs.
[2] *Ibid.*, p. 14.

153

'veteran,' he must pay for his insurance rates that reckon with such rivalry.

Meantime, pre-War patterns weave on unbroken through the post-War web. Lemon, in his day, developed his liaison with the G.A.R. until the G.A.R. Commander publicly acknowledged him as his aide-de-camp.[1] In these latter years the incident is re-enacted to the life, between the modern Lemons and the Legion.

Not only what the Legion leaders have done, but what they desire to do, displays the bond. Their move to wipe out time-limits as to when insurance suits may be filed; their proposal to increase the fee of that attorney who, though successful in prosecuting his suit, gains judgment of no more than $5000;[2] above all, their design to win for these same attorneys free access to Government files concerning their clients' medical, service, and personal record — things such as these show only too clearly the old mutual aid association.

The project to open the files to claims agents' eyes seems gross enough; the Lemon that has access thereto has nearly won his case, for he has only to discover what lacks in his client's position and then to make up the deficit. But a thing even grosser is already established by law. That protected privacy in personal matters that should be the due of every man from his Government, and as such be firmly defended, has been eaten away

[1] Cf. *ante*, p. 33.

[2] H.R. 15621, Sections 30, 304, 305, 500 (a) and (b). Introduced January 5, 1931. The attorney's fee, as fixed, is a maximum of 10 per cent of the amount recovered, both on immediate payment and on later instalments. Under this 10 per cent limit, the exact fee is discretionary with the court. But the custom has been to assign the maximum. The Legion would raise the fee to 15 per cent, when the award does not exceed $5000.

until scarcely a shell remains. Our law now facilitates examination of the files by 'recognized representatives' of the Red Cross, of the Legion, and of several smaller ex-service organizations; by any person believed to bring written authority from the man in question; and finally, by *any* member of Congress concerning whom the man in question has *not* notified the Veterans' Administration that this particular member of Congress is *not* his agent! [1]

In a word, the unfortunate whose history lies in those cards and folders has no safeguard, worthy of the name, from friend, enemy, or gossip.

The natural results have followed. All of them.

[1] World War Veterans' Act, Sections 30 and 500. *Regulations and Procedure*, Veterans' Administration, paragraphs 5585–5592.

CHAPTER XVII

HAND OUT THE BONUS!

THE American World-War ex-service man has been provided by his Government with two special insurance schemes invented to serve him and him only. In the first, the War Risk Insurance, he has paid a small premium. In the second, the Bonus, he has paid nothing at all, receiving his policy as a free gift.

The Bonus is a straight endowment insurance, bearing its terms printed on its face.[1] These terms state that the policy is payable in twenty years from its date. Further, they provide that no Bonus policy can become effective earlier than January 1, 1925. Therefore, no Bonus policy can fall due earlier than December 31, 1944, excepting by the death of the holder.

It was the Legion that invented the Bonus. It was the Legion that, over the protests of two Cabinets and over the pleas and vetoes of two Presidents, Mr. Harding and Mr. Coolidge, saddled the Bonus upon the Nation; while President Coolidge, recognizing that the Legion's gains are never a finality, but always a stepping stone, had, it will be recalled, embodied in his Veto Message this declaration:

> No one supposes the effort will stop here. Already suggestions are made for a cash bonus in addition, to be paid at once. Such action logically would be encouraged if the bill became law.

[1] For the earlier history of the Bonus, see *ante*, pp. 83, 93–94.

True to that presage, it was the Legion that, in the second year of the present economic depression, demanded the surrender to a class numbering some three and a quarter per cent of the people, of a huge slice of the whole people's tax money.

This it proposed should be done by raising the loan rate of the 3,389,000 extant Bonus policies,[1] valued at $3,418,000,000, from 22½ per cent, as then authorized, to 50 per cent, of their face value.

President Hoover, when this proposal came before him as a measure already accepted by both Houses of Congress, spoke faithfully:

> The sole appeal made for the reopening of the bonus act is the claim that funds from the National Treasury should be provided to veterans in distress as the result of the drought and business depression. There are veterans unemployed and in need today in common with many other of our people. These, like the others, are being provided the basic necessities of life by the devoted committees in those parts of the country affected.... Inquiry indicates that such care is being given throughout the country, and it also indicates that the number of veterans in need of such relief is a minor percentage of the whole.
>
> ... The breach of fundamental principle in this proposal is the requirement of the Federal Government to provide an enormous sum of money to a vast majority who are able to care for themselves and who are caring for themselves.
>
> Among those who would receive the proposed benefit are included 387,000 veterans and 400,000 dependants, who are already receiving some degree of allowance or support from the Federal Government. But in addition to these, it pro-

[1] The number of policies extant as of December 31, 1930. Up to December, 1932, 142,000 policy holders had died. As of June 30, 1933, the account stood thus: Number of policies (adjusted service certificate) in force, 3,549,503. Maturity value of certificates in force, $3,519,064,638.

157

vides equal benefits for scores of thousands of others who
are in the income-tax class, and for scores of thousands who
are holding secure positions in the Federal, State, and local
governments and in every profession and industry. I know
that most of these men do not seek these privileges... that
they do not want to be represented to our people as a group
substituting special privilege for the idealism and patriotism
they have rejoiced in offering to their country through their
service.... It is a fundamental aspect of freedom among us
that no step should be taken which burdens the Nation with
a privileged class who can care for themselves.[1]

He then vetoed the measure raising the borrowing
power of the Bonus policies.

With one gesture of cool insolence, the National Commander of the Legion crushed the President's effort. In
an official letter laid upon the desk of each member of the
Senate and the House, he announced, simply,... 'I desire,
as National Commander of the American Legion, to request you to promptly repass [the measure] over the
veto.'[2]

Congress obeyed. The new law became effective on
February 27, 1931. Under it, within the next six months,
$1,080,000,000 was withdrawn from the Treasury.

Meantime, much earlier, in January, 1931, the National
Executive Committee of the Legion, still true to President
Coolidge's fore-vision, had published its next objective —
immediate cash payment to all the three and a half million
Bonus policy-holders, of the full face value of their policies.
This, the Committee gravely affirmed, 'would be an ap-

[1] Veto Message on H.R. 17054, February 26, 1931. House Document No.
790, 71st Congress, 3d Session.
[2] *Proceedings of Thirteenth National Convention of The American Legion*, 1931,
p. 169. Letters delivered February 25, 1931.

HAND OUT THE BONUS!

propriate demonstration of the gratitude of the Nation
to those who carried its arms in 1917–18.' [1]

The comment of the Secretary of the Treasury, was: [2]

... the total cash surrender value which [the proposal] con-
templates exceeds by over $375,000,000 the present-day value
of the certificates outstanding, and in effect would constitute
a grant of this additional amount.

As to the logic of the proposal, consider the prospects
of John Doe, who, having on Tuesday received of the
Prudential Company a twenty-year insurance endowment
policy of a thousand dollars, should on Wednesday stroll
into the Prudential office and say: 'On second thought,
I don't care to wait twenty years for that thousand. Hand
it to me now.'

In September, 1931, the National Convention of the
Legion met in Detroit. The main question then before
it was this very demand for immediate cash payment of
the Bonus. The President of the United States himself
came on from Washington — an unprecedented step —
to plead on behalf of the distressed and endangered Nation.
But the Legion's Executive Committee had already declared for the raid, and an unfortunate species of Congressman was there, to mislead, inflame, and betray his
hearers.

Then it was that a shining miracle intervened. The
old A.E.F., so long suppressed, found voice. Four men,
in four little speeches, uttered words that ought to be cast
in eternal bronze, as proof that, despite all neglect, all
abuse, all deception, temptation, false leadership, no

[1] *Ibid.*, p. 165.
[2] Letter to the chairman of the Ways and Means Committee, House of Representatives, January 19, 1931.

leadership, the manhood of the War survives. Two of them, at least, were members of that too-silent company, the battle-wounded.

Said one of these — Broon of California: 'I left a leg in France and most of my right arm. This urge for the full payment of this certificate is not right. The American Legion has a job to do more important than this. Forget yourselves. We gave in 1917. Give in 1932.' And with that, Broon of California sat down.

Wally Williams of Maryland, beginning, 'I haven't any business to be here arguing with brilliant minds from the Congress,' said his brief say — and before he had finished, brilliancy from Congress might well have gone out and hanged itself. Then John McCall of Tennessee, and Jim Morris of Florida. Those four so roused the spirit of the men before them — that glorious spirit so long and so wickedly wronged — that it saved the Legion Convention, that day, against the disgrace that had almost swallowed it up.

Nevertheless, by the next Congressional session the machine was obeying the wheel again, and 'a tremendous pressure was brought for the full cash payment' of the Bonus policies.[1]

In June, 1932, while a bill to that purpose lay before both Senate and House, Washington was infested by some twenty thousand 'Bonus Marchers,' a motley crew from here, there, and everywhere, bent on swaying the vote.

Congressman Fish, of New York, declaring in debate that 'the United States does not owe the able-bodied

[1] *Reports of Fourteenth Annual National Convention of American Legion*, 1932, p. 139.

'eteran a single penny at the present time, directly or in-
lirectly, now or tomorrow, or until 1945, on their [bonus
policies]' affirmed, 'we do not propose to be coerced by
any veterans in Washington or any other group in the
United States.'

Major La Guardia, his colleague from New York,
asserted: 'With 8,000,000 unemployed men and women
in this country, I for one refuse to sacrifice them for any
uch sordid, selfish purpose.'

But Mr. Cox, of Georgia, lamented, with poignant
ruth, 'the tragic part about this whole thing is that the
oldier has been told that the Government owes him
noney that it will not pay, and in most instances he be-
eves it.... Things said upon the floor of this House
ave filled his heart with a feeling of distrust, and he is
nade to despise the thing he once... risked his life to
ve.'

The following account, from the lips of a United States
enator who witnessed that whereof he speaks, may lack
mething of the sympathy that some spectators felt, but
least it is the honest utterance of a serious man.

> One of the most pitiable sights I ever saw was the Bonus
> Army's 'death march' around the Capitol. All day and all
> night, they shuffled around the plaza in single file, perhaps
> 1500 yards long. Determined-looking fat women, thin men,
> tired, whining children dragging after. Shuffle, shuffle, never
> stopping, at the rate of a mile an hour. Every sort of creature
> was there, inspired by selfishness, blinded by ignorance,
> minds choked with rubbish, and yet with something terrify-
> ing in their very stupidity. I am *afraid* for the country, when
> I realize that that moron type have votes and can and do put
> political terror into — yes — into Senators of the United
> States. As for the House, it turned tail before them, as its

vote shows. . On the night when we voted in the Senate[1] the front steps of the Capitol and the paved part of the plaza were packed tight with these service men. As the vote was taken, their yells were piercing into the Senate Chamber through two sets of locked doors. The bill was defeated, 62 to 18, but we of the 62 certainly expected to be manhandled before we reached home that night.

The country has wandered far from the purpose of Government and one of the two greatest menaces to the very survival of our form of Government today, is the ex-soldier lobby.

But so long as the Legion Lobby continues to exist, it is well for every American citizen to remember that that Lobby is a good Lobby; that it does its work faithfully, taking its orders from its employers, the little group that originates the Legion's official policies; and that what it once undertakes, it may through shrewd strategy defer; but it never gives up.

The prepayment of the Bonus was urgently opposed by the President of the United States and by his Cabinet officers, on grounds of extreme public necessity and distress. It was defeated in Congress, where honest men, disregarding their personal fortunes and their physical safety, gave sound reason for refusal to cede more ground.

And yet, the body of the Legion, whose controllers had permitted it one brief hour of awakened moral revolt in the convention of September, 1931, was well drugged and quieted again before the next autumn. The Convention of 1932 resolved, 'That the American Legion endorses

[1] While the Senate Gallery was occupied by emissaries of the Bonus Marchers, men, such as Senator Thomas of Oklahoma and Senator Robinson of Indiana, had been throwing oil on the flames in demagogic speeches from the floor.

and urges the full and immediate payment [of the Bonus] and that the National officers be instructed immediately to proceed before Congress toward enactment of this legislation.'

CHAPTER XVIII

THE MAN FORGOTTEN

> Do you not think it almost time that somebody commenced to pay some attention to the men who were actually wounded in the War? (The Honourable Royal C. Johnson, Washington, January, 1930.)

CONGRESSMAN JOHNSON, when he asked that disconcerting question, was presiding over a Congressional Committee Hearing on a new amendment still further to swell the World-War pension roll with names of men who had suffered in World-War service nothing at all.

> We are losing sight of the actual battle casualty... he is getting lost among a sea of gold-brickers [pursued Mr. Johnson relentlessly], because he is in such a small minority... nobody seems to be looking after his interest any more.[1]

The phenomenon was not new. Every succeeding President of the United States since the World War had pointed out, denounced, and deplored it, vetoing 'gold-brickers' legislation. But our World-War battle casualties have had no lobby to push their cause.

In truth they have needed none, for the Nation at all times has asked but the word to surround them with whatever their welfare could require.

Who, though, was to speak that word? Never the men themselves, for the true type does not talk. And how

---

[1] Hearings before the Committee on World-War Veterans' Legislation, 71st Congress, 2nd Session, H.R. 7825, January, 1930, pp. 46–47. This was the bill that proposed to declare presumptive War-service origin for any 'chronic, constitutional, or analogous disease' developed by any World-War ex-service man to a 10 per cent degree before January 1, 1930.

could the Legion Lobby have built a master political machine on a list as meagre as this:

RECIPIENTS OF COMPENSATION FOR INJURIES INCURRED IN ACTION AT SEA OR OVERSEAS IN THE WORLD WAR [1]

TYPE OF INJURY [2]	NUMBER OF INJURED
Double Permanent Total	7
Permanent Total	2,855
Permanent Partial	49,275
Total	52,137

As far as provision of money goes, the record is good: Compensation for War-incurred or War-aggravated injuries had been fixed in the original War Risk Insurance Act of October, 1917, thus:

1. Total disability, incurred in line of duty............$30 monthly
2. Extra allowance for those in need of constant attendance...................................... 20 monthly
3. Loss of both hands, both feet, both eyes, totally blind, helpless or bedridden............................100 monthly

Vocational rehabilitation for the less seriously injured, and insurance for the totally disabled, as provided. in the Act, were, it will be recalled, to round out the compensation figures, making together a sufficient whole.

These rates, however, were soon raised by a series of amendments that entirely ignored the original factors of

[1] As of December 31, 1929, Hearings before Sub-Committee of United States Senate Committee on Finance, 71st Congress, 2nd Session, on H.R. 10381, May, 1930, p. 167. These figures include derivative cases, such as the neuropsychiatric and tuberculous, as well as the medical and surgical cases.

[2] The following definitions are cited by the Veterans' Administrator: 'Any impairment of mind or body which renders it impossible for the disabled person to follow continuously any substantially gainful occupation shall be deemed... total disability. Total disability shall be deemed permanent whenever... it [is] reasonably certain that it will continue throughout the life of the person suffering from it.'

vocational rehabilitation — cost to the Nation $644,900,-
000 — and insurance. A general rating schedule, as already
described,[1] working on a scale of 100 degrees, now awarded
compensation of a dollar a month for each percentage of
disability recognized. Independent of this stood certain
compensations fixed by statute.

By statute, every man in hospital for a temporary ailment, regardless of its nature, got $80 a month, free from
all charges, during the period of his stay; and if he had
dependants, additional grants were made to him on their
account — $10 a month for a wife, $10 for a father, $10 for
a mother, $5 for each child. These awards were implied in
a statute assigning $80 monthly for total temporary dis-
ability,[2] since disability is reckoned by its effect on earning power and since a hospitalized man is interrupted in
earning. Other statutes raised the blind man's monthly
award to $150; granted $200 a month to a blind man
who had lost a limb; raised the rates for attendant's
pay; added $25 a month to any compensation drawn by
the man who had lost a hand, a foot, or a creative organ, in
active service in the line of duty; gave $200 a month to any
man suffering from two of the injuries appearing in the
third section of the list of October, 1917; assigned $50
a month for life to everyone recognized as having arrested
tuberculosis; and a minimum of $25 a month to cases of
tuberculosis 'apparently cured' — which latter decree included every person in whom the X-ray could discover
a sign of those tuberculous affections obscurely harboured
in childhood, which give no later hint of existence other

[1] *Ante*, pp. 62–64, and United States Appendix II.
[2] World-War Veterans' Act, Section 202 (1).

than the X-ray's trace, and from which few of us, it is said, are free.

These provisions, among others that arbitrarily attached War origin to certain diseases, seemed to establish our War-pension disbursement on the level of liberality — an assumption not put to the blush by the following comparisons:

TOTAL EXPENDITURE ON BEHALF OF WORLD-WAR EX-SERVICE MEN, IN THE YEAR 1931–32

France	$277,015,071	
Germany [1]	285,840,000	$803,115,795
United Kingdom	240,260,724	
United States of America [2]		860,635,000

In this connection it is useful to turn again to other figures already cited: [3]

NUMBER OF MEN, AS OF 1919, DISABLED BY WOUNDS OR SICKNESS, IN THE WORLD WAR

France	2,052,984	
Germany	4,202,028	8,124,579
United Kingdom	1,869,567	
United States of America		192,369

From which it appears that, to care for a combined number of War-disabled men exceeding those of the United States by over 7,900,000, the three European countries together expended, in 1931–32, a sum smaller by $57,500,000 than that spent by America in that year, for her World-War ex-service men.

Finally, a third glance shows this contrast:

[1] The German total is that of 1930–31, the latest available.
[2] Statement of the Administrator of Veterans' Affairs, Joint Congressional Hearing, December 10, 1932.
[3] See ante, p. 128.

167

SOLDIERS WHAT NEXT!

ANNUAL EXPENDITURE FOR WORLD-WAR EX-SERVICE MEN AND
THEIR DEPENDANTS, BASED, PER CAPITA, ON
DEAD AND WOUNDED

United States............... $2,668.66 [1]
United Kingdom............ 104.50 [2]

But these are figures that need critical reading. The
European countries, curiously enough, in many instances
have actually pensioned their heavily disabled men more
generously than has America, if due allowance be made
for the difference in the buying power of money. The
English soldiers' widow and orphan, the orphaned Italian
children, are distinctly more liberally cared for than are
ours. The pension of the French *grand invalide* has been,
in effect, better than that of his American counterpart.
And all this has been accomplished, for a number of beneficiaries far exceeding ours, at a fraction of our outlay.
The reason? The European Governments, with one partial exception, have confined their War-disablement benefits to War-disabled men and the dependants of the War
dead. Their pension roll is an honour roll. And the difference that makes in moral values exceeds the power of
money to show.

The European Governments have been gifted to understand that nothing on the physical plane can compensate
a man for the loss of his eyes, his legs, his bodily competence; and that his best comfort lies in serious respect
accorded to one who has heavily suffered for his country.

[1] Figures as of the previous fiscal year, given by the Administrator of Veterans'
Affairs, Joint Congressional Hearing, Washington, December 10, 1932.

[2] Figures as of 1930–31. Authority of the Ministry of Pensions. The sum
given is computed at par of exchange. Great Britain did not go off the gold
standard until November, 1931.

THE MAN FORGOTTEN

Our American effort, on the contrary, while generously inclined on the material side, has given little effective heed to the higher aspect. Instead, we have let the honour of our War-wounded men be sacrificed. We have let them be used by unscrupulous gangs as certain other types of mobs use women — pushing them to the front to serve as shields behind which mischief may be the more easily accomplished. We have allowed their name to be rendered suspect by the ever-growing multitude of hangers-on accepted by our laws. And so far has this abuse progressed that today a War-wounded man of pride and sensitiveness may well shrink from confessing the source of his hurt, lest he be thought another pretender.

General Hines, Administrator of Veterans' Affairs, recognized this when he vainly urged:[1]

> If we are so to liberalize [the law] as to take in [many thousands of] non-service-connected cases, then most certainly we should consider putting a premium upon those who have actual battle disabilities.... That force that served overseas, in action — and they are a small number compared to the total number — should be rewarded so that the inequality will not be so great.

And again General Hines pointed out that if the compensation of every battle-disabled man on the rolls were raised by ten per cent, the sum added to the budget thereby would be only about $2,800,000 annually.[2]

Let us keep that figure in mind for a moment, while picking up another to set against it:

[1] Hearings before Sub-Committee of United States Senate Committee on Finance, on H.R. 10381, May, 1930, p. 165.
[2] Letter to the Honourable Roy G. Fitzgerald, March 12, 1930. See *Congressional Record*, April 17, 1930, p. 7263.

In 1932 we carried on our pay-rolls as 'disabled World-War veterans' some thirteen thousand men who did not come to enlist until after the Armistice — after all the fighting was done. This we did because, although hostilities ceased on November 11, 1918, Peace was not officially declared until July 2, 1921. But for that technicality, the thirteen thousand would be drawing, not World-War veterans' compensation, but the considerably lower pension of the Regular Army. If, now, that thirteen thousand were transferred to the Regular Army pay-roll upon which they justly and reasonably if not technically belong, the annual savings effected would reach $3,649,000, or enough to raise the compensation of every one of our World-War battle-disabled men by ten per cent, with $849,000 left over.[1]

But it is increasing the number of pensioners, not increasing the pensions of battle casualties, that has aroused our practical enthusiasm. And if proof were needed as to the quality of our interest in the men who truly suffered in the country's cause, it lies stripped bare to the sun in our attitude toward the dependants of the World-War dead. Can it be questioned that their special care should have been accepted and welcomed as a sacred duty by the people of America?

How have we met that duty?

Our World-War Army was so young that a large percentage of those who were killed left, as dependant, a mother, not a wife. The widowed mother, in the original law, was allotted, on proof of dependancy, $20 a month.

---

[1] Hearings before Joint Congressional Committee on Veterans' Affairs, 72nd Congress, 2nd Session, vol. I, p. 95. (December 16, 1932, Testimony of General Hines.)

That sum has never been augmented, while the veterans' original basic pension was soon increased by over 166 per cent — from $30 to $80.

No one, seemingly, has taken thought, to an effective degree, either to add to the old mother's mite or to bless it with humanity. In some cases it may be enough when added to co-existing resources. Or, again, it may not suffice to save a poor, friendless soul, broken in health, advanced in years, and unable to work, from real suffering. If there are two surviving dependant parents, the pair may have $30 between them; but only in case the $30, added to whatever sum is paid to widow and dependant children, does not exceed $75 monthly.

As to actual conditions in a given case, if they are very distressful, the Red Cross, the Church, or the American Legion Post or Auxiliary, whose good works abound, may step into the breach as an act of charity. But our laws themselves provide no certainty, no control, no watch, nor any contingent relief. And that healing touch of respect that only Government action can give we have not troubled ourselves to offer.

Again, as to the widow: Under the original War Risk Insurance Act she was allowed, as the relict of a soldier dead from injury incurred in line of duty, $25 a month for herself, $35 if she had one child, or $47.50 if she had two children to support.

If the dead husband carried War Risk Insurance, the income thereby was increased by from $5.75 to $57.50 for 240 months. If he died uninsured within 120 days from his enlistment, the widow was entitled to $25 a month for 240 months as from automatic insurance, besides her $25 in

widow's compensation. But for the widow of the man who
volunteered in April, 1917; who, happy-go-lucky, took out
no insurance; and who was killed at Château-Thierry,
nothing was allowed beyond her $300 a year, and no more
concern was exhibited at the moment.

Some eight months later,[1] however, Congress recalled her
to mind, pondered her prospects and decided, in a moment
of thrift, that she had been over-lavishly promised.
Forty-seven dollars and a half for a widow with two
children was surely five dollars too much. Congress withdrew the excess.

Happily, our men in France could scarcely have learned
of that tribute when, eight days later, on May 28, 1918,
they went into our first American battle, in which they
were to leave four hundred and forty dead.

On these laurels we slept for quite six years, then awoke
and stirred again — this time to raise the widow's portion
to $30 a month. At the same stroke we gave her $10 to
maintain her eldest child, and added all of an extra monthly
dollar, making the sum $6 instead of $5, wherewith to feed
and clothe and house each other child, besides the first,
that the dead man left to her care.

If her husband had lived, but had lost one thumb, he
would have received, monthly, from $20 to $44 to console
him for his vanished thumb, supposing him to have been
a private soldier. Or, if he was an emergency captain,
that same lost thumb, thanks to the Legion's hard-
fought legislative victory for ex-service officers,[2] would

[1] Act of May 20, 1918. Public 151, 65th Congress, Amending Section 301 (c)
of the War Risk Insurance Act.
[2] See pp. 110-11, ante.

172

bring him approximately $165 a month in retired pay. But the widow has no rank. The average price of a private's thumb is enough for her, whoever she is or whatever her condition — and four or five times too much for any little orphan!

Of the World-War widow, Congress and the Legion have not necessarily assumed that in all parts of the country — town, farm and village alike — a woman can decently provide for herself and two children, educate the little ones as their father's service warrants, and meet all their vital needs on $46 a month. Rather it seems to be held that if the woman has no other resources, she can labour to earn the necessary remainder. The idea that she may not have bodily strength to do this; and that, if she does it, she probably must go from home, leaving her children, the while, without a mother's care, has seriously disturbed no one. In fact, as an individual human being with individual problems, and with a major claim on the country's solicitude, the widow of the actual World-War casualty has not been conspicuous.

We used at least to demand of her that she should not resort to the Ancient Trade to eke out her means, on pain of forfeiting her widow's rights; but that requirement has not applied since June 7, 1924, and for a reason peculiarly our own: We find personal observation and contact — regardless of any help that might result — too troublesome and too expensive to handle.[1]

'Think what a staff it would take to superintend the domestic relations of cotton-field darkies!' — with this exhausting thought we fade from the whole subject.

[1] Cf. for another conception, *post*, pp. 383-84.

By our original World-War Law the woman whom a War-disabled man married within ten years of the date of his injury could claim widow's compensation if his death, whenever it occurred, was the result of War-disability.

Then came our successive 'presumptive' amendments, adding doubtful cases by the many-score thousand to the list of 'War-disabled veterans' — adding correspondingly, therefore, to the potential number of compensable widows. Next, in 1925, we extended the time-limit of marriage to July 1, 1931 [1] — a minimum of over twelve years beyond that permitted by the European nations. But when 1931 arrived, the Legion Lobby, at its principals' command, occasioned the introduction in the Lower House of an amendment extending to July 2, 1941, the period within which a World-War veteran may marry, yet leave his widow eligible for compensation.[2] Widows have votes.

Up to this point our law has retained its original provision that the widow's title to pension rests on the husband's death from War-incurred injury. That provision must now be wiped out.

That it be so wiped out, and that the widow of every man who ever wore our World-War khaki, whenever he dies and whatever he dies of, shall hereafter be pensioned by the Nation, is today a declared major item on the Legion's legislative agenda.[3]

[1] Act of March 4, 1925. Public 628, 68th Congress.

[2] The 'unmarried wife,' as such, has no claim to compensation. Legality of the marital relationship is established under the law of the place where the contracting parties lived at the time of marriage or where the right to compensation accrued. Common-law marriages hold when duly contracted in States recognizing such relationship.

[3] Cf. *Proceedings, Thirteenth National Convention*, 1931, pp. 188–91. *Reports to*

the land it should ensure us a World-War
oll active in the year 2000 and well beyond.[1]
the woman whose husband left her and her
:o France — the widow of the man killed in
ad of combat injuries — has still her dollar
o bare hands — and her memories.
p with easy sentiment, we Americans. We
on impulse — and often, a little later, call
world at large to come help us marvel at
giving. But we are better at lighting grass
maintaining the eternal flame on the altar.
xpending thought and effort in defence of
sts as the honour of dead men and cripples,
s a practical world we live in — Is not'
y enough?

National Convention, 1932, pp. 22–23. Resolution adopted by
nal Convention in Chicago, October, 1933.
ʃar ended 1848. In 1932, Mexican War soldiers' widows to the
w pensions to a total of $326,124. *Annual Report, Adminis-
Affairs*, 1932, p. 30.

CHAPTER XIX

DEAD MEN CAN'T VOTE

Now let us take up the case of a dead soldier's children —
those whom the French Government surrounds with
honour and affectionate care, crowning them with the
name 'Wards of the Nation.'

While their mother survives, our law grants her thirty
cents a day for the first child, twenty cents for each other
child, until they reach the age of eighteen, wherewith to
provide for all their necessities.

If the mother dies, we give the eldest orphan $20 a
month. If there is a second, we allow $30 between the
two. For a third, another $10 is added.

These allowances may be continued for three additional
years to a child pursuing an approved course of advanced education. Or, for one physically or mentally
incapable of self-support, payment may continue for the
duration of its incapacity.[1] But no provision is made for
liberalizing the sum to meet actual need in individual
cases; no account is taken of the child's special abilities
and requirements; no thought is bestowed on the probable
education that the father would have provided had he
lived to fill a father's place. In this, other nations leave
us far behind.

Under our Rehabilitation scheme of the early post-War
period, we lavished thousands of dollars upon any young
man who had acquired a War-injury, to give him any

[1] World War Veterans' Act, as amended, Section 201.

176

DEAD MEN CAN'T VOTE

form of education that he desired. We would pay his way — maintenance, tuition, books, and all, through our major universities or post-graduate schools; and we disdained to enquire as to his private means or those of his parents, which, it is said, were often large.[1] Yet at the same time our law-makers were, as they still are, content to bestow, for the care and education of the son of a man killed in battle, the sum of $120 a year — that or less, but no more. And here, equally, we disdain to enquire the relation of our munificence to the needs of the case in question.

In Civil Service appointments, widows and orphans of soldiers and sailors are accorded certain preferences.[2] To the United States Military and Naval Academies the President may appoint a certain number of sons of men who died before July 2, 1921, of injuries acquired in the World War. But before either of these advantages accrues, the boy must somehow have been got through his tender years and his earlier education.

As to full orphans: Such attention as our first World-War laws bestowed upon them concerned only the actual payment of money into their guardians' hands. The War Risk Insurance Act allowed the Director of the Veterans' Bureau no further discretion in the matter. His business was simply to pay, not to ask what happened thereafter; and the attitude of the States and of the State courts, if

[1] See *ante*, p. 63.

[2] Widow's preference is now extended to women who were married after the husband's discharge from service; and to women remarried any number of times after the death of the soldier-husband, whether the subsequent marriages ended in death or in divorce 'without fault on the part of the wife.' See *Veterans' Preference*. Form 1481, June, 1931, U.S. Civil Service Commission, Washington, D.C.

177

attempt was made to follow up, was commonly one of resentment toward what they were prone to regard as offensive Federal interference in State affairs and an attack upon the State Judiciary.

Yet few States have shown much zeal to relieve the Federal Government of the financial burden involved; and too many have yet to provide adequate and reliable supervision of their own either for the spending of the money granted by the Nation or for the general welfare of child wards. As to their sense of responsibility, it has too often seemed entirely exhausted in the effort to defend State dignity.

After some years of such procedure, the American Legion, informed through its local posts and women's auxiliaries; the Red Cross, informed through its local branches; and other co-operating agencies, began pouring in upon the Veterans' Bureau urgent complaints. Investigation followed, which, says a recent Veterans' Administration departmental statement,[1] soon revealed the fact that 'aside from actual embezzlement — and this was no unusual occurrence — the ways in which a guardian could misuse the funds of his ward were legion.'

Then the Federal authorities, still incredibly handicapped and prevented by State jealousies, attempted to intervene. In the year 1927, the year's embezzlements and misappropriations in the handling of orphans' and incompetents' pensions, amounted, as uncovered, to $1,615,775. In the second year $1,162,124.39 were found thus diverted from proper use. In the third year (1929)

---

[1] For transition of Bureau into Administration, and history of structure, see United States Appendix I.

the sum discovered as stolen fell to less than half a million dollars.[1]

Since that time the annual figures of theft have dropped and risen again.

As to personal watch over the child itself, apart from mere tracing of funds paid in its father's name, and checking fraudulent accounts, the Veterans' Administration Guardianship Service inspector, under present procedure, makes one original visit. If the visiting agent is then reasonably satisfied with conditions in evidence, he asks a local clergyman, or the local postmaster or doctor, or the local Legion Post, or the Red Cross branch, if such there be — all of them, be it noted, without delegation of authority to act, whether from Federal or State Government — to keep an eye on the child, and to inform the Chief Attorney of any signs of abuse that may chance to be seen. Besides this, social workers on the employed staff of the Veterans' Administration's Medical Department, pursuing their ordinary travels on other business, will look in upon pensioned orphans in whose neighbourhood they may find themselves. But, in order to visit each ward once a year, the Administrator's staff, it is said, would have to be increased over fifty per cent above its present strength.

Nowhere more clearly than in this general connection does one see the virtue and the fault of the American Legion. Working diligently through its State branches, it has of late years forwarded improvements in the guardianship laws of several Commonwealths, and has been

[1] *The Developments and Functioning of the Guardianship Service*, Veterans' Administration, 1932. Unpublished.

instrumental in securing in twenty or more States educational aid for World War orphans.[1] Working through its local posts and its women's auxiliaries, it has rendered great help in individual cases, as it does in many another community need. But, working in Washington as a central political machine, on policies determined by a small group of men ambitious for power, it has behaved as do other big machines fighting for class advantage at the moral and material expense of the country, and with little time to spare for serious effort in the interests of politically negligible elements.

Where a strong Legion post or a strong Red Cross branch is found, there the World-War orphan has a protecting friend. But neither is omnipresent.

Here is one actual case, to suggest what spectres may enter the door unguarded by the law of the land.

The soldier-husband was killed in the War. The widow, left with two baby girls, seems to have been, in the beginning, a well-meaning, fairly careful mother. She married again. More children came rapidly. The second husband turned out worthless — an idle, dangerous scamp who could not be made to work. Even if she would, the wife dared not hold out against his insistence, nor could she deny the growing family's hungry mouths. So the money provided by law for the care of the soldier's children was spent, not for them, but for the whole household. Meantime, worn out by hard work and rough usage, discouraged and broken-spirited, the mother

---

[1] State scholarships are commonly confined to orphans between the ages of 16 and 21. Those awarded by California, reaching to $450 a year, exceed almost twofold those granted by the State next in liberality.

was taxed to her limit by the man's and the younger children's demands. The soldier's two little girls, unhappy at home, neglected and unrestrained, ran loose in the streets.

Time passed. The soldier's two daughters are now in their teens. One is infected with a social disease, the other is said to be a common prostitute.

This condition was reached gradually, during a period of years through which, month by month, Federal funds, unguided by intelligence and defeated of useful result by State pride, irresponsibility, and selfishness, had been dribbled into that unhappy household.

From afar off, the townsfolk had seen or guessed what was afoot. But they had no positive knowledge, they felt no personal responsibility, nor did any of them care to pursue enquiry, still less to make complaint. The man's character was such that either course might mean a vengeful attack upon the complainant's life or property.

If in that locality there had chanced to live some citizen or group of citizens so militantly minded that they would have interfered for those two little girls, while yet there was time, their fate might have been other than it is today. But the vital point would nevertheless remain untouched — that no means was commanded and provided by State, by State Court, by local or by Federal power, to watch over those children with personal care, as their dead father's delegate, and to see the thing through.

The theory that such care can not be ensured by any Government falls defeated before the record of England and of Italy today.

It seems sufficiently clear that our guardianship laws

need radical reform; that all dead men's children, not those of dead soldiers alone, need, in this our America, a protection at present denied them. But most of all it seems clear that the time has come when we as individuals and we as a people must emerge from our hiding in the disclaimer of Cain.

CHAPTER XX

CONGRESSMAN LEWIS DOUGLAS

WHAT are Congressmen?

It is time to think what they are, before sitting longer in judgment on their works.

First of all, many of them are people who took the job because you, who are better equipped to serve your country, were not willing to do so whether as a whole-time or a part-time effort. You said 'American politics are too dirty to touch' — as you might have said, 'My hands are too dirty to wash.'

The truth was, you found your own amusements too amusing or your use for money too robust, to be put aside for the country's service. What you said was, that your business responsibilities were too weighty to permit you to give time to public affairs. How ridiculous that looks, put down in ink! Nevertheless, you did say just that, and, what is far worse, your friends allowed you to say it in the hearing of their own growing and impressionable boys and girls, as though it were a decent and reasonable utterance.

So, awarding to yourself the rôle of free and non-responsible critic, you have left the country's work to be done either by better men than you, or by what you call an inferior type. And naturally the latter preponderate — though whence comes your right to call them so? A large percentage of them are plain, small-town folk, unsophis-

ticated, with rudimentary education, having no slightest
vision of the far-echoing effects of the things they do.
Sitting there in that little Congressional Chamber, this
type plays with big words, parrots stock phrases, and pro-
poses or supports or denounces pregnant measures with as
much awareness of what he does as a child would bring
to driving an airplane. You, who know better, or should
know better, put the control in his hands. You went
away and left him there. Never have you turned your
head since, to see what he is about. Never have you
helped him with support or advice. Even to write him
a letter as crises approach has been beyond your energy
— unless some organization pushed you to it. Whose
fault is the smash?

The Congressman of this type is forty-five to fifty years
old. He has left the country town in which, in his younger
years, he married his wife and made his living — left the
stream in which he could swim independently, abreast of
his neighbours and by his own power. The pay of a Congressman looked good to him then. A Washington hotel
looked grand to his wife. So he hired a lawyer to write
campaign speeches for him — and he has a good radio
voice. Also, he combed the district for any and all sorts
of local organizations that he might enlist in his support.
Among others, he visited the Legion in its posts over
bakers' shops or billiard rooms or in its own halls or houses,
throughout the constituency, slapped the comrades on the
back and told them what he would do for them if they
would send him to Congress. 'This is the richest country
in the world,' he never failed to repeat to them — 'and
you boys that went over the top for us all, you deserve the

best it has to give. Only tell me what you want, and then just watch me, when I get to Washington.'

The constituency sent him to Congress. That was years since. Now he is afraid — afraid to offend anyone who shouts — afraid to let go.

If he has not, through careful merchandising, established useful connections while in Washington, worth some little Government clerkship, he must, if he loses his seat, slink about at home, a shame-faced derelict — a man without a reason. He is too old to start afresh. His wife would have to work for them both at whatever she can find — stenography, perhaps, or shop-keeping.

'It is easy to blame us,' said one of them. 'Try it on yourself: Suppose you had to choose between writing a book that you knew to be false or being a down-and-outer and letting your dependants starve.'

He must hold on as long as he can — and meantime, perhaps, his salary is overdrawn.

In the lush years that ended with 1929, figures, that meant little enough to any of us, meant nothing to the average Congressman. As one of them has phrased it, 'We'd have passed a bill then, to cover with gold leaf every filling station in the United States.'

As for the people of the United States, some of them heartily desired gold-leaf legislation to cover their personal filling stations and almost all the others were too much absorbed in their private affairs to see what was going on.

One day on the lip of 1930, four men sat at luncheon in a New York club. Three were presidents of great banks. The fourth was a distinguished Government official. Old friends, they had not met since the War. Now they were talking of economic catastrophy.

'You three,' suddenly demanded the official — 'have you the foggiest idea what this country is paying out to the ex-service man, and how it compares with the numbers of our really War-disabled?'

'Not the foggiest,' answered one banker, speaking for the rest, 'but no doubt it is plenty!' — and all three laughed.

'That is exactly the terror of it,' said the other — 'you don't know, but you laugh.'

Then they all laughed again.

Two years later these same three bankers, as members of the militant Economy League, were fighting hard to defend the solvency of the Nation from the attack of the organized ex-service body. But they began their work too late. Thirteen years earlier they could have acted as friends powerfully. Instead, having no friendship to spare and no sense whatever of personal responsibility in affairs of State, they left the field open to the professional racketeer and his able cumulative work. Today the racketeer's pupil truly believes in the justice of his claim and in the unmitigated hostility of capital; furthermore, the pinch of the times impels him. 'Banker' means 'enemy,' now, to the man whom, until their own shoes pinched, the three that ate lunch had wholly forgotten.

For the rest, indeed, few of us were given to thinking much or clearly about unpleasant things. We had enjoyed easy money for a long time. Just now, certainly, there appeared to be a lean spot. But surely that would soon pass. Is not this the greatest and richest country

186

in the world? Only look at our size, our position, and our natural resources! Let us then show our confidence and spend money freely, whether we have it or not, leaving to Nature, who abhors a vacuum, the filling of our emptied pockets.

Thus the Legion Lobby, in spite of the times, was able to credit the short Congressional session preceding the Legion Convention of 1931 with 'more legislation beneficial to veterans' than had been enacted by any Congress before it. And the Legion Convention itself, in that year of national disaster, was emboldened to adopt one hundred and seventy-six resolutions, later embodied in bills, demanding yet further tribute from Congress and the country.

But in taking this action the Legion National Executives, drunk with long success, went against the shrewder judgment of its Lobby. Noise followed. The Nation, already partially awakened by a nightmare of thieves in the house, stirred, sat up and rubbed its sleepy eyes. The first thing it clearly saw was, that it stood on the edge of financial ruin and that twenty-five cents out of every one of its dollars had been snatched by a small body of people the great majority of whom had no sort of right to their loot.

Then general chatter began. Books appeared. Editorials in the major press. A few Legion posts, before they could be quashed, shouted out protests against the tar with which their name had been smeared. Ex-service men who were neither Legionnaires nor members of any other ex-service organization, called upon the country to realize that the Legion's commonly claimed membership of a

million men meant less than a fourth of America's World-
War ex-service body; and that not even that fourth part
did, in fact, belong to the Legion.[1]

And finally the House of Representatives, shivering a
bit under the shrewd new bite in the air, appointed a
House Economy Committee to review the position. This
was in February, 1932.

The Committee met behind closed doors, admitting no
ex-service lobby to its hearings. In that unmolested peace
it planned, as to the budget for ex-service men's benefits,
a cut to be effected by diminishing a few of the most
flagrant abuses. The Senate Finance Committee, meantime, adversely reported fifty of the newly proposed
'veterans' bills, and, as the Legion Lobby put it, 'strangled
109 more without a hearing.' 'For the first time in our
history,' confessed the Lobby, 'we were placed on the
defensive.' [2]

Alarmed at last, the Legion high command mobilized
its whole machinery. Through all its channels of publicity,
direct or sinuous, it now shot forth its story and its orders.
'The rascals are after your bone! Growl! Show your
teeth!' As by clockwork, in every constituency teeth
gnashed, growls rumbled, while Congressional hearts
quaked.

It was before a House thus distempered that, in April–
May, 1932, the Economy Bill came to judgment. Pitiful
cowardices, pitiful trucklings and crawlings it evoked.
Things more sickening.

[1] The paid-up membership of the Legion, in September, 1933, was 758,430.
National Commander's statement at the Annual Convention, 1933.

[2] *Reports to the Fourteenth Annual National Convention of the American Legion,*
1932, p. 139.

CONGRESSMAN LEWIS DOUGLAS

A few men, standing fast, speaking out like men, shone
bright against that background: Simmons of Nebraska,
Johnson of Dakota, hitting straight and hard.

Then arose a third — the man who himself had framed
the provision now under attack. When he began to explain its details, the usual interruptions, nagging or futile,
ensued. But presently the House awakened to the fact
that the event of a lifetime was happening. It was being
confronted with a great moral challenge. A prophet stood
before Israel. It hushed itself to hear. A young man,
slender, very quiet. Trained and finished and poised, a
man of the world. Something about him that meant a
sure seat in the saddle, and the habit and nature of the
open. Courage, physical and moral, and the trenchancy
of a flexible Damascus rapier. Simplicity. The blood
that tells. A thoroughly dangerous gentle courtesy. A
man who, when he came home from France, had said,
'If this America is good enough to live in, it is good enough
to fight for at home as well as abroad' — and, in season
and out of season, untiring and unafraid, had since made
good that word. A man as yet little known, but, if he
lives, of incalculable hope to the Nation. A man not
soon to be matched. Lewis Douglas of Arizona.

With clarity, with dignity, he told them what they
needed to know about the measure before them. Speaking
with all a soldier's sympathy for the truly War-disabled,
he showed them the monstrous and disastrous burden
that had been heaped upon the country by indecent and
unjustifiable class legislation, trading upon and dishon-
ouring the ex-soldier's name. Then, standing motionless,
his hands clasped behind his back, with a concentrated

quiet more telling than any oratory, he threw his whole strength into a final challenge to the manhood in the men before him.

Were the ex-service men of this country... who followed their flag into battle, to become cognizant of what has been put on the statute books of the country, they would rise up in arms and say, 'This thing must stop!' and if they will not, then I say to you here, as an individual, that this thing must stop. Were I to take any other position I would consider that I, as an individual... were unworthy of the flag I once followed; that I would be unworthy to sit in this House.:...

This is no time to consider our own petty political careers. This is no time to set ourselves up individually above our country. On the contrary, this is a time when you and I are under the guns. It is for us to decide whether we have the courage to stand under fire.

All the great political philosophers — Voltaire, Hume, and Locke — prophesied the day when under a democratic form of government the power of organized minorities would be greater than the resistance of the legislative body. I submit to you that that time has almost arrived.... Unless you and I now have the courage to stand firm against these organized minorities, to exercise our best judgment in the interest of our Nation as a whole, I say to you — and in this respect I will assume a prophetic rôle — the democratic form of government... which has made this country great, will crumble into dust.

As for myself, as long as I am a Member of this House I will ... oppose every organized minority that attempts to impose on the United States a burden which cannot be justified and which the United States cannot and should not carry.

Upon that came drama such as might draw tears from the heart of any true American.

The House, by common and spontaneous impulse, rose as one man and stood in respect, while the speaker returned to his place. Then it broke into long applause

Afterward — so it is reported — men came up to him to seize his hand — 'You are right. I know you are right. Would to God I could follow you! But I dare not. I have to go home and face my constituents. I can't afford to lose my seat.'

In the vote that followed, 211 to 116, they struck from the Economy Bill the whole section effecting cuts in World-War ex-service men's 'benefits.'

CHAPTER XXI

PRESIDENT HOOVER'S LAST CARD

So, THE House having shorn the Economy Bill of all reductions in the ex-service budget, the *amputé* on its stretcher was borne away to the Senate.

The Senate, in a Special Economy Committee, restored the limb that the House cut off.

Whereat, to quote its proud Lobby, 'once more the Legion sprang to the attack.'[1] The Senate retreated before it. The Economy Bill was enacted bared of ex-service cuts. All things oozed quickly and quietly back to their former level, and again the victory of Legion over Nation seemed complete.

Nevertheless, the leaders' sense of security was shaken. The Lobby, prefacing its *Annual Report* rendered at the end of the year, used urgent language. No expressions of divergent opinion within the Legion could henceforth be permitted. 'As a matter of organization, it behooves the members... to abide by the will of the majority and play the game according to the rules.' Only so could a minority hope to win legislative success. 'We cannot and will not agree to a ruthless slashing of veterans' benefits in the sole interest of economy, and allow our disabled war comrades and their dependants to ponder upon the gratitude of the Republic.... The Legion's fight for those who cannot help themselves has just begun.'[2]

[1] *Reports to Fourteenth Annual National Convention*, 1932, p. 172.
[2] *Ibid.*, p. 141.

192

This statement gives a sample of the good faith of the Legion central control toward those who accept its teaching. By the great majority, the distinction in meaning between 'disabled War Comrades' and 'War-disabled Comrades' would pass unobserved; any normal human being will rise on behalf of the War-disabled.

The proposal now was, it is true, even in the case of the actually War-injured man, to reduce the basic pension, for permanent disability, to $80 from $100, scaling down the lesser degrees in accordance. But 'the gratitude of the Republic' was not at fault here. The Legion had long ago and many times been warned that their insatiable rapacity, masked in their legerdemain of phrase, would one day recoil upon those whose credit it exploited — the truly War-disabled.

The following comparisons, as of the year 1932 (see table on page 194), exonerate the country from intentional neglect of its ex-soldiers.

But it is always essential to realize that, of the total number of men drawing American compensation as for service-connected disabilities, approximately one-third only are suffering from the result of combat with the enemy.

It were both needless and wearisome to detail the story of the Economy Act much further. A joint Congressional Committee was appointed to review the possibility of reducing the ex-service drain on the National Treasury. The Committee sat in December and January, 1932–33. Meantime, the United States Chamber of Commerce and a volunteer emergency organization called the Economy League started a country-wide campaign to rouse support

SOLDIERS WHAT NEXT!

WORLD WAR

	NUMBER OF MEN IN COMBAT SERVICE	NUMBER OF MEN PENSIONED IN 1932	EXPENDITURE ON EX-SERVICE MEN'S BENEFITS, 1932
U.S.A.	1,390,000 [1]	771,399 [6]	$417,738,652 [7]
United Kingdom	4,970,902 [2]	480,840	240,260,724 [8]
Italy	5,600,000 [3]	210,000	60,758,885 [9]
France	7,932,000 [4]	1,098,047	297,842,031 [10]
Germany	12,000,000 [5]	900,000	285,840,000 [11]

for ex-service budget retrenchment. Certain local Legion posts, again revolting against the gag-rule, broke out in open denunciation of the Legion's official stand and were, for their pains, silenced or ejected from membership by the cancellation of their charters. Two or three new organizations came into being composed of ex-service men who desired to clear the name of the old A.E.F. from complicity in the scandal in progress.

The Legion's attitude, under these circumstances, may

[1] Ayres, *War with Germany*, p. 101.

[2] *Statistics of the Military Effort of the British Empire During the Great War*, The War Office, March, 1920, p. 363.

[3] Authority of the Italian Government, March, 1933.

[4] Edmond Michel, *Les Dommages de Guerre de la France et leur Réparation*, Editions Berger-Levrault, Paris, 1932, p. 497.

[5] Authority of the German Labour Ministry, August, 1933.

[6] Hearing before the Joint Congressional Committee on Veterans' Affairs, December, 1932, p. 26.

[7] *Annual Report, Administrator of Veterans' Affairs*, 1932, pp. 156 and 160. This figure does not include Bonus or insurance expenditures, or hospital construction. The figures for the other countries include all expenditures, excepting only the figures of Italy, which omit the costs of the three great Institutes. See *post*, pp. 316–17.

[8] Authority of the British Ministry of Pensions, 1933.

[9] Authority of the Italian Government, 1933.

[10] Authority of the French Ministry of Pensions, March, 1933.

[11] Authority of the German Ministry of Labour, 1933. Figure of 1931.

most fairly be self-described. Said the Lobby's *Report* for the year just ending: [1]

> ... Heretofore at each [Congressional] session your National Legislative Committee and the Legion throughout the country had pressed onward from accomplishment to accomplishment. Then came the panic of 1929, with the resulting financial depression.... Selfish interests... turned their big guns at last upon the benefits accorded disabled. The attack came from a dozen different sources, but nearly all were inspired by the financially great, or by the little brothers of the rich.... The disabled were to be the victims of economy....
>
> Selfish financial interests are determined that the cost of war veterans' legislation be drastically reduced....
>
> The Legion should, therefore, be on its guard as never before and should prepare to resist, to the last ditch, the restrictive proposals which will be brought forward during the coming session.

Soon the Lobby signals the Legion body for attacks upon Congressmen from their home towns. Bulletins sent out to commanders of local posts carry explicit directions: The local people, whether in town, country, or State, must be made clearly to grasp that if the Federal Government does not take care of this section of their needy for them, they surely will be obliged to do it themselves, and to pay for it out of their State and local taxes.

As a stimulus to the brain an alphabetical list is furnished [2] showing, for each State, the amount of money sent into it in 1932 by the National Treasury in the shape of World-War disability allowances — $2,462,345 into Alabama, $3,693,991 into California, $3,075,824 into Mississippi; into Pennsylvania $4,911,017, into Texas, $2,698,-

[1] *Reports to the Fourteenth Annual Convention of The American Legion*, September, 1932, pp. 176–77.

[2] *Weekly Bulletin*, No. 1, December 10, 1932, p. 4.

753; to a total of over $75,458,000. Shall all these golden rivulets be turned aside?

Also, grocers, butchers, milkmen, coal-dealers, landlords, must be visited by energetic Legionnaires and educated by the local press. Such as these should be made to understand, and above all to make their Congressmen understand, that the men to whom money is voted will have money to spend. 'You should bring home to your merchants and your storekeepers... that disability allowances are now paying the cost of food, heat and rent in thousands of families.' [1]

It is not, however, suggested that anyone should bring home to the storekeeper the fact that he himself has exactly as sound a right to that Government subsidy as has the 'disability allowance' man. The very word 'allowance' means that the disability for which allowance is drawn is a disability incurred in civil life, such as the storekeeper himself may today be carrying, or tomorrow may acquire, equally without relation to War-service.

Perhaps the storekeeper and every other citizen, when means, health, and earning power are insufficient to procure the vital necessities, has a moral right to sickness stipend and hospital care, to old age and unemployment insurance built up, not as charity but with the aid of public funds. That may be. Other countries think so. But until such right is faced, accepted, and translated into American law, what title have our 'disability-allowance' ex-service men to preference as a class apart, above and at the expense of their often poorer neighbours?

[1] *Weekly Bulletin*, No. 2, December 17, 1932, p. 6. Issued by the Legion Lobby. Cf. *Bulletin* of October 8, 1932.

PRESIDENT HOOVER'S LAST CARD

The Government deficit in 1931–32 was $2,100,000,000.
The budget item of which the Legion, in the face of that
deficit, successfully defied reduction, was $945,988,000.

> Unless... the veterans stop their constant demands for more
> money from the Treasury, there is going to be a reaction in the
> country against veterans' legislation that will make the thing
> that the Economy Committee proposed to do look like a pea-
> nut stand. We can not go on forever in demanding continued
> and enlarged payments out of the Federal Treasury in the
> name of veterans without justification and without end.

So had said Representative Robert Simmons of Nebraska.[1] But the warning which other of his fellow-legislators,
both Congressmen and Senators, had expressed in no less
emphatic words went all for naught. The Legion faced
the country and the incoming Roosevelt Administration
without abating one jot of its demands. 'The fight,' it
repeated, 'has just begun.' It dwelt on 'the accepted
principle that the Federal Government owes an obligation
to veterans apart from payment for actual war injuries,'[2]
and always, directly and indirectly, it spread its old, bitter
teaching — curious in an organization loud against communism — that its real opponents, whether under cover
or in the open, were the stupid, selfish, and malevolent
rich deliberately banded to rob the poor.

But President Hoover, although he had signed an
Economy Bill that left undiminished the huge ex-service
budget, had still one card to play on the country's behalf.
On March 3, 1933, his last day in office, he played it.
He cancelled the appropriation voted by the Seventy-

[1] House of Representatives, May 3, 1932.
[2] Legion press sheet, December, 1932.

Second Congress to feed the Administration of Veterans' affairs for the next fiscal year.

This move forced upon his successor in the Presidency, forced also upon the new Congress, decisive action before June 30, the end of the fiscal year. In default thereof the Administration of Veterans' Affairs must stop functioning.

The rest is recent history. The entry of the new Administration. The sudden collapse of the country's credit. The great national banks shut down. The fall of the dollar. The desperate, groping sallies into dark and unmapped tunnels, if perchance way may be found out of our pit of smothering fear.

CHAPTER XXII

TO MAINTAIN THE CREDIT OF THE UNITED STATES

IT WAS while the banks were still closed that a frightened Congress, on the request of the new President, approved 'An Act to Maintain the Credit of the United States Government.'[1] Not with deliberation, as in Mr. Wilson's day, but in precipitate speed, driven by present disaster, did this second Democratic Administration of the century move to shake off the vampire that in fifteen years of sucking the vitals of the country had grown to monstrous size. The Act signed by President Roosevelt annulled and superseded all previously existing World-War pension legislation.[2] Yet, if truth be faced, it set in its place not a clean-cut, thoroughbred War-pension, but a mongrel with a dangerous bar-sinister in its pedigree. Largely War-pension, but partly special privilege for a limited civilian class, the lesser strain may prove the stronger blood.

Reform measure though it is, the new law still allows to ex-service men, as a class apart, rights and perquisites that no other Government, with one single and partial exception, has conceded.

It leaves, in particular, the ex-service men of the Spanish War, as a small favoured caste, in possession of an

[1] Public, No. 2, 73rd Congress. Approved, March 20, 1933.
[2] This Act dealt also with pensions of the Spanish War, the Boxer Rebellion and the Philippine Insurrection, with which this chapter is not concerned.

199

unconditional old-age pension, without regard to War-injury, to financial need, or to physical condition.[1]

The Act, therefore, contains within itself the charter and pledge for renewal of our old game of leap-frog.

It does, however, even while violating the principle, reassert the world's standard — that entitlement to War-pension must rest on injury or disease aggravated or contracted in line of duty in active military or naval service. It does insist on honourable discharge as prerequisite to pension. It does emphatically reiterate the misconduct clause and make it of inclusive application, robbing the Spanish War ex-service men, in that respect, of their special privilege. It does fix the end of the World War, for pension purposes, as November 11, 1918, the end of hostilities. It does reduce the rates of compensation for the lower grades of war-incurred disabilities, while heavily increasing some of those in the high categories. It does insist that the 'disabled emergency officer,' drawing retired officer's pay for an ailment that he did not contract as an officer during the War, must be put off the retired officers' pay-roll. It does say that $15 a month is money enough for a single man without dependants to draw as pension while being maintained and treated in hospital at Government's cost.[2] And it does remove from the World-War pension rolls all classes of non-service-connected cases save one: Persons who enlisted before November 11, 1918, who had given ninety days active military or

[1] Public No. 2, 73rd Congress, Title I, Section I (b).

[2] Hospitalization costs, in Veterans' Administration institutions, are reckoned as averaging $120 per month per man. The single man without dependants had been drawing, while in hospital, $80 a month compensation, free of charges.

naval service, who had been honourably discharged, and who were now totally and permanently disabled, might continue on the pay-roll, although at a lower pension rate, on this one further condition: that their physical decay was not the result of a social disease nor otherwise induced by their own misconduct.

This final condition demands notice for the reason that, where no second compensated ailment existed, it compelled the extinction of pension to venereal cases; and that if some of the worst of these cases were shortly advertised over the country as 'battle-scarred wrecks,' now inhumanely mishandled,[1] no official explanation was offered — since explanation must openly pillory the man. The public, therefore, was left to draw its own conclusions, easily erroneous.

As to persons pensioned for disabilities 'presumptively' of World-War origin, the new President's Regulation would curtail their number.[2] It would reduce the period allowed for the development of the 'presumptively' war-incurred malady to one year from the date of discharge

[1] Some such cases so adduced had in fact good War records; which records were cited in Congress and in certain newspapers, with the suggestion that the present physical condition was due to War service. For the new law's connection of the term 'misconduct' with social diseases, see Executive Order, March 31, 1933, Veterans' Regulation No. 10, Section IX.

[2] Regulation Number 1, Part I, paragraph 1 (c), 'authorizes a presumption of service-connection for chronic diseases becoming manifest to a 10 per cent degree or more within one year of separation from active service, but the Government is authorized to rebut such presumption where there is affirmative evidence to the contrary, or evidence to establish that an intercurrent injury or disease, which is a recognized cause of such chronic disease, has been suffered between the date of discharge and the onset of the chronic disease, or in case the disability is due to the person's own misconduct. It is required that a person, to be entitled to this presumption, must have served at least ninety days or more in the active service. (*Regulations Relating to Veterans' Relief*, Document No. 19, 73rd Congress, 1st Session, April 10, 1933, p. 38.)

from service instead of permitting it, as in the law superseded, to run until January 1, 1925. And it would entirely abolish diagnosis by Congress, in favour of diagnosis by medical science.

Other things the new Act did as well. Certain things also, it left undone: It left the widows and the orphans of the War-dead just where they stood before; and it left the case-files exposed, as before, to multiple inspection. But in all its doing the Administration made clear from the start that its scheme was tentative, not rigid — an open plan, to be changed as further examination and trial might suggest. By May 11, before Congressional stir had arisen, it was announced that the cuts, as proposed, cut, at points, too deep dealing, too severely with the War-disabled; and that those points would be modified.[1]

Meantime, behold a half-million or more men drawing World-War pensions for maladies whose connection with the War was either dubious or frankly not claimed. For years they had built on that pension, framing their scheme of life on its permanence. Now, in a period of unprecedented unemployment and money shortage, it is suddenly threatened with reduction or extinction, to take effect in a few months' time. The dismay, the shrieks, the curses that greeted the news were not without excuse. A cruel trick had indeed been played them — played by unworthy leaders and false friends. Not any President of the United States, not any Federal Treasurer, not any National Budget Director carried that guilt upon his shoulders. Each in his time had laboured and prophesied

[1] For the first scale, set up on March 20, 1933, and for the modifying scale of June 6, 1933, see United States Appendix V.

truly to save them from the Day of Wrath that now was come.

Now, in all this making of new history, what had been the rôle of the American Legion? To answer the question means to turn backward a page:

The President, in planning his policy as to pensions, had realized that it must, for a time, work hardship to many — had realized their need, therefore, to be braced to meet the shock in a spirit of courage and patriotism.

So, he made it one of his first acts, as President, to express his confidence in and dependence on the men who had once served the country in arms and to ask their loyal help in the battle before him.

He sent forth that call in a brief and simple radio talk, addressed to the American Legion and all veterans, delivered on the day after his inauguration — March 5:

'I am glad,' he began, 'that this, the first word addressed by me to the people of this country from the White House, can be dedicated to the great ideal of sacrifice and service,' and, 'I invite the support of the men of the Legion and of all men and women who love their country.'

The President's appeal was promptly and warmly answered in a public declaration by the Legion's National Commander. The American Legion, this official declared, had no desire other than to serve now as they served in 1917–18. The President could count absolutely on their loyalty.

And yet, within half a week's time of that public pledging of good faith, the Legion's innermost control, its Washington Lobby, was deep in the work of launching a general attack upon the President's position.

Congressmen were dealt with frontally: Did·they fondly imagine they could escape the consequences, if they allowed the President free hand with veterans' money? Congressmen were dealt with from the rear: Legion posts were ordered into action. 'Situation requires you to put down immediate barrage on all Senators and Congressmen insisting they vote against Administration Bill.'[1] Whereat, to quote a later Lobby bulletin, 'the Legion put up a tremendous fight... literally poured in telegrams.' 'I tell you the Legion has responded magnificently,' declares the Legion National Commander, again stepping before the curtain... 'the vast majority... have pledged their support to our President.' Meantime, under cover of that *divertissement*, the Lobby, behind the scenes, is working as only a master-lobby can.

Letters and telegrams from constituents and from strangers, pleading or threatening, spontaneous or to order, come raining down upon Congress. Terrible, shocking visitors appear. What can Congress do, with all the pack at its heels? Impossible to admit its own part-authorship of the high-stacked trouble that now, as long predicted, had toppled over upon everybody's head. Impossible, man for man, swallowing medicine and pride together, to declare: 'This infernal situation is largely of my own making. For my own little mess of pottage, I, even I, did it.' Triply impossible to surrender, meekly, one of the richest sources of patronage.

What, then, can Congress do?

The Senate, in this *impasse*, devises an expedient. It

---

[1] Telegram from Lobby to Legion Post Commanders. See 'The Counter-Attack,' Roger Burlingame, *Atlantic Monthly*, November, 1933.

produces an amendment of the new law, to curtail the wide rights conferred upon the President only thirteen days earlier. He shall be permitted to cut no pension for service-incurred disability more than twenty-five per cent.

At this, the major press of the country lets fly in sheer rage.

Not the press, not any normal citizen, would willingly see serious or lasting cuts in the pensions of truly War-disabled men. But all know that the President himself is like-minded; that his present moves are mere necessary preliminaries to establish an even base on which to build; that to work out his plan to a sound conclusion, he must be given liberty and time. And they recognize, in the Senate's step so quickly to check and limit him, the Senate's passion — to conserve its own power, though the country fall.

Said an editorial of the *New York Herald Tribune*, on June 6:

> The hundreds of thousands whose names now pad the pension rolls have been sending in their letters and telegrams. The hundred millions out of whose pockets the dole must come have been silent....
>
> ... No one should be under the slightest misapprehension as to the meaning of the present Congressional attitude.... We are right back again confronting the basic issue of whether pensions are to be poured out by Congress whenever a minority large enough to exert political pressure chooses to demand them.... If Congress will vote such a measure, at such a time as this, for no reason except that the Congressmen are afraid of the 'soldier vote,' then Congress will do anything. The public should make no mistake. Here is a fundamental issue which the President ought to go to the mat on,

and which the public, whether the President does or not, must go to the mat on. There is only one way to do that — by letter and telegram to Washington, and by letters and telegrams sent now.

But the amendment checking the President's liberty became law.

The *Herald Tribune* had been faithful and diligent throughout the crisis in calling citizens' attention to the need and duty of individual action — specifically of letter-writing. Yet on the day when the editorial just quoted reiterated its alarum, the following colloquy took place on the Senate floor:[1]

Mr. Walsh of Massachusetts: 'I think the public sentiment of the country is overwhelmingly in favour of the action taken by the Senate.'

Mr. Cutting: 'I think so, too; but the Senator from Massachusetts will agree with me that we would not get that impression from reading the editorials in the Metropolitan press.'

Mr. Walsh: 'I am sorry to say that I have to agree with the Senator; but, as for myself, I have not received a single, solitary letter of criticism of my vote in that matter.'

Mr. Cutting: 'Neither have I.'

Mr. Walsh: 'The only criticism I have heard is that we have delayed too long before acting.'

In other words, the only constituents, the only American citizens who had taken the trouble personally to acquaint these United States Senators with their views on the matter were persons interested in the defeat of the President's plans.

The Senate, nevertheless, could not relish the tone of the press. Feeling the need of a scapegoat, it had already

[1] *Congressional Record*, June 6, 1933, pp. 5188–89.

206

turned, therefore, where at such moments it always turns
— to attack the Administration. 'In order to do this
terrific injustice to the defenders of the Nation the
President of the United States sent that infamous measure
here to us labelled "A bill to maintain the credit of the
United States." It was of course misrepresentation of the
worst hue... trickery... weasel words...' So declared
one Senator.[1]

'The most infamous act ever passed by the Congress of
the United States. I believe it ought to be repealed from
top to bottom,' agrees another voice from the curule
chairs.[1]

'One of the most disgraceful things that has ever occurred in the history of our country,'[2] adds Senator Huey
Long.

Their thunder might well have taken to itself bolts
but for the certainty of evoking a Presidential veto which
for the moment, the country would scarcely endure.

Then, on June 6, the President, pursuing his intention
as originally announced, issues new Executive Orders.
These orders contain definite easings of the Orders of
March; raising of the pension rates; extension of the
rating schedule.

Senators, nevertheless, keep up their clamour. They
produce curious and gruesome stories of men wrecked by
battle wounds, now barbarously cut off from means of
survival — stories whose essential part they may omit to
tell. The President, it is said, privately confronts them

[1] Robinson of Indiana. *Congressional Record*, June 1, 1933, p. 4832.
[1] Bronson Cutting of New Mexico, *ibid*, June 2, 1933, p. 4906.
[2] *Ibid*, p. 4901.

with records. But the record is aside from their purpose.

Next comes an announcement that boards will be set up all over the country to review 'presumptive' War-disabled cases, and 'resolve all reasonable doubts in favour of the veteran, the burden of proof in such cases being on the Government.' The Legion and other ex-service organizations, as well as State and municipal authorities and non-service local interests, are invited, in each section, to submit names of candidates for reviewing-board membership. The President himself often checks and approves the members. In every case to be reviewed the pension will be continued until the case has been decided.

'How good will all this be?'

As good as the boards prove at rendering honest judgments. The question before them is otherwise clear. For the Legionnaire board-member it could be, quite simply, 'Shall we contribute to the reduction of our corporate prestige as the country's most flourishing plum-tree?' For the local interests, it could be, equally simply; 'Shall we bear on our own shoulders burdens that we could shift to the Nation? Shall we turn away Federal funds that would be spent in our community?'

If local men reject the burden, declaring it a Federal responsibility, they can safely count, as in years past, on the resounding support of many Senators, many Representatives, as soon as Congress sits.

Meantime, the organized ex-service element, although the Legion itself is for the moment officially hushed from loud public complaint, finds other means of expression. The President, it declares, is already weakening. By

208

degrees — as swiftly as he can while saving his own face, he will surrender unconditionally to the mighty power that, to his sorrow, he has presumed to challenge. As for those who have aided him in his folly, their heads will shortly be required of him, nor will he dare to refuse. What happened, they ask, in the old days, to dreamers in office who, counting on Presidential support, espoused the cause of the people against the G.A.R. machine and its Lemon? Is not every President's master-concern his own re-election?

Nor is there lack of individual speculators to fan the flames for the coming fight, advertising themselves in advance as champions worthy of note. Out to Legion posts goes a condensed reprint from the *Congressional Record*, carrying certain Senatorial speeches delivered in early June. These sow dragons' teeth: The provisions of the new scheme 'are the most illiberal, the most fraudulent and the most perfidious provisions which have ever been written into a statute'; the Administrator of Veterans' Affairs, General Frank T. Hines, and the Director of the Budget, Mr. Lewis Douglas, 'are regarded by the ex-service men throughout the Nation today as the two most rabid enemies they have in the world'; 'we know the outrages which have been perpetrated and the brutality which seems to bring pleasure to the sadistic hearts of these men.' And if this, for the moment, is as far as the speaker will go, lest he awaken and shock the innate decency of the men whose favours he is courting — one has but to look back into the *Congressional Record* to forecast his next step — 'The President of the United States,' he declares, 'never can escape responsibility for the injustices that have come about as a result of the so-called "Economy Act." ' [1]

There are in the country today thousands of obscure men to whom such words would come as suggestion — as a call to self-immolation on the altar of human rights — thousands of border-land minds. The police and the doctors know some of them, but not all. If the world ever learns their faces, it will be in one instant, in the light of a revolver's flash. But will the guilt be theirs?

[1] Senator Bronson Cutting, *Congressional Record*, June 1, 1933, p. 4834.

CHAPTER XXIII

THE PRESIDENT OF THE UNITED STATES

CHICAGO, turbulent city, in the throes of a World Exposition, crowded to utmost capacity by strangers from all the earth. A vast hall packed with humanity — twenty thousand, they say — and the room veiled blue with their smoke. The American Legion in National Convention — over a thousand delegates.[1]

And the rest? Their friends. Or — people that came. Who knows! No care could wholly determine, no wisdom tell.

Ten minutes to noon. For hours they have sat there, listening to this and that, waiting, fidgetting, waiting, to witness the act of a man.

In all the world, that day, that room was the only place into which, as far as human knowledge could judge, the President of the United States would enter at special peril of his life. Here were men who had been cunningly incited to believe him their merciless enemy — men surely for the most part steady, happy, good-humoured and sane. But it takes but one to go mad. And there in that room were packed thousands to produce the one.

Those charged with the President's personal safety had most earnestly besought him not to go to Chicago — not to enter the Convention hall. Aside from threats and warnings received, they knew, as it was their business to

[1] The Fifteenth Annual National Convention of the American Legion opened in Chicago on October 2, 1933.

know, the risks involved. The National Commander of the Legion, it is true, had bespoken Legion support of the President in his attempt to lift the country from its economic morass. But the work of years could not be wiped out in a few months' time by one official's shift of note. The fires of distrust and class hatred, so long fanned, had spread beyond Legion ranks — had swept afield through unknowable hosts. Now there were hungry men in our land of milk and honey. And hungry men see ghosts.

Yet President Roosevelt, rejecting all caution, all advice, all pleas, had himself insisted on going to Chicago to enter that very hall. These were the men whose class privilege he was taxing for the Nation's sake. These were the men whose help he needed for the Nation's sake. That they might the more surely understand their own higher importance and grasp the purpose and gravity of it all, he must go before them, meet them face to face.

Ten minutes to noon. The gathered thousands waiting, patiently waiting, crowded in the great hall, suddenly catch, from the street without, a sound of tumultuous cheers. Instantly every creature is alert. On the high platform the presiding Legion official springs to his feet.

In a great voice he cries out: 'The President of the United States!'

The whole house, rising, roars applause.

Then, curiously, falls a moment of silence — quick stillness — while five Secret Service guards, each with both hands thrust deep into his pockets, come swiftly to the front of the speakers' platform, sweeping and searching the smoke-veiled audience with their eyes.

THE PRESIDENT OF THE UNITED STATES

As openly as that. For the danger is so real as to mock disguise.

Five minutes to noon.

Leaning on the arm of an aide, the President appears, while the band breaks into the National Anthem. The President stops short — stands at salute. Then, from the rostrum, he begins to speak, in his steady, significant voice.[1]

> ... I want to talk with you about the problem of government, the difficulties which you and I as Americans have faced and solved and those which we still face.... I want to talk to you about national unity... a living thing — not a mere theory resting in books or otherwise apart from everyday business of men.... There are two enemies of national unity — sectionalism and class; and if the spirit of sectionalism or the spirit of class is allowed to grow strong or to prevail, it means the end of national unity and the end of patriotism.... You and I are well aware of the simple fact that, as every day passes, the people of this country are less and less willing to tolerate benefits for any one group of citizens which must be paid for by others.
>
> ... For several years past the benefits of American life were threatened. The crisis came in the spring of this year. It was necessary to meet that crisis.... Millions were out of work, the banks were closed, the credit of the Government itself was threatened. The car was stalled. Obviously the first objective was to get the engine running again... to restore the credit of the Government.... The great human values... for all American citizens, rest upon the unimpaired credit of the United States.
>
> ... We undertook to take the National Treasury out of the red and put it into the black. And in the doing of it we laid down two principles which directly affected benefits to veterans — to you, and to veterans of other wars.

[1] *New York Herald Tribune*, October 2, 1933; *New York Times*, October 3, 1933, and the press in general.

SOLDIERS WHAT NEXT!

The first principle, following inevitably from the obliga_
tion of citizens to bear arms, is that the Government has a
responsibility for and toward those who suffered injury or
contracted disease while serving in its defence.

The second principle is, that no person because he wore a
uniform must thereafter be placed in a special class of bene_
ficiaries over and above all other citizens. The fact of wearing
a uniform does not mean that he can demand and receive from
his Government a benefit which no other citizen receives.

It does not mean that because a person served in the
defence of his country — performed a basic obligation of
citizenship — he should receive a pension from his Government because of a disability incurred after his service had
terminated and not connected with that service.

... It does mean, however, that those who were injured in
or as a result of their service are entitled to receive adequate
and generous compensation for their disabilities. It does mean
that generous care should be extended to the dependants of
those who died in or as a result of service to their country.

To carry out these principles, the people of this country can
and will pay in taxes the sums which it is necessary to raise.
To carry out these principles will not bankrupt your Government nor throw its bookkeeping into the red,... Furthermore, it is my hope that in so far as justice concerns those
whose disabilities are, as a matter of fact, of War-service
origin, the Government will be able to extend even more
generous care than is now provided under existing regulations.

To these two broad principles the time has come, I believe,
for us to add a third. There are many veterans of our wars
to whom disability and sickness unconnected with war-
service have come. To them the Federal Government owes
the application of the same rule which it has laid down for
the relief of other cases of involuntary want or destitution.

In other words, if the individual affected cannot afford
to pay for his own treatment, he cannot call in any form of
Government aid. If he has not the wherewithal to take care
of himself, it is, first of all, the duty of his community to take
care of him, and next, the duty of his State. Only if under

214

these circumstances his own community and his own State are
unable to care for him, then, and then only, should the
Federal Government offer him hospitalization and care, and
the Federal Government stands ready to do that.

... Your task and mine are similar. Each one of us must
play an individual part in our own field... but at the same
time we must realize that the individual part belongs to a
closely related whole — the national unity of purpose and of
action....

... You who wore the uniform, you who served, you who
took the oath of allegiance to the American Legion, you who
support the ideals of American citizenship, I have called you
to the Colours again. As your Commander-in-Chief and your
comrade, I am confident you will respond.

As the President, finishing his address, withdraws,
cheers follow him.

But how will the Legion answer the summons of this
their Commander-in-Chief, once the cheers have died
away?

How should the Legion answer? His call to the Colours
is an out-and-out summons to abandon their entrenched
position and the heaped-up winnings of all their campaigns. His liberal intentions toward the War-disabled
could not but leave them cold; that small contingent,
though often named, has never greatly engaged their
minds. His denunciation of the spirit of class privilege is,
in effect, an attack upon the very life-springs of their
corporate being. His assumption that they are ready,
now, to act on a basis of altruism and idealistic citizenship, kindly as it is couched, throws a devastating light
on their record of years past.

Men there must have been, sitting in that hall, who felt
the pull of the President's words. But they, for thirteen

215

years, had been steadily drilled by machine-makers —
deserted and forgotten, the while, by those who could,
perhaps, have kept their souls alive. Generous youths no
more, they are professional 'veterans' now — veterans
by trade, veterans for profit. Flaccidly, cynically, they
take their cue from the handful of managers they employ.

Those few men, well used to weathering storms, did
the job they were paid to do — and did it with skill. In
advance of the President's arrival, and with an engaging
frankness, they had made public this acknowledgment
of recent events:

> Before the American Legion ... can hope for enactment of
> any major legislative program to extend benefits, it must
> above all resell itself to the American people.[1]

Now that the President had said his say and gone, they
did not, therefore, fling their defiance, bare, straight in
the President's face. They veiled its nakedness. But the
veil was thin.

The President had told the Legion in convention assembled that the spirit of class, if allowed to prevail, would
mean the end of national unity and the end of patriotism.
So, in the resolutions presently adopted they did not
baldly repeat their old demand for full and immediate
payment of the Bonus — a sum approaching $2,305,000,-
000.[2] Instead, and for the moment, they requisitioned
merely an annual gift to their class of fifty million dollars
of the people's money; this in the form of remittance of
interest on Bonus borrowings.

[1] *Annual Report of the Legion's National Legislative Committee*, September,
1933.
[2] *Annual Report of the Administrator of Veterans' Affairs*, 1932, p. 37.

Again, the President had just told them that 'the people of this country are less and less willing to tolerate benefits for any one group of citizens which must be paid for by others.' So they did not call at once for restitution of pensions for non-service-incurred disabilities. They declared, instead, merely for free hospitalization and medical care for all their future ailments; for class pension, also, on behalf of widows and children of all ex-service men.

Further, the President had told them, as more than one of his predecessors in office had done, that when a man serves in the defence of his country he is performing a basic duty of citizenship; that the mere fact of having once worn a uniform does not entitle him to benefits from his Government that no other citizen receives; and therefore that if, in later life, he finds himself burdened with disabilities not occasioned by war-service, for which he lacks means to care, his proper recourse is not to the Federal Government as a member of a class apart, but to his local and State authorities, as a citizen among citizens, to receive the relief provided for all.

To this last principle the Legion responds, however, with defiance categorical and direct. Restating the President's position the better to repudiate it, they declare:

> Whereas, the responsibility for the care of disabled and destitute veterans has now been placed upon the community and State, now therefore be it
> Resolved, that... it is the policy of the American Legion that the care and treatment of War veterans is the responsibility of the Federal Government.

And here it is useful to recall that of the hospitalized or domiciled 'disabled War Veterans' for whose benefit,

217

in 1932, $41,739,618 [1] was expended, 79 per cent [2] were men whose ailment had no connection whatever with their one-time soldiering. And the increase, both as to percentage and as to costs, was rising by leaps and bounds.[3]

Other resolutions the Chicago Convention passed. But those just indicated suffice to show the effect of the President's appeal.

Finally the assembled delegates chose their new National Commander. For this position the Legion has never sought men of high rank, of distinguished leadership in war, nor of outstanding administrative or executive achievement in civil life. The choice, rather, has been dictated by Legion internal politics. This time it fell upon a man with no Overseas record.

In accepting the distinction at their hands their new leader, as reported, thus proclaimed his intent: ·

> I pledge to God and my comrades to bring every eligible World-War veteran into the American Legion, and to see that all of us are saying and doing exactly the same thing on... American Legion objectives.[4]

It remains only to recall the hitherto well-justified boast of the Legion Lobby: [5] 'The Legion takes all of its objectives'; to mark that, as of October, 1933, it has officially

---

[1] *Annual Report of the Administrator of Veterans' Affairs*, 1932, p. 24.

[2] *Ibid.*, p. 13.

[3] The hospital construction appropriation authorized by Congress in 1931 (Public No. 868, 71st Congress) was $20,877,000. This was suggested by non-service-connected requirements only. See *Proceedings of the Thirteenth National Convention of the American Legion*, 1931, pp. 207–09.

[4] *New York Herald Tribune*, October 6, 1933.

[5] *Reports*, Fourteenth Annual National Convention, 1932, p. 265.

defied the President of the United States as it has defied all Presidents of the United States since the time of its birth; and to remember that Congress reconvenes.

'And what will happen then?' One put the question to a United States Senator — a man among the best.

'What has happened before?' he replied. 'The fight will begin at once, under cover and in the open. The President and those of us who stand by him in this effort will get little support from the country — not nearly enough to uphold our hands. Criticism we shall have, when it is too late, but no steady wheel-horse help. Compromise and concessions will result, until the tax-yoke grows so heavy that the younger generations throw down their tools and say, "Why should we work when all our earnings are taken from us to keep this class of privileged parasites?" It is a vicious circle, without end. But given the nature of our people it is inseparable from our form of Government.'

Let no one who has read this narrative think that the tracing of it can have been a pleasant task to any American; the less so because its historic unity, running through the years, shows itself born not of changing circumstances but of continuing spirit. That spirit, before it raised a monster, drove out an angel — the Angel that came with our boys home from France. That spirit itself, not any one of its numerous brood of offspring, is America's deadliest enemy today. For such a cause this present survey has been compelled to show it in the raw, rather than to try to shield and excuse it because it is our own.

SOLDIERS WHAT NEXT!

And now, having followed America's story through to the current hour, let us turn to those of our sister nations, who, since the World War's end, have been travelling the same road.

FRANCE

FRANCE

CHAPTER I

THEIR LAND AND THEIR DEAD

If the soldiers of France who died in the War could come back to life and were to march again in serried ranks of four abreast, 10,500 of them passing a given point every hour, more than six days and five nights would elapse before the last of them had passed. — The Honourable A. Piatt Andrew, M.C., House of Representatives, Washington, D.C., January 19, 1925.

In other words, by the eleventh of November, 1918, when the guns ceased firing, France had already sustained the loss of one man out of every six whom she had called to her colours on land and sea. Men of every rank, quality, profession, or trade; men in the flower of their youth or their prime; men wrenched out from the heart and the sinew of the race to be awfully destroyed.

But look once more toward that tragic scene. See now exposed, by the passing of the dead, a multitude still more numerous — helpless, weeping — infirm old folk, young wives and little children, suddenly robbed of their natural support — the strong young arms that are gone.

And see, again! Yet another array, less happy, perhaps, than the dead — the army of the maimed and the broken, lingering wreckage of war.

'What good, now, could victory bring to France?' moaned the pessimists of France, during those black days when the issue hung in the balance. 'What use, now, could victory be to France? Flowers on a corpse!'

Then Victory, herself descending, put an end to words. There was work to be done if France was to rise again to her normal vigour.

And surely the country's first duty — a twofold charge — lay toward the disabled defenders of the soil and toward the dependants of the slain. Crippled and invalided men, old folk, widows, little children, some four and a quarter million victims awaited the succour of the State.[1]

But, though the loss of her men was the bitterest sorrow of France, it was not the only loss she had endured. Ten of her most prosperous departments, home of an eighth of her population, had been laid waste. Fields, forests, orchards, vineyards, flocks, herds, horses, oxen, barns, stores, tools, machinery, all were destroyed; all mills, all factories demolished, coal-mines flooded, high-roads wrecked, while bridges blasted into rubble-heaps blocked the course of the streams. Inns, markets, churches, schools were gone. Cottages and châteaux alike had vanished. Over half a million homesteads were homes no more. And in the grey ocean of crumpled masonry that blotted out their sites, only a fire-gnawed leaf from a book — a bit of brown fur that some woman had worn, the round-eyed face of a child's doll peering out from between lumps of shattered concrete — remained to drive home the completeness of desolation. Elsewhere in France

---

[1] Edmond Michel, *Les Dommages de Guerre de la France et leur Réparation*, Édition Berger-Levrault, Paris, 1932, p. 503. The exact figure, 4,245,000, is as of August 1, 1928. This book will hereafter be referred to as *Les Dommages*.

224

bomb and shell had done their impartial work. All of France had suffered. But this area of the Front, whether for domestic life, for industry, or for the tillage of the soil, lay dead as the unpeopled moon.

Measured as a financial asset, not only was its contribution stricken from the nation's resources, but by no possibility could that contribution be resumed save at heavy outlay. Trenches, dug-outs, shell-craters, their lines for four years swinging back and forth with the tides of war, had turned the earth upside-down. Great stones, blown from beneath, encumbered the present surface, mingled with the débris of battle. Mines, shells, hand-grenades, buried alive, threatened life and limb in any attempt to clear the ground.

Then, 'This is a practical question,' said Government to people — 'a question for engineers. The land must be surveyed, to determine where it can pay back the labour and expense of reclaiming. Would you order your shoes resoled if resoling would cost you more than a new pair?'

Soon followed decision: 'Here and here we will clear and rebuild or recultivate. But here and here the game is not worth the candle; yet, since the soil is full of the bones of our dead, we may shroud it in forest and leave it, forever untroubled, a silent witness to the grief of France.'

And so, on the sixth of April, 1919, the edict went forth across the land. On the seventh of April, the mayor of the little commune of Roeux called the head men together to hear the command.

'Forbidden— to clear away — the ruins! Forbidden — to recover — *our fields!*' They stood as if stunned, mechanically repeating the words, slow tears gathering in their eyes. Then one broke out vehemently: 'That is impossible! We will not obey!' And by common impulse off they rushed, their mayor at the head, straight to their demolished market-square.

There, in the fading April twilight, gathered on the heap of stones that had been their bell-tower, they solemnly swore before God that, despite any human edict, any law, or any cost, they *would* restore their village and the soil of their immemorial love.

What happened in Roeux happened in many another desolated place. And of that fierce loyalty of each Frenchman to his own familiar bit of earth is built the composite patriotism of France.

To serve his year in the Army, learning to do his part in his country's defence; and then, to rush to her call when the ever-dreaded war-cloud bursts — so much, to the average Frenchman, is his natural law. 'He performs that service,' says his distinguished compatriot, Monsieur Bernard d'Été, 'as one of the logical requirements of civilized society, but his preoccupation is with the ways of peace. Soldiership, militarism, and all that these represent are not part of his ideology and are even distasteful to his spirit.' His heart is always with his hearth and his own familiar scene. Throughout the Great War, whenever he got a scrap of leave from the trenches, back he hurried to the land, to sow the wheat, to cultivate the crop, to guide the plough. In his horizon blue you saw him, a lonely, laborious figure, plodding the furrows as long as daylight's memory served. That night, huddled with his kind, he would sleep in the aisle of a racketing railway wagon. On the morrow he plodded furrows

226

again — trench-furrows — on the way to the Front. Whether in that day's work a shell-splinter tore off his legs; or took his life; or whether, at the end of the War, he would return unmaimed to the land, was a matter of personal fate — the chance shared by all Frenchmen alike, inherent in blood and birth. Whatever befell him, he took it as it came, yielding no tears to Fate.

CHAPTER II

THUS RUNS THE LAW

AND now, the Great War being ended, upon this background was projected a question of expediency devoid of romance — the question of what must be done for disabled men, for the relief of their families, and for the dependants of the dead.

Up to 1914, the old Law of 1831, framed, not to serve a nation in arms, but to provide the retired service pay that is part of any Government's contract with its regular army, had remained the only pension law of the land; and in principle it was still unchanged. By this law, soldiers disabled while in service were entitled to anticipated retirement pay; in other words, to a pension; but such entitlement could be attained only by proving a permanent service-incurred disability to a degree not less than 60 per cent.

The amount of the award was scaled according to rank, neither family circumstances nor private means affecting it. But the highest pension to which a totally disabled private could establish legal right was 780 francs ($156) [1] a year. Gratuities might be granted for other or lesser occasions, at the authorities' discretion. But no legal right to a military pension existed save as above indicated [2] and save that of the soldier's widow.

[1] The franc, at the outbreak of the War, stood at 19.3 cents. See United States Appendix I, for fluctuations in exchange.

[2] Edward T. DeVine, *Preliminary Economic Studies of the War*, Carnegie Endowment for International Peace, Oxford University Press, New York, 1919, pp. 25–27, 240–41.

This Law of 1831, somewhat relaxed, somewhat cush-
ioned with stop-gaps, continued in force throughout the
Great War. In the French Parliament, during that period,
commissions were set up to examine and recommend,
measures bloomed and withered on the floor of the Chamber, and long arguments were worried through, looking
to the creation of a new pension code. Yet while, one by
one, all the other great belligerents took action, France
still delayed. For, as her statesmen early reminded her,
her children yet unborn would be chargeable with the
costs of the scheme she adopted, whatever the scheme
might be. For their sakes, therefore, it behooved her,
before casting the die, to know well and surely who was
to pay the bill. Would it be a ruined and exhausted
France, groaning under the goad of a conqueror, who
must carry this burden too? Or would the debt and the
goad be laid upon another's back? Upon the answer
might well depend both the scale and the embrace of new
pension legislation.

So France made shift and marked time, till the end of
the War, till she knew beyond peradventure the decision
to be embodied in the Treaty of Versailles in the famous
Part VIII, Annex I, paragraph 5, which reads:

> Compensation may be claimed from Germany for all losses
> caused to the peoples of the Allied and Associated Powers, for
> all pensions or compensation of that nature to the military
> victims of the war (land, sea, or air forces), whether maimed,
> wounded, sick, or invalided, and to all persons of whom these
> victims were the support....

'Compensation may be claimed *from Germany...*'
That point safely established, the French Government

could at last sit down with a free spirit to write its bill of particulars — now no pinch-penny task forced for neces-sitous Peter's sake to skimp necessitous Paul.

Here are the main headings that the French Government assembled under which to compute the account to be handed to Germany.[1]

Pensions to ex-service men of the land, sea, and air forces who are suffering from infirmities occasioned by the War; and to widows and orphans of those who died for France.

Allowances for the parents and grandparents of the dead and missing ex-service men.

Extra allowance, to pensioned men or to widows, on account of each child below eighteen years of age; and for children yet to be born.

Free medical and surgical care, and free medical supplies, to be guaranteed both to ex-service War-victims and to their dependants, together with their travel expenses and the costs of necessary apparatus.

State aid to pensioned men who, because of their wounds or infirmities, are unable to pursue their former calling.

Running expenses of the pension boards and of the national bureaus for the care and the re-education of the War-maimed, and for the care and education of orphans.

Annuities to the *compagnes* — the 'unmarried wives' — of dead or missing men.

Emergency relief and additional allowances required for the families of dead or missing soldiers, sailors and merchant sailors.

[1] *Les Dommages*, p. 499. See also Robert Murray Haig, *The Public Finances of Post-War France*, Columbia University Press, New York, 1929, vol. I, pp. 297–98 and 416.

THUS RUNS THE LAW

Upon this simple base was raised the Law of March 31, 1919, the 'Great Pension Law' of France today extant. Each of its entitlements rested either upon the death or disability, incurred under arms, of a man fighting in his country's service.

This basis has survived, but from the time of its enactment until the present day, the Law of March 31, 1919, has undergone so many other modifications that these present pages can make no pretension to cover them, or indeed to do more than suggest the general concept. The principal provisions now extant are, however, as follows:

Every soldier [1] is entitled to pension if he is afflicted with infirmities attributable to his military service, which infirmities disable him to the extent of at least 10 per cent. The rate of his pension rises with the degree of his disablement and with his rank. All disablements are classified and assessed by a fixed scale, rising from 10 to 100 per cent — total disability. But no account is taken of the actual importance to a given individual of the physical diminution that he has suffered. Thus, by the French law, the loss of the first joint of the right thumb arbitrarily constitutes a 10 per cent disability. Whether the thumb is a Paderewski's, a sculptor's, or a ditch-digger's makes no difference.

In case of multiple infirmities, their several assess-

---

[1] France mobilized, in addition to her home troops, 260,000 Senegalese troops and 215,000 native troops from her other possessions. These lost a total of 71,100 killed. The dependants of the dead and wounded of these conscript coloured troops are pensioned under special laws, although the costs are understood as included in the clause of the Versailles Treaty above quoted. See *Les Dommages*, p. 497; and Jean Souquet, *Code des Anciens Combattants et des Victimes de la Guerre*, Charles-Lavauzelles & Cie, Paris, 1932, pp. 243–45. This volume will hereafter be referred to as *Code des Anciens Combattants*.

ments are so controlled that their sum shall not exceed 100 per cent. But a man afflicted with multiple infirmities, of which at least one entails in itself a condition of absolute invalidism, may be granted, over and above his regular pension, an annual allowance ranging from 240 to 2400 francs.[1]

Pensions are fixed for life, permanently, where disabilities are established as incurable. Where incurability is not established, the disabled man must be medically re-examined after a two-year period, at which re-examination his pension meets one of four fates: It is cancelled, reduced or increased, made permanent, or continued as temporary for a second two-year interval. After the fourth year, it must either be cancelled or rated as permanent. Once made permanent, it can never be decreased. The disabled man retains under all circumstances the right to demand medical re-examination, with a view to prove his worsening. He can also at any time demand examination on a new claim for disability arising from military service. Appeal from Ministry decisions can at any time be taken.[2]

In principle, the claimant of a pension must himself show proof of the service-origin or service-aggravation of his disability, whether wound or sickness.

Nevertheless, in view of the difficulties which many mobilized men would have experienced in so doing, it has been conceded that, save where proof to the contrary can be advanced by the State, disabilities established during the period of six months following the decree promulgating

---

[1] Title I, Article 12, of the Law of March 31, 1919.
[2] For the machinery dealing with the right of appeal, see French Appendix IV.

the Law of September 4, 1919, as well as those recorded before demobilization shall be considered as attributable to War-service. This is called the 'legal presumption of origin.' [1]

Ex-service men were originally allowed a time limit of five years in which to claim pensions. But, by a series of legislative changes, the limit was gradually moved forward until it reached December 31, 1932, and a new measure now pending will probably extend by two or three years more the period during which Great War pensions may be claimed.

The Law of March 31, 1919, set up pension rates for all ranks of the service; and for all degrees of disablement, from 10 to 100 per cent. [2] A private soldier 50 per cent disabled was thereby entitled to an annual pension of 1200 francs; a colonel, under the same disablement, could receive 4200 francs, and a general commanding an army division, 6300 francs. With the fall of the franc and the rise of the cost of living, it was found necessary to add a temporary supplement of 140 per cent to all pension allotments. This was done in January, 1929. Today they stand, for the 50 per cent disabled private, colonel, and general, at 2880 francs, 5880 francs, and 7980 francs a year, respectively. [3]

Furthermore, special legislation in behalf of the *grands invalides* — as the blind, the paralyzed, the men who

---

[1] Manuscript statement of French Ministry of Pensions prepared for the author August, 1932.

[2] For number of men pensioned under each degree of disability, see French Appendix VII.

[3] *Code des Anciens Combattants*, pp. 330–31, 333, and 221–23. For table of pensions of officers and non-commissioned officers, see French Appendix VIII.

have lost arms or legs, the advanced cases of tuberculosis
— placing them in a superclass, has bestowed upon them
pensions reaching, even for the private soldier, as high as
39,700 francs ($1556) a year. In addition to this, the
grand invalide as such, regardless of rank, receives a
yearly allowance of 1028 francs for each minor or infirm
child, while each descending grade of invalidity brings
to the father a correspondingly diminished allowance for
his children, down to the 72 francs per capita alloted for
those of the 10 per cent disabled man.[1]

Other provisions acting to improve the financial condition of certain classes of pensioners include such items
as the privilege of reduced rates of travel by land or sea;
certain rebates of taxes; provision of cheap food and lodging for heavily disabled workers; governmental help in
meeting the annual dues of insurance associations, with
the object of securing old-age assistance from that source;
small loans toward setting up in business; and special
grants of from 5000 to 15,000 francs to enable invalided
ex-service men to acquire cheap and suitable homes of
their own. Upon this last count, the national budget of
1932 presented an item of 70,000,000 francs ($2,744,000).[2]

During a period of ten years dating from July 21, 1928,[3]
certain paid positions in the gift of the State and of local
administrations go by preference to the War-disabled

[1] The franc is here computed at its post-War parity, 3.92 cents. For pensions
of private soldier and his dependants, see French Appendix IX. *Tarifs des
Pensions de Guerre*, furnished in manuscript by the French Ministry of Pensions
to the author.

[2] These relief measures are administered by *L'Office National des Mutilés* and
L'Office National des Combattants. See French Appendix V.

[3] Law of April 26, 1924, and Law of January 30, 1923, modified by the Law of
July 21, 1928. *Emplois Réservés aux Victimes de la Guerre.*

pensioner. And, further, private commercial or industrial enterprises employing more than ten salaried persons, and lumbering and agricultural enterprises employing more than fifteen salaried persons, must award a minimum of 10 per cent of their paid jobs to War-pensioners. Concerns employing thirty or more hands must give one third of those places to War-pensioners of reduced earning powers, an employé, rated as disabled to the degree of 80 per cent or more, counting as two.

Failure to obey this law, which is exceedingly detailed and complicated, entails punishment by fine, the fines going into a fund in *L'Office National des Mutilés* to assist unemployable War-disabled men.

Government's object has been, however, not to make idleness easy, but to make work possible. And nothing is farther from the mind of France than the idea that a War-injury can entitle any man to be set up, at the expense of the common purse, in a position in life beyond that which he occupied or stood in line to attain before the War.

The point is well illustrated by the French concept of re-education. Some 500,000 mutilated men, when the fighting was over, stood in seeming need of re-education if they were to earn their bread. But a large part of this half-million, spurred by their natural energy, thrift, and spirit of independence, found their way, unassisted and with speed, back into the earners' ranks.[1]

Of the remainder — 76,081 men — it is officially stated that fully 75 per cent have been returned to self-supporting status. And this end has in general been accomplished, not by training the disabled man to a strange or more

[1] *Les Dommages*, p. 514.

ambitious calling, but by helping him to adapt himself either to some suitable phase of the calling he followed before, or to other work so closely allied thereto that it carried the impetus of accustomed thought.

Such handling evoked swift responses, conscious and subconscious, mental and physical, on the part of the learner. And it demonstrated, in the end, the value of avoiding the shock of uprootment from the natural place, condition, and sphere of life.[1]

Of the mobilized forces of France, during the Great War, over 45 per cent were farmers, and nearly 30 per cent industrialists.[2] To these same ranks her system of re-education, better called re-adaptation, aimed to return their disabled members as active working men.

The major part of the task of re-education naturally fell to the period immediately following the War. But with the breaking-down of wounds, and with the normal development of some disabilities due to increasing age, new candidates for re-education still come forward.

The War-disabled pupil in Government industrial training schools [3] has received free tuition and board and a daily allowance above his pension of not less than two or more than four francs. The cost to Government has averaged at the rate of 3500 francs a year per capita, reaching the rate of 4000 francs in schools for the blind, the tuberculous and nerve cases. Men choosing to acquire their re-education as apprentices to a private employer have been allowed, beyond their pension, ten francs a day

[1] *Les Dommages*, pp. 514–16. The work of re-education is carried on by *L'Office National des Mutilés*. See French Appendix V.

[2] *Les Dommages*, p. 498.

[3] Maintained under *L'Office National des Mutilés*.

in the provinces, or twelve frances a day in and about Paris.[1] The duration of apprenticeship has varied from six to eight months, for some callings, to eighteen months for others.[2]

It follows that the largest average sum expended by the French Government on the industrial re-education of a disabled ex-service man has totalled about 7096 francs.

Students, denominated 'intellectuals,' whose education was interrupted by the War, were allowed a lump sum of not more than 5000 francs to aid them to complete their studies.[3]

According to the French law, with regard to War-incurred injuries and those only, every pensioner is entitled for life to free medicine, and also to free appliances and their free replacement and repair. He may go to a clinic for his troubles, or he may, if he prefers, consult a private physician. He may get his artificial leg or arm, or his orthopædic shoe, his brace, or his wheel-chair, from some commercial dealer; or he may elect to use Government-made goods, which he will find at the most conveniently situated of the fourteen surgical equipment centres and forty-six sub-centres maintained by the Ministry of Pensions. Throughout he retains his independence of choice, and Government, under safeguards, pays the bill.

The War-disabled ex-service man is also entitled to treatment in hospital or sanatorium. But, in the case of a pensioner who goes to hospital merely because he is so maimed or crippled that he is immobile and cannot per-

---

[1] *Les Dommages*, p. 513. *Code des Anciens Combattants*, pp. 268–69 and 521. But cf. Title V, Article 76, of the Law of March 31, 1919, as modified by the Law of March 23, 1928.

[2] *Les Dommages*, p. 513.   [3] *Code des Anciens Combattants*, p. 521.

form unaided the essential acts of life, the cost of his
hospital keep and care is deducted from his pension;
whereas, if he elects to remain at home, he is entitled to a
25 per cent addition to his pension, toward the expense
of the necessary personal care.[1]

Men certified as requiring treatment that cannot be
given in clinics or at home are, however, entitled to free
hospitalization without deduction of costs, and may choose
among the ordinary public hospitals or sanatoria of the
jurisdiction in which they live. Or they may go to authorized private establishments. In the latter case, Government will contribute to their expenses a sum equal to the
charges current in the nearest public hospital.[2]

But in all the above cases the benefit may be claimed
only for conditions arising in or from that specific service-
contracted wound or malady that in itself occasioned the
granting of the pension.[3]

In this connection it is worthy of remark that France
maintains but one national soldiers' hospital, *Les Invalides*, famous as containing the tomb of the Emperor
Napoleon I, and still, as in his day, providing for one
hundred men.[4] Government has set up no other hospitals,
no sanatoria for ex-service War-invalids. But in 1931 the
French Parliament voted an appropriation of 60,000,000

[1] Title I, Article 10, of the Law of March 31, 1919. See also *Code des Anciens
Combattants*, pp. 254, 296.

[2] Title V, Article 64, of the Law of March 31, 1931 (modified by the Law of
Finance of December 31, 1920, Article 54; the Law of July 21, 1922; the Law of
March 30, 1923; the Law of August 1, 1924, Article 36, and by the Law of Fi-
nance of December 19, 1926, Article 102).

[3] Article 64 of the Law of March 31, 1919.

[4] Inmates of *Les Invalides* must be War-pensioned at or above 80 per cent disability. They pay a modest price for their board and lodging.

francs for the building of a model village at Salagnac (Dordogne), to be inhabited by War-veterans who contracted tuberculosis while in service. This village, which drew its inspiration from the British Legion's village for the tuberculous at Preston Hall, in England, is now close to completion.

The tuberculous, as a rule, however, remain in their private dwellings with their families, being allotted, in advanced stages, an annual 10,000 francs ($392), supplemental to their pensions, to provide themselves with suitable food and to enable them to abstain from work.[1]

Mental cases, including all the neuro-psychiatrics, when asylum is necessary, are sent to the ordinary public institutions for the insane, where Government pays for their maintenance at the medium rate.

Even the badly mutilated face cases — and these seem to have aroused less special concern in France than elsewhere — go their own way.[2] Associated, self-styled as *Les Gueules Cassées* — 'the smashed jowls' — they give an annual banquet in Paris; and, to raise funds for mutual benefit, they run, each year, public lotteries under official patronage. Also, friends have assisted them to acquire a pleasant country house and estate, where comfort and green peace receives them.

---

[1] The Report of the Finance Commission of the Chamber of Deputies, July, 1930, on the Pension Budget for 1931–32, Document 3878, p. 138, cites Professor Léon Bernard, of the *Academie de Médecine*, as stating that there were then, in all France, 20,000 beds, whether in sanatoria, in hospitals or in special wards of hospitals, for pulmonary tuberculosis.

[2] It should, however, be noted that the decree of May 20, 1925, adds to the pension awarded the *gueule cassée*, for functional disablement occasioned by his wound, a separate award on account of disfigurement. See *Tableau Synoptique Résumé des Divers Barèmes à Appliquer aux Infirmes et Malades de la Guerre 1914–19*, Charles-Lavauzelle & Cie., Paris, 1930, pp. 185–92.

CHAPTER III

THEY THAT MOURN

THE laws governing pensions of ex-soldiers' widows have undergone several changes since the enactment of March 31, 1919. A detailed statement concerning them will be found in the French Appendix of this book. There, also, will be found a statement of the Ministry as to pensions of widows, orphans, and the parents of the dead.[1]

In brief, the widow's pension follows her husband's rank, the widow of the private soldier at present drawing a minimum of 1920 francs or a maximum of 2880 francs a year ($75.26 or $112.90).[2]

The widow must show, in order to establish her claim, that her husband died of wounds or disease attributable to service; or else that, although his death resulted from a non-service-connected cause, he was at the time drawing for a service-incurred disablement pension of at least 60 per cent. In the former case her pension will be higher than in the latter. But the higher always goes to the widow of a helplessly disabled man. She must also show that her husband's state of health, at the date of marriage, did not warrant expectation of his death within a short time, and that the marriage lasted at least two years. Many qualifications and exceptions affect the law; but no divorced woman, nor one against whom a decree of separa-

[1] French Appendices II and III. Prepared for the author, August, 1932.
[2] *Tarifs des Pensions de Guerre*, 1932. See French Appendix X.

tion has been granted, nor one who has forfeited her parental rights, can either establish or maintain entitlement.[1]

The State offers several privileges to the soldier's widow; as employment in certain State and local governmental posts and in those private enterprises that are obliged to give a percentage of their jobs to War-victims; as education provided by the State; or as apprenticeship,[2] facilitated by the State, in a gainful industry under the same conditions that pertain to the re-education of War-disabled men; as little loans toward setting up in business; and as aid in getting a cheap home.

But the object of each and every privilege thus offered is to help the woman to help herself and her children; and the spirit and character of the whole effort, its frugality and meticulous adjustment of detail to occasion, may best be savoured in a human example.[3] Let that example be the case of the Widow Ledoux. The Widow Ledoux is poor. Her two small children are hungry, yet she wants no charity. If she might somehow lay hands on a sewing machine for herself, she could, she thinks, keep the wolf from the door by her own industry. She asks the authorities how a sewing machine can be had. And here follow the requirements they invite her to ponder:

A sewing machine may be given, 1st, to war-widows who have not remarried and who have, at fewest, three children dependent upon them.

[1] Law of March 31, 1919, Title II, Article 14, modified by the Law of March 23, 1928. Instruction of March 23, 1897, Article 65; Law of June 25, 1861, Article 6.

[2] Law of March 31, 1919, Title V; Article 76.

[3] *Code des Anciens Combattants*, pp. 533-34, Annex 8.

2d. To war-widows who have remarried, but have a very numerous family.

The request for the machine... must be accompanied by a certified copy [of some official document] establishing the fact that the applicant is a war-widow; and by a certificate supplied by the mayor, giving the facts regarding the children.

When the request is granted, the sewing machine will be sent to the beneficiary at the expense of Government.

The war-widow, having obtained a sewing machine, pledges herself to preserve it, to use it, and to take good care of it.

If she fails to use it, or, if she abuses it, it may be taken from her, by order of the Prefect of the Department.

The sewing machine does not become the actual property of the widow until after the lapse of five years.

In case of the widow's death before this period, the sewing machine must be returned to Government.

The Widow Ledoux, having slept on this matter, perceives that the getting of a sewing machine is not to be undertaken in a light spirit.

The *compagne* or unmarried wife of a service man who died or disappeared in the course of the Great War is not entitled to a regular pension, but may receive a relief grant. To qualify for relief, she must have lived with the man for at least three years previous to the declaration of war; the *liaison* can have been broken only by his death or disappearance; the woman can have made no later marital connection, regular or irregular; her conduct and morality since the man's death can have afforded no ground for unfavourable remark; and her situation must be established as really necessitous and worthy of interest. These conditions being duly met, and all circumstances continuing unchanged, the Ministry of Pensions may renew the grant annually. Its amount is, in principle, 600 francs a year for *compagnes* of privates and

non-commissioned officers, 1000 francs for those of subal-
terns, and 1200 francs ($47.04) for the *compagnes* of
superior officers. *Compagnes'* applications are made
through the general commanding the subdivision, who
himself transmits them to the Ministry of Pensions,
adding the necessary details.[1]

As to War-orphans, the pension is not affected by the
father's rank. Based on an original allowance of 300
francs a year for the minor or infirm child, it can reach,
through various additional grants, a total of 1028 francs
for each child.[2]

The French War-orphans, however, are not left to the
care of the paymaster only. 'Because they have suffered
both a moral and a physical loss,' says a French writer
on the law,[3] 'the Nation owes them a double debt. To
meet the moral loss, it has chosen to confer a sort of moral
ennoblement, through the bestowal of one of the most
glorious of titles: The death of the father, "on the field
of honour," is tantamount to the birth of the child as a
"ward of the Nation."'

To give substance to the phrase, the French Government has set up a permanent establishment, called *L'Office
National des Pupilles de la Nation*, 'The National Office
of the Wards of the Nation,'[4] the dedicatory sentence of
whose establishing Act reads: 'France adopts those
orphans whose fathers, mothers, or the supporter of the

---

[1] *Code des Anciens Combattants*, circular of September 22, 1919, pp. 162–63,
and footnotes, p. 163.

[2] *Tarifs des Pensions de Guerre*, see French Appendix X.

[3] Jean Souquet, *Droits et Avantages Réservés aux Pupilles de la Nation*, Charles-
Lavauzelle & Cie, Paris, 1929, p. 11.

[4] See French Appendix V.

family has perished in the course of the War of 1914, a military or civil victim of the enemy.'

That was in 1917. By 1920 it was officially estimated that the number of children embraced in the law would reach 653,500. The event proved the number to be nearer 710,000; but not more than half of these actually appealed for financial help to the Office established for their benefit.[1]

Illegitimate children, conceived before the event that gave rise to the father's pension and recognized by the father within two months of their birth, or before March 5, 1920, if reasonable grounds for delay could be shown,[2] are entitled to the same pension as that accorded to the lawfully born.

Finally come the *ascendants* — the forebears — of men who died for France. Whether or not a pension has already been allotted to the widow and children of the dead soldier, his father and mother are entitled to pension on his account, if they are, respectively, at least sixty and fifty-five years old. But if either parent is incurably infirm in health,[3] the age condition disappears.

And if more than one son has been lost through battle wounds, or through sickness contracted or aggravated in War-service, the parent's pension is augmented on that account. An additional one hundred francs yearly is allowed for each son, beginning with the second to die.[4]

If, however, neither parent is living, the grandparents

[1] *Les Dommages*, pp. 519-20.
[2] *Code des Anciens Combattants*, p. 171.
[3] Title III, Article 28, of the Law of March 31, 1919, as modified by the Law of Finance of December 9, 1927, Article 53.
[4] Title III, Article 31, of the Law of March 31, 1919.

may draw the pension.[1] Or it may lawfully be claimed by any person who can prove that he or she brought up the dead boy and stood, toward him, in a parent's place from childhood to his majority or to his summons to the colours.[2]

The highest pension due to any *ascendant*, on account of the death of a private soldier, is 1920 francs annually, with an addition of 240 francs for each minor or infirm dependant child.[3]

Small sums indeed. But the thrift of the French people in dealing respectfully with small sums has gone far to make France a rich nation.

[1] Title III, Article 32, of the Law of March 31, 1919, as modified by the Law of March 31, 1931.

[2] Title III, Article 33, of the Law of March 31, 1919, as modified by the Law of Finance of December 9, 1927, Article 53.

[3] *Tarif des Pensions de Guerre*, 1932. *Taux de Soldat*. See French Appendix X.

CHAPTER IV

CHANGES

IF, NOW, we turn from the law itself to the number of its beneficiaries, it must be remembered that French statistics of the Great War, as regards its earlier periods, are, perforce, often surmise rather than statements of known fact. Not until January, 1916 — not until the War was seventeen months old — did the War Ministry set up a central control of reports of losses; the information supplied from army divisional staffs was full of mistakes; and the Bureau of Administrative Archives possessed no means of checking its figures.[1]

Under these circumstances, the guess of the *Journal des Mutilés et Réformés* [2] was probably as good as any regarding the number of persons who, on January 1, 1927, were drawing Great War pensions. Its estimate stood:

Disabled soldiers	1,060,000
Widows and orphans	630,000
Parents and grandparents	875,000
Total	2,565,000

But as late as September 21, 1928, it was stated that the Ministry of Pensions still remained without records to determine the number of its beneficiaries who had died.[3]

[1] *Les Dommages*, p. 498.

[2] Paris, April 2 and 9, 1927, quoted in *Les Dommages*, p. 505.

[3] *Les Dommages*, pp. 505–06. Report of Deputy Nogaro to the Commission of Finance.

CHANGES

The following figures come directly from the Ministry
of Pensions.[1] They represent the number of Great-War
pensioners living at the given dates:

	January 1, 1929	October 1, 1932
Disabled men	1,030,000	1,159,936
Widows and orphans	630,000	691,524
Parents and grandparents	860,000	833,901
Total	2,520,000	2,685,361

Perhaps the most significant feature in these two
columns, taken with the table preceding, is the slightness of
change observable over a period of six years ending thirteen years after the War. Cures and deaths of disabled
men, remarriage of widows, and coming of age of children
seem scarcely to have played their normal part. But the
explanation lies elsewhere.

The effect of the law's progressive changes has been,
in the main, twofold — to increase the size of pensions
and to widen the field of entitlement. So, while natural
causes have diminished the number of pensioners whose
claim rested on the original basis, new classes of beneficiaries have been added to the pension rolls. Nor may it
be forgotten that the passage of years too often is marked
by the growing worse of old wounds and the awakening
of dormant maladies contracted in the fighting service;
whereby men are continually being forced to ask for
help.

As to changes in the law, these have chiefly been
effected through political pressure exerted upon the
French legislature, occasionally in the name of one or
another ex-soldiers' organization. But the organizations

[1] By courtesy of the Minister to the author, March 4, 1933.

show little tendency to pull together and have only once acted as a unit. Several hundreds in number, only five or six among them have large or important memberships, and the great majority are merely social groups, assembled without religious colour, political purpose, or class discrimination. Certain few represent the effort of some candidate for election to the Chamber of Deputies to tie together and earmark for himself a bundle of votes. Deputy Jean Berger observes in his constituency a number of blinded men. So he pledges himself, if re-elected, to introduce a bill removing the tax from blind men's dogs. Pursuing his idea, he organizes a Blind Men's Association sworn to work for Jean Berger, drawing into it all blind men's families and friends. Successfully re-elected, he introduces the bill. Because no fellow-deputy wants to stand before the country as a churl who would collect a dog-tax from a blind man — especially a War-blinded man — the bill goes through. The same thing has happened as to extensions of the field of entitlement.

Many of these bits of tinkering are thus in themselves slight. When the Chamber of Deputies decided, as late as 1925,[1] to make a gift equivalent to three months' extra pension to every War-pensioned ex-service man who had lain as a prisoner in a German hospital, and when it also decided to make a present of 5000 francs to every non-hospitalized tuberculous ex-service man already pensioned as 100 per cent disabled, the gift to the individual was not large.

But the sum total of these and other excursions into bypaths attains proportions distinctly visible. Given

[1] Law of July 13, 1925, Articles 201 and 198.

248

such tendencies, it is scarcely necessary further to explain
the steady rise in the annual budget. The figures follow: [1]

1926	3,871,398,674	francs.
1927	4,154,535,203	
1928	4,401,650,000	
1929	5,071,870,000	

But the principal and great changes in the French
pension system have been brought about, not by ex-
soldiers' organizations, not by single political aspirants,
but by the political parties, one and all, exerting pressure
upon each successive Government that has come into
office since the War. These rival elements, locked in the
desperate hazards of a general election struggle, at last
made a common discovery: a grateful nation would no
longer brook delay in expressing its gratitude to a still
larger class of ex-service men.

One and all — however gladly each would have kept the
bait for its own hook — one and all, every party therefore
promised, if elected, to abolish entirely the condition of
service-contracted disablement as essential to the drawing
of a War-pension. They proposed to extend War-pension
rights to ex-service men:

First, on account of any War-wound whatsoever, without regard to its gravity.

Second, on account of having belonged during a period
of three months, whether consecutive or not, to certain
combat units, although no wound or illness was incurred.

Third, on account of having been accredited to one of
these combat units for any length of time whatsoever, although withheld from actually joining the command by
some service-contracted malady.

[1] *Les Dommages*, p. 511, first and second tables.

Other enablements were included in the measure, which was called *La Retraite du Combattant* — the Service Man's Pension. Also, it carried a fringe of new benefits, as reduction of telephone rates for certain classes of pensioners, and a raising of the pensions of widows and of the heavily disabled.

But the point of the appeal lay in its opening of the gates to the multitude.

The effort succeeded. All the Great War ex-soldiers' organizations, united for the first and only time in their existence, gave it their support. The measure passed both the Senate and the Chamber of Deputies by unanimous vote. Enacted in the Law of Finance of April 16, 1930, it became the law of the land.

The awards conferred by *La Retraite du Combattant* are individually trifling — $20 annually to men between 50 and 55 years; $48 to those aged 55. But their total, because of the hosts involved, at the present moment adds 1,140,000,000 francs ($44,688,000) to the yearly burden of the public Treasury. And in fifteen years' time, as the ex-service men of 1914–18 come successively within its operation, it will load three extra milliards of francs ($117,600,000), upon the annual budget payable by the French people.[1]

It is meet to remember, however, that at the time of the enactment of this law, France still supposed that the bill would be paid by Germany.[2]

This measure at one stroke destroyed the base of the

---

[1] Estimate of the Ministry of Pensions, August, 1932, and revised March, 1933, for the author. See French Appendix VI. The exchange is here computed at 3.92 cents to the franc.

[2] Cf. *ante*, p. 229.

system and proclaimed on the grand scale the
of political interference. Under such conditions
n's liabilities as to War-pensions must and do con-
rise; and the end is impossible to foresee.

eficit in the French national budget for 1932 was
0,000 francs. The War-pensions budget for that
7,598,011,000 francs ($297,842,031.20).

he character of the Ministry of Pensions, it stands
ched. Its permanent officials are uniformly cred-
h integrity, devotion, and self-immolating re-
lity, to a distinguished degree. Their duty is to ad-
the law as it is given them. And this they do, with
de, to the extent of their reach.

eir reach does not extend to the individual pen-

dministrative scheme is one of marked centrali-
The law is applied, under strict surveillance of
y agents who are directly responsible to the Cen-
ninistration in Paris. By such control, procedure
ironized and kept uniform in all the provinces
out the country.

riginal concept of the French War-pension con-
o idea of recompensing a man for the performance
y that he shared with every other male citizen of
e — a duty to which he was born and for which
e had trained him at public expense. When war
ll must suffer in some degree, male and female,
nd old, without choice, therefore small reason ex-
singling out one particular class to be petted above
. When the Great War was over, Government
each man, with his honourable discharge, a little

present — a little bonus, of 250 francs,[1] thereby closing accounts with those in health.

As to the disabled men and the dependants of the dead, their pension was not intended as a recompense or reward, but merely as the minimum allowance that, eking out the recipient's diminished earning power, could suffice to provide bread and a roof.

This point of view in itself explains the practical non-existence in France of citizens' volunteer social welfare work for the benefit of the ex-soldier. The thought is apart from the position. Sisters of religious orders beg alms for their hospitals, and therein nurse the sick for the love of God. American and English friends, out of admiration for French bravery and sympathy with French suffering, have established and financed, in France, various relief works. But to the minds of the French — individualistic, logical, hardy — War is no stranger nor does she wear the garments of romance. As she has come before, so she may come again. Therefore, in peace as in war, each and every Frenchman squares his shoulders to his own back-load and asks no odds from the man at his side.

[1] Approximately $50 by the exchange of that day.

GERMANY

GERMANY

CHAPTER I

DER STAHLHELM

Who made the War?

You may hear many answers, all advanced with fervour, some supported with learning, most more or less at variance each with each. But one thing, at least, is certain: no nation made the War. No people, as such, hungered and thirsted to kill and be killed; not the German people more than the rest.

But the German Emperor lost the War, and the helpless German people, who could not, like him, escape to safety, have taken his punishment for him, through the years, blow on blow, a terrific penalty.

It is true that the guns of the Allies had levelled no German towns; that no German homes had been demolished, no wheat-fields sown with iron, nor vineyards uprooted, nor forests laid low by axe or shell; true that no German factories had been smashed into heaps of rubbish, no mines flooded, no bridges blown up. And yet, it is also true that the position of Germany, at the end of the War, was worse by far than that of France.

For over two years Germany had starved. The blockade had early shown her that she must live on her own substance till the end of the War. Gradually, therefore, she rationed herself. Her bread and meat she doled out by ounces — so much a day a head. Then the ounces grew

255

fewer and the days farther apart. Then there was no more bread and no more meat, and the milk that had been saved for the babies ran low, because the harvest had failed and milk cows were killed by order, for lack of fodder. And the winter of 1917–18 was called 'the Swede winter,' because, having no more meat, nor bread, nor milk, nor potatoes, the people lived mainly on turnips, so that children and frail old folk died, and tuberculosis and diseases of malnutrition crept over the land.

Food-cornering, meantime, mocked the hunger of the masses, war profiteers lived in open and insolent luxury, and Government failed to stay that abuse — a failure in itself disastrous to public courage and discipline.

So food riots broke out. Munition workers, already fed and favoured above the rest, struck for still higher wages and were allowed their claims. Confidence in Government wavered and died. Confidence in the invincibility of the German arms, in the beginning so vehement, wore thin. War-weariness rose and spread in a dank, grey tide. Malcontents became agitators; agitators grew bolder; internal dissensions tore the State. As early as 1916, Russian agents working among the populace saw proof of their success and redoubled their labours. By the spring of 1918, partly aware of the defection behind them, the men in the trenches were saying bitterly: 'If we lose this war, it will be because our own people have stabbed us in the back. We shall not be beaten in France.'

Meanwhile, the policy of the Government had been to shut all news of disturbing tendencies and incidents out of the press, keeping each region in the dark about the troubles in the rest of the Empire. And so far had the policy succeeded that Berlin, for example, was taken completely by surprise when, on the afternoon of November 9, 1918, strings of motor trucks rolled into the city filled with armed workmen, mostly young boys, flying red flags and shouting the fall of the Government and the advent of 'the Revolution.'

Others of that enterprise seized the barracks and the castle from the hands of their helpless guards; for orders from somewhere had reached all military posts that 'massed workmen' were not to be fired upon.

The men of the fleet at Kiel, rotted out with idleness and Red propaganda, had already mutinied — on the rumour that they were about to be ordered to fight their ships. The War Lord himself, on November 10, fled to Holland and personal safety. Rapidly now the lesser German sovereigns abdicated. Central authority vanished, and in the heaving jelly that oozed into its place, the most vital embryo appeared to be the Spartacus League, with Liebknecht and Rosa Luxemburg at its head and the 'dictatorship of the proletariat' as its birth-cry.

Workmen and Soldiers' Councils, unopposed, seized the administrations of towns and villages and did as they pleased with the resources thereof, until they split in the middle because of the soldiers' disgust at the workmen's riotous squandering. And so new upheavals, always without progress, while the great mass of the bourgeoisie stood, hands down, irresolute, staring, helpless. Its rudder and compass had carried away. Not a lighthouse cast a ray through the whirling storm. Old Germany was adrift and sinking.

Meantime, out in the mud and the cold, in the trenches beyond the Rhine, battered, deserted, sore at heart, but never broken in spirit, Germany's best manhood stood fast.

Seven times disciplined, purged of its weaker element by desertion or surrender to the enemy; cleared by long hardship of its physically inferior part; bound together by ties of suffering endured shoulder to shoulder for four ghastly years; careful no longer of dignity or rank, of parties or of personal ambition, the front-line army asked of no man whether he was banker or peasant, barrister or factory hand, servant or official, Protestant or Catholic, but only, was he a faithful comrade, a good soldier, and a steady fighting hand.

Fighting for what? Did he know? Who knows? — Sometimes he may even have thought he was fighting to save the world for democracy. But of this at least he was sure; he was fighting because his flag had led and called him — fighting for no conceivable personal reason or profit — fighting for Germany. And up to the very end — up to the moment when, as he put it, 'peace broke out' — his tenacity was magnificent.

And now, he could go home — home to the country and the people that he had done his best to serve — carrying the flag and his honour with him.

But, as he was shortly to find, neither that flag nor his honour meant anything whatever to the present drivers of Germany. Their flag was the red flag, and for their purpose, the honour of the front-soldier must be quickly branded shame, lest it touch and arouse the stunned soul of the people. So the 'Soldiers' Soviet,' meeting him in strength on the threshold of his own home town, tore the black-white-red cockade from his cap, cut the epaulettes from his shoulders, and seized his arms, 'because, comrade, your day is done and you have no more leaders to lead you.'

And because also, perhaps, you cannot withdraw the best manhood of any country for a period of years, leaving at home only its women and its young boys, its old men, its unfit and its skulkers, without seriously endangering that country's sanity.

The same thing was happening everywhere. In Magdeburg it happened. In Magdeburg the 'Soldiers' Soviet,' unable to await the return of the local regiment, boarded troop-trains in passage, pulled officers out of the carriages and shot them on the station platform, merely because they were officers and represented a tradition of discipline. The sight of the uniform in the streets was a signal for attack. The spirit of disorder and violence spread. Neither life nor property was safe. A reign of terror set in with exotic wild men directing the storm — and still the bourgeoisie stood, hands down, helplessly staring, while all their world crumbled.

Meanwhile, among this paralyzed Magdeburg bourgeoisie was one man awake and thinking. His name was Franz Seldte, and he owned a chemical factory which gave him his living. He was about thirty-six years old, of medium height and complexion, broad-shouldered, clean-shaven, hair cut Prussian-fashion — short behind and parted on the left; and his mouth and nose and eyes and jaw, together with the shape of his head, declared unanimously three things — balance, clarity, and firmness. For the rest, he looked exactly what he was — a plain, ordinary German provincial business man, like hundreds of thousands of others. And like those hundreds of thousands of others his early life had been spent. The usual ordinary schooling, supplemented by a business course and a course in chemistry. The usual year of army service. Then into his father's factory, to learn how to stoke the furnace, and how to brew the stuff; then to the road as travelling salesman, and finally, the step into his father's shoes as owner of the plant. Meantime, he had read more or less, filling his mind with travels, history, and literature rather than politics; and he loved sports, whether fencing, mountain-climbing, snowshoeing, riding, or the oars.

So came August, 1914 — and Franz Seldte, lieutenant of machine-gunners in the Sixty-Sixth Regiment, went with that regiment to France. Two years of steady front-line service followed. Then the Somme — the last week in June with its six days and nights of unbroken hell culminating in the moment when, from 'behind a vapour of smoke and after a gas attack, the thoroughly organized English storm columns seemed to arise from the ground.' Wave upon wave, they crashed against the Sixty-Sixth's resistance, smashing the line to bits — bits that somehow pulled themselves together and fought on the bodies of their dead. And Lieutenant Franz Seldte fought like his mates, grinding his machine-gun until that moment when gun and man, shattered together, pitched down into the pulp.

After that came nine months in hospital — a hospital penetrated by the dark and dubious spirit of the land.

260

DER STAHLHELM

The little chemist lay in his bed and thought; thought
unhappily of his comrades in the trenches, braced shoulder
to shoulder, closing the lines above their dead, muttering
through clenched teeth, the while, the very words of those
they confronted — 'They shall not pass'; thought then
of the German people for whom his comrades were dying
and had died — of that people's obviously weakening
fibre, their distraught faith and wavering mind. And he
did his best, with such brains as he had, to discover
the meaning and the answer to it all.

Then, one day, the doctor said, 'You may go.' So
with his empty left sleeve hanging, away he went to the
front again; for now they knew where to use even one-
armed men — who could think. And there at the front
he stayed until the beginning of November, 1918, when,
by chance, they sent him home to Magdeburg on a few
days' leave.

Thus it happened that Franz Seldte was present in
Magdeburg on November 9, when the revolution broke
out and the field-grey uniform was assaulted in the streets.

The next few days were torment to him. Was it for
this that for four long years, through misery and all
sacrifice, the field-grey front had held! Was the Germany
they had died for a broken, rotten thing, their Germany
no more? Then he thought of the old Sixty-Sixth. Scarred,
weary, ragged, heavy-hearted, the little that was left of
it would soon be coming home. By any hideous possibility
could it, in the streets of Magdeburg, meet the incredible
welcome that earlier comers were receiving?

Then, all at once, light broke. The old Sixty-Sixth
had never faltered, whatever duty had confronted it. It

261

would not falter now. What fool had said that the War
was ended! The War was just begun!

That night, November 13, in his factory office, Franz
Seldte laid his idea before four friends — his brother, his
old sergeant major, and two privates from the front.
During the next ten days they perfected the plan. On
Christmas Eve, the Sixty-Sixth, marching, swung into
Magdeburg — only too well and bitterly aware, from
experience along the homeward route, what reception to
expect.

But before the ranks had broken, messengers had
spread among them an invitation to meet at ten o'clock
next morning for a 'welcome gathering' in a public hall.

Christmas Day dawned bleak and grey, between squalls
of snow and rain. The shabby old hall was cold as death,
and bare of furniture. The men, trooping in, stood shivering in their overcoats, chilled alike in body and soul,
waiting in silence to learn why they had been summoned
to a 'welcome' such as this. At last, when all had arrived
— a round thousand — one man, Franz Seldte, stood
forth and quietly, soldier-fashion, said just this: [1]

In the middle of November, in the office of our factory,
seven of us men decided not to allow this filthy revolution to
go any further. This 'revolution' is no manifestation of
strength and nationalism. It is a breaking down. It is vile.
What will become of Germany nobody knows today. But
this is certain: You cannot extinguish a nation of seventy
million people. Eventually, therefore, we shall rise again.

But whenever this resurrection comes to pass, it can never
be the work of screaming revolutionaries or fat sailor mutin-
eers. It will be the work of front-line soldiers who will give

[1] Sigmund Graff, 'Gründung und Entwicklung des Bundes,' *Der Stahlhelm,
Erinnerungen und Bilder*, Stahlhelm Verlag, Berlin, 1932, p. 26.

their last breath to save Germany. Therefore, we intend to organize a league of fighters from the front. We suggest as a name for the league 'The Steel Helmet!' We suggest as its symbol the representation of our grey steel helmet from the battle-field. And we propose, for our colours, our proud old black-white-red banner, and in the centre of the white the steel helmet again. Will you join?

Half an hour later, when that meeting broke up, *Der Stahlhelm, Bund der Frontsoldaten*, 'The Steel Helmet, League of Front Soldiers,' had been born.[1]

For Franz Seldte, certainly not a Junker, certainly not an aristocrat, simply a wounded and gallant common man, using their own language and the language of the Front, had expressed for them their highest subconscious thought. No demagogue to work up brief enthusiasm, he had given them a live idea to live upon — a hope, a purpose, and a new campaign. Still *Frontsoldaten*, their duty, now, was to forget themselves, to ask nothing for themselves, but to protect Germany from enemies in her midst and from her own confused thought. Careless of parties and politics, they must stick together and stand fast for the common good. With all life and property in danger, with law, order, and religion alike the target of Communist fury, they must defend whatever of value remained to be saved.

'Nothing for ourselves. Germany is sinking. Then, *Front heil!* It's still our job!'

The bleak sternness of the call brought them together with a rush — the best of the returning front-line men. From all over the country, as the weeks rolled on, they

[1] The soldiers in the trenches drew an iron line between themselves and those others safely sheltered behind them and out of the mud. Membership in the Stahlhelm is still limited to the *Frontsoldaten*.

declared for the old comradeship in new duty — thankful
for the courage and self-respect it gave them back. No
thought of choice or type of government was in their
minds. Monarchy or what not made no matter. The
one object was, to protect and steady the people, to
exorcise 'the man from the East,' to save the Fatherland.
And though their work, in those mad days and madder
days to come, meant steady fighting against high odds,
their immediate personal reward transcended reckoning.
For they escaped that loathly sickness that elsewhere —
yes — in victorious America poisoned men who, coming
home from the War with dreams in their souls, found no
leadership, no understanding, and no work hard enough
for souls to live on.

Today there are many other ex-service men's organizations in Germany most of whom have for their prime
object the betterment of the fortunes of their members,[1]
and, in practically every case, each has its strong party
affiliations. The Stahlhelm, however, has carried on as
it began. It aids its needy members and the general needs
of the community from its own fund or by its own exer-
tions. But it has never besieged the public Treasury,
whether for itself or to facilitate its work for others; nor
has it flung its weight in the field of partisan politics. Its
object has been, in very fact, not to get, but to give. And,
thanks to the sovereign power of that appeal, no organization in Germany can show so high a type of membership from so wide a range of classes. Princes serve as
rankers. Neither place nor name nor fortune counts.

[1] It is well to remember that the great *Reichsbanner*, political in origin and
purpose, and now perhaps ninety per cent Socialist, is not an ex-service man's
organization.

The original leader, unchanged in his simplicity, still holds the helm, keeping the movement going straight and strong 'till the nation shall need the men again.'

Meantime, a curious mixture of democracy and authority, vitalized and welded by constant effort in a purpose too unselfish to admit debate, the Stahlhelm has become a great national stabilizing force.

A Stahlhelm annual meeting is, for a foreigner, a sobering sight. Of the vast throng that it assembles, most are poor men who, during the past year, have put away perhaps ten cents a week, to be able to attend this gathering. Also, during the whole year, they have kept up their gymnastics, and, where their bread-winning allowed, have done two or three long marches, just to prove to themselves that they still measure up. The youngest of them is now a little over thirty years old, and his field-grey uniform is half his age. But he wears it with pride that is almost reverence. From their homes they have travelled twelve, fifteen, eighteen hours, jammed in third-class railway carriages, sitting on wooden planks. Now, to the number of 150,000 or so, they will spend two days hearing their leaders speak, repledge their comradeship and purpose for future work, do a drill and a march past — and so quietly away home again.

Seen thus together, they show what they are, a primal force, consciously driving to a single end. And somehow the sight, laying sudden grip on the spectator, wrings out the cry: '*Front Heil!* God see you through!'

Meantime, encamped beside them, has lain another organization of the utmost significance to Germany. This is the Junior Stahlhelm — boys too young to have known the War, but to whom the Stahlhelm itself has sworn, through the devotion of its picked men, to hand down the moral values of the Army — not the pre-war Army, but the *Frontsoldaten* — 'to preserve the spirit of self-sacrifice, patriotism, and comradeship that was so strong in the trenches.'

Happy is the country that so ensures its future! To watch the young Stahlhelm at work, under the guidance of the Stahlhelm itself, is to feel almost with awe the real strength of Germany.

These boys, also wearing the old field-grey,[1] show the snap, spirit, and discipline of professional soldiers. Yet years of Saturday-Sunday training and holiday work in the hands of their Stahlhelm mentors is the only discipline they have known. Their bodies, hard and supple, are splendidly developed. Their faces are clear, intelligent, vital, firm. In companies they have learned to live in the open, to swim, to run, to jump, to fence, to ride, to box, to cook, to wash and cobble and mend, to build real houses and bridges, to harvest crops, to work in the forest, to handle and repair machines, to use rifles, to read maps, to dig trenches, to put shot, to drill, to obey, to be good and faithful comrades, to help their neighbours wherever they can, to think of and serve their country — and to do long marches with full kits on their backs.

When the convention met in Coblentz, in 1930, some hundreds of the Junior Stahlhelm, 'just to make it seem real,' marched all the way from Berlin with full kits on their backs and steel helmets on their heads. It was a

---

[1] Each boy buys his own uniform, which costs about $4, and usually pays for it by instalments.

266

twelve to fifteen days' stretch and they had a little under-
estimated the distance. So they tramped twenty-four
hours in the last day, to arrive, stiff with pride, exactly
on the dot.

Here are some of the pronouncements of Franz Seldte,
simple and definite as himself; addressed, not to the world,
which does not know him, but to his own men: [1]

> The Stahlhelm stands positively for the Christian religion
> and for our culture. It is determined to maintain German
> principles in the education of youth, in clean living, in art....
> The Stahlhelm is a thing born alive, natural and necessary.
> Therefore it must grow, operate and fulfil its aim.... From
> its ranks and its creed will come the new German leadership....
> The German nation is one of the youngest and most vital
> powers on earth. Because she is so young, she behaves in a
> youthful and awkward manner. She is unaware as yet of
> herself and of her strength.... We, the German people, did
> not want the War.... And what about the others, so much
> older and more experienced than we, who had been united
> nations for centuries? They also did not want it, yet they could
> not prevent it.... If, however, those others are also blameless,
> then surely all together, we should declare it to have been a
> catastrophe of nature... and the horror of Versailles therefore
> becomes impossible and void.... A Germany that has recovered
> will overcome Bolshevism by herself, but not a dog-tired
> Germany. Germany is the bulwark against Bolshevism.
> France is mistaken if she thinks that Bolshevism, having
> gone through Germany, would halt at the French frontier....
> There is no peace in Germany, no happiness, no life, and no
> more sunshine until we have withdrawn from our healthy
> flesh the thorn which is called *Marxismus* within, and Ver-
> sailles without.... A state is like a large, important, and cleanly
> conducted firm. Politics is the prudent leadership of the firm
> itself.... So we guide the work of the Stahlhelm until we have
> accomplished our aim, the inner and the outer freedom of
> Germany. *Front heil!* Hail to the Front!

[1] *Der Stahlhelm,* 'Foreword,' by Franz Seldte, pp. 16–18.

SOLDIERS WHAT NEXT!

The Stahlhelm, we are assured, is non-political.[1] Yet here is Seldte himself publicly denouncing Versailles. Which leads to the true conclusion that denunciation of Versailles belongs, in Germany, not to the realm of politics, but to that of the principles of being.

Says young Germany — says the Young Stahlhelm; 'We weren't even in that old war of yours. We had nothing to do with it, or with the Kaiser. We want to build a new world for ourselves. We won't be punished for what we didn't do. And, *we are not going to stand any more of it.*'

Franz Seldte had no need to teach them that. Life has taught it — even the little they have seen. And from the look in their eyes as they speak — their quietness, their power, their united and profound certainty — one cannot but feel that the very angel of the race speaks through them — an angel strong in battle, ill to engage, whose enmity would be a tragedy, whose defeat would be a poison to all the world.

[1] In the election of 1931, in the belief that Field-Marshal von Hindenburg, as Reichspresident, was falling under radical influence, the Stahlhelm for the first time put up a candidate of their own. This move, it is said, they later considered a mistake, and Seldte emphasized anew their separation from politics.

Herr Seldte is now, however, Minister of Labour, in the Hitler Cabinet.

CHAPTER II

FRAGMENTS AND FIGURES

THE story of the Stahlhelm, as far as it goes, shows fairly well the position, in Germany, of the newly demobilized citizen-soldier.

In France the *poilu* stepped straight back into his normal place — his own home, his own work, which save in the devastated region, the War had interrupted rather than stopped. And the life of the country rolled on its way, bringing its old habit of thought to the handling of new problems. But Germany, at the end of the War, was 'without form and void,' and darkness brooded over her. Nothing material remained of what had been before — nothing of assured stability. And, weighing against her invisible asset — the basic character of her people — stood the fact that the nation had forfeited the right to direct its own destiny.

Old Germany was gone. Central control was gone, and in its place wild foreign furies — spectres of destruction, and discord — drove hither and yon the unhappy people. Thus was the stage set to receive the home-coming citizen-soldier.

Twelve million Germans, white men all,[1] had been called to the German colours. Of these, some two million had been killed. And now, when the fighting was over, there remained over a million and a half disabled men and

[1] Germany called no colonial troops to her colours in the World War.

more than a million dependants of the dead and the heavily wounded somehow to be carried on the shoulders of an exhausted nation.[1]

The Army as a whole, in the act of disbanding, got a 'bonus' toward a new start in civil life — fifty Marks [2] to each man — and the right to retain and wear his uniform to cover his bones and keep out the cold. That applied to all alike, regardless of rank or condition.

For the disabled, also, some comfort yet existed. The old pension law, built in 1906–07, had proved wide enough to support the spread of the World-War burden up to the final crash; and under that law, through the dust and noise and wreckage that followed, a faithful secretariat managed to carry on, giving some degree of service, until, in May, 1920, a new measure was enacted.

In any pension legislation, the most important feature must always be its 'entitlement' — the base condition that it lays down as essential to pensionability. Entitlement to War-pensions, under the German law today, rests squarely and solely upon disablement incurred in War service. The idea that War-pensions could be claimed without War-injury seems, in fact, to jar upon the German sense of the tolerable.

Where the French law, in fixing an ex-service man's pension, considers his army rank and raises the pension therewith,[3] the German law takes no note of rank, but

---

[1] For number of War-disabled ex-service men and dependants of the War-dead, see German Appendices, VIII and IX.

[2] At the pre-war rate of exchange, $12.50. The French gave 250 francs — $50 at the pre-War rate of exchange. For the rate of the Reichsmark later established, see German Appendix I.

[3] For the French position, see *ante*, p. 231.

considers, instead, pre-War status. If the subject, in pre-War life, was a skilled man, not a common labourer, he is entitled to 35 per cent more than the combined sum of the base pension and the heavy disability supplement of the unskilled man; and if he was not only skilled but also an active and responsible executive,[1] he may receive a 70 per cent addition. These two latter provisions are called 'Compensation Pensions.'[2]

Continuing the comparison of French and German law, a further difference is found in the minimum degree of disablement for which a pension may be granted. The Germans, like the French, began rating from 10 per cent. But, while the French continue that rating, the Germans, in 1920, paid off, with lump sum gratuities, all their 10 per cent disabled, and in 1923 similarly dealt with those of 20 per cent, thereby reducing the numbers of War-pensioned disabled to 900,000 men, exclusive of officers. Since 1923 they have accepted no disablement of less than 25 per cent as War-pension entitlement.[3]

Another example of Germany's individuality appears in her recognition of local variations in the cost of living. In Germany, as elsewhere in the world, a considerable difference exists in the minimum cost of living as found in a great city, a minor city, a village, a hamlet, or in the

[1] Germany's ex-service War-pensioners are found in three categories as follows: Unskilled labourers, 11.1 per cent; skilled workers, 87.7 per cent; responsible and active executives, 1.2 per cent. A Ministry table relating to the upward and downward post-War shift, under these headings, will be found in the German Appendix X.

[2] *Handbuch der Reichsversorgung*, Ministry of Labour, Berlin, 1932, vol. 1, Part 1, Article 28. This publication will hereafter be referred to as *Handbuch*.

[3] The monetary pension scale begins with 30 per cent disablements. Physical disabilities of 25 per cent are rated as 30 per cent, for payment.

open country. The Labour Ministry[1] has mapped the
whole land with a view to these differences, and all War-
pension awards are determined with place of residence
(*Ortszulage*) as a factor.[2]

Further, in the case of men who are 50 per cent or more
disabled, and whose individual circumstances involve
special need, the Ministry possesses discretionary power
to add an emergency allowance — *Zusatzrente* — whose
highest figure is 504 Reichsmarks,[3] or $120.05, annually.

But the *Zusatz* pension cannot be paid in full to any
pensioned ex-service man in receipt of transitional relief[4]
whose monthly income exceeds 80 Reichsmarks, if
resident in a super-class district, 75 Reichsmarks, if he
lives in a Class A locality, 70 Reichsmarks in Class B, 65
Reichsmarks in Class C, or 60 Reichsmarks in Class D.[5]

If, being 50 per cent or more disabled, the ex-service

[1] German War-pensions are handled by the Ministry of Labour.

[2] *Handbuch*, Article 51. The localities are graded according to rental scales
therein prevalent, as follows:

ADDITION TO PENSIONS

S. Super-Class	24 per cent	30 per cent
A. Class	18	25
B. Class	12	22
C. Class	6	18
D. Class	0	14

Pensioners rated as 90 per cent or more disabled receive the higher addition
indicated above.

Pensioners having no established residence are rated as of D class.

In the sense of this law, the pension upon which the additional percentage for
cost of living is to be computed is composed of, (1) Base Pension; (2) Heavy
Disablement Supplement; (3) Compensation Pension; (4) Maintenance Allowance for wife and children. For (4) see *post*, p. 274.

[3] *Handbuch*, Articles 88, 89 and 90. For table of allotment of *Zusatzrente* see
German Appendix VI.

[4] *Uebergangsgeld*. See *post*, p. 277.

[5] *Handbuch*, Article 90.

man has a wife, he is entitled to an annual maintenance addition equivalent to 10 per cent of his Base Pension, and also of his Compensation Pension, if such he enjoys.[1] Pensioners having minor children receive an additional twenty per cent of their pensions for the maintenance of each child.[2]

To determine the pension due to an ex-service man in any given instance,[3] the German system takes as its starting-point the case of an unskilled labourer living in a 'D' class locality in the open country. His pension is the fixed minimum, or Base Pension, on which the structure rests. To it is added a Heavy Disablement Supplement, in case his disability involves a physical reduction of or exceeding 50 per cent.[4] These two basic scales run as follows:

YEARLY BASE PENSION	HEAVY DISABLEMENT SUPPLEMENT
Disablement 30% — 129.60 Reichsmarks	
40% — 172.80	
50% — 270	36 Reichsmarks
60% — 324	42
70% — 378	54
80% — 432	72
90% — 486	108
100% — 540	168

This means, done into American terms, that a German unskilled labourer without wife or children, suffering from a War-service-incurred disablement of 30 per cent draws an annual pension of $38.59. If 40 per cent disabled, he

[1] *Handbuch*, Article 29. No maintenance for a wife is allowed to men disabled less than 50 per cent. The lower grades, however, carry children's allowances.
[2] *Handbuch*, Article 30.
[3] See German Appendix VII for extended table.
[4] *Handbuch*, Article 27, as affected by information from the German Ministry of Labour, given August 14, 1933.

273

gets $51.46; if 50 per cent disabled, he gets $64.31 plus
$8.58, his heavy disablement supplement; and from that
point on as follows:

BASE PENSION		HEAVY DISABLEMENT SUPPLEMENT	TOTAL
60% disablement	$77.18	$10.00	$87.18
70%	90.04	12.86	102.90
80%	102.90	17.15	120.05
90%	115.77	25.73	141.50
Total	128.63	40.02	168.65 [1]

To see how all this works out, let us take an extreme
case, that of a helpless paralytic, 100 per cent disabled,
and in circumstances warranting the Emergency Allowance. Before the War he was manager of a large factory.
He has a wife and three minor children, and he lives in
Berlin. His pension will be built up as follows:

Base Pension	540.00 RM	$128.63
Heavy Disablement Supplement	168.00	40.02
Compensation Pension	495.60	118.05
Maintenance Allowance for Wife and 3 children	842.52	200.69
Highest Zone Allowance	613.84	146.22
Special Zone Allowance 2 per cent	53.19	12.67
Emergency Allowance with Special Allowance	844.56	201.17
	3557.71 RM	$847.45

If to this is added an attendant's or nurse's allowance,
since he cannot perform necessary acts of life without
aid, that allowance will be from 600 ($142.92) to 1500
($357.30) Reichsmarks, according to the discretion of the
Ministry. The total reaches from $990.37 to $1204.75
annually. Not only is it the highest War-pension paid in
Germany, but only about two thousand German ex-
service men exist today in condition to draw it.[2]

[1] For table of disablement percentages attached to the various types of muti-
lation, see German Appendix V.

[2] Statement of the Ministry of Labour, Berlin, September, 1932, to the author.

274

In May, 1932, there were in all Germany 349,372 ex-service men[1] whose War-wounds or War-incurred malady had reduced their capacity by 50 per cent or more. Of these, 310,060 were drawing extra pension on account of their wives, while their minor children, to the number of 891,778, were receiving assistance.[2]

A Compensation Pension, as we have seen, is awarded to the man who, before his War-disablement, was a skilled artisan or a master of his trade. It is bestowed after the disabled man has exhibited the utmost energy and will-power in the attempt to overcome his handicap, and has thereby proved that no lack of determination on his own part delays his return to civilian occupation.[3]

This policy rests on a principle adopted early in the War by the German chief surgeons. Laying great stress on the psychological element in physical reconstruction, they fought the 'hero-cripple' idea from the start and launched a vigorous campaign to teach the general public not to ruin a maimed man's morals by doses of destructive sympathy.

'We have the medical skill, the practical experience, and the earnest desire,' they said, in effect, 'to restore our mutilated men to useful life. One thing only is needed to ensure success in the great majority of cases, and that is, that the man be considered, by himself and those about him, as a capable citizen. Experience has taught us that

---

[1] *Die Zahl der versorgungsberechtigten Kriegsbeschädigten und Kriegshinter-bliebenen Deutschlands im Mai 1932.* Sonderdruck aus dem Reichsarbeitsblatt, 1932, No. 21, Teil 2. Von Oberreigierungsrat Foerster, Berlin, p. 2. This publication will hereafter be referred to as *Die Zahl.*

[2] *Die Zahl,* p. 2.

[3] *Handbuch,* Article 28.

even the most heavily maimed can do good work if he has the will. And to help a man into a "pension psychosis" is to do him worse harm than ever he got from the enemy.' Upon this principle the German reconstruction experts founded an extraordinarily successful war work.[1]

Returning to the comparison of the German and the French pension system, a conspicuous difference appears in the matter of hospitals. While the French Government maintains no special hospitals for its ex-service pensioners, the German Government supports eight thermal bath sanatoria [2] and six tuberculosis hospitals for War-service invalids.

Medical, surgical, and nursing care, residence and treatment in general hospitals, in sanatoria, and in thermal bath institutions are today provided for the disabled ex-service man without cost to him, on condition that his trouble is unquestionably service-incurred; and that, under treatment, he faithfully co-operates with his doctors and is either improving or prevented from getting

---

[1] Cf. Edward T. Devine and Lillian Brandt, *Disabled Soldiers and Sailors*, Oxford University Press, New York, 1919.

[2] Their capacity averages as follows:

TUBERCULOSIS HOSPITALS		THERMAL BATH SANATORIA	
Potsdam	150 beds	Wiesbaden	150 beds
Minden	70 beds	Nauheim	70 beds
Hanau	80 beds	Kissingen	100 beds
Weingarten	120 beds	Homburg	110 beds
Nagold	150 beds	Wildbad	120 beds
Davos	80 beds (Ministry)	Mergentheim	80 beds
Total	550 beds	Landeck	110 beds
		Driburg	80 beds
		Total	850 beds

In the year 1931, 2800 ex-service men were sent, for periods of three to four months or more, to the above mentioned Tuberculosis Hospitals, and to private Tuberculosis Sanatoria, while the general cases cared for in the Thermal Baths somewhat exceeded 8000.

276

worse. Pension payments continue during hospitalization. and are, under some circumstances, supplemented
by maintenance allowance for the family. Sickness allowances are also sometimes granted to men temporarily
unable to earn wages.

Artificial limbs and supports, orthopedic shoes, wheel-
chairs, crutches, special clothing, etc., are also supplied
free by the State, and are repaired and replaced without
charge unless their deterioration is due to misuse or
gross neglect on the part of the recipient.[1]

Every ex-service pensioner whose physical condition
has not reached a fixed stage is required to report periodi-
cally for re-examination in a Government medical centre.
If his state is then found less good than before, his pension
may be raised. If he has improved, his pension may fall
even to the point of cancellation. Thus, a man sent to a
sanatorium for rheumatism or for tuberculosis may, at the
end of his cure, be found so much better in health that his
disability drops below 25 per cent — the minimum pensionable disablement—and his pension therewith vanishes.[2]

Disabled men in definite need of re-education were
recognized as entitled thereto at the State's expense. At
the Ministry's discretion, such training might run on for
a year, more or less; and meantime, subject to the same
conditions, the man might receive as maintenance or 'transitional relief,' an *Uebergangsgeld*,[3] to tide him over the
interval. This sum could not exceed $112.43 yearly.[4] But

[1] *Handbuch*, Article 4, *et seq.* and 13.

[2] For the French practice, see *ante*, p. 232.

[3] *Handbuch*, Article 32.

[4] The amount of the *Uebergangsgeld* was limited to two-thirds of the base
pension plus the heavy disablement supplement.

every effort was made to induce the disabled man to refit himself either for his pre-War calling or for something as like it as may be. Few, it was found, even amongst the seriously maimed, were really unable to do this; and when they threw themselves into the attempt, the concentration now required, added to the mental familiarity with tool or problem, tended to produce a skill equal or sometimes even greater than that which the man had possessed before his injury. This re-educational work is now practically discontinued.

Two other advantages belong, in principle, to the German War-pensioner; First, if over 50 per cent disabled, he is entitled to consideration for certain places in the Civil Service. Second, he may, if he can satisfy the Ministry of the soundness of his scheme, capitalize a part of his pension, to improve his business or his property. The younger he is, the higher the capitalization permitted; but he may not go beyond two-thirds of his pension, the remaining third being held as a fixed income for daily needs.[1] And, as the utmost capitalization of pension would in itself scarcely suffice to build a house, it has been customary for German cities and large institutional plants to issue loans at low rates of interest, to enable such building — 'in order that the heavily disabled and the blind may stay at home and have gardens.'

Capitalization of War-pensions was suspended in July, 1931, for lack of funds in the Treasury. Since June, 1932, it has been resumed, on a minor scale, to pay debts and prevent bankruptcy sales.

When a War-pensioner dies, the Ministry, regardless

[1] *Handbuch*, Articles 72 *et seq.*

of the cause of his death, grants a definite sum of money to meet the funeral expenses. This sum is fixed according to the district in which he lived, as follows:[1]

Super-Class.............................. 210 Reichsmarks
Class A.................................. 195
Class B and C............................ 180
Class D.................................. 165

And after the War-pensioner's death, his pension is continued for three months to his dependants, in order to help them through the adjustment period.

The widow of an ex-service man whose death was the direct result of a service-incurred disablement for which, up to his last day, he was drawing a pension, is herself eligible to pension.[2]

But the *compagne*, the 'unmarried wife' recognized in the French system,[3] has no existence in the eye of the German law and the idea that an irregular relationship of that nature could be recognized by the State appears to be irreconcileable with the ruling type of German thought.

The Ministry proper deals only with laws and their administration — takes the laws as enacted and applies them in uniform sense. The individual cases are prepared and presented through a network of Pensions Offices — *Versorgungsämter* — eleven regional, seventy-four local, distributed over the country, each containing a medical department. In these centres, physical and mental conditions are tested, their nature scientifically determined, and the findings set up as a clear statement of fact, ready for the Ministry to name the law that fits it.

[1] *Handbuch*, Article 34.
[2] For further information as to pensions of widows, children, orphans and forebears of War-disabled men, see German Appendices I, II, and III.
[3] See *ante*, pp. 242-43.

279

'But,' hazards the foreigner, 'the law, naturally, is capable of more than one interpretation — the law allows exceptions.'

'We are not hunting for trouble,' replies the Ministry. 'Governments cannot step forth to defend or explain themselves when attacked. And the moment we made our law theoretical or subject to plural interpretation, the moment we began to recognize exceptions, no matter whom we favoured, we should run counter to the public sense and find every organization in Germany arrayed against us.'

The ex-service man, however, always retains the right of appeal from Pension-Office decisions as to his condition.[1] He had also the right to present a new claim for service-incurred disability up to the year 1931, when that right was abolished, to be reopened in May, 1933.

As to the burden of the German War-pension upon the national budget: Its peak was attained in 1928, when it touched 1,700,000,000 Reichsmarks ($404,940,000). Declining thence, by 1931 it had fallen to 1,200,000,000 Reichsmarks ($285,840,000). Of that reduction, about 400,000,000 was due to cures or deaths of ex-soldiers, to deaths of their dependants, to remarriage of widows, or to the coming of age of children. The remaining decrease was effected by an economy measure — the Emergency Decree of 1931.

For the collection of fragments and figures brought together in this chapter, it seems scarcely necessary to disclaim any pretension to embrace the German Pension

[1] For construction of the Provision of Review, see German Appendix IV.

Law. Rather, its purpose has been to suggest, through examples, something of the law's character. And to that end further material will be found in the German Appendix.

CHAPTER III

SHEER KINDLINESS

MANY, alas! are the cases of War-born distress that no War-pension system covers.

When Field Marshal von Hindenburg, nearing his eighty-first year, was asked what he would like for a birthday present, wistfully he replied: 'I see so much misery amongst my old comrades, for which no help exists! More than anything I should like to have means to help them.'

So the people got together, by nation-wide contributions, a purse of 10,000,000 Reichsmarks ($2,382,000) — then an enormous sum in Germany — and gave it to their friend to use as he saw fit.

Today, six years later, it is more than half spent. Questions of politics or of religion have never affected its mercies. And great is the good it has done.

Other funds had been raised for similar work, such, for example, as the 100,000,000 Marks endowment set up for aid of widows and orphans of ex-service men. But most of these, caught in the national currency inflation, went up in smoke, together with the incomes and the savings of the German people. The Hindenburg Fund alone, created after the stabilization, remains today good money.

The details of the Fund's administration are handled in a special bureau whose chief is one of the Ministry coun-

282

cillors. Himself an old soldier full of humour and humanity, Dr. Karstedt still confronts, as he comes to his office
morning after morning, some hundreds of letters of appeal
new since the night before. Each one of these must be
examined, not only for its merits, but also for its relative
importance; for yearly disbursement is limited to 1,000,000
Reichsmarks, and the most painstaking care is needed
to make every penny do its work.

The attitude of the Field Marshal Reichs-President
toward his fellow-campaigners is known far and wide.
And all the wild asses of the desert, in return, believe him
their soul's twin brother, needing only to hear their
trouble in order to wipe it away.

Take, for example, the man who recently wrote, for
sympathy and help, from a State's prison in which he is
doing ten years at hard labour for a truly uninteresting
crime. His War-pension had been stopped, as all German
War-pensions are stopped when hard labour is imposed.[1]
But this injustice he was sure his distinguished brother
campaigner the Field Marshal Reichs-President would
undo, the moment he learned of its existence. How much
more seemly were it for a less fortunate comrade-at-arms
to find, on return to social life, the accumulated evidence
of the nation's gratitude!

Or, take that other recent appeal, from a Bavarian
woman whose plea rested on wider grounds: She had
borne, she said, twenty-six children and now was desirous
of settling down; but as no two of the twenty-six, save

---

[1] Entitlement to War-pension, resting as it does upon disability incurred
through service already rendered, is not cancelled by mere sentence to jail.
Conviction of heinous crime, however, such as is betokened by the sentence to
hard labour, destroys entitlement.

283

only the twins, had the same father, she stood in doubt how to fix upon final establishment. Two points only were clear to her; some of the fathers must have been soldiers, and an all-wise Field Marshal must know the proper course for a lady in her dilemma.

But the majority of the petitions laid upon Dr. Karstedt's desk are less easy to handle. Where so many honest ex-service men, disabled and unemployed, are, in spite of their pension, burdened to the breaking point; where so many widows and orphans of gallant soldiers are without the reasonable necessities of life; and where the available sum cannot possibly reach more than a fraction of this multitude, the difficulty is, which to choose to aid.

A scrap of coal here, an overcoat there, fifty Marks a month to help educate the little orphaned son of a famous Ace; [1] twenty Marks a month to bridge the deadly deficit of some struggling household — such, in effect, are the answers of the Hindenburg Fund to its daily applicants; answers based on individual study and understanding, worked out in a spirit of intelligent frugality that means devotion.

Simple, homely friendliness is a characteristic that must often strike the foreign observer of these German relief conceptions. Frederick the Great obviously had such an ideal in mind when, 185 years ago, he built the *Invalidenhaus* in Berlin. 'Laeso et Invicto Militi' — 'To Wounded and Unconquered Soldiers,' he carved, grandly,

[1] Proper education of the ex-service men's orphans is one of the acknowledged duties that the German Government has been forced to let lapse, of recent years, because of its drained treasury. The small sums now available for that purpose are in the nature of assistance rather than provision.

above the entrance. But once the door is passed, all
grandeur vanishes. Frederick, himself, a kind-faced,
frail and bent old man, clad in a dressing-gown, sitting
in an armchair, his hand on the head of a dog whose
chin rests lovingly on his master's knee, presides at the
stair-head. (He sat for the statue, they say, a few days
before his death.) And one feels that he, too, chooses
with contentment, for his latter days on earth, the company of battered 'old comrades' home for good from the
wars.

As for the house itself, the King with his own hand
designed it all, even to the arrangements of suites; for
he wanted his men to have their families about them, if
such they possessed. So there are single rooms for single
men, and suites of two, four, five, six rooms for men with
wives and children. All of them are ample in size, strik-
ingly well-proportioned, airy and filled with pleasantness
and sunshine. There is a lecture hall, a library, a little
recreation room, and a Protestant and a Catholic chapel.
There are also sixty individual gardens, of dimensions
varying from, perhaps, twenty-five by fifty feet to seventy
by ninety feet; each enclosed in its high hedge, each with
its trees and flowers, each the private domain and personal care of a separate old soldier. Charming little
gardens, neat, gay and flourishing.

One hundred and twenty-five ex-soldiers, officers and
men, all disabled fifty per cent or more, and all with
records of conspicuous gallantry, today inhabit the place
— some of them dating from the World War, some from
earlier campaigns; and their wives and children bring the
combined household up to 450 persons.

Thus the German *Invalidenhaus* actually entertains but few more men than are domiciled in *Les Invalides* in Paris. But the atmosphere of the two places differs fundamentally. And the nature of the difference is epitomized in their several representations of their patron-monarch — the one by a glorious classic sarcophagus encompassed with stands of arms and flags of victory, the other by a kind-faced, frail old man, sitting in his dress-ing-gown, in his armchair, fondling a dog that loves him.

This same spirit shows conspicuously in the typical German military hospital. Take, for example, that in Potsdam. Built in 1893, it lacks much in modernity. But to the lay eye and mind, its intimate, homely pleasant-ness weighs on the other side of the scale. Its buildings are scattered through its private park whose tall pine trees are headed high enough and grouped broadly enough to let down floods of sunlight upon riches of flowers. Cut flowers in abundance brighten every ward, every room, even the kitchens. 'Oh, we *must* have flowers!' says the Surgeon-Chief — as one might say 'We must have food and drink' — half in protest against the banality of the assertion. And little painted garlands of flowers, simple and gay in the Dresden china fashion, festoon pavilion windows that look out through the pines.

All summer long the men lie under the pines, on cots or reclining-chairs, or, when the sun is too hot, under three-sided shelters, these, too, flower-filled, and neat to the point of wonderment.

Pavilion, ward, day-room, each apartment inhabited by patients, faces to the south, with ample window-space. From kitchens and lavatories to wards and pavilions radiant sweet-smelling cleanliness reigns. Pleasant pictures of landscapes, children, birds, flowers hang on the walls, and the chairs and lounges are easy and wide.

Daily chorus-singing at the piano in the cheerful music-room is given the lung cases, as therapy, under a trainer. Out-of-door games, as ball and croquet, are also part of the cure. And, whenever weather permits, the men live their outdoor life in shorts with the upper body bare.

Four doctors, including the Surgeon-Chief who is also the general business administrator, four orderlies, and thirteen nursing deaconesses, compose the entire staff save cooks, laundry-people, and the general domestic service.

The beds in this hospital number 157. Their occupants come in for observation and the re-rating of pensions, for operations on old wounds newly broken down, for re-education of injured and flagging muscles, or for any physical malady that is the outgrowth of War-service.

Neurasthenic cases, however, are regarded with reserve. 'At all times,' says the Surgeon-Chief, 'we have considered such disorders primarily constitutional. And now, so long after the War, while new cases of War-occasioned neurasthenia *may* develop, we receive such claims with extreme doubt — a doubt that must be well offset indeed before we burden the Ministry with their care.'

A sub-section of the Potsdam work deals with the blind men and their dogs. The World War left Germany a legacy of 2900 totally blinded soldiers, of whom two thousand now have the companionship of 'leaders.'

Bred by Government, these 'leaders' are all of the

German *Schäferhund* strain — the small, dark police type. When a youngster has reached the proper age, he is taken from his breeding kennel to a Government school, such as that in the Hospital Park at Potsdam, there to receive his professional education. In the autumn of 1932, the Potsdam school had on hand fifty scholars, with whom a corps of trainers was working daily.

The dog, while on his job, wears a belt to whose top is attached a stiff leather ball, shaped like the handle of a wooden bucket; so that the blind man, gripping the ball rather than a flexible leash, is in close contact with his leader and conscious of his every movement. The dog is taught to walk, always, in the middle of the sidewalk; to watch for obstacles; to swerve from oncomers; to pick up and give back anything that his man drops; to stop short and stand fast at the head of descending steps; to pull back at a rail-barrier, as at a railway crossing; to sit down at the kerb and stay sitting till he gets the attention of the policeman on duty before consenting to take his man across a city street; to bark if anything is wrong; and always to steer a wide course around letter-boxes, which, being fixed to the wall, might easily fell a wayfarer who should crash into them.

When a set of dogs is trained and ready for service, a set of blind men desirous of 'leaders' is called. These, in the Potsdam school, are domiciled, for their stay, in a comfortable bungalow in the park near the training kennels.

Then comes the task of fitting dog to man, and man to dog. A high-strung, nervous man must not be given a leader of the same temperament; nor must a slow-walking,

slow-thinking man be given a dog whose movements are
too deliberate to even the balance. In the bungalow, each
man has his separate bedroom, where by his bed at night
sleeps his dog, just as it attends him constantly by day.
And no small essential of the experiment lies in discover-
ing whether, all other points being adjusted, man and
dog, as individuals, really like each other.

For the relation of blind man and leader dog, like the
relation of man and wife, is too exacting, at best, to be
begun with an unnecessary handicap. 'His ears don't
stand up straight enough!' complains the blind man.
Whereto the official in charge responds, not 'Nonsense
and rubbish!' but 'Try another dog,' experience having
shown the long reflexes of an original trivial prejudice.
'I don't think much of that fellow,' confides the dog, as
to the man he slept with. 'Right,' says the official,
'forget him.'

About a fortnight is commonly allowed for the training
of right man and right dog together, so that the man may
grasp the dog's technique and the dog may take on his
master. But the dog never becomes the blind man's
property. He is always the State's dog, loaned on the
blind man's good behaviour. A proper food-money allowance goes with him.[1] If the food is diverted, if the dog
shows lack of care or any sort of ill-usage, the Government inspector withdraws him promptly.

In the long corridors of the Ministry you meet blind
messengers walking rapidly, led by their *Schäferhund*

[1] The annual food-allowance for the dog is, in Super-Class localities, 240
Reichsmarks; in Class A districts, 216 Reichsmarks, in Class B and C, 198
Reichsmarks, and 180 Reichsmarks in Class D, the open country. *Handbuch*,
Article 7.

companions; and these dogs are ready for caress. But in such places as the great Siemens Machine Works, where the blind and other disabled form an established percentage of the working staff,[1] the leader dogs wear another expression. Sitting by the workbench, close at their master's side, where steel-filings and brass waste fall thickest, they look out at strangers sternly. 'You may be all right, but keep away from my blind man. This is *my* responsibility, and I intend to discharge it.'

But the German War-blinded are not as a whole a tractable folk. The bent of their particular ex-service organization is well to the Left, and when it became known that Government would reduce the 1932 pensions budget, a deputation of the League of Blinded Soldiers, led by their radical president, descended upon the Ministry.

'Maybe you think,' announced they truculently, 'that you can beat us all down forever, to get money to pay fat War-pensions to foreigners that fought us — even to the last French nigger in Africa. But *we* say you can't. And if you dare cut *our* pensions, we blind men will make a big demonstration in Unter den Linden, and show you up to the nation.'

'Very well,' said the Ministry, 'but if you do that, we must publish in the newspapers the figures of your pensions. And when the unemployed read those figures and

---

[1] The Siemens Works, near Berlin, in normal times employs 130,000 hands. By September, 1932, the number had been reduced to 100,000, working at normal day's pay in shifts of two days a week. This establishment gives employment to a definite percentage of maimed men, amongst whom are twenty-five totally blinded. The blind man's earnings about equal those of the seeing girl. 'A blind man's work is women's work,' say the managers, 'and his advantage lies in his concentration. Unlike the girl, he does not raise his head every time there is a stir in the room.'

290

then see you "demonstrating" for more money still, do
you think you will be quite safe?'

The blind men thought: On the one hand, over six
million men unemployed in Germany — really hungry,
almost desperate, often homeless, many of them with
wives and children on their hands, and getting, there in
costly Berlin, about 50 Reichsmarks a month from the
public relief. On the other hand, behold the War-blinded,
commonly living in the country, snugly settled in his
own house, with his own garden, his goats, pigs, poultry.
He does no work whatever, unless he likes, and he gets his
350 Reichsmarks a month with the regularity of sunrise;
while the farmer, his neighbour, cannot make 300 Reichsmarks by toiling with all his family from dawn till dark.

Country neighbours or Berlin jobless, what would either
say or do, when, grasping those facts, they saw the Unter
den Linden 'demonstration' for more cash?

The League of Blinded Soldiers decided to go home
quietly, leaving Unter den Linden in peace.

More than once in these lean latter years has Government been forced to cut its budget, War-pensions with
the rest. And each time more or less outcry has arisen
from the ex-service men's organizations: 'We know our
country is poor,' they complain. 'We know there isn't
money for everything. But we see that Government is
spending in other fields. Let them economize there before
cutting War-victims' relief. All we ask is just enough to
keep soul and body together.'

'Where would you make that other economy?' you
enquire.

'In the Reichswehr — the present army. In the police.'

Yet they realize, even as they speak, that whatever else suffers, those two services no Government will cut; the first, because its pay is fixed by contract — even as its shape and rule of being is fixed by Versailles; the second, because it is the State's first line of defence for law and order.

'Then damn Versailles! Away with Versailles!' growl the ex-service men. But they know all too well that the real question no longer is, 'Does our pension suffice?' but, 'Can any pension survive?'

Meantime, War-pensioned ex-service men have this steadying satisfaction: With their own eyes they see that every Government salary has been heavily pruned, that governmental expenditures have been cut to the raw, and that throughout the departments, administrative costs have been pared to 5 per cent, or less, of the total disbursement. In other words, they know that their straits are the nation's straits, fairly shared by all. Nor have the ex-service men, by attempted group-grabbing or otherwise, raised their hand against the country.

As for our own 'Bonus Army,' its 'march on Washington,' and what happened thereafter, all Germany read of it first with incredulity, then with amazement, and at last with whole-hearted if unflattering mirth.

ever
cut;
n as
ond,
and

rowl
the
ice?'

ITALY

ITALY

CHAPTER I

A PEOPLE BETRAYED

Before the Great War, Italy's spirit lay sleeping — sleeping the sleep of the drugged. Material poverty had been fastened upon her by the long absorption of her politicians in their personal fortunes, by their indifference and incompetence as to her economic distress, and by each statesman's willingness that the country should endure all misery rather than that he himself should risk offending any power or person capable of reprisals at the ballot-box. And her outward and visible condition reflected her dormant mind.

The nation — a mass of humanity rather than a nation — lay limp behind her seas and mountains, little aware of the world without, dreaming herself apart from it, absorbed in her own pains and sloth, acrawl with decay bacteria that she had neither eyes to see nor conscious health to repudiate.

Then came May 24, 1915, and Italy's entry into the Great War.

In all their backings and fillings before that step, egotistic, timorous, doctrinaire, those who ordered the position of the country had taken little thought of the men who must fight their war should they decide to declare it. Now, untrained in new methods already nine months old, short of officers, short of uniforms, armed with rifles of the pat-

tern of the previous century and with cannon more dangerous to their own gun-crews than to the enemy, the
youth of Italy were flung to the frontier. And there, for
forty-one months, they fought the fight of the damned.

What were its elements? A wild terrain among mountain
peaks and passes, where every road and trench and dug-
out must be hewn from living rock; the task of dragging
munitions and supplies up into such fastnesses to fight
battles above the clouds; ice, deep snows, and bitter cold
of the long winters; shortage of men to hold a line almost
as long as the whole Allied Front in France against a
skilled, well-armed, and active enemy; with little or no
help from the Allies; heavy losses; much sickness, including strange contagions brought in by prisoners from the
East; low and scanty rations; little and scanty leave; lack
of welfare work [1] or of any sort of diversion to key up
weary minds; and, worst of all, continuing home news of
soldiers' families left hungry and destitute while overpaid
munitions workers and gross profiteers flaunted their cal-
lous extravagance in the eyes of the people; and while the
men who had planted the nation in this wretched plight
had still small thought to spare from their own interests
and theories.

Also, as an English historian [2] puts it, the Central Powers had left nothing to chance:

[1] Don Giovanni Minozzi, chaplain of the Knights of Malta, originated and
maintained, almost from the first, a series of soldiers' reading- and writing-
rooms in the forward zone, a most valuable service. But the help of the American Y.M.C.A., offered in 1917 and eagerly accepted by the Italian Army's High
Command, was withheld until fifteen months later. The needs of the armies in
France occasioned the delay, but the loss of opportunity was tragic. See *Service
with Fighting Men*, Association Press, New York, 1922, vol. II, pp. 369-79.

[2] John Buchan, *A History of the Great War*, London, 1922, vol. IV, pp. 49-50.

A PEOPLE BETRAYED

For months they had been sowing tares in Italian fields. A secret campaign was conducted throughout Italy which preached that peace might be had for the asking, and urged Italian Socialists to throw down their arms and fraternize with their brothers from beyond the mountains. If Austria attacked, it was said, it was only to enforce the views of the Vatican and establish the brotherhood of the proletariat; let her advance be met with white flags and open arms and the reign of capitalism and militarism would be over. This appeal, insidiously directed both to the ignorant Catholic peasantry and to the extreme Socialists of the cities, worked havoc with the Italian morale. Orlando, the Minister of the Interior, was averse from repressive measures, and enemy propaganda had for the moment almost as clean a field as in the Russia of the Revolution. The poison had infected certain parts of the army to an extent of which the military authorities were wholly ignorant.

Never were wickeder plots laid against a hapless people.

And so, in such a day, came Caporetto, dark-robed mother of Glory.

The Austro-German High Command had planned the thing with the utmost care, with long preparations, with supreme skill and strategy. In the wild mountain peaks, the jagged gorges, the tragic traps and chasms of Italy's northeastern border, Italy's frontier guards, strung thin along the cloud-wrapt miles, were already spent in body and mind through long and unbroken service. One colossal, unexpected blow, struck on that weary line, should utterly destroy the Italian forces, should deliver Venice into the hand of the stranger, should open the road to Rome; above all should set free the entire Austro-German strength, until now divided, for a united decisive attack upon the Allied Front in France.

On October 23, 1917, the blow was struck. Picked and

297

experienced German and Austrian troops, heavily supported by artillery, were flung in a surprise assault upon the Italian positions about Caporetto. The Italian Second Army, holding sixty-three miles of the most difficult country, had only two corps, and those the weakest, on the section chosen for assault. They gave way. The enemy poured through. Familiar with the treacherous terrain, he swept and circled down the narrow passes, isolating positions, dislodging commands to whose desperate valour in hand-to-hand fighting both the German and the Austro-Hungarian despatches of the day bear witness. But the struggle was too unequal. Soon great masses of troops were in full retreat along routes choked with their own batteries, transports, and ambulances. The people of the countryside fled behind them, laden with household goods. Close on their heels rode the Austrian cavalry, pausing only to apply the torch. And while flames and smoke of the burning towns made horrible the northern sky, the German commander swooped toward the south, to cut off escape.

But if parts of the Second Army at first succumbed to panic, the very bitterness of the truth drove men in its midst to toss away their lives in acts of doomed and transcendent gallantry.

Such [says the historian] as that of the Alpini in Monte Nero, who held out for several days and died almost to a man. Such as the troops in Monte Globococ who defended successfully the gate of the Judrio till it had ceased to matter.... But the greatest glory of all was won by the cavalry, troops like the Novara Lancers and the Genoa Dragoons, some of the finest horsemen in Europe, who again and again charged the enemy and sacrificed themselves with cheerfulness that the retreat might win a half-hour's respite. Said one Colonel to his officers: 'The *canaille* have betrayed our country's honour; now we, the gentlemen of Italy, will save it,' and wheeled his squadrons into the jaws of death.[1]

Yet the honour of Italy was safe. Again and yet again the enemy was checked, until, after days of rear-guard fighting at the point already chosen in the Italian general's plan, the retreat stopped short. By the river Piave the pursued turned at bay, to deliver one of the most amazing battles in history.

Austrians and Germans together hammered the new line with sixteen heavy divisions, some of them fresh troops, all hot and confident and furious with victory. Yet, worn as they were, and many of them raw boy recruits, and all with the psychology of retreat to conquer, the Italians held fast or counter-attacked. And so, through twelve days and nights, from November 11 to November 22, with unsurpassable brilliance they fought to its determining point an action of crucial weight in the fate of the Allies and of Western civilization.

When British and French divisions came into line as relief, on December 2, the crisis was already past, won out of the pit of death by a miracle of naked will and courage.

Had the issue of the Piave been otherwise, had the enemy succeeded in breaking through, Italy's sun would have set, and the dusk of the gods must have brooded over France. Said Winston Churchill, 'The falling away of Italy, a people of forty millions, a first-class power, from the cause of the Allies at that time, would have been an

[1] Buchan, vol. IV, pp. 53 and 58.

event more pregnant in consequences than all the triumphs of March 21, 1918.[1]

As for the tragedy of Caporetto, it poured blood and fire and iron into the veins of the nation. It awoke and unified the whole people. From that point forward they knew but one impulse. Before the next year was done they had won back all their lost ground, they had destroyed the enemy armies that had attempted the destruction of Italy, and they had regained their historic provinces of Trentino and Trieste, for centuries under the hand of Austria. From the Piave until the crowning glory of Vittorio Veneto, Italy's youth stood fast.

The Italians came into the War nine months late. But they came in time to teach the Austrian commanders, at terrible cost to both forces, that it was suicide to weaken their Italian Front. They came in time to prevent Austria from reinforcing the Germans before Verdun. They came in time to offset the loss of Russia. They came in time, as Ludendorff admits, to hold Ludendorff's head in the East and in Italy, while his heart strained toward the Western Front.[2] And, having come, they so behaved that the Austrian Empire at no period thereafter dared to take its eyes from the Italian line, or fling its weight to its German mate against the Front in France.

Fifty, fifty-five, seventy Austrian divisions the soldiers of Italy held in their grip facing to the south. If, through the dark years, that grip had once really broken, dare anyone say who, today, would be master of France?

---

[1] Winston Spencer Churchill, *The World Crisis, 1916–18*, Charles Scribner's Sons, New York, vol. II, p. 54.

[2] Erich von Ludendorff, *Ludendorff's Own Story*, Harper and Brothers, New York, 1919.

And here a few figures, set in comparison, help to point the picture.

	Population Exclusive of Colonies	Troops Mobilized 1914-1918	Killed and Missing	Wounded
France.............	39,604,992 [1]	7,932,000 [2]	1,393,388 [3]	2,052,984 [4]
Italy...............	34,700,000 [6]	5,600,000 [5][6]	700,000 [6]	1,000,000 [6]
British Isles.........	46,331,548 [7]	6,554,821 [7]	812,317 [8]	1,869,567 [9]

Length of Front Held

By the Allies in France............ 700 kilometres
By Italy alone.................... 650 kilometres [6]

Meantime, what was happening in civilian Italy?

Anarchism and kindred types of social philosophy had honeycombed the body politic, and succeeding statesmen had been content to woo the favour of that element, if only by closing their eyes to its progress. Now, after the Armistice, these coddled enemies of the State stood boldly forth with bared teeth. The winter of 1918 became a *crescendo* of confusion, of political strikes, of seizures of public and private industries, of general attack upon order, commerce, and the economic structure of the country. Life and property became increasingly insecure. The people went hungry and bewildered, while bullying gangs of Commun-

---

[1] *Statesman's Year-Book.*
[2] Exclusive of coloured and colonial troops. *Les Dommages*, p. 497. Of this total, 6,830,000 were combatant troops.
[3] *Les Dommages*, p. 497.
[4] *Ibid.*, p. 501.
[5] Italy mobilized no coloured or colonial troops.
[6] Authority of the Italian Government, Rome, March, 1933.
[7] *Military Effort*, p. 363. For full title see *post*, p. 368.
[8] *Whitaker's Almanack*, 1933, p. 381.
[9] House of Commons, *Report*, May 5, 1921.

ists sprawled in the midst of superabundance that they knew only how to abuse.

And still Government remained supine — or intervened only to favour the disturbers and to tie the hands of citizens who would have resisted them. Private soldiers coming home from the War, especially if wearing decorations for wounds and valour, met insult or violence in the streets of their own towns, while officers, not seldom murderously attacked, must fight for their lives. Yet Government's only response was to pardon and set free all army deserters; to order all officers, save when on duty, to keep their uniforms out of sight and to carry no arms, lest the Communists take offence; and to refuse permission for a Victory Parade.

Under such handling, the tide of crime rose fast, while the country lost all semblance of dignity.

Meanwhile, some hard thinking was being done, not in high places, but among the newly friendless and despised. As for example, the Arditi.

The Arditi were a small picked force of super-shock troops, self-invented during the War. All volunteers, they gathered, uncalled, man by man, from the Army's regular branches. Their rules were peculiar to themselves. They asked little about the physical perfection of any suppliant for admission to their ranks. They asked, only, how great was his desire. His degree of enthusiasm, his nerve, his will — these alone interested his judges, and stiffly they tested all three before accepting him. The fruit was a corps whose unique fame for dash and daring was the pride and the spur of the entire Army.

The Arditi had their own technique and their own mo-

ment. They led the attack; they preceded the ad
Strung out in a long line of couples, spaced with yar
tween, each man carrying bombs and a knife as his
weapons, they rushed forward, crouching, under a
creeping barrage from the Italian guns. That ba
rising as they ran, covered them just to the lip o
enemy's trenches. Then, as it lifted, in they jumped
ing *A noi!* their battle-cry — 'For Us This Victor
worked fast with bomb and knife, and, if they sur
fell back within the Italian advance as it overtook the
await in reserve the break of the next action.

They first took the field in July, 1917, numbering
only four companies. By the end of the War they ha
come a full army corps of 32,000 men. And they ha
27 per cent killed, while 83 per cent of the survivors
more or less disabled.

Their hymn was *Giovinezza*, 'Youth.' Their fla
a small black flag. Their uniform, as worn in the last
of the War, was a black shirt with grey breeches.

And it happened, in the four months between Armi
and demobilization, that the Arditi, out of a job, per
idle in the mountain-top fortresses, had time to con
what it was they had been dying for, in their own pec
fashion, for the last fifteen months. Was it, by any p
ble chance, to save their Italy as a maggots' paradis€

The Arditi concluded that their job, far from l
finished, was only just begun.

Therefore, as soon as the Army released them, in M
1919,[1] they re-formed as a National Federation of A

[1] The Arditi, after the Armistice, had returned to their several original br
of the service, and were thence demobilized.

Associations, with a post in each province of the country, having, as their object, to fight Bolshevism. In the following month, in Milan, occurred the first assembly of that body of crusaders which, in its later growth, would determine the fate of Italy.

Of the two hundred men who that day took the Fascist oath, 79 per cent were furnace-tried Arditi. *Giovinezza*, the Arditi's hymn, *A noi!* the Arditi battle-cry, the black Arditi flag, and the black Arditi shirt, became the hymn, the battle-cry, and the uniform of the Fascist organization. And the first-formed Arditi unit flung itself heart and soul to the support of the Crusader Chief — Benito Mussolini.

CHAPTER II

IL DUCE

As AN American turns to the figure of the great Italian leader in those early days, a familiar prelude seems to fill the air — the cradle-song of our own race who in their time have risen from bare rocks, alone and of their own will, to fight the Dragon. Think of Il Duce's childhood home — a poor man's cottage in the hills. Think of the father— blacksmith to the countryside, honourable, industrious, sober, stern, much given to reading, and a hot reformer, studying the public questions of the day; sometimes imprisoned for his bold speech, yet sought by neighbours, far and near, for the visions of his mind. Think of the mother — village schoolmistress, singularly lovely to the eye, with spiritual intelligence, inherent refinement, truth, probity, and gentle, reticent femininity written in her face. Think of the boy, her adoration and anxiety, her hope and prayer — a boy omnivorous of great books, a boy so full of life and fire and power of intellect and will, so full of eagerness to learn, to know, to understand, to grip, to conquer, that he casts himself headlong at every obstacle he meets till that obstacle breaks. Think of a life, as it widens before him, that uncovers, each day, new public wrongs, new squalid, evil, dangerous things, threatening his country — things that the home talk of the elders has led him to take to heart as every honest man's concern and cause for action. Think of those elements gathered

305

into one story and say if you are not reading such a page as might be torn from the heart of our own highest saga?

The new Fascist organization failed in its first effort. In the election of November, 1919, its candidates were defeated. At the opening of Parliament, the King in person was flagrantly insulted by the now dominant Socialist members, whose party directorate had recently declared that 'Our fatherland is Russia, our capital is Moscow,' [1] taking the sickle and the hammer as their emblem. The Red press now flamed out untrammelled, attacking all established institutions — religion, the family, property, preaching class hatreds. Disorders spread. An impotent Premier feared to act except in behalf of the Reds, conceded demand after demand upon the State's Treasury, while he extended little or no protection to the unhappy people. Police at times dared not show themselves in public unless in disguise. Rioting, looting, blackmail and murder multiplied, constant strikes paralyzed industry and commerce, property was seized by force without warrant, and the Socialists' declaration against private ownership of land showed itself as deadly to the peasant who tilled his own farm as to the extensive landholders.

In January, 1920, when the action of citizen volunteers, coming suddenly forward in numbers to replace striking railway personnel, broke the back of one Bolshevist attempt, the Premier made haste to disown that temerity, lest it cost him his office. Yet the mere fact that volunteers had at last so acted was a sign that a wiser man might have seen as a writing on the wall.

[1] Luigi Villari, *The Awakening of Italy*, Methuen and Company, Ltd., London, 1924, p. 74.

For Mussolini, up in the north country, had been working. From boyhood a journalist-publicist, since 1914 he
had owned and edited his newspaper, *Il Popolo d'Italia.*
All through the War, while himself a soldier in the combat
zone, he had used that powerful vehicle to broadcast the
fact that Italy's own demagogues, in Parliament and out,
were responsible for her woes. Now more than ever determined to arouse the nation and consolidate it as a single
creative will for its own redemption, he was steadily building his means; he was gathering, all over the land, a body
of serious, fearless, and passionately devoted youth, his
Fascist squadrons, to drive the new gospel home.

And so the victorious Frontier Army, that the little
folk in office had continuously offered up in sacrifice and
that the Bolshevists in control had as continuously pil-
loried — the victorious Frontier Army, reborn — arose
again to fight for Italy.

The organization grew fast, offering as it did both form
and leadership to the sounder instincts of the people.
Only the tried and surest were accepted for enlistment in
the actual Fascist squadrons. But each new Bolshevist
assassination, each new anarchist bombing, burning, or
confiscation, swept more citizens of all classes into Fascism's wider ranks. And whether with thrashings, with
bullets, or with the peerless castor oil, the Fascist soldiery,
growing in discipline, dealt with each several case as its
quality required.

In the middle of this year the demagogue Nitti was succeeded as Premier by another as devoid of weight — Giolitti, a man too small to feel or to trust the submerged virtue of the nation that would have surged to his support

had he shown courage and energy to call it from its deeps. So he, too, trod warily, while the crops rotted in the fields, while the wheels of the mills stood idle, and while trade deserted the seaports because in all of Italy there remained no freedom for peaceful men to work.

Yet, as the summer merged into autumn, even such eyes as Giolitti's could not avoid a glimpse of new life astir in the people. And so, to throw it a sop, he declared that the demobilized Army, such of it as could still be collected, might now hold a Victory Parade — might, two years after the Armistice, be suffered to bring its ragged battle-flags to Rome, for one day's honour.

To this the Communists, surprised and affronted, replied with new explosions of violence, culminating locally in a plot to seize Bologna, massacre the townspeople, and declare Red revolution. This plot the Bologna Fascisti discovered in time to anticipate. But the horrors of the scheme in its stripped atrocity, the list of its actual victims, dead and wounded, the staunchness of the local Fascist squadron, and the fact of its organized presence as a rallying-point on the spot, gave another forward drive to Mussolini's effort.

During the following month, December, 1920, the tide set in that swept the Reds from office, not only in the Province of Bologna, but also in the neighbour provinces to the east and north — the immediate home zone of Mussolini's labours.

In January, 1921, the Italian Socialist Party held a week-long Congress. To it Moscow, enraged at news of revolt in a country that it had regarded as its definite conquest, sent orders demanding, on pain of excommunication, a categorial subscription to the full Moscow revolutionary code. From that point forward the battle raged with greater fierceness, while Fascist squadrons grew in strength, numbers, and discipline, and their leader still perfected his system.

By November, 1921, enough ground had been gained to make possible a national religious memorial service, in Rome, over the body of the Unknown Soldier. And two days later, in Rome, the National Fascist Party, in congress assembled for the combined occasion, heard its leader formally proclaim its birth and declare its code 'a moral code as well as a rule of conduct.' In the speech that followed, Il Duce pronounced the death-warrant of Italian demagoguery.

The immediate sequel, however, was another ten months' campaign against Red violence and tyranny, during which the Communist strategy included attacks upon children and the bombing of theatres and railway trains.

Destructive strikes continued, with the avowed purpose of annihilating all property values, of wearing down the country to complete despair, and of forcing revolution. And so 1922 bade fair to hobble its course like 1921 — save for the fact that the head of the Fascisti had further developed his method.

Now, when a city government showed itself pulp in the hands of Communist agitators, or when Reds, filling all municipal offices, had paralyzed a city's works, be it railways, trams, docks, post, light, the supply of milk or bread, the burial of dead, the local Fascist squadron silently marched in, put the fear of God into whoever resisted, and ran the service itself until some sort of regular governmental machine decided to function.

Yet, significant of its own ripeness for doom, the Italian Parliament could neither be stung nor kicked into action. With the air of marble Senators aloof in the majesty of their office, the nation's legislators sat as before, talking — always talking.

With a treasury drowned in deficits, they still refused to make economies in their own machinery or to abolish any of their own perquisites or patronage. Costs of administration soared to new heights. And while they shovelled out bonuses and relief funds and voted relief works for unemployed whose very unemployment was the fruit of legislative sloth and folly, their only expedients for financing their projects were such as these: to clap higher and higher duties upon imports; to tax capital, industry, and the professional classes to extinction; and to extinguish agriculture, while leaving so-called 'workers' without participation in the country's burden-bearing.

So came August, 1922, and the calling, by the Socialist and Communist Parties, of a general strike of all governmental services and of all labour, throughout Italy, the object now being, not revolution alone, but also the overthrow of the Fascisti.

Mussolini's response was a sudden out-flashing of accumulated power — the order for immediate mobilization of all Fascist squadrons throughout the country. At the same time came this ultimatum from the Fascist Directorate:

> We give the State forty-eight hours in which to prove that it possesses authority over all its employees and over those who are attempting to destroy the very existence of the nation. At the end of that period, Fascismo will assume full freedom of action and supplant the State, which will once more have proved its incompetence.

During those forty-eight hours of grace, all over Italy the black-shirted Fascisti gathered to their standards, fully armed, perfectly disciplined now, the picked Arditi of this their nation's deadliest war.

At the end of the appointed interval, the Government, having duly and fully 'once more proved its incompetence,' the General Strike began. True to their leader's word, at once the waiting Fascisti stepped in and took over public services. Next morning, Mussolini published his order for the occupation by Fascist squadrons of every provincial capital in the land unless, before that nightfall, the Central Government had proved an intent to restore law and order.

Within a week's time cities like Milan and Genoa, long abject victims of Red municipal control, had been purged of that dominance. Order reigned in Italy. And now, with the prestige of the Government dead by slow suicide, and with that of the Socialists and Communists weakened by the failure of their supreme effort, even labour unions joined the rush to the Fascist camp.

The Fascisti now laid before Government their definite demand: there must be a new Cabinet, in which five portfolios — Foreign Affairs, War, Navy, Labour, and Public Works, as well as the Commission of Aviation, should be allotted to Fascist Ministers; and there must be a complete reform platform; or else, a general election forthwith.   The Government answered dodderingly.

Mussolini replied in a public speech at the great Naples Fascist review, where forty thousand Fascisti paraded:

> I tell you with all the solemnity which the moment de-mands — it is a question of days, perhaps hours — either the Government will be given us, or we shall seize it by marching on Rome.

That was on October 24, 1922. On October 27, the simulacrum Giolitti Cabinet resigned. By the twenty-ninth, a hundred thousand Fascisti, marching in orderly columns from every quarter of the land, were closing in upon Rome. On the morning of the thirtieth, they began entering the city. And in that same hour, summoned from Milan by royal command, came Mussolini himself to receive from the King's own hand the Premiership of Italy.

'I bring to Your Majesty,' he said, 'the Italy of Vittorio Veneto reconsecrated by the new victory, and declare myself the devoted servant of Your Majesty.'

Then he turned to his squadrons whose work for the moment was over. And first they marched to the tomb of the Unknown Soldier to make their reverence there; then to the Quirinal, with a superb outburst of loyalty to pay homage to the King; then for a review by Il Duce; and so, dismissed, their duty done, quietly away to their own homes, near and far, all within a few hours of that crown-ing hour of triumph, their entry into their Eternal City.

And the morrow was the Second Day of Newborn Italy.

Now, what was this thing that had happened?

For long Italy had lain inert, flung down on the throne

of the Cæsars, a poor, strange, half-dead thing, 'the slut of the Mediterranean.'[1] Imperially descended, she had lost all trace of that lineage. Miserably she survived, 'resigned to her lot, content to abide in infamous poverty.'

And those that were charged with her care and defence were beard-waggers, mostly — garrulous, timorous, old-minded folk, chiefly concerned with their comfort. Whenever robbers broke in, as robbers did, and a young man, shouting in their ears, roared out a warning, these old folks pushed him away, testily: 'Leave us alone! Only fools vex robbers. Give them what they ask, lest they grow angry and hurt us.'

Then came War to the land — and young men marched away so that old men now could live in peace; and so, as well, could robbers, who forthwith sat down at their ease, greasily growling, like curs to meaty bones.

And the young men, far away, keeping the border castles, lived bitter lives of hardship, fighting a strong enemy, subject to such stern discipline as neither they nor their fathers before them had ever known.

At last, out of hardship and discipline and long night watches in the presence of death and fighting shoulder to shoulder, deep down in their secret hearts a vision was born. And the Vision, in form, was like that famous statue, the Samothracian Victory — a beautiful, valiant Being with great, strong wings, but alas! lacking a head. It had no head — and so, for all its beauty and power, it led nowhere.

Now, among the young fighting men was one unlike the rest — one who had fought as none else had fought —

[1] A. Beltramelli, *L'Uomo Nuovo*, A. Mondadori, Milano-Romo, 1923, p. 161.

fought and sought and prayed and hammered at the gates of earth and heaven, in one long, lonely, endless battle.

For upon him alone it had been laid to find and to awake the lost and sleeping soul of Italy.

Seeking everywhere, he had trod many roads — and when he proved them wrong had left them, pursued by the curses of the dwellers thereby. Sometimes hungry and homeless, always alone, often in prison or hunted, still he pursued. Now a soldier and covered with wounds, he yet relaxed no effort. And at last, because his purpose was single and not for himself; because his faith and his courage outlived the years and all trials, God vouchsafed him that knowledge that he sought, with great power of the spirit. With speed, then, he came to tell the young fighting men, his brothers. And they shouted aloud with joy, for they knew that the night of inaction was past — that the day of their Vision was come. '*A noi! A noi!*', they shouted, 'For *us* this Victory!'

So they called him Il Capo, The Head — Il Duce, The Leader. And he led them, the youth of the nation, tested young fighters, marching shoulder to shoulder, straight down through the land, and purged it.

And when they came to the Eternal City, they drove out the robbers with thongs. And then, their hearts dark with love, they knelt at the throne of the Cæsars and put forth the hilts of their swords.

CHAPTER III

THE ROUNDED TRIBUTE

WHEN the new Prime Minister took the helm of Italy, the economic sky looked black indeed. The outgoing administration's budget for 1921–22 — the coming year — showed an estimated deficit of 15,760,000,000 lire, against a total revenue of only 19,701,000,000 lire. The morale of the country had sloughed away from its old standard of laborious thrift; industrial and agricultural production had been garroted, and the foreign market killed. Less than two years later, to be sure, Mussolini had balanced the budget and set all wheels whirring. But meantime no wrongs could be righted by the passage of fat appropriation bills.

One wrong cried for redress with a voice that went straight to his heart: The soldiers of Italy, home-coming from hard-won victory, had been shamefully received — dishonoured, persecuted; and their wounded, more spitefully attacked than the rest, had found no place to lay their heads. Now this must be righted, though not by outpouring of money. Nor is it, indeed, in the manner of Il Duce to put a price on the loyalty of men.

His Fascist squadrons he dealt with at once, disbanding them as such, to be reassembled in a few days' time [1] as the 'Volunteer Militia for National Safety,' under oath to the King — a part of the Government's defence forces.

---

[1] Decree of January 15, 1923. The new organization continues to wear the Black Shirt, and still serves without pay except for a few full-time units.

315

As promptly now, he turned to the maimed and the sick
— *mutilati ed invalidi* — the physical wreckage amongst
his fellow ex-service men of the Great War. They would
have pensions, of course; but the Prime Minister's immediate concern was for something more precious than
pensions — for the men's own self-respect and for their
dignified and contributory status in the nation. He would
establish their position as of acknowledged merit because
of service rendered and sacrifice made. Yet he would
establish it, not as an idle, retrospective thing, apart and
of the past, but as an active, integral, driving force in the
great, united forward drive of the nation.

Perhaps his plan was matured even before the March on
Rome. In any case it was ready for materialization
directly thereafter — and it wiped off the record, with one
broad stroke, the ex-soldiers' case against Italy.

Il Duce's design, characteristic in its simplicity and
completeness, falls under three main heads, represented
by three great Government-controlled and Government-
financed Institutes. The first of these cares for the disabled fighting man and his family. It is called the National
Institute for the Protection and Aid of the War-Disabled.[1]
The second deals with the interests of the non-disabled,
and is called the National Institute for Combatant
Soldiers.[2] The third, charged with the welfare of dead
soldiers' children, is the National Institute for War
Orphans.[3]

These three National Institutes, each having its own

---

[1] *Opera Nazionale per la protezione e l'assistenza degli Invalidi di guerra.*
[2] *Opera Nazionale per i Combattenti.*
[3] *Opera Nazionale per gli orfani di guerra.*

316

central office in Rome, are conjointly supervised and controlled by one master office [1] directly responsible to Il Duce,[2] and kept well aware of his intense and observant interest.

Allied with each several Institute as part and parcel of its being, is a complementary National Association.[3] While each Institute represents the Fascist Government, from which it derives its authority and its means, its complementary Association, on the other hand, represents the beneficiary body. To vitalize the connection of Institute with Association, delegates from the Association directorate sit in every meeting of the corresponding Institute, to present the needs of the beneficiary body. And it is the business of the Institute to determine in what manner those needs can be met.

The National Institute for War-Disabled receives from the Fascist Government an annual appropriation of 25,000,000 lire,[4] to which is added 5,000,000 lire from investments, a total amounting to about $1,578,000.[5] Not a large sum, as such things go in America; but enough, handled as Mussolini handles public money, competently to meet the need and to produce, in some respects, the finest system in the world. Here, after ten years, are

[1] *L'Assistenza Reduci e Famiglie caduti in guerra.*

[2] Royal Decree of April 19, 1923, n. 850. For structure of Scheme see Italian Appendix II.

[3] *Associazione Nazionale fra Mutilati ed Invalidi di guerra; Associazione Nazionale dei Combattenti; Associazione Nazionale delle famiglie dei Caduti in guerra.*

[4] Statement of the Director-in-Chief of the *Opera Nazionale per la protezione e l'assistenza degli Invalidi di guerra*, Rome, September 26, 1932, to the author.

[5] As of 1932, before the fall of the American dollar, one lira, stabilized par value, was equal to 5.26 American cents.

some of the blessings it has brought forth for Italy's War-disabled ex-service men:[1]

1. For the tuberculous — and the Fascist Government has strained many a point to admit, as War-incurred, late-developed tuberculous cases — three fine sanatoria ultra-modern in design and equipment, for free care and domicile of ex-service patients. Of these, the two major houses are, the one in Aspramonte, in the Alps, the other near Trieste. The three together offer 650 beds. It is felt that this number of beds is now rather more than sufficient to care for all remaining War-incurred cases. Therefore no further building for such use is intended; overflow applicants being sent to the Government's provincial tuberculosis sanatoria maintained for the use of the general public. The principle of isolation from family and society, and of segregation in the sanatorium, immediately a case is identified, is heavily stressed. The working power of arrested cases is thoroughly tested in after-cure sanatoria before returning the men to outer life.

2. A series of rest and convalescent camps and colonies newly built at the seaside and in the mountains, ideally planned, placed and maintained for the toning up of the mental and physical machine.

3. Courses of treatment in mud baths, thermal baths, and medicinal water cures, in the various Italian resorts where such exist. These, like stays in the rest camps, are provided as and when the case indicates.

[1] For the Fascist Government's important anti-tuberculosis war for ex-service men and the nation, see Italian Appendix XIII. See also *Relazione tecnica sulla attività svolta dall' Ufficio Costruzioni Sanatoriali*. Silvio Guidi, Rome, 1932.

4. For the totally blinded by War-wounds, four excellent establishments that are home, club, school, and workshop combined; or, to him who so prefers, a comfortably furnished house for his own use, and a uniformed soldier of the present army detailed to live with him and escort him to and fro upon his occasions.

5. A country-wide network of diagnostic centres free to all ex-service men.

6. For the super-disabled a specially beautiful and luxurious home, the Villa Demidoff, in Florence, where nothing is spared that can brighten their lives.

7. For the paraplegics, a separate hospital, in Arosio, Milan, where under cheerful surroundings they receive that particular treatment that their case demands.

8. For the mutilated requiring re-education a system of schools whose success has now largely destroyed their own necessity, their pupils having been absorbed in Government or private employ.[1] During the last three years, only fifty-four hundred have been so re-educated, but before 1929 these schools had restored over one hundred thousand War-disabled men to self-supporting status in lines meeting market demands, the effort being to return them, as far as possible, to their original callings.

9. Thirty-five plants for fitting, manufacture, and repair of artificial limbs, crutches, orthopædic shoes, wheel-chairs, etc. This work is done under supervision,

[1] The Fascist Government obliges every public enterprise or bureau to include among its employés ten to twenty per cent of disabled ex-service men, while requiring all private concerns to reserve for disabled ex-service men five per cent of their jobs. With industries which cannot take on that number of disabled men, the percentage is made up by the employment of War-orphans between fourteen and twenty-five years old. Breaches of the regulation are punished by fine 'imposed,' as one official put it, 'less to get money than to get action.'

in pleasant and comfortable conditions, chiefly by mutilated soldiers who themselves use artificial limbs. The product is distributed free, to War-disabled ex-service men, through a network of fitting and service stations covering all of Italy. The expenses of the recipients in journeys to these stations, or to hospitals, sanatoria, or camps, are met by the Institute.

10. Suitable cottage homes, provided on almost nominal terms, for poor and disabled ex-service men; and aid toward obtaining rural mortgages, up to 30,000 lire, by the War-disabled agriculturist, through Government's payment of his mortgage interest up to the rate of five per cent.

11. Aid to co-operative home-building by War-disabled men through part-payment of interest on building loans. Large co-operative apartment house in each city, built solely for disabled soldiers and their families and for War-widows and orphans; the family pays a trifling amount monthly, and at the end of fifty years will own its flat — a prize keenly desired in a country where the family, not the individual, carries the greater weight.

12. Club-houses, scattered through the country, which disabled men now use as such, and which, when their working days are done, will become the permanent homes of those that have no home.

This list suggests the nature, but by no means names the working varieties of a most human and intensely practical enterprise. But it should not be closed without naming another example of Il Duce's personal relation to his people. Here and there, in the four quarters of Italy, he, son of a mother beloved and remembered, has established pleasant, comfortable houses of repose for the widows and parents of the War-dead. To these they come, when need arises, for periods of rest, for convalescence and peace, always under the benediction of beauty — as in the favourite villa of Queen Margherita in Bordighera, now dedicated to that use. The significance of this, profoundly suggestive, invites lingering thought.

Among the stronger impressions received by the foreigner in examining these things, perhaps the most immediate arises from the qualities of beauty, of order, and of intelligence governing all; a beauty, not only of form, but of thought, choosing material perfection as a means to convey an exalted idea; an order that exhibits self-respect and dignity as the first fruit of discipline; an intelligence that, divining the higher essence of each need, has not been content to choke off its demand with material care only.

Disabled soldiers' homes and workshops are installed in ancient palaces. Grand old salons are now dormitories, their wealth of murals, their bossed and frescoed ceilings looking down upon rows of cots; but the cots are as white, as smooth and set as straight as human hands can make them. The lofty banquet hall, with its slender carven columns, its glorious doorways and windows and mantels, is now the dining-room of common men; but there are flowers around the room, flowers and clean white cloths upon each table. And while the men sit at their meal, one of themselves may play great music, perhaps upon a pipe organ built into the wall. The workshops, in cloister or in ballroom, are beautiful. The work that the men produce therein is often of itself beautiful. Always there is the determination that it shall be beautifully done. But above and through all, without cant or pose or any sort of cheapness, is the purpose to find the inmost heart of every thing and creature, and to unite and consecrate them all as a single driving force for the greater honour of Italy.

We have glanced at workshops housed in ancient palaces. Turning now to the new-built structures of the service, you find the same ideas. Nothing is jerry-built, nothing is wholesale or impersonal, nothing is ugly. Faithful workmanship has gone into it all; faithful art or craft striving to honour the purpose it has been set to serve; and a constant quality of dignity.

The new House of the War-Blinded in Rome is a case in point. Its wide, airy spaces, sun-filled or shaded, its big curves, its freedom from corners and obstacles and sharp edges, its plentiful guard-rails, the planning of each room for elimination of the unnecessary and for the comfort and handiness of the required, all show study and understanding of the special needs of the case. But the men who live in this house are sightless men. Beauty is hidden from them.

And yet, no visitor can walk through their home without praising its beauty. None will pass along the upper corridors looking into their bedrooms without remarking the charm of color and design. Above all, no one can enter their chapel without catching his breath before its grave and piercing loveliness. All this for blinded men; and all this definitely reflected in their quiet and uplifted minds.

The purpose of this particular effort, as originally announced, was: to provide industrial re-education and remunerative work for the War-blinded of Central Italy; to set up special workshops adapted to the capacities of the blind; in the cases of men who desired to work in their homes, to find the necessary tools, materials, and market; [1] and finally, 'as a moral, intellectual, and economic contribution,' to establish a house of entertainment for War-blinded men sojourning in Rome, with lodgings, as well, for their detailed soldier escorts [2] and for the assistant personnel.

The 'house of entertainment' has just been slightly described. The workshops are under the same roof. In them are made, among other matters, a type of machine-knitted underwear used by the Army Aviation Service. And the product turned out is not merely 'good for blind men,' but good. In quantity per man per day, it equals about three quarters of that of a seeing operative; and it brings an average knitter about thirty lire for a day's work. A corps of War-widows and orphans make the yarn. And the supervision of all, like the care of the house and its guests, lies in the gentle hands of the Sisters of Dorothea of Vicenza.

An auxiliary body, headed by one of the Queen's ladies-in-waiting, Marchesa Anna Guglielmi di Vulci, and chiefly composed of the wives of principal members of the Fascist Government, concerns itself with friendly offices. Each day one or more of these ladies comes in to read aloud; or to visit the men and keep in touch with their personal and family needs, in order that upon occasions,

[1] The pension of the totally blinded ex-soldier precludes the necessity of work. But work is encouraged as a moral necessity.

[2] See *ante*, p. 319.

such as sickness or death, marriage or childbirth, or any anxiety, interest and help may not be missing. Many little parties are given for the families of the blinded, and especially for their children, with children's dances and songs, little comedies, seasonal gifts, and simple feasts. And in the auditorium, which seats four hundred persons, is arranged, at intervals of ten days or less, a series of recitals, concerts, lectures, or readings of poetry or drama for which the ladies of the auxiliary frankly compete to secure the most able artists or speakers, and the best programme in Rome. Seats not occupied by the blinded men and their families are gladly filled by distinguished Romans whom it is later a stimulus for their blinded hosts to meet in conversation.

It has seemed the more worth while to speak particularly of this feature in that such volunteer friendly work, organized, reliable, and utterly human, is not readily discovered in France or in Germany, whereas in Fascist Italy, in many shapes, it is budding into flower and spreading fast.

Also in Rome is the *Casa Madre dei Mutilati*, the 'Mother House' of Il Duce's whole scheme for Italy's act of contrition and amends for her period of coldness toward her War-maimed sons.

In another country such a place could hardly exist; in its stead would be an office building, more or less severe or ornate, barren or out-at-elbows, according to the habit of the land. But here, where everything is a symbol, this too is a symbol — a double creature, having, in an active able body, a soul of fire. No Italian puts that into words for you, but the fact is scarcely to be missed.

324

The office part, in which the records and varied business
of the entire big enterprise are handled, is practical,
business-like, plain. But the rest is simply a Presence-
House, where dwells the Apotheosis of Pain. Each piece
of wood and marble has been handled like a prayer. The
whole place breathes deep with some stern power that,
having paid the price, has conquered both self and the
sting of death, and now, unshaken and unshakable, is
satisfied — satisfied to the point of joy.

Il Duce conceived it all. And his friend Carlo Delcroix
understood — he whose eyes and hands were blown
away by an Austrian shell, yet who, today, is one of the
ablest and most respected of Italy's statesmen patriots,
and certainly the most brilliant orator in the Fascist
Parliament.

Bitterness can come to the maimed — a final outrage
blasting them downward into cynics and enemies of
mankind. Or, their suffering may be sublimated to a
challenge and a benediction.

Il Duce desired that challenge, that benediction, for
Italy. The force of his aspiration cast the die. Delcroix
could contribute his own superb example, presence, and
devotion. And so the *Casa Madre*, where Delcroix and
his comrades in courage meet, is an altar upon which
pain is laid as a thank offering and where faith and un-
swerving efforts are repledged to the greatest of all
victories.

CHAPTER IV

HONOUR MEANS HONOUR

THE present War-Pension Law of Italy was enacted in 1923, Year II of the Fascist régime. Its base is simple, imperative, and final: death or disablement in war; but the degree of disablement, to be pensionable, must reach 30 per cent.

Italy's Great War disabled ex-service men numbered 1,000,000. Of these 210,000, being less than 30 per cent disabled, were immediately awarded a lump sum indemnity and their class closed and dismissed; 275,000, being above 30 per cent disabled, were pensioned; and the remaining 515,000 refrained from presenting their claims upon the State, because of a certain pride that exists in the country concerning it.[1]

The Italian War-pension rate is, with a solitary exception, affected by two considerations only — rank, and the zone of service in which the disablement was received. Disablement incurred in the combat zone brings entitlement to higher pension than that awarded for the same injury when incurred elsewhere; as in the zone of support or supply. Thus, a colonel totally disabled in front-line action may receive an annual pension

[1] Official statement of the Director-General of the Bureau of Pensions, Ministry of Finance, Rome, September 26, 1932, to the author.

The average lump sum indemnity paid to soldiers less than 30 per cent disabled, was 1500 lire. The sum was reached by multiples, from one to six, of the pre-War annual pension of 378 lire, awarded to soldiers of the lowest pensionable disablement. See Italian Appendix III, Eighth Category. *See also* Appendix IV, Table B.

f 15,000 lire ($789), whereas, had he received that wound
hile serving in some less advanced position, his pension
ould be 825 lire less. In the case of a private soldier
tally disabled, the zone difference would figure as
etween 4080 lire ($214.61) and 3240 lire ($171.42).[1]

And, to drive the principle early home, Article 1 of
itle I of the Fascist Law of July, 1923 — the basic
ension law — expressly excludes from pensionability
ose members of the military whose service was performed
s workmen in any sort of dépôt, dockyard, or manufactur-
g plant, whether governmentally or privately run and
gardless of their having been detailed by command to
at service. As to 'swivel-chair soldiers,' Article 2 of
itle I deals with them thus: 'Sedentary [2] service carried
    outside the zone of war operations, even though in a
rritory declared to be in a state of war, will never be
onsidered as war service or relating to war.' [3]

To men whose disablement reaches certain fixed super-
ypes — and this is the 'solitary exception' alluded to
bove — a super-pension is accorded, in addition to that
ttaching to the case as 100 per cent disabled.

For example, a man who has lost both hands above
he wrist and both feet above the ankle; or a man whose

[1] *Riforma Tecnico-Giuridica delle Norme Vigenti sulle Pensioni di Guerra.* Regio
ecreto in data 12 luglio 1923, n. 1491, Tipografia Ditta L. Cecchini, Roma,
able C. This publication will hereafter be referred to as *Riforma Tecnico-
iuridica.* For the full table of pensions according to rank and degree of disable-
ent, see Italian Appendices V and VI.

[2] Article 3 of the Royal Decree, n. 1383 of 1924, defines the term 'sedentary
rvice' as used in the Law of 1923, above quoted, to signify any type of office
ork.

[3] In reckoning seniority in the civil services, one year spent in the zone of
ombat counts as two years, while service in garrison, dépôt, or bureau carries
o advantages.

sight is completely and permanently destroyed and who also suffers from another super-disability; or a man totally paralyzed by a wound on the spine, is entitled, irrespective of rank, to an additional yearly 14,400 lire ($757.44). Similarly, the totally and permanently blinded man who has lost both hands and one foot; or whose legs have been cut away in such fashion that he cannot use artificial limbs, may receive a super-pension of 9600 lire ($400) yearly in addition to his base pension as a totally disabled man. And so down by degrees of 8400, 7200, and 4800 lire, to the 2100 lire super-pension allotted to the tuberculous whose malady renders him wholly incapable of profitable work.[1]

For the rest, the law is clear and brief. It was written with the single purpose of meeting just claims justly, always balancing the claimant's needs against the country's ability to pay. It has been little altered since its enactment.

Except in cases where no possibility of improvement exists, the pensioned man is called up for medical re-examination every two years. The doctors then rate him as they find him, indicating if his allowance is to be raised, lowered, or left as it is. If his condition is discovered to be so much bettered that his disablement no longer amounts to 30 per cent diminution of earning power, the allowance automatically disappears and in its place a lump sum is given, finally closing the case. But if the increase in earning power is due, not primarily to improved

[1] *Riforma Tecnico-Giuridica, Assegni di Superinvalidita*, Article 17, and Table E; modified by Royal Decree of May 27, 1926, n. 928, Article 2. For the specific physical conditions to which these super-pensions are applied, see Italian Appendices VII and VIII.

health, but to diligence in re-education, the allowance remains as before.[1]

If he thinks his case warrants it, the pensioner may himself apply for review before the lapse of the two-year period. But the right does not survive a second exercise, although right to re-examination in due course by the State's doctor is inalienable.

After the eighth year of observation, the pension must, in principle, be fixed for life; yet the State retains its title to reopen cases at any time if an important improvement is indicated. Once the pension is fixed for life, a sick man, as distinct from one wounded, must wait five years before asking for revision and increase. But the wounded may at any time ask, and promptly receives, re-examination.

As for new claims, a man with a War-wound may always present himself. But the consideration of new appeals on grounds of War-incurred or War-aggravated sickness, closed finally on January 1, 1924.

Cases of mental disturbance, neuro-psychiatric and other, when established as War-disablement, are domiciled in the regular provincial asylums, of which special sections are amplified for ex-soldiers' accommodation. Such cases are also maintained on a per capita basis in private sanatoria. But the Fascist Government has found it neither necessary nor desirable to incur the overhead of special mental hospital building for a limited and passing use, preferring, rather, to spend the means and effort on improving hospitals available, not only to the ex-service man, but to all the people.

[1] Law of July 12, 1923.

Malarial fevers, which the Italian troops serving in Albania contracted heavily, cannot produce a claim to pension.[1]

Provisions for dealing with criminal and misdemeanant War-pensioners are mainly as follows: During imprisonments for lesser offences, when of more than a year's duration, the pensioner's pay is, in principle, cut in half. But if he has a wife, or minor children, the State retains a third of his pension, and pays the remaining two thirds to the family; or, if he be single, payments, during his imprisonment, may be made to his parents, or to his minor brothers and unmarried but not widowed sisters who would be his heirs should he die.[2]

The conviction of grave offence — an offence that debars in perpetuity from the holding of public office or from the honour of service in the National Militia — means at any time total and final forfeiture of pension.

And, in conclusion, no man found guilty of having, in time of war, committed a traitorous act or an act of cowardice, of having deserted to the enemy, or of having wounded himself in order thereby to escape service, is eligible to receive or permitted to retain any War-pension, indemnity, or allowance, even though amnesty, pardon, or even reinstatement has been accorded him. To this, one exception is possible, that of a man who, after committing his crime, has displayed distinguished gallantry in action against the enemy in the combat zone, for which

[1] Statement of the Director-General of Pensions, Ministry of Finance, Rome, September 23, 1932.
[2] Law of July 12, 1923, Title V, Article 49, and special decree of October 13, n. 926.

gallantry he has been recommended for a medal for Military Valour.[1]

As to money awards aside from the pension, accruing to the ex-service man, these were two:

First: Italy, like the other belligerent nations, granted each soldier a gratuity, or bonus, on demobilization, its amount determined by his rank and by his years of service. All below commissioned rank received 300 lire, down, with a complete civilian suit and change of clothing.

Second: Paid-up insurance policies were made available to ex-service men under certain conditions.[2] A 'simple' policy of 500 lire for a private, of 1000 lire for a non-commissioned officer, and of 1500 lire for the commissioned officer was granted to men whose War-service was active, but rendered under conditions of lesser risk. A 'mixed' policy of 1000 lire for the private and the non-commissioned officer and of 5000 lire for the commissioned officer was offered to men whose exposure had been of character more severe.

A 'simple' policy was payable only to the soldier's heirs, and at his death. The 'mixed' policy might be so paid, or might be drawn by the ex-soldier himself, thirty years after its issue. When the policy was issued in favour of a man already killed in battle, its benefits took the form of a payment of 500 lire to each of the orphaned children of men below commissioned rank and of 1000 lire to each orphan of an officer, on its coming of age. If the beneficiaries were parents, they received 1500 lire, or 1000 lire for a single parent.

[1] Law of July 12, 1923, Title V, Article 46.
[2] Decree Law of December 10, 1920, n. 1970, as modified by Decree Laws of June 7, 1920, n. 738, and January, 1922, n. 522.

With regard to the widow's pension, the salient points are these:

It is affected by the husband's rank; and it is awarded in two degrees, dependent upon the zone of action in which the late soldier's service was rendered. A 'privileged,' or higher, pension goes to the widow of a man dead in consequence of injuries received in an offensive or defensive front-line action, or otherwise at the hand of the enemy at the front; or, if he died because of injuries received from the enemy while serving elsewhere with mobilized troops, *provided* that he had already rendered good service in the zone of combat.[1]

No War-pensioner's widow can establish claim to pension if her marriage was contracted after her late husband received the service-disablement from which he died, unless the intention of marriage was published before the disablement occurred.[2] Nor can any children conceived of such marriage draw pension as a soldier's orphan. No claim can arise based on a marriage contracted after the man's discharge from military service.[3]

The widow who remarries loses her pension thereby. But the pensioned widow remarrying within fifteen years of her soldier husband's death may receive in lump payment a sum equivalent to certain multiples of her annual pension, their number depending upon her own age, thus:

Under 25 years old	seven times her annuity
Between 25 and 30	six times her annuity
Between 30 and 35	five times her annuity
Between 35 and 40	four times her annuity
Between 40 and 50	three times her annuity

[1] Law of July 12, 1923, Title II, Article 15; and Title III, Article 23. And see Italian Appendices IX and X Tables G and H, for the amount of widow's pensions.

[2] Law of July 12, 1923, Title III, Article 24.   [3] *Ibid.*, Article 29.

The widow who remarries after her fiftieth year can claim nothing.[1]

The widow who becomes a public prostitute or who has been convicted of seduction permanently forfeits her pension, as does the widow or any pensioned heir of an ex-soldier convicted of crime of the degree that bars from public office.[2]

As to the *compagne*, the 'unmarried wife' of the dead soldier: Under the pre-Fascist code she received, not an 'assistance,' as in France, but a regular pension, provided no lawful wife existed. By Fascist law this feature was abolished, except to beneficiaries already established. Today, therefore, the *compagne* who drew pension before 1923 still receives her pay. But the principle is extinguished and no such claim can now be established.

If, besides the lawful widow, there are minor orphaned children to be considered, the pension, in the case of a private soldier, is increased by 200 lire annually for the first child, 175 lire for the second, and 150 lire for each succeeding child; while the increase for children of officers, of whatever rank, is, respectively, 300, 275, and 250 lire.

If the widow dies, or forfeits her right to pension, her pension is continued to the minor orphans.[3]

The Fascist Government's Institute for the care of war-orphans, *Opera Nazionale per gli orfani di guerra*, as mentioned in the preceding chapter, is operated by a central control seated in Rome. This control maintains

[1] Law of July 12, 1923, Title III, Article 25, as modified by Royal Decree of May 27, 1926, n. 928.

[2] Law of July 12, 1923, Title V, Article 47.

[3] Law of July 12, 1923, Title III, Article 29, as affected by Article 23, 26, and 27.

a commission in each province; while in each commune of each province, under the chairmanship of the *podestà*, the municipal judge, a working committee is charged with the duty of keeping in close personal touch with the individual child, its needs, condition, and development.

For children who are ailing, the Institute has its own children's colonies, both in the mountains and by the sea; in 1930, 12,627 War-orphans were so happily domiciled. For those who need special hospital treatment, special children's hospitals are provided; or sometimes the patient is sent to a general hospital having children's wards for such cases.

Children who are mentally non-normal are cared for in two homes, one in Rome, the other in Leghorn.

Children who are ill, but who can be properly cared for at home, are looked after by the visiting nurse and supplied with medicine and food.

As far as possible, the child is left with its relatives. But if such are lacking, or if, for any reason, they are unable or unsuited to have the care of a child, excellent orphanages have been established by the Institute, where the child may remain until its eighteenth year, and where it is given an education and a trade or calling, chosen in accordance with the aptitude and intelligence developed in the individual case. The child of an agriculturist, however, must follow agricultural lines. Otherwise the question of birth and parentage affects nothing.

Great importance is attached to the development of agricultural skill in all its branches, and the Institute maintains no fewer than forty-nine agricultural school colonies for War-orphans, both boys and girls, where

are given a good home and where, with a common
ation, they are taught practical farming in all
ches.

on marriage, the Institute gives the War-orphaned
dowry, as a nest-egg for the new household; and
e boy, at his majority, a gift of working tools and of
all farm.

l this work is done at the expense of the State. It
justly be described as intelligent, sympathetic, prac-
, and constructive. Funds are used with economy,
the children are led through a happy, wholesome, and
ected minority into a useful and competent citizen-
—are handled, in a word, not only as sacred trusts
the dead, but as precious assets of the State — fur-
ing thereby a contrast devastating to the credit of
rica.

hen a War-pensioned man dies leaving neither widow
children, a maintenance allowance equal to a widow's
ion may on certain conditions be granted on his ac-
t to his father, to his mother, or to his minor brothers
sisters, the amount allowed being, as always, greater
e dead man's pension was won in the zone of combat.[1]
he conditions are as follows:

he father may claim if he is over sixty years old;
f he himself is an ex-soldier 100 per cent disabled and
pable of earning money by his labour. The mother
claim if she is a widow. The minor brothers and sis-
may claim if both father and mother are dead. But
hese claims rest on the proviso that the person or

r the amounts of the maintenance allowance see Italian Appendices IX, X,
nd XII, Tables G, H, I, and L.

335

persons concerned lack means to acquire the necessities of life, that this condition exists through no fault of their own, that the dead soldier was their essential support, and that the local governmental authorities so certify.[1]

But parents who have lost more than one son in battle may receive, for the first son lost, an annual allowance of either 990 or 810 lire ($52.07 or $42.61) according to the zone wherein the dead soldier received his injury;[2] to which foundation allowance is added, for the second boy killed, 300 lire a year; for the third, 2000 lire; and 2000 lire annually for each additional son who lost his life through War-service.

Occasion naturally recurs, in the course of the inquiry, to compare the procedure of the two Latin countries, France and Italy. At this point it is of interest to recall that while the Great-War pension roll of France, like that of America, carries a heavy weightage of men disabled less than 20 per cent, Italy's War-pension entitlement, like that of Germany, begins at 30 per cent disablement.

As has already been stated, Italy originally pensioned 275,000 Great-War-disabled ex-service men. By 1932, that number, through improvement in health or through death, had fallen to 210,000. The annual pension of these 210,000 men, for the year 1931–32, amounted to 555,000,-000 lire ($29,193,000), while annuities of dependants of the dead — parents, widows, orphans, and others — raised

[1] Law of July 12, 1923, Title IV, Article 37. In the absence of father or mother, grandparents or adoptive parents may make the claim, if they stood *in loco parentis* to the deceased.

[2] See Italian Appendices IX and X, Tables G and H. The base figure given above is that for the private soldier.

the total War-pension budget of 1931–32 to 1,155,000,000 lire ($60,753,000).[1]

The war-pension budget chart, followed through the years, shows a continuous downward trend, due, among ex-service men, to death or recovery; due, among dependants, to remarriage of widows, to coming-of-age of children, or to mortality. This downward trend, in the experience of other nations, is definitely to be expected of any War-pension system successfully defended from political interference. And the Fascist Government, up to 1932, considered its budgetary item for War-pensions as one whose rate of decline and date of closure could be forecast with almost mathematical certainty.

In the earlier half of 1932, however, began a new phenomenon. As stated in the outset of this chapter, the Italian Government's records showed the existence, at the end of the Great War, of 535,000 disabled ex-service men who refrained from claiming pension. These were people who took their War-service as a natural and rightful part of their citizenship, their disablement as a personal affair to be dealt with as such; and who, quite simply, considered it unmanly to bring wounds got in the nation's service to the door of the National Treasury. No propaganda had been put forth to create the idea; rather it was a part of the people's mind, existing of itself, without regard to rank, from officer and gentleman to simple peasant; and without regard to means, among all degrees of fortune or lack of it.

But in the early spring of 1932 came a break. Un-

[1] The figures in the paragraph rest on the statement of the Director-General of the Bureau of Pensions, Ministry of Finance, Rome, September 23, 1932, to the author, and by him corrected as of March, 1933.

employment and the pressure of the times, long resisted
by the tightening of the belt, drove an increasing number
of men, out of the half-million till then silent, to ask for
War-pensions. By the end of the summer they were coming in at the rate of between three and four hundred a
month — coming reluctantly, with gritted teeth, driven
by the needs of their families.

All of these were wounded men. Seventy-five per cent
were granted pensions at once, on the indisputable status
of their cases. And practically the whole of the remainder
were turned away, not because of bogus claims, but because their degree of disablement fell beneath the 30 per
cent by law required.[1]

The opening of so large a source of possible War-pension
claimants, uncertain in number and not included in earlier budgetary estimates, throws out the earlier Italian cal-
culations. The Great-War pension, which reached its peak
of expenditure in 1923-23, is still falling. But the men who
fought the War are yet young; for another half-century
some of them will be living and entitled to come forward.
Yet the Fascist Government's drive toward economic betterment, already so successful as to command its major
place in any speculation as to Europe's future, bids fair to
stop this movement, by enabling all men of good-will to
live without appeal to their country's bounty.

[1] Statement of the Director-General of the Bureau of Pensions, Ministry of
Finance, Rome, September 26, 1932, to the author. The Director-General adds,
as of March, 1933, that new applications at that period continued to be made at
the rate of about five hundred monthly. The Great War Army of Italy did not
undergo medical examination when demobilized. But for proof of War-origin as
to these later wound-pension claims, the official notes of wounds as shown in the
applicant's military record, or the record of the War-hospital where his wounds
were treated, is required in evidence.

CHAPTER V

IN HOC SIGNO

ITALY at the end of the War demobilized, aside from her million of disabled soldiers, nearly four million men-at-arms, most of them poor. These it was Il Duce's desire to acknowledge, yet not with a bonus, not with money in any shape.

The demobilized millions included millions of farmers. Italy is a country of farmers, her prosperity hinging largely upon agricultural success. Also she is a great consumer of cereals; yet she had never raised cereals in quantities approaching her own needs. Further, she has long and miserably suffered from malaria, a disease that saps the mental and physical vigour of any people upon whom it preys; and her malaria travelled by the wings of mosquitoes bred in her widespread marshes. Finally, there had not been enough arable land in the country to give her small farmers, bone of her bone, homes of their own.

In Il Duce's vision, the combination solved itself thus:

All marshes should be effectively drained, cleared of mosquitoes and prepared for occupation. Ex-service farmers, brought from crowded districts, should be comfortably settled on the land. And these, still disciplined soldiers of Italy, should fight for Italy 'the Battle of the Grain.'

The thing sounded simple enough. But since the days

339

of the Roman Republic, two centuries before Christ, marshes had poisoned Italy. Roman Emperors had tried to cure them. Popes had fought them, and died of them. The monks of Cluny and the Cistercians had sacrificed their lives to the task. Through the Middle Ages and into our times, the struggle has gone on. Sometimes man gained, sometimes the malady, and the graph of the two trails makes a pattern of countervailing curves. Of late some progress had been achieved. But that progress was not synchronized with the speed of Fascist Italy. Il Duce said it must strike a new gait — said that in fourteen years the entire redemption must be completed.

That was eight years ago. Since that day, through the length and breadth of Italy, some six million acres of pestilent marsh have been turned into healthful, productive fields. And eighteen million acres more, with the aid of splendid engineering construction, aqueducts, roads, dams, drainage and irrigation schemes, and the turning of river-courses, rapidly being brought under intensive cultivation, are already scattered over with small farmers' prosperous homes. In six years more, at the present rate of doing, the last mosquito marsh in Italy will have become a grainfield, a vineyard, or a market-garden, giving food to the country, good homes and a present and a future to the erstwhile poor.[1]

But let us turn to a specific example yet in process of development:

Since the beginning of recorded history, the Pontine Marshes have spread their accursed skirts to the south of

[1] See *Les Services Sanitaires et d'Hygiène dans les Régions Rurales en Italie et la 'Bonifica Integrale,'* published by the Ministry of Foreign Affairs, Rome, 1931, pp. 56–79.

Rome. Their victims in unnumbered myriads have died deaths swift and slow, and their evil work, since books were written and since travellers talked, has blackened the name of Italy.

Il Duce, coming to their case in the course of his plan, did them the honour to inspect them. What was there to inspect? A vast and miserable flat, backed almost perpendicularly by the Lepini and Volsci Mountains, and stretching from their foot to the Tyrrhene Sea. Steeped in stagnant mountain water which it lacked slope to drain away, it lay bare of everything save birds and scrub forest, mosquitoes and ooze. Yet, here and there at wide intervals, stuck on a tussock among the reeds, squatted a round grass hut with a roof like a candle-snuffer, or a square grass hut like a microscopic haystack, all dun brown like the marsh itself, invisible as a muskrat's nest, and not fifteen feet across. In those huts lodged nomad shepherds — some hundreds, perhaps — whose sheep miraculously survived upon the wretched swamp grass. As to the shepherds themselves, they seemed to exist in order that the swarming mosquitoes might have handy hosts in which to brew that poison thence dispensed through Italy.

Mussolini, having seen, gave orders. That was late in October, 1931. On November 7 arrived the first trainload of workmen — thirteen hundred ex-service men into whose web of life malaria had been so woven that this new exposure meant naught. More trainloads came, and more. In April, Il Duce returned. The forest had completely disappeared, except as represented by charcoalburners and their work; the drainage secret had been solved; fine roads had been built; five hundred houses were in process of erection, of which two hundred were already roofed; and an ample supply of good water had been established for the use of the coming colony..

'Your Excellency, could we have, here, a telegraph and telephone station and a post-office?' ventured the engineer. 'It would speed the work!'

'Next morning,' said the man who told the story, 'the telegraph-telephone men were on the spot, and in a fortnight all we had asked for was up and in working order. In other régimes, before Il Duce's day, it would have taken years to get that service. Dozens of Deputies would have made dozens of speeches, and nothing would have happened. The modest advantage of avoiding errors, proud boast of our earlier method, was modest indeed, compared to this present joy of seeing work jump.'

By October, 1932, five months after Il Duce's second visit, Littoria, as he had named it, was showing form. Around a wide central plaza, shortly to be gardened, the main buildings essential to a town were already erected, to the number of twenty-five: a church, a town hall, a post-office, a hotel, a hospital, a large schoolhouse, a theatre, a public bakery, a police headquarters, a boys' club-house; and beyond, a fine stadium for football and other games. All these public buildings, dignified and decorative, are faced with Travertine marble, like that which faced the Colosseum in Rome, 'because,' explained the chief architect, 'its slightly pitted surface gives greater sympathy of light and shade.'

As far as possible, all tributary work was being done on the spot: stone- and marble-cutting, brick-making, carpen-

342

tering and joining, structural and ornaméntal ironwork, and sculpture of fruit-filled urns, Roman eagles, and symbolic groups destined for the plaza gardens, terraces, and façades.

Around this town centre runs a broad and well-paved road. A similar road encloses the outer limits of the territory; and a working network of lesser roads opens the whole, while a drainage system of main, secondary, and tertiary canals at last effectively disposes of the excess mountain water.

The land is divided into five thousand parcels of from fifteen to thirty hectares each (about thirty-seven to seventy-four acres), the size depending upon the quality of the soil. Each of these parcels has its dwelling-house, either erected or in process of erection.

The houses, all of pale blue stucco with pink tiled roofs, are of five types, governed by size. Within they are well-proportioned, well-lighted, and airy. Floors are of hard cement; walls plastered. Shapely iron hand-rails guard stairs and stair-wells. All windows are screened, all outer doors protected by screened vestibules.[1] Each house has its stable, definitely well-drained, lighted, and ventilated,

[1] The Rockefeller Foundation, in 1925, supplied the means for the Italian Health Department to carry out demonstrations of methods, new to Europe, for the prevention of malaria. In the hands of the Italian doctors, these methods have worked out in success, and the Fascist Government is now relying on screening and larvæ control as the principal anti-malaria weapon. The Foundation is now withdrawing its assistance, but that of the Government is increasing and the work is spreading. Italy now leads Europe in malarial control.

For methods employed and results attained, see Professor A. Missiroli, Director, *La Prevenzione della Malaria nel Campo Pratico*, Relazione 1925–26, Industria Tipografica Romana, Rome, 1927. And also L. W. Hackett, M. D., Dr. P. H., Assistant Director, International Health Board, Rockefeller Foundation, *Transactions of the Royal Society of Tropical Medicine and Hygiene*, vol. XXII, no. 6, April, 1929.

with separate stalls for four or eight cattle, and for horses; it has also its storage place, its bake-oven, its chicken-house, its pig-sty, its wagon-shed, and its excellent manure-pit, all of concrete.

In that month of October, 1932, ten thousand workmen were busy in Littoria, preparing it for the coming of its future tenants. In accordance with Il Duce's plans, all ten thousand were ex-service men, with the exception of a few necessary specialists not to be found in ex-service ranks. They were getting free barracks lodging and a wage of thirty lire ($1.58) for a ten-hour day. They were running a co-operative kitchen, and buying their own food. Malaria, although perhaps ninety per cent reduced, was not yet quite extinguished, some drainage yet remaining to be done. So the police were rigorously enforcing curfew at sundown, at which moment the ten thousand, to a man, retired for the night behind mosquito screens. For sickness could not be afforded. Only one month later, Il Duce was coming formally to open Littoria and to welcome the first lot of colonists.

'You can't possibly finish in time!' one ventured to say to the chief builder.

'But we shall,' he replied.

'How can you seriously say so, in view of the mountains of work still in sight?'

'I say so, because Il Duce has willed it. And what Il Duce wills, happens.' He spoke with a half-suppressed thrill of intense pride. And indeed, all over the place, from decorators to diggers, the men were pulling with the snap of the crew of a racing-shell.

That section of the land intended for the first five hun-

344

dred tenant families, which duly arrived next month,[1] was all cured of its salt, all ploughed and ready for the harrow. 'Not before in two thousand years has it been stirred. Like all Italy, it has reposed too long. Now it, too, must wake up!' said the chief engineer. The soil looked heavy and cakey, lying there under the sun, but, rubbed in the hand, it showed a considerable element of sand. 'Good humus,' said the chief engineer; 'much better than the soil of Isola Sacra, down by Ostia, that we have already redeemed from marsh. And you saw what fine crops they grow there.'

Enormous stacks of straw and hay, brought in for the coming cattle, stood ready, square-edged and brown, like mammoth barns, at intervals all over the section. And at Azienda Elena, the Government's 4500-acre cattle-breeding farm some miles to the south, a great herd of broad-horned Maremmano bullocks awaited distribution to the new colony. For when the families arrive, they find draught cattle, cows, and a horse supplied to each house, together with tools, cart, seed, and all simple implements needed in cultivation.

Each newcomer, beginning as a tenant of the State, will, in time, become owner of the house that is meanwhile his home and of the land that meanwhile feeds his family. The instalments of payment, assessed at first very low, rise by degrees as he works up his production. By or before ten years, the tenant will hold his property in his own right, at a paid price much below anything possible by private purchase; and the State will be reimbursed, without profit, for its expenditures.

[1] By December, 1932, Littoria was housing in comfort 17,800 colonists.

345

But the manner of working the land is not left to the individual, to be well or badly handled according to his personal knowledge or lack of it, or according to his own choice of methods. The cultivation of the whole territory, mapped and planned by practical agricultural experts, is under one director; and to each section of one hundred dwellings is allotted a sub-director charged with the supervision of the performance, condition, and morale of that hundred families. Wildcat farming, if persisted in despite admonition and advice, would, equally with wildcat behaviour, cost the offender his privilege to stay.

But rarely has such an offender been found in any of these great new enterprises; for the Italian peasant, by nature sober, industrious, and thrifty, is not lacking in wit to recognize obvious butter on his bread.

Now, as we have already seen, Il Duce's purpose in pushing this nation-wide land-redemption scheme contains several elements, none of which is greater than his desire to encourage ex-service men. To ex-service men is given the work of preparing the land and of building the houses. And, when it comes to choosing the inhabitants for these new worlds, again he turns to ex-service men, applying a process of selection:

First, a region is chosen wherein unemployment weighs heaviest. Then its men who fought with credit in the zone of combat are reviewed. And from among their numbers are picked those poor men of good character and habits, who are agriculturists, yet who own no land and who have the largest families.

The families number from ten to eighteen members. The selection of such units serves a double end — that of relieving congested sections, of counteracting the tendency to move into the cities, and of providing the greatest number of workers for the new enterprise, since, from grandparents to little children, each individual in the Italian peasant household lends a hand to the family task.

The education of children, however, is by no means overlooked. Both religious and secular, this is a matter of special solicitude in the whole Fascist plan of life, and Littoria is no exception to the rule. Il Duce, however, believes in education that leads into necessary jobs, rather than into proficiencies for which only a luxury market exists. And Italy's great need is for intensive agriculture.

The pupils in Littoria's schools are all heirs to good farms. Il Duce, as an established principle, takes no farmers' sons from the land.[1] Consequently, the boys, in addition to a sufficient common schooling, are thoroughly grounded in such practical scientific knowledge as will enable them to better their father's agricultural work. The girls, with equal thoroughness, are groomed for farmers' helpmates; added to their three R's, they are trained in domestic hygiene, the care of the house, simple nursing, the care of children, the care of bees and the smaller animals, and the culture of fruit trees and vegetables. When their time comes, they will not go begging for husbands.

As for the boys' club, the 'House of the Balilla,' with its gymnasium, its baths and lockers, its auditorium, its movie-room, its first-aid clinic, and all the rest, it is one of the best of the many good buildings in Littoria Plaza.

Littoria will, within two years' time, be supporting 5000

[1] It is customary, however, in the case of children showing marked promise along special lines, to give them special educational opportunities in accordance therewith.

347

ex-service men and their families in a safe and useful life, with all their reasonable needs and ambitions satisfied.

Meantime, two similar development centres, Sabauda and Pontina, are repeating its history in other sections of the same redeemed tract. And all these throw their strength into the Battle of the Grain.

Il Duce, in his seven years' campaign, has already so reduced grain importation as to ensure the issue of that battle — a new triumph soon to be added to the roster of his victories.[1] The rate of progress is most easily grasped through contrasted figures:

	1910–1917 (cwt.)	1925–1932 (cwt.)
Average annual total production	49,000,000	63,600,000
Average annual production per hectare	10.3	13.4

Italy's total grain production of 1932 was 75,000,000 hundredweight, with an average annual hectare production of 15.2 hundredweight, rising to a maximum of 70 on choice ground. Intensive cultivation is strongly emphasized.

The scheme displayed in Littoria is by no means the only method devised by Il Duce to benefit non-disabled ex-service men. Many different avenues have been opened, all under State control, through the National Institute for Combatant Soldiers. But their general spirit may be gathered from the one instance just roughly described.

On the whole, Fascist Italy has done more for her able-bodied ex-soldiers than has any other European nation. But she has done it all through giving, not of bonuses, but of the opportunity to work as before they fought, with all

[1] Since the writing of these words comes news that in October, 1933, the victory is won. Italy has achieved the production of all grain needed for home consumption.

their heart and strength, for the good of the whole nation. She has conferred upon her sons the honour of assuming that they are not mercenaries — that their pride is still in giving, not in getting, where their country is concerned.

And no one breathing Italy's air today could so mistreat his own intelligence as to imagine either her government countenancing or her men stooping to pick out of the mud that sorry label that America's able-bodied ex-service men have wrung from Congress or have extorted from the nation — the 'disability allowance' for peace-time ailments given merely because the man once served.

The capital appropriated by the Fascist Government for this whole work for non-disabled ex-service men was 1,500,000,000 lire ($78,900,000). The results achieved, in relation to the sum, are amazing. The same thing is true of the Government's work for the War-disabled, described in a preceding chapter.

'How is it possible to have done so much with so little money?' I addressed the question to an American resident in Italy, one eminently placed, whose public responsibilities over a period of years have ensured his knowing whereof he speaks.

'"How was it done?"' he repeated; 'it was done by a poverty stricken people living on the edge of starvation and paid for out of taxes. It was done for them by a leader who has killed graft and shiftlessness out of his Government, who sees to it that not a penny in transit sticks to any fingers; and who imposes discipline and gets efficiency all along the line. My colleagues who come here from work in America and other parts of Europe say that this is the only country in the world whose Government is planning for the future. Before Mussolini, we had here a mass of ignorant voters controlled by bosses, and a Government that was merely a private battle, while all the country's business was paralyzed by jockeying and debate.'

'How is it possible to have effected so much with so little money?' Again I asked the question, this time of a distinguished scientist.

His face lighted. 'Before this day,' he said, 'public money ran in streamlets, branching, branching, and always sticking by the way. Now it flows in one big stream, and a million lire spent means the full million's worth accomplished. No good idea, now, is denied fair trial. No obstacle is thrust in its way to success. All energies press in one single direction. Everything helps. If a man fails now, it is because he deserves to fail. Oh, this is a great time to be in Italy — a glorious day for work!'

'But you have lost your liberty — your precious liberty of speech?' This question was addressed to an Italian whose life is spent in constructive public work of a high order of humanity and effectiveness.

He smiled, whimsically: 'We had an indigestion of liberty before,' he replied. 'You know that peasant proverb: "Where there are two cocks to crow, the sun never rises"? Surely cocks and to spare were crowing their heads off, in pre-Fascist Italy! And what came of their noise? Our sky was black. Are you quite, quite sure that free crowing for everybody is as important as sunrise?

'Fascism is the opposite of anarchy. It means discipline, order, and pride in one's own work. Think of Fascist Italy not as a soldier, but rather as a worker — a good worker in all fields — moral, intellectual, industrial, agri-

350

cultural. Under Il Duce we have become a morally strong and disciplined nation. Our people are sober, responsible, knowing their business, united in a will to produce the country's highest good. Even those thousands of labourers you saw in the Pontine Marshes — even they work seriously, respecting the orders of their engineers. If they should be required to become soldiers again, they would do that also in the same spirit of conscious responsibility, purpose, and discipline. They consider their country's business their business and are proud of it.'

One day opportunity was granted to inquire of Il Duce himself [1] his judgment on the right relation between a National Government and its ex-service men. Without a wasted syllable, his answer covers the case.

'Governments have a duty toward their ex-soldiers who have served the country.

'The Fascist Government recognized that duty as to its ex-soldiers. Therefore it established two Associations, one of the *Combattenti*, the other of the *Mutilati ed Invalidi*.[2]

'Both these Associations are very calm. They are confident that the Government has given them help to the extent of its power.

'We have no problem of ex-soldiers in Italy. It does not exist. Our ex-soldiers are the supporters of the Government. The most important feature in the coming celebration, in Rome, of the Tenth Anniversary of the Fascist Revolution, will be the parade of mutilated veterans. On that

[1] Palazzo Venezia, Rome, September 29, 1932, in private audience.

[2] The Prime Minister, in speaking here of the Association, rather than the Institute (cf. *ante*, p. 316), was emphasizing their representation of the ex-service man, rather than of Government. To say that 'these Associations are calm' is to say that the ex-service men are content and satisfied.

day, the twenty-eighth of October, sixteen thousand of them will gather to take part as a body in that celebration.

'This is in manifestation of their sympathy with the Fascist Government.

'All members of the Fascist Government are veterans. All have been wounded, all decorated for gallantry in the field.

'I myself am a *mutilato* [smiling faintly down at a scarred left hand]. I do *not* draw my pension. I renounced it.

'*Our old soldiers are a strong moral force in the nation.*'

It seems difficult, to many of us Americans, to accept the sincerity of Italy's talk of spiritual rebirth. Does our difficulty arise from the fact that we, as a people, have not as yet completed that descent from which Italy is so rapidly mounting? Italy, long misgoverned by egoists, weaklings, cynics, and theorists, lived the doctrine of 'self-expression' straight down its successive stages until she rotted apart and dropped into hell — whither the way is easy for others to follow. But the fires of hell did her this service — they burned away much vanity; they forced her to measure those values that accrue when each man follows his own fancy, goes his own way, seeks his own advantage as pictured by his own little brain.

Then came one calling — calling till heaven rang back the call, in words as plain as this: 'You shall rise from pursuing personal ends. You shall join to build one continuing will, for the service of God Eternal and of our Italy.' Those whose ears had been opened understood and obeyed.

That is why, today, words of fiery faith are spoken in all sincerity by the men whose united strength and exhilara-

352

t is evoking in Italy an upward thrust found in
tion of our time.

in the *Casa Madre dei Mutilati*, on the wall of
:oom, hangs a relief sculptured in white marble.
ent work of an ex-soldier totally blinded in the
his votive offering. Before his blinding — and
ι glimmer of light — he was a simple stonema-
ιt of the sculptor's art.

ntre of the relief, dominant, is the figure of
ιe Cross. From behind and beyond, hosts of
ress forward. As they near, more and more
are revealed as soldiers, till the foremost, steel-
le before Him. Until they reach the foot of the
keep their soldiers' garb. But as they pass be-
helmets disappear, the heads are bared, and
ιe shoulder is a spade, a sickle, a matlock, or a
ε column swings on and away.

s carved the inscription, *In Hoc Signo*.

es it mean?' I asked — for the blinded sculp-
side me.

— the soul of our new Italy.'

ENGLAND

ENGLAND

CHAPTER I

STRONGER THAN DEATH

EARLY in 1916. A hillside on Gallipoli Peninsula, swept by
Turkish guns. A British officer just regaining consciousness, vaguely struggling to rise. He turns on his side —
tries to stand — but his throat chokes with blood. Shot
through the head — and through the back of his tongue.
He drops on all fours. Stretcher-bearers approach — some
sort of hospital people. The wounded man raises imploring
eyes. 'Half an hour to live if you stay as you are, sir. Ten
minutes if you move' — and they pass on.

'Funny thing, this War —' thinks the man on all fours,
foggily. 'We have a row with Germany — and here am I,
fighting *Turks!* What for?... Mix-up somewhere. Who's
to blame? The Kaiser?... Something wrong with this
crazy world.... In a couple of hours they'll scoop a hole in
the ground... right here... roll me in, uniform and all...'

Presently he feels for his pocket — draws out a pencil
and a bit of paper — marks on it, somehow, 'Hospital' —
and pushes it toward another stretcher-team that comes
along.

'Sorry, sir. Orders are to bring in those that have a
chance. You'd be dead before we got you there. Sorry,
sir' — and these too pass on.

'I don't want to die' — protests the man on all fours, arguing to himself within his shattered head. 'I don't want to die. I want to be in London to see the Peace Parade.' Nor does it occur to him, in that half-choked dream, that the Peace Parade may be in Berlin.

Then he wants to pray, yet forbids himself — 'It isn't fair — you haven't prayed for years, and now you come whining around for notice when you're in the last ditch!' But the need conquers him — he *must* pray. 'Well, then — not for something for nothing — *God — if You give me my life, I'll try to make it count toward Your other men.*' Then, testing the bargain, he starts to crawl. Crawls on hands and knees, choking, falling, fainting, up and on again, half a mile to a dressing-station — and there blots out.

Three blank days and three blank nights in the same muddy bandages all the way to Egypt. Then, because of some odd chance, they shove him aboard a transport full of wounded New Zealanders bound home.

Men without legs, without arms, without eyes, lying around the deck — so many that the doctors and the nurses can scarcely handle their jobs. But the man with a bullet through his head begins to mend. 'A bargain's a bargain,' presently he says to himself. 'My legs and arms, my eyes and ears must be good for something.' So he turns in to help those no longer so fortunate.

Day after day through the long voyage, doing odds and ends for the helpless, he learns the others' minds — young New Zealanders, farmers' sons, doctors' sons, sons of all the land, big, sturdy, open-air boys flung down on this deck like so many felled trees. What had it all been about? They didn't know. Around and around in their patient, puzzled heads they were turning the question. How had it happened? Well, word had come one day that the Empire was at war and needed men. So, of course, in their thousands, they had down-tooled and run to sign up. What was the War about? What did that matter? Empire's business. The War was in France, against Germany — so much they understood. And they started out on ships. But then why, when they started for France to fight Germany, had they arrived in Gallipoli to fight Turks? And why, before they had time to do anything at all for the Empire, were they here on this deck, like logs banked in rows, without arms, without legs, without eyes, going home? They hadn't even a story to tell the home people — it had all happened so quickly; nothing but bandages and flattened kitbags to show for their trip. Nothing else to show.

'I've got a few snap-shots. If you'd like copies I'll have some made and send 'em to you. Give me your address,' said the man with the bullet through his head. And then he would add — for he was a senior officer on board — 'If there's anything I can do for you, in New Zealand, within the next few weeks, let me know.'

The voyage over, they all scattered — some carried away by their people, some dropped into hospitals, and the rest who knows where? But the man with the bullet through his head, having sent the snap-shots, began getting letters: 'You very kindly said, on the ship, I was to write you. I'm in hospital, away in the South. My friends are all in the North. Why can't I go North?' — and *vice versa;* dozens of letters like that. Or: 'When I landed I had a kitbag full of things I need and care for. It has disappeared and everything is lost. Could you possibly start an

359

inquiry?' Or: 'When I went overseas I made an allocation of pay to my mother. She never got anything. Could you find out why?' And: 'Before, I was a farmer. Now I've lost a leg. What am I to do? I've lost caste. I don't want to live.'

'Why don't I tour around and visit them all?' thought the man with the bullet through his head. So he toured New Zealand, finding forty, fifty, sixty wounded men in each town. And this only from the first shipload sent home.

'There'll be plenty more ships and plenty more problems,' said the man to his new friends. 'We all started out all right, with our minds made up to serve the Empire. It'll take more than Turks to stop us now. How about forming an Association to stick together and get on with the job?'

And that was how such things began.

But this particular man with the bullet through his head reported back to England on New Year's Eve, 1917, for orders to the Front.

CHAPTER II

SOLDIERS COME HOME

WHETHER from Gallipoli or from France, whether from
Baghdad or from Palestine, the Briton's homeward road
was short, and, as the War wore on, increasing multitudes
of broken men travelled it — men unfit for further fighting. The country received them as best it could, but its
major thought — its life-or-death effort — was outward-
directed toward the struggle in the field. And the old pre-
Great War pension law and system had not yet been adjusted to the needs of a new day.

So the men themselves, disabled, discharged, and
largely thrown back on their private devices, began to
form little groups — little relief organizations of their own
— in various parts of the country. Three or four such organizations took shape and increased in size before Armistice Day, before demobilization began, before the great
wheels of the War Machine, arrested in their course with a
sudden, dislocating shock, could start turning in the opposite direction. Then more men — millions more men —
came trooping home to the country they had helped to
save, believing with gladness that the good life lay ahead;
that when they had rested a bit, good jobs would come to
their hands in the good, new, remade world.

Alas, the disappointment that awaited them! The work
of the country during their absence at the Front had multiplied and gone forward with desperate energy. Every
place had of necessity been filled. That necessity needed

361

no argument. Production of munitions and supplies had meant survival or destruction to the whole nation. And yet, now the fight was over, now the tension was relaxed and the wreckage exposed, the thought of high wages long enjoyed by able-bodied munitions workers safe at home bred a resentment, as natural and as bitter as it was illogical, in the minds of demobilized fighting men at loose ends for livelihood, sick at heart and out of step, suddenly cast up as no better than embarrassments and superfluities to their own people.

The men that had been kept under cover and paid much cash still held the jobs — the jobs other men had left to go to the War, and now in vain asked back again. Women held the jobs. A younger generation held the jobs. The Southern Irish held the jobs — a people whose loyalty was spotty, who had refused conscription, who had but thinly volunteered, and who then, awaiting their chance, had swarmed over like locusts to occupy the land and the fatness thereof when its own men's backs were turned.

Also, inequalities developed in demobilization itself. Some men who had come out late were called back early, because of good reasons insufficiently explained. Some men who had friends seemed to escape sooner than others, creating thereby a feeling of unfairness, quick to spread in the post-Armistice atmosphere of rumour and discontent.[1]

[1] See Winston Churchill, *Aftermath of War*, Charles Scribner's Sons, New York, p. 19.

See also, *Ministry of National Service, 1917–1919. Report upon the Physical Examination of Men of Military Age*, His Majesty's Stationary Office, London, 1920, vol. 1, p. 5.

Large numbers of able-bodied men of military age needed in agriculture, mining, ship-building, and munitions works were retained at home, exempted from recruitment until the casualties among the fighting forces compelled the gradual

In a word, general conditions favoured the breeding of disaffection; busy Communist agitators sought and found their openings; the new ex-service organizations began taking on political colour, and one, at least, tended distinctly to the far Left.

Well before the War ended, men at the Front had scented danger. 'We must look after this thing,' they said to each other anxiously. 'When we get home, we must pull the men together for the new start.'

Major-General Sir Frederick Maurice formed an association of officers with that purpose chiefly in view. The National Character responded, and the normal Briton, returned to civil life, carried with him his sense of responsibility toward the common weal.

Then Field Marshal Sir Douglas Haig came home — Commander-in-Chief of the victorious British Army — a gallant, simple soldier, a great figure. And when, following tradition, the King, welcoming him, would have expressed the Nation's gratitude by raising him to the peerage, he quietly refused that honour. He could accept nothing for himself, he said, until his men had been properly cared for — until Parliament had enacted a general pension law adequate to the needs of the War-disabled. His declaration undoubtedly hastened an already impending step. That step assured, he took his title.

'Bonus' payments were fixed and paid at a rate higher than those adopted by any other of the nations treated in

combing-out of all home workers. The process did not reach its height until the fourth year of the War. When the War ended and demobilization began, industrial 'key men' so recently come out, were among the first recalled. The advisability of explaining this movement was possibly somewhat overlooked; misunderstanding resulted.

363

this book. The following 'statement of measures on behalf of ex-service officers and men who served in the Great
War' put into effect at the time of demobilization, comes
from the British War Office, under date of October, 1932:

1. *Gratuities.*
    (*a*) All temporary officers received on demobilization a
substantial gratuity to assist them in returning to civil life.
This was based on rank and length of service and was calculated at the rate of 124 days' pay for the first year of service and 62 days' pay for each further year or part of a year.
For example, an infantry lieutenant with 2½ years' service
received £142.12.0 ($962).[1]   (Cost: £30,000,000.)
    (*b*) A special war gratuity, varying according to rank and
length of service from £5 to £39 ($24.30 to $189.54), was
also paid to men who served in the ranks.
                            (Cost: £100,000,000.)
    (*c*) In addition, nearly 4,000,000 men were granted on
dispersal four weeks' furlough on full pay and allowances
to enable them to seek employment. (Cost: £40,000,000.)

2. *Clothing.*
    Plain clothes, or an allowance in lieu, were given to all
men on demobilization.   (Cost: £10,000,000.)

3. *Repatriation.*
    Officers and men who came from abroad to join the Brit-
ish Army were repatriated to the numbers of approximately 11,000 and 24,000, respectively. Free conveyance
was also granted to their families, and widows, and orphans,
to the number of 13,000.   (Cost: £1,119,000.)

4. *Unemployment Insurance.*
    During the period of demobilization, ex-soldiers (and cer-
tain members of the Women's Corps) were given free policies entitling them to special allowances during periods of
unemployment within twelve months from the date of demobilization (or 25-11-1918 in the case of individuals who

[1] The pound sterling is here computed at the parity of $4.86. See
Appendix I.

364

had already been demobilized before that date) and this period of eligibility was subsequently extended in many cases.

But these steps, liberal though they were, scarcely affected the greater issue. Thoughtful men were more than a little anxious concerning the morale of the demobilized millions now confronting bad economic conditions, difficult mental readjustment, and the insidious poison of preachers of class hatred. In their anxiety, they came to Earl Haig for help. Would he, they asked, become president of a new association of ex-service men, to combat such disintegrating forces?

He would, he replied; but on certain fixed conditions only: all the several existing organizations must come together in one. To make an Anglo-American brotherhood would be best of all; but in any case there must be no competing of interests, no invitation to vendettas between one ex-service organization and another in the same English town or Scots workshop or Welsh hospital. Fighting the Germans abroad was enough of fighting and in that they had stood together, comrades and friends. They must not now start rivalries at home, confusing the public and the press while befogging the clarity of their own ideals. To perpetuate the old comradeship; to carry on in peace as they had in war; to be loyal to the King. That was enough.

Yet, if they wanted Haig for their leader, three things more they must do: they must pledge their new organization to maintain true democracy; to keep clear of politics in any form; clear, too, of sectarian religious partisanship.

Keen to serve again under their old Commander-in-Chief, by degrees the original organizations surrendered. One by

one they discarded their machinery, accepting his conditions, until at last the road was clear for a unity embracing
all. On July 1, 1921, the British Legion came into being,
with H.R.H. the Prince of Wales as Patron, Field Marshal
Earl Haig as President, and, as Chairman, Corporal Thomas
Frederick Lister.

As it started, so has it gone on. Says Major-General Sir
Frederick Maurice,[1] its present President:

'It was the great force of Haig's personal character that
carried the thing through into final steady form. He was
no speaker. He could do nothing from the platform. But
men felt, of Haig: "Here is a man who served through the
entire War with honour. He is well entitled to sit down in
enjoyment of his honours and to rest. Instead, he devotes
his whole energies, first to getting the men taken care of;
and then, to winning them to the ideal of service, not gain,
as the purpose of their union."

'He was a deeply religious man, and that fact shone
through everything. He was also extremely simple-
minded and sincerely unaware of the country's admiration.
Once, while the Legion was yet unformed, we went on a
tour together. Passing through Wales, we approached the
district of the great Rhondda mines, known to be much affected by Communism. The news of Haig's coming preceded us. As we drew near the mines, the colliery whis-
tles declared the fact, the little Welsh miners in their thousands trooped out of their pits, and for thirty miles the
road was lined with his old soldiers, cheering their hearts
out at the sight of his face. At which he was overwhelmed
with profound amazement.

[1] Statement to the author, London, October 17, 1932.

'There can be no question that his tireless work for the Legion and for the post-war interests of the men shortened his days.'

Yet, at the very first it was obvious that the appeal of the British Legion, addressed to all ex-service men, to join the organization, was finding its quickest response among those who wanted something for themselves; eliciting less attention from such as were comfortably established in their various ways and stations. This tendency Lord Haig attacked in a vigorous challenge especially directed to ex-service men who were happily circumstanced, adjuring them to join the Legion, not only to help finance it, but, more, to convince the public of its unselfish purpose.

And in this he had the help, all over the country, of officers of his old army now returned to civil life, but animated as keenly as himself with a sense of continued personal responsibility; quick, therefore, to see and discourage false starts. Hundreds of instances illustrate it — as, for example, that which occurred in a town in Buckinghamshire, when a mass meeting of ex-service men was called to hear a speaker sent down from London to recruit for the infant Legion. Captain George Bowyer [1] held the chair. All went well until the guest speaker, warmed with his argument, uttered this final phrase:

'And besides, every man of you should join the Legion, because, you know, *you never can tell what you may get out of it.*'

Instantly the chairman, white with anger, sprang to his feet. 'I dissociate myself from the speaker's last words. If we men here tonight join this organization, it will be for

[1] Now Captain Sir George Bowyer, M.C., M.P.

what we can put into it for the country, not for what we can get out of it for ourselves. The opposite suggestion is an affront to the old uniform.'

Next day the misfit speaker, duly reported, was sacked by Legion Headquarters. But young Captain Bowyer, running true to breed then, as since, in that one sure loyal stroke had cast the die and coined the gold of Buckinghamshire.

The general aim of the British Legion, as phrased in brief by Major-General Sir Frederick Maurice, is 'to keep alive in the country the spirit that saw us through the War, and to set an example of service and comradeship.'

Eligibility lies with the following persons: All ex-service men and women [1] who have served at least seven days with the Colours in His Majesty's Navy, Army, Air Force, or any Auxiliary Force, excepting conscientious objectors: all men and women of the Merchant Marine afloat during hostilities; all men and women of St. John's or St. Andrew's Ambulance Association or of the British Red Cross Society who served with Crown forces.[2]

The annual Conference takes place at Whitsuntide each year, beginning with a vast and profoundly impressive open-air religious ceremony at the Cenotaph in London, led by the King.

The main governing body consists of a President and Vice-Presidents, a Chairman, Vice-Chairman, and Treas-

[1] Seventeen thousand, one hundred and eighty women served with the British Expeditionary Force in France, as nursing sisters, ambulance drivers, canteen workers, etc., including 842 American women working with the Royal Army Medical Corps. *Statistics of the Military Effort of the British Empire During the Great War, 1914–1920*, The War Office, March, 1922, p. 93. This publication will hereafter be referred to as *Military Effort*.

[2] British Legion Royal Charter, Section 7.

urer, and a National Executive Council, all elected and all
voluntary workers — men, it may well be added, who are
not figureheads, but who take their work seriously. These,
when on duty, are entitled to actual travelling expenses,
but receive nothing whatever beyond. In addition there is
a small paid secretarial staff in Central Headquarters in
London and in each of the thirteen areas into which, for administrative purposes, the country is divided.

The funds, aside from membership dues, come from two
main sources, the first being the surplus capital that remained with the War Service Canteens when they closed
their accounts. These canteens had done an enormous
business, in food, clothing, etc., with British troops in the
battle areas. The end of the War found them with a credit
balance of over £16,097,000 ($78,231,420). This was di-
vided [1] among the benefit funds of the several branches of
His Majesty's Forces — Home, Dominion, and Indian —
whom the canteens had served, a portion going to America
on account of American troops that had fought in British
sectors.

When the distribution had been made in due proportion,
there remained about seven and one quarter million pounds
sterling. This, christened the United Services Fund, was
dedicated to ex-service relief work in the United Kingdom.
Provided with a charter of its own, this organization is entirely distinct from the Legion, although Legion members
form a majority on the directorate, and the United Services Fund furnishes a part of the Legion's resources.

Lord Haig, as President of the Legion, soon saw, how-

[1] War Service Canteens (Disposal of Surplus) Act, 1922 [12 & 13 Geo. 5,
ch. 53].

ever, that needs would arise beyond the powers either of membership dues or of the United Services Fund to answer. He himself then, to raise more money, invented 'Poppy Day.' And Poppy Day has struck so true a chord in the Nation's heart that, as regularly as November 11 dawns, the people each year, until calamitous 1931, exceeded all previous records in their buying of red poppies. In view of the straits through which the country has meantime been struggling, the figures are sufficiently remarkable: [1]

1921	£106,000	1927	£442,326
1922	158,307	1928	503,348
1923	203,364	1929	518,489
1924	272,426	1930	524,650
1925	338,560	1931	501,000
1926	360,256	1932	481,000 [2]

The collection of these great sums is accomplished, each year, in a single day's effort. Every Armistice Day a quarter of a million volunteer poppy sellers, directed by four thousand volunteer committees, do the work. And the cost of organizing and selling has uniformly kept below five per cent of the amount collected.

As for the making of the poppies, that provides year-round occupation, in the British Legion Poppy Factory, for 276 ex-service men 80, 90, or 100 per cent disabled, among whom some 200 limbs are missing, as well as a considerable number of other normal belongings.

In the first six months of 1932, these men turned out 30,000,000 poppies, 36,000 wreaths, and a general supply

[1] They do not include the contribution of Scotland. These, always handsome, are collected and disbursed by the British Legion in Scotland, a semi-separate and autonomous body.

[2] Figures uncompleted.

of similar beautifully made hand-work. They earn, individually, up to £3.10s. a week — sums which, in addition to their disablement pensions, make them and their families amply comfortable. A charming little settlement, with its model dwellings, its park, bowling green, and gardens, built by the Legion for the Poppy Factory men, adjoins the plant, which is in Richmond near London. Here also is a cozy club-house for the families' enjoyment, with card-rooms, billiard-rooms, library and lounges, and with special rooms for the boys and girls — both Scouts and Cubs, Girl Guides and Brownies.

For these it was — these little children of his old soldiers — that Lord Haig made his last earthly effort, coming to spend a happy hour with them the day before his death.

In his own Scotland they buried him, in the crumbling ruins of Dryburgh Abbey, out in the open under the sky. And they marked the spot with a common soldier's wooden cross bearing his name on a tag of metal, such as, by hundreds of thousands, mark his soldiers' graves in France.

Over the sod that covers him lies always one red poppy wreath, made by his soldiers' hands.

CHAPTER III

THE BRITISH LEGION

ANOTHER conspicuous enterprise of the British Legion, and one to which Poppy-Day money has largely contributed, is Preston Hall [1] and its surrounding 'British Legion Village.'

Preston Hall, lying in the midst of England's 'garden county,' Kent, is a large private country house converted to hospital uses. It is intended for ex-service patients only, whether War-pensioners or men lately broken down by tuberculosis not demonstrably service-connected. Patients are admitted irrespective of the stage of the disease. Its beds number two hundred and thirty-five, of which some seventy-five are now occupied by non-pensioners. But if vacancies chance to occur, it is the Legion's present policy to fill them with tuberculous male dependants of ex-service men, on the understanding that they must give place if the room is needed for service cases.[2]

As a hospital, Preston Hall is, in atmosphere, exceedingly homelike. But its outstanding feature is the use of work as therapy. Close at hand are a series of shops in which is conducted the building of portable dwelling-houses, poultry-houses, motor caravan bodies, etc., and

[1] The British Legion assumed responsibility for Preston Hall in 1925. The prototype of the scheme was Sir Pendrill Varrier-Jones's pioneer work, still continuing, at Papworth.

[2] Non-War-pensioned patients are paid for on a capitation basis by the health authorities of the counties whence they came; for the care of pensioned patients the Ministry of Pensions reimburses the Legion.

fine cabinet work; wood-graining; the marbling of asbestos
panels; the making of leather and fibre suitcases, and various other manufactures. Here also is a printing department that does 80 per cent of the British Legion's work,
almost all that of the United Services Fund, much of the
Red Cross's printing, and an increasing amount for the
general public — and does it extremely well.

If Preston Hall be taken as the centre of a circle one
hundred miles in diameter, that circle embraces a population of twelve and a half million people. In other words,
being near London, it can reach a large market. In 1931
the total cash turn-over in Preston Hall industries was
more than £80,000, with a total profit of 16s. 8d. With approximately the same turn-over, 1932 showed a loss of
£300. But the payroll, in wages, was £16,500; and all of it
went to the men who had done the work — the patients.

Says Dr. J. B. McDougall, Medical Director and Superintendent of the whole enterprise, a man of contagious vitality and enthusiasm: 'A stranger might object: "This is
a factory, not a sanatorium." But suitcases and poultry-
houses are medicine at heart; and their selling is of small
importance compared with the curative value of giving
the sub-normal man, under hygienic conditions of living
and working, and under careful medical supervision, a way
of earning his living. In six years we have not had one man
unemployed who was fit for work.' [1] And he has quoted
with sympathy the criticism of an eminent English medical
health officer: 'Many of our modern Sanatoria might be

[1] Statement to the author. See also J. B. McDougall, M.D., M.R.C.P., *Occupational Therapy: an Adjunct in the Treatment of Tuberculosis.* British Journal
of Tuberculosis, April, 1927; cf. the *Rehabilitation Review*, January, 1932, The
American Rehabilitation Committee, Inc., New York.

named "The Lounger's Paradise," where men eat and sleep, drink and smoke, and then, when they can muster energy, play a game of cards.'

'"How long are you in for?" one sulky patient asks of another,' adds Dr. McDougall, 'And the second yawns as he sighs, "Three months."'

No visitor to Preston Hall shops can fail to be impressed with the rising tide of life there visible, nor to see the upward shove that a convalescent gains when he finds he can work like other men, match them and get forward. Trades are there to suit any taste, each man taking his choice. And when, one day last autumn, some genius among themselves found out a brand-new industry with market complete, the whole place sparked with excitement.

The British Legion Village, a mile or so distant from Preston Hall, is a nucleus settlement of one hundred and thirty small modern cottages implanted in a two-hundred-acre estate, gradually built by the Legion with Poppy-Day money. These cottages are one-family homes for ex-service men who served at the Front, and whose tuberculosis has been arrested by treatment in Preston Hall. The rent averages six shillings a week. Each cottage sits in its own garden of vegetables and flowers. The settlement also has its hotel for unmarried men, its school, its cinema-house and concert-hall, its club-house, its mothers' clinic, its child-welfare centre, its medical attendance, its post-office, its general store — whose turn-over is £250 a week — and its abundantly productive farm.

Residence in the village is granted only to the man whose treatment in the hospital has expired with satisfactory results, who is able to work at least thirty-eight

374

hours a week, who is relatively efficient in the work he has
been doing while under treatment, whose chances, under
care, are reasonably good and who, the Director feels, is the
right type for a settler as regards industry, character, and
temperament. Such may keep their cottage homes as long
as they like; enjoying meantime the certainty of steady employment in the workshops, all under medical supervision.

If a settler suffers a relapse of his old malady, he returns
to Preston Hall hospital for treatment. But the likelihood
is minimized by the constant attention under which he
lives, both in his home life and at work.

It may well be said that these men are ideally circumstanced — pleasantly and comfortably housed, earning
sufficient money, paying very little rent, their families well
cared for, no doctors' bills to meet, and the whole British
Legion behind them. Not least, they are enjoying the
companionship of their children in the knowledge that no
child, in the history of the village, has become infected.[1]

But Dr. McDougall adds this statement: 'I say that
every man who has the bacillus in his sputum should be
pensioned as not less than 80 per cent disabled. His expectation of life is such that he should be freed from all
economic worry.'[2]

In view of the more general practice — Italy's being
the distinguished exception — by which the tuberculous
patient, having been hospitalized and his disease arrested,
is without precaution thrown back or allowed to go back

---

[1] Dr. McDougall considers more striking the fact that among the births that
have taken place in the village, since 1927, there has been no case of tuberculous
meningitis.

[2] Statement to the author, Preston Hall, October 21, 1932.

into the competitive labour market, there often to relapse and break down under the strain, meantime infecting his neighbours, the British Legion Village demonstration is of world significance. Its principle seems likely soon to be adopted as a part of England's general public health procedure.

Although both the Poppy Factory and Preston Hall, with their contingent settlements, are of peculiar interest, they by no means form the major part of the British Legion's work — a matter too extensive even to be indexed here. With branches [1] all over the country, it penetrates the whole social structure, bringing relief in many forms to ex-service men and their dependants in cases beyond the scope of State agencies. Thus, it facilitates emigration to the colonies, first investigating and preparing the candidates. It gives small business loans and grants. It maintains many employment agencies, conscientiously patronized by employers of the better class. It provides business training for widows and orphans. Through the Officers' Department it aids ex-officers' needy widows and dependants, not only in their physical necessities, but by advising and intervening in difficult situations. It does a great work in caring for special needs in the education of children. Through the Prince of Wales's Fund, it relieves ex-service men and women prematurely aged as a result of War-service hardship; in general, it serves as the ex-service man's friend in matters beyond the Ministry's Warrant, helping him and his to find their way out of troubles and mystifications of whatever sort.

[1] 'Branches' correspond to the American Legion 'posts.' No attempt has been made here to deal with the British Legion in Scotland.

THE BRITISH LEGION

Toward the Ministry of Pensions, with whom the
Legion's relations are co-operative, it acts as the ex-
service man's advocate, investigating his case and
presenting its strongest aspect. In that capacity it
renders the Ministry much valued and much appreciated
assistance.

And yet, with all this varied scheme of benevolence,
so admirably dovetailing with the work of the Government, the Legion's steadfast moral weight is its greatest
contribution to the country at large.   There are, of
course, malcontents, 'sea-lawyers,' trouble-brewers in
the ranks, but these are the exceptions, not the representatives nor the guides. In almost every town and
village in England, the Legion operates as a lively constructive factor, in many smaller towns practically
running the place. All social service boards, all civic
committees, have their active Legion members. When
the mayor sees a piece of useful work to be done, he sends
for the local Legion branch. 'This would be a good
thing for the town; what about it?' Then the Legion,
if it agrees with him, puts the thing through.

In the General Strike of 1926 the Legion exercised a
strong restraining influence.   In all times of stress it has
proved a steadying element. And except for one brief
flurry, quickly repented and as soon repudiated, it has
kept strictly to its platform of abstention from politics.
Not only does it refrain from approaching any Member of
Parliament to advocate legislation on its behalf, but, by
strong unwritten law, it permits no discussion of political
matters in any Legion quarters; nor will the branches so
much as rent their rooms for political or religious meetings,

although they could, in some localities where good halls are few, make useful money by so doing.

And yet, in reading the Constitution and Rules of the British Legion, one cannot but see that, fine as they sound, they could easily be interpreted as licence to political brig_andage. Why, then, in the wracking, disheartening, hungry decade through which the country has just passed, has this not happened? Why are the Legion's hands still clean of any breach of its founder's high and simple creed? Why has its true democracy survived untainted by any class rancour, any attempt at class grabbing, any bullying of Government and Nation, through years of unparalleled distress?

The answer admits no doubt: It is because, from its in_ception, the British Legion has commanded the devoted leadership of the Nation's best men of all ranks. Earl Haig was no figurehead, but a constant, active, labouring spirit. The Prince of Wales has exercised a deep, strong personal influence. To quote Captain Ian Fraser,[1] the War-blinded leader of Saint Dunstan's: 'Old soldiers see in the Prince of Wales a fellow who went with them to France, who shared, just as far as they would let him, all their dangers and all their hardships, and who now is not only their Prince and their Patron, but their devoted, hard-working, deeply understanding friend. Wherever he goes amongst them, all his accumulated good-will and prestige go with him.'

'Wherever the Prince goes, up and down the land,' says the Legion's President, General Sir Frederick Maurice, 'he makes it a point to visit the local Legion branch. He

[1] Statement to the author, Saint Dunstan's, London, October 8, 1932.

378

goes to ex-service men's hospitals and Homes and talks to each patient and inmate with sure understanding. Whenever he sees a chance to help in any way — and he has personally invented not a few — he is unsparing of himself in thought and deed. But his constant appeal to the Legion, as to the whole Nation, is still for effort, still for service, and that each and every man shall pull his own weight in the boat, for the good of all, in peace as in war.'[1]

Admiral of the Fleet Earl Jellicoe, Lord Derby, Major General Sir Ian Hamilton — one could go on calling a long roll of eminent men that have stood for steady yeomen's service in the Legion's name. But the spirit is the spirit of the country, irrespective of rank. It is the National Trait, the inborn sense of personal and individual responsibility and pride, regardless of class or condition, to contribute toward the common weal, that has kept the whole people of the United Kingdom through all their sufferings unembittered and one at heart. Here is a tiny final straw that may help to show how that big current flows:

One evening, in the autumn of 1932, a party of friends who had been dining together in a quiet London hotel were going up in the hotel lift to the flat occupied by the host. As they debarked at their proper floor, the lift-attendant, an old ex-service man, spoke quietly to one of the guests.

'Might I have just a word, Sir?' he asked.

The guest stepped aside. A few moments later, rejoining the party, he remarked, casually, 'That man only wanted news of an old friend.'

Next day one of the party, seeing the lift-man again, was

[1] Statement to the author, London, October 17, 1932.

curious enough to ask, 'Did you know who the gentleman was to whom you spoke last night?'

'No, madam.'

'That was one of England's most distinguished soldiers, Field Marshal Sir Claud Jacob, late Commander-in-Chief in India, and with a long and splendid war record.'

'Thank you, madam,' rejoined the lift-man, with gentle interest. 'He is certainly a most kind gentleman.' And then in a flash up flamed his still smouldering excitement: 'But here, right here in this lift, *he actually spoke my old Colonel's name!* I hope you didn't mind, madam, but I *couldn't* let *that* pass! I knew he must love my old Colonel. Ah — and we had a fine talk!'

Prince, Field Marshal, Colonel, disabled Tommy, the endless chain that unites them all holds strong in every link — forged of humanity as simple as deep, of mutual loyalty and of self-respecting trust.

CHAPTER IV

A PECULIAR PEOPLE, ZEALOUS IN
GOOD WORKS

For a sound opinion of any British administrative performance the last person to consult is an average member of the British public. For he, while taking all its virtues as a matter of course, continually imputes to it shortcomings that, were his perspective longer or his bias less, he would see in another light.

For example, he is not thankful that political interference and group grabbing have never caught toe-hold in War Pension Ministry affairs. As soon would it occur to him to give thanks that Hyde Park is not infested with cobras.

Neither is he proud that a Department of his Government distributes, weekly, nearly £1,000,000 among over 1,180,000 separate beneficiaries, at an administrative cost of less than two per cent. That sort of honesty and competence seems to him part and parcel of routine dealing with public money, or of serving the injured and the poor.

Nor is he impressed with the fact, so striking to the foreign observer, that the Ministry's attitude toward pensioner and petitioner is definitely humane, liberal, and painstakingly considerate. That element, to him, is dubious or non-existent. All of which is again a logical development from the great National Trait — personal responsibility in citizenship.

So strong is the trait that it rather more than threatens

that other racial attribute — love of Justice; for it automatically creates a critical bias amounting almost to hostility toward any British administrator working in the field of human relations. Be he far or near, the English public seems incapable of remembering that he is one of its own breed, minded like itself, and therefore conscience-goaded to the same effort. Neither can it retain the fact that Parliament makes the laws, not the administrators, whose duty it is to apply them. It intensely desires that all things be done in fairness and in mercy; — so intensely as to ensure to itself the place of first transgressor. For on the flimsiest of testimony, on the weakest of say-sos, without evidence, without hearing, it leaps to the conclusion that its own good men, the admiration of the world, are, if not unjust and wrong, at least hard and merciless.

The obsession is constant — the defect of a great quality — and bears no necessary relation to fact.

'Bureaucratic,' 'cold,' 'without generous impulses' — such phrases one hears applied on general principles to the Ministry of Pensions by good English citizens who are blankly incredulous when one tells them that their position, as judged by an outsider examining the facts, is untenable.

The truth, nevertheless, shows clearly enough in many details, small and great. To touch them lightly, here and there, take the practice of paying pensions by the week, instead of by the month as other countries do; or quarterly as was the pre-War British Army system. This innovation was adopted because of the heavy enrolment in the Great War Army of citizen-soldiers whose whole family system was built on the weekly pay-check. These people, the

esently saw, would find it difficult to gear their
longer income-period, and the families' affairs
nce might suffer. So Government took the bur-
ts own shoulders, with all the extra work in-

ain; the system devised to enable those men
e shrinks from the name and fact of pension-
et whom necessity robs of choice, to draw their
onveniently to themselves, but without their.
having knowledge thereof.
the patient indulgence that meets the whims of
in one typical case, last summer, paying his
t his request, through twenty-nine different
in as many consecutive weeks.
example lies hidden away in the handling of the
low. The Royal Warrant says,[1] flatly, that the
hall suspend or stop the pension of any widow
duct, he considers, shows her 'unworthy of a
public funds.' But the Ministry, so far is it
y fulfilling the letter of the Warrant, interposes
he law and the woman every protection that
lawfully devise. Nor is it satisfied with that;
h tact and with delicacy, to befriend her toward
safer lines.
ing his people in the field, the Minister says
woman is really endangering her position, they
'personal persuasion, judiciously exercised.'
ds, they are not to constitute themselves detec-
to invite evidence against her. If charges of
onduct are brought, such must be made known

rant of 6th December, 1919, Article 10 (1).

to as few persons as possible: 'It is of the utmost importance that the woman should be given every facility to meet whatever charges are made,' and this opportunity must be arranged for her as a quiet private interview with one chosen person. Briefly, the Ministry recognizes that it cannot pay out the people's money as maintenance to a woman living either promiscuously or at the expense of a lover. But it is loath to punish the widow of one who died on his country's behalf, or in any way to worry, affront, or perhaps harden her. It refuses to encourage mere local gossip or unnecessarily to pry into her affairs; yet it is not content with posting her pay-checks downhill to perdition. In a word, it accepts the full duty, or privilege, of making the most of its own ability really to help her in the best way it can, however much trouble that costs.[1]

Such was the general course laid down in 1921, such is the course followed today. It is the antipodes of 'bureaucratic coldness' or of moral snobbery. It is characteristic of the Ministry's work as a whole and it closely follows teachings to be found in a little book called the New Testament.

And if one asks how it happens that this particular country overflows with phenomena of this particular quality, one must turn again to the National Trait — individual responsibility in citizenship — and rehearse a bit of history.

Beginning its task in the year 1917, the Ministry of

[1] Cf. *The Local War Pensions Committees' Handbook*, His Majesty's Stationery Office, London, January 1, 1921, Paragraph 96. Hereafter referred to as the *Handbook*.

Pensions, during the Great War, never quite caught up with its daily descending fresh avalanches of work. The guns were never still. Hospital ships with their tragic freight were always crossing from France. By Armistice Day, 1918, the United Kingdom's loss in soldier dead had reached a total of 750,000. War-disabled men to the number of 600,000 were already pensioned. And by the end of March, 1920, 820,000 more wounded or injured men had emerged from hospital in a state requiring pension, or after-care, or both.[1] Behind the dead or disabled men stood their multitudes of dependants, awaiting help. All this confronted the Ministry of Pensions.

Meantime, many citizen committees and many private efforts, financed by large privately subscribed funds, had sprung up to labour each at its own chosen type of emergency relief. The combined expenditure was heavy. Overlapping and waste were also heavy. And the outcome, taken with the country's need, proved two things to a finish: the good-will of all concerned and the necessity of bringing about as soon as possible a maximum of system and control.

The first attempt to co-ordinate such private efforts began in 1916, even before the Pension Ministry's birth, with the setting-up of volunteer Local Committees, to the number of two thousand,[2] in every county, town, and district of any size. The main work of these bodies, at the time, was to look after the families of the fighting men and to supplement their allowances from the Army and Navy

[1] *Medical History of the War — Casualties and Medical Statistics*, p. 315.
[2] Naval and Military War Pensions, etc. Act, 1915 [5 & 6 Geo. 5, Ch. 83], Section 2.

385

Departments. With the end of the War, however, the Committees quite naturally fell into position as aides to the Ministry of Pensions. As such they played a large part in handling demobilized men returned to their towns and villages; in listening to their claims of disablement; in giving them immediate help, whether in cash or in care; and often in helping them to get back into jobs. How large was that work in its material sense may be guessed from the fact that, a year after the Armistice, the Committees were still spending over £21,000,000 in a twelve-month.[1]

But this effort, being still of the essence of War emergency, cried aloud for more ordering yet, to fit the wear of peace. Sir Laming Worthington Evans, coming into office in 1919 as Minister of Pensions, made use of the whole two thousand Local Committees as a part of a new and most efficient scheme. Today, however, with the steady and natural reduction of work that comes from freedom from graft and political interference, 166 Local Committees suffice to serve, in their own highly important field of activity, the entire United Kingdom.

The make-up of these Local Committees is an interesting and a significant thing. Fixed by statute, their members cannot exceed twenty-five. Of these twenty-five, not fewer than four must be women; not less than one fourth must be ex-service men disabled in the Great War or women pensioned as widows or dependants of men who lost their lives through Great War service; not less than one fifth must be members of the local Government; not less than one fifth must come from local voluntary associations

[1] *Third Annual Report of the Ministry of Pensions*, p. 25.

for the care of ex-service men and their families, such, for example, as the British Legion, or the Lest We Forget. Three other representative persons are added, on the strength of special qualification.

These people are drawn from all social grades, men and women of station and of the labouring class serving together on equal footing, without pay and with equal responsibility and devotion, through the years.[1]

The Local Committees' duties are: to keep themselves informed about the interests and actual conditions of all pensioners in their district, especially of children, for whose care children's sub-committees are appointed; to hear and consider complaints; and to make recommendations in administrative matters within their respective areas.[2] They hold no power other than to recommend, and the Minister, who has also his own official inquiry officers, says to them, in effect, 'You are not asked to decide cases, but you are expected, in every question, to get the man's side, on the spot, and to put it up to the Ministry as strongly as possible.'

Another and vitally important duty incumbent upon the War Pensions Committees is the selection and appointment of suitable residents in each parish, especially in rural parts, to serve as 'voluntary workers.' 'The main function of such workers,' says the Minister,[3] 'is to deal with the more personal aspects of certain types of cases...

[1] The regulations say that committee members may claim compensation for wage-earning time actually lost, up to 1s. 6d. an hour, but not over 10 shillings a day; and for travelling expenses by bus or third-class rail. (*Notes on War Pensions*, p. 52.) But such claims are not generally entered.

[2] Cf. War Pensions Act, 1921 [11 & 12 Geo. 5, ch. 49], Sections 1 and 2.

[3] *Notes on War Pensions*, Ministry of Pensions, London, March, 1926, p. 6.

which call for sympathetic and personal handling, rather than for technical investigation. Such matters as the visitation and oversight of orphan and neglected children who are boarded out by the Ministry; cases where a widow's pension has to be administered in trust; cases of claim to compassionate allowances from the Special Grants Committee, call for inquiries and reports which require the exercise of discretion and can, in general, best be made by persons in the locality.'

The names of the voluntary workers are put up in their nearest town or village post-offices,[1] so that no person, man, woman, or child, may be at loss to know where to turn for a ready and qualified friend and adviser. Thus the timid and the ignorant are quietly helped over the stile and the women and the children are cared for by one who lives among them, whom they see as their familiar friend, and who understands their needs and natures, having known them or their kin forever. It is they, the voluntary workers, who turn impersonal law into personal protection; it is they who know the widow's troubles; they who with intelligence and sympathy discover and serve the real needs of the home. The good that they have done and are doing is incalculable. They minimize the chances of hardships, erase misunderstandings, and cancel injustice and beliefs in injustice. They multiply the Ministry's sidelights on personal lives and express its real attitude toward the people. They are another manifestation of that National Trait that makes of the Nation a united people.

Neither money nor compulsion, neither of which enters into the matter, could produce such service as these people

[1] There are 22,124 post-offices in the United Kingdom.

have rendered, unflagging through the years. In 1932, their number was 16,516.[1] Nor is it conceivable that they will ever be fewer than the Nation's work requires.

But among the Ministry's critics — and in England it has severe critics — some of the most resentful are found in the ranks of the voluntary workers.

The thing could scarcely be otherwise. Voluntary workers are warm-hearted people or they would not give themselves to such service. Because of the closeness of their contacts with individuals, their sympathies catch fire. Because of their position, working in narrow fields, always as advocate, never as final judge, those sympathies flow unchecked by realization as to the wider bearing of whatever precedent may be set up. Finally and emphatically, the Ministry sometimes possesses, concerning the ex-service man in question, decisive personal knowledge that it will neither impart nor indicate; and the voluntary worker, being without that knowledge, is now and again reduced to pulp by the Ministry's 'inhumanity.' Yet here is a fact, usually forgotten and never officially suggested, that signifies much:

Every British War-pension, whether of an ex-soldier or of his dependants, rests on a man's death or disablement through War service, that death or disablement '*Not being due to the serious negligence or misconduct of the discharged man.*'[2] The condition is repeated in every basic clause of the Law. Its complement is this fact:

The complete Army and Ministry record, medical and other, of every man to whom or on whose behalf a War-pension is paid, is kept in the Ministry files. And that rec-

[1] *Fifteenth Annual Report of the Minister of Pensions*, p. 6.
[2] See Royal Warrant of 6th December, 1919, Articles 1 (1) and 11.

389

ord is never exposed or divulged to anyone whatsoever. Members of Parliament on the floor of the House, demanding to know why a pension is denied to or in respect of an ex-service man whose case seems to them deserving, have never yet elicited the reply that their question is answered in the proviso just quoted. No Member of Parliament, no non-Ministry official, no social worker or agent, no outsider of any sort is permitted access to these confidential case-history files.[1] The Ministry under no circumstances, however violently attacked, defends or explains its own decisions by recourse thereto.

This policy, here emphasized because of its grim contrast with the American practice, has bred for the Ministry much condemnation, where, had the underlying purpose and fact been understood, only the heartiest support could have been found.

[1] The confidential character of these files is insisted upon by the Minister even where proceedings before Law or Police Courts are involved: in such cases it is usual to plead 'Crown Privilege'; i.e., that the production of documents would not be in the public interest. Exceptionally the Minister occasionally consents to the production of documents where such production is essential in the interest of justice. Further, the Pensions Appeal Tribunals (see pages 434-35) are entitled to have before them, for the purpose of deciding a statutory appeal, all the relevant documents; and at their instance an appellant is supplied with a *précis* of all material facts of the case he has to meet.

CHAPTER V

A MESSAGE TO AMERICA

THE Star and Garter, Home for disabled and incurable ex-service men, lies on Richmond Hill overlooking one of the finest views in England — down Turner's 'Petersham Reach' of the shining Thames, past Twickenham Ferry to Windsor Castle, with the background of Windsor Great Park and the Surrey hills.

The management of the Star and Garter rests in the hands of the Red Cross, but the money to build it was raised by the women of the Empire, as their Great War Memorial. Naturally, therefore, it is as splendid, spacious, massive, imposing, as the Ministry's own buildings are simple and economically built. But the life the men lead in that grand Star and Garter seems incredibly jolly. Technically speaking, they are all dying; some fifty or sixty have even to be hand-fed. But they are dying with extreme deliberation. And meantime, they are living an interesting life. 'We always treat everyone, no matter how hopeless,' said Sir Arthur Stanley.[1] 'The first War-paralytic that came to me — that was in 1916, the year we began — was totally paralyzed — a doomed case. But we treated him as vigorously and continuously as if we expected results of the first order, lest he be discouraged and so discourage the rest. After three years of this, he suddenly said: "I believe I feel something!" Today he is walking about on sticks.'

[1] The Honourable Sir Arthur Stanley, G.B.E., Chairman of the British Red Cross Society.

SOLDIERS WHAT NEXT!

The men have all the books, and whatever books, they want to read, regularly served by the ever-faithful voluntary workers as librarians. They have frequent and varied entertainments from many sources. The London Stock Exchange provides them with a monthly concert. Other organizations and individuals arrange theatre parties, garden parties, river trips; and none of these volunteer contributions have diminished or become irregular since the War. The men have their own orchestra and singers, patients all, gratuitously trained by professional teachers; they have their camera club and dark room, doing beautiful photographic work. They raise poultry with much success and sell chickens and eggs to the Home. They have a tailoring and a cobbling shop, where they mend each other's belongings. They make baskets of woven reeds, feather ornaments for hats, leather purses and bags, painted boxes and lampshades, children's toys. They make what they like, on their own designs if they like, sitting up in bed or in their wheel-chairs. Whatever they produce is sold for them, they receiving in return all but the cost of material purchased.

Five of the patients now in the Star and Garter, trained engineers before the War demolished them, make walking-machines or repair wheel-chairs. All five have spine-wounds that paralyze them completely from the waist down. But, in the workshop, the thing to be made or mended is held in a hoist at the proper level above them; they run their own chairs under it and there you are!

There are no hard-and-fast rules in the Star and Garter. The men may drink what they like, play cards as they like (the question has been raised and thus answered), and go

392

where they like — such as are mobile. 'But if you keep them busy and interested here at home, there is not much pub-going,' says Colonel Gowlland, the Commandant.

They do go, however, with unflagging enthusiasm to football matches all over the neighbourhood. Men whose legs are dead burdens — paraplegics and arthritics — heave themselves into their trusty motor-driven chairs, seize the control and rush off, alone, away to the Midlands, or north or south, wherever a great game is scheduled, the police and the public cheering them on their way.

Sometimes in like fashion they rush for a change to their other Home, the Star and Garter by the sea, near Folkestone. Ample opportunity is given for them to stay with their own people — from which excursions the paraplegics, in particular, only too frequently return the worse, having inevitably missed the daily skilled institutional care so necessary for such cases.

For the treatment that prolongs a paraplegic's life is one that requires attention such as only trained nurses and orderlies can give. Without it the patient would probably die in three years' time.

'Perhaps some practical-minded countries have decided against that special attention, in view of the economic value of the lives at stake ——' The remark was addressed with less doubt than its form might convey, to the Chairman of the Board of Governors.

'England is not one of them,' said he with quick brevity.

The original purpose of the Star and Garter was to receive totally disabled Great War pensioners only. Now only about half its patients are Pension Ministry-maintained men. The rest are ex-service incurables discovered here and there about the counties, whose cases, not being demonstrably service-connected, fall outside the Ministry's sphere. These are the border-line needs, these are the unavoidable gaps, that the Star and Garter so admirably fills.

The report of the Financial Chairman, Sir Edgar Horne, shows the average weekly cost for each patient, including all overhead as well as all treatment, to be less than four pounds. In estimating the meaning of this, it should be remembered that the Star and Garter, like Scio House, the neighbouring Red Cross Home for officers in advanced stages of tuberculosis, is deliberately a haven *de luxe* — not maintained by public taxes — where private benevolence may indulge its impulse toward a limited group.

Not far distant is another somewhat similar institution, known as the Queen Alexandria Hospital, Gifford House, established in the late War years in memory of Lady Ripon, for cases similar to those that the Star and Garter receives. Here live some fifty severely disabled men. And the big house that holds them, formerly a private mansion, both looks and feels, not like a hospital, but like a cheerful, happy home. Terribly injured as most of the men are, they are far from idle, busying themselves, with obviously keen interest and enjoyment, in a variety of occupations that, without the evidence of one's own eyes, it would be difficult to believe that men so mutilated and crippled could possibly undertake. Many of the family — as many as can use such things — have been supplied by the Pensions Ministry with tricycles, in which they vary a contented and courageous life by little trips into the surrounding country. The moving spirit of this institution is Mrs. Algernon Hay, who takes a motherly interest in every one of the inmates.

394

The Home is shortly being transferred to the South Coast, where its useful functions will continue.

But the national passion for volunteer social service finds expression not only in Ministry Committees and their tributary workers, not only in the Red Cross, not only in such blessed isles as Gifford House, but in a great number and variety of other voluntary associations, or single private donors, using their own capital and labour for auxiliary relief purposes. The Housing Association for Officers' Families beautifully contributes to a true need. The 'Haig Homes' organization, in memory of Lord Haig, is erecting in various parts of England admirable groups of practical small houses for disabled ex-service men, chiefly of lower than commissioned rank, and for War-widows; the rental, adjusted in each case to individual means, averaging 5s. 5d. ($1.32) a week outside London. A third beneficence takes the form of villages for disabled ex-service men, where they and their families may live under protected conditions while provided with medical care, vocational training, and wage-earning work. The War Seals Flats afford good homes at minute cost for War-pensioners and their families. The Ashtead Pottery, in Surrey, Sir Lawrence Weaver's conception and care, provides interesting and profitable handiwork for a colony of neurasthenic War-pensioners.

The Lord Roberts Memorial Workshops give employment at a minimum of thirty shillings a week to some 375 men above fifty per cent War-disabled, none of whom has any other chance of getting a job, and none of whom had training in any trade previous to his disablement. One of these men, a former gardener's boy, having lost both legs and an arm, works regularly as a time-keeper, earning thereby thirty shillings a week. He could live on his two pounds permanent disablement pension. But the difference between surviving as a subsidized log and living as an earner of daily bread doing a real job is the difference between self-respect and damnation. The Lord Roberts Workshops men, scattered all over England and Scotland, turn out much product, beautiful, useful, or both, and always of a high grade of workmanship; they earn up to 1s. 10d. an hour; and the entire enterprise lost, in the bad year of 1931–32, 1s. 6d. (36 cents) per week per disabled man.

As a demonstration in economy the Lord Roberts Workshops do not exist. As a demonstration in humanity they tower. And the fact that, year in, year out, they have been handled at so little cost, is again largely due to the quality and the faithfulness of unpaid voluntary workers who carry the burden of the job.

Another distinguished soldier's memorial — that to Lord Kitchener — provides scholarships in universities, colleges, and technical schools for some four hundred sons of officers and men of the fighting forces. The United Services Fund meets countless emergencies of countless sorts. The King's Fund is another gap-filler. That the Lest We Forget Association and others like it have never forgotten is daily proved to the disabled ex-service man in terms of practical friendship. And so, skipping a long, fine list unnamed, and with a passing salute to the great figure of the Order of Saint John, one comes to the world-famous name of Saint Dunstan's.

Here, at Saint Dunstan's, one may pause, perhaps, to

396

pick up certain less familiar threads not always distinguished.

Saint Dunstan's was founded early in the War by Sir Arthur Pearson, the publisher. Sir Arthur Pearson, an active man of affairs, himself totally blind, conceived the idea of turning his own misfortune to the aid of War-blinded soldiers. Knowing that the question of morale was the key to the future, he made it his personal business to meet each freshly blinded victim sent home from the Front, at the earliest moment possible, presenting himself as a living proof that a man without eyes may go forward in useful working life if only he wills to do so. Sir Arthur Pearson it was who devised Saint Dunstan's, to be a ready asylum, a training school, and a home for Britain's War-blinded men.

Sir Arthur Stanley recalls the incident of one such man who, somehow escaping this watchful friend, got straight away from the hospital ship that brought him across the Channel into some lair of his own finding in a London purlieu. There he struck root in solitary bitterness, refusing to stir. 'But I got him — in the only way he could be got,' laughed Sir Arthur Pearson, telling the story. 'I sent one of our blinded men for him. He wouldn't have listened to a man with eyes. This Saint Dunstan's fellow simply said: "What *are* you fussing about? Be ashamed of yourself! I'm as blind as you are and I've come way across London, alone, to get you. Stop your silly grousing and come along home." And he came. Now he's as right as anyone.'

The whole purpose of Saint Dunstan's is to make men face and overcome their accidents. 'Just because you've lost the gift of sight' — so one man put it — 'you can't

397

chuck your hand in. Anyway, if you do, it's not sight so much as guts you're short on.'

And here again is displayed England's great good fortune in leadership. After the death of a Pearson, to find a War-blinded man of like spirit and power to step into his harness as pump-master of courage and vitality, was certainly a grace of God. Captain Ian Fraser, C.B.E., M.P., late First Battalion, King's Shropshire Light Infantry, lost his eyes on the battlefield by means of a German shell. That happened in 1916, when he was nineteen years old and just out of Sandhurst. And he read in that incident, as did Sir Arthur Pearson, as did Carlo Delcroix, no retirement orders, but rather special assignment to active service on a new front. Like the gallant Italian,[1] Fraser has gone into Parliament to put his shoulder to his country's business. Like Delcroix, like Pearson, Fraser has given the rest of his life to personal work and close constructive association, day by day, with other War-blinded men, less gifted at birth than he. Therefore, and because Saint Dunstan's, of which he is Chairman in Sir Arthur Pearson's place, has gathered to itself the care of all the Nation's War-blinded ex-service men, Captain Fraser's word and opinion command respect and carry authority.

'We are looking after nearly two thousand men,' said he.[2]

---

[1] See *ante*, p. 325.

[2] Statement to the author, Saint Dunstan's, London, October 8, 1932. The Ministry of Pensions furnishes the following information, as of October 8, 1932: 'Number of ex-service men (of the United Kingdom only) pensioned as having no useful vision and therefore assessed at total disablement: 2050. This number includes those having perception of light. The number of cases of total blindness included in the above is: 970. The number of eyesight cases which have been pensioned, all assessments, is 31,592, or 2.4 per cent of the gross total of pensioners.'

'Almost all the War-blinded come here, even from the Dominions, for training. Last year we had forty new cases of
slowly developed total blindness resulting from War-injuries. This year, thus far, we have thirty-three new men.
In our hospital in Brighton, out of its hundred beds about
a third are given to men so badly shattered that they will
never again be able to do anything useful. Taken all in all,
we have several hundred men so shattered as to be permanently incapacitated for work except as a paying hob-
by. But the majority of the rest, being only blinded, and
otherwise mentally and physically fit, are engaged in some
handicraft or profession that enables them to make a
substantial addition — say two pounds weekly — to the
pension, varying from two to three pounds a week, that the
Government gives them.

'Saint Dunstan's scheme is based on this principle: a
blinded man should become a normal person. He must not
think of himself as disabled. He must not be put in segregation. To segregate is not to rehabilitate. He must be retained to work and to play. When he is trained, we equip
him with whatever special facilities he needs and, where it
is possible, send him back to his old home — first making
sure that his home is fit to receive him. We have established almost all our men in the town that they know — in
the place and amongst the people whose looks they remember. And there they have settled into normal life in normal
scenes and relations.

'If you were to follow them to their villages, you would
find them not only earning their living, but going in for
sports — rowing, swimming, road and track racing, skat-
ing — and attending soccer and cricket matches with en-

thusiasm. If you were to visit our hospital in Brighton, where old Saint Dunstaners can always go for a free holiday rest of a fortnight or a month, or whatever is needed, you would find the place full of cheerful, laughing, joking men.

'We in England, having so many War-disabled to care for, could not make them all comfortable in idleness even if that were desired. But we are sure it is not good to award War-pensions so high that the man has no incentive to work. If you remove the necessity to earn a bit in the early days of blindness, you produce a situation like that of the young son of a rich man who isn't made to pull his own weight in the boat. There is a restorative pride in work or a trade. It gives a man his courage back.

'Roughly, our problem of training and rehabilitation is about over. We have trained 120 masseurs — they are especially good for deep massage — and the same number of telephone operators. Both are doing extremely well. About two hundred blinded men are running poultry farms of their own, under guidance. Our central farm organizes, supplies, directs, and markets. Our production is only for breeding eggs, and our hens must lay a high quota a year. The central farm pays the men three shillings a dozen for the eggs, incubates them, sells day-old chicks, and turns over £12,000 ($58,320) a year. The whole thing just pays for itself.

'Others of our men do cabinet-making, cobbling, basketry, etc., each in his own home, with his family about him. Saint Dunstan's gets him his working materials and helps market the product. Saint Dunstan's, in fact, maintains responsibility in the after-care and general welfare of each and every one of its people.

400

A MESSAGE TO AMERICA

'We have never had, here in England, a single War-blinded soldier begging on the street. That is not because they have been so abundantly cared for — though they have been generously cared for. It is because of the spirit of pride and independence inculcated by Saint Dunstan's under Sir Arthur Pearson's leadership.

'We all know that you can't blow £7,000,000,000 into the air, as we did in the War, and have things go on as before. Every creature left alive has to take his or her share of the consequences in one shape or another, and take it cheerfully.

'So, don't be too sentimental and heroic about the blinded soldiers,' Captain Fraser concluded; 'we don't like that. High explosives, like rain, fall on the just and the unjust alike. But' — and here he paused wistfully, his handsome head, his tall, athletic, young figure thrown into changing reliefs between the flickering firelight and the shadows of the deep chair in which he sat — 'But — if your words reach my American comrades who stood alongside of us in France and were disabled, tell them to watch out lest the privileges they enjoy as a result of their disability be whittled away by encroachments from the millions who had their names on a list, but didn't really serve — at any rate, not in any War area. Anyway, give them my best wishes and encouragement.'

CHAPTER VI

DULY AND IN ORDER

The medical problem that confronted the Pensions Ministry at the close of the War was nothing short of appalling. In the first post-War year, in the United Kingdom, 1,051,102 cases of War-disablement came up for care.[1] As one closely identified with the work has phrased it:

The limbless wanted limbs, face wounds required plastic surgery, 'shell-shocks' demanded a remedy for their multitudinous complexes and complications. The insane needed mental institutions, and the tuberculous sanatoria. Men from the East brought with them malaria, dysentery, bilharziasis, and other tropical diseases. The blind sought training, the paralyzed a home. The situation was without precedent, analogies were few, and doctors, whether clinicians or administrators, found themselves launched on a little-charted sea.[2]

The Ministry recognized its permanent responsibility toward them all, to provide free remedial treatment, both

[1] The numbers of medical examinations of ex-service men conducted by the Ministry in subsequent years in connection with awarding pensions are as follows:

1920–21	1,259,899	1926–27	89,837
1921–22	888,026	1927–28	46,127
1922–23	613,171	1928–29	47,424
1923–24	457,555	1929–30	62,500
1924–25	288,012	1930–31	25,500
1925–26	137,132	1931–32	25,503

Medical History of the War — Casualties and Medical Statistics, chapter xxi, p. 312, and Minister's *Annual Reports*. The number of examinations made in connection with applications for medical treatment is estimated to have been equally large.

[2] *Medical History of the War — Casualties and Medical Statistics*, chapter xxi, p. 313.

medical and surgical, for every War-incurred injury. Yet how to handle this flood?

The Ministry's first step was to arrange with civil hospitals, large and small, throughout the country, for the reception of ex-service men and for treatment of their War-injuries. This the hospitals agreed to do as far as they had room, the Ministry meeting the costs. Men were thus enabled to enter hospital near their homes, where their friends could easily visit them — an admirable and humane arrangement continued to the present day wherever ex-service beds are still available.

But these civilian hospitals were not equipped to treat all War-bred ills. For that reason as well as because of the pressure for space, it was all too clear that the Ministry must make haste to acquire facilities of its own. Having no time to build, it took over some of the best of the emergency War-hospitals; adapted large private houses, here and there, for hospital use, surrounding them with quickly built War-type bungalow-pavilions and opened many out-patient clinics.[1]

The first Ministry hospitals set up were special orthopædic and limb-fitting centres, and centres for dysentery and malaria. Hospitals for mild and advanced cases of

[1] In 1920–21, the peak year of the Ministry's activities, there were 113 hospitals in which accommodation, amounting to 17,389 beds, was reserved for Ministry cases, the majority of these institutions being under the Ministry's own management. The Ministry was also using military and civil hospitals throughout the country, and operating 507 clinics, whether surgical, neurasthenic, aural, ophthalmic, cardiac, or for tropical diseases. At the end of that year the Ministry had under treatment 26,342 hospitalized patients, as well as 106,005 out-patients — a total of 132,347. (For table showing in-patient hospital accommodations provided by the Ministry of Pensions from 1919 to 1929, see British Appendix V.) *Fourth Annual Report of the Minister of Pensions,* pp. 8, 9, 35.

neurasthenia were soon added. And in the early stages —
1919–20 — the Ministry opened a number of 'convalescent
treatment and training centres' where the man whose
War-disablement would prevent him from resuming his
pre-War occupation started training for a new one, while
still receiving remedial care. These centres were maintained until 1925, when their special work was completed.

In addition to such vocational training, equipment
was installed in many Ministry hospitals for occupational
treatment of a curative sort, such as carpentering, in order
to assist a man to recover the free use of a limb after
fracture, or to regain command of muscles weakened by
disuse. Today, however, scarcely a workshop exists in
Ministry hospitals, save only in those caring for neuras-
thenics of the two types, ordinary and severe.

In the treatment of mental cases, both of neurosis and
of psychosis, the Ministry has met marked success, re-
storing many to normal life. And because the way to
success was exceedingly obscure, because it was felt out,
step by step, at cost of much time, skill, and patience, the
methods used and the conclusions reached are particularly
interesting.

First and always, with the keen co-operation of its
medical men, the Ministry has strained many a point and
faced no slight risks to keep the stigma of 'certified luna-
tic' from the ex-soldier; yet some six thousand War-cases
remained whom no effort could save.

These, like all persons certified insane, automatically
came under the provision of the Lunacy Acts, and therefore were received into county and county borough mental
hospitals. But the Ministry of Pensions early effected an

arrangement with the Lunacy Authorities whereby 'ex-service patients,' paid for by the Ministry on capitation basis, enjoy the legal status of private patients, with special privileges. For example, the more hopeful cases, who can safely be trusted with some degree of freedom, are domiciled in separate wings of two special mental hospitals set aside for 'service cases' only, where exceptionally favourable conditions may be enjoyed. All the six thousand are regularly visited by Ministry specialists, and the discharge of many a 'service patient' has been facilitated by an arrangement with the Board of Control, the National Lunacy Authority, under which the man was first transferred for a short stay in a Ministry hospital, in order to break the speed and jar of return to ordinary life.

In a word, while the Ministry has raised no budgetary mountain of outlay and overhead by building special hospitals for the War-deranged, it has provided more than ordinary care and comfort, at no expense to the taxpayer beyond the actual maintenance cost per capita.

As to the care of the tuberculous, that, like the care of the insane, is at all times, and for all people, assumed by the county health authority, under supervision of the Ministry of Health. The Ministry of Pensions has therefore made use of existing county facilities in providing for service-incurred tuberculous cases, reimbursing the county for each ex-service pensioner provided with sanatorium treatment. But the Ministry, in its own hospitals, treats surgical tuberculosis, observes and diagnoses doubtful cases, and sometimes sends men abroad for special cures.

By the year 1929, 'only 26.8 per cent of living cases of originally appreciable War-disablement [were] still disabled to the extent of more than 30 per cent. The remaining 73.2 per cent [had] ceased to be assessed at more than 30 per cent or [had] died whilst in receipt of pension.... [The deaths numbered] about 120,000 [of which] only 60–70 per cent were associated with the effects of War-service.' [1]

This great decline in needs produced its logical results — corresponding reduction of the number of Ministry hospitals and clinics.

In the year 1930–31, the number of Ministry hospitals in the United Kingdom was reduced from 17 to 14, the number of medical institutions under direct ministry control dropped from 37 to 33, the clinics from 27 to 24, and the total number of beds from 5098 to 3941. In 1931–32, the figures again fell, for Ministry hospitals, to 11; for controlled institutions to 31; and for beds to 3582, the clinics remaining unchanged.[2]

Costs naturally dropped accordingly, as the following table will suffice to show:

EXPENDITURES ON HOSPITALS [3] AND CLINICS

	1928–29	1929–30	1930–31	1931–32
Hospitals	£395,000	£345,000	£302,000	£240,000
Clinics	33,000	27,000	25,000	20,000
Capitation payments for Ministry patients in civil hospitals	307,000	277,000	224,000	202,000
Total	£735,000	£649,000	£551,000	£462,000

But all this record of steady decline implies steady watchfulness. British War-pension entitlement, it will be remembered, rests not alone upon injuries of War-origin;

[1] *Medical History of the War — Casualties and Medical Statistics*, pp. 347–48.
[2] *Fifteenth Annual Report of the Minister of Pensions* for 1931–32, pp. 3–4.
[3] See *Fourteenth and Fifteenth Annual Reports of the Minister of Pensions*.

it can also be established on account of aggravation of pre-War disability by War-service. Of the hosts of men between forty and fifty years old [1] when they joined the fighting forces of the United Kingdom, how many had escaped a touch of bronchitis, a twinge of sciatica or rheumatism until that time? And who dares assert that the bronchitis or sciatica or rheumatism from which they today suffer is not a development of a long-latent pre-War slight ailment, aggravated by lying in the mud of the trenches? Such connections are as hard to disprove as to prove. No one wants to reject the rightful claim of a needy man. The Ministry's unenviable task is to judge between the effects of the Great War and of unaccelerated Anno Domini; realizing the while that each false judgment in favour of the claimant adds to the tax upon the public which, if for its generous spirit alone, deserves the most considered justice.

All this, the Ministry holds, serves to emphasize the importance of making and keeping an accurate medical record of the physical status of each recruit at the time of his entering the service. The neglect of this precaution, difficult indeed to observe in the rush of war, piles up trouble for everyone concerned, invites bitterness and disaffection in years to come, and costs the State, in the end, much unnecessary labour and expenditure.

In concluding this topic, it is well to emphasize again the smallness of the amount of building done by the Ministry of Pensions in view of the great numbers of the wounded and sick. Apart from adaptation and additions

[1] Men between 41 and 51 became liable for military service under the Military Service (No. 2) Act [8 Geo. 5, ch. 5], of 18th April, 1918.

407

to temporary and permanent War-hospitals already existing, the Ministry has built only three hospitals of its own.
Each of these was attached to an already existing private
house which it fitted for administrative purposes. The
three are:

(1) *Chapel Allerton, Leeds*, with 157 beds, of which on June 15,
1933, 134 were occupied. This hospital is built on two
floors and is of concrete, some of the roofing being permanent and some temporary.

(2) *Dunston Hill, Newcastle-on-Tyne*, with 120 beds, of which
96 were occupied on the date above mentioned. The buildings are of temporary construction, with brick footings.

(3) *Rookwood, Llandaff, Cardiff*, with 86 beds, of which 83
were occupied in mid-June, 1933. Also of temporary construction, with brick footings.

And any visitor will stand willing to testify that whatever these buildings may lack in grandeur, they more than
make good in efficiency and true homely cheer.

CHAPTER VII

BLESSED BE THE MERCIFUL

In the United Kingdom on the thirty-first of March, 1932, about forty-eight per cent of the men drawing Great War pensions were wound cases — stabilized cases, one might have supposed at this late date, with nothing further to be done about them. But, to the surprise even of the specialists, enough troubles still arise from Great War wounds to keep War Pensions Ministry surgeons busy.

A glance at the work of an individual Ministry hospital may best illustrate the facts. And Queen Mary's Hospital in Roehampton, on the outskirts of London, is a fair example.[1]

Here, as in many of the Ministry's institutions, the nucleus was a largish private house seated in its own good grounds and gardens. One-story War-type wooden pavilions for wards and for various other needs of the service, hastily built in the first days, still perform their original duties. As quarters for patients they are pleasant, bright, airy, and in every way sufficient. But it is noticeable that the Ministry has spent no money, here or elsewhere, on matters non-essential to the comfort of its invalids.

[1] Prior to 1925 this was purely a limb-fitting hospital. In that year it was enlarged to act also as the Ministry's chief in-patient treatment centre in London. The hospital itself is administered by an independent committee, but the Ministry pays the whole of the costs and controls the medical staff and nurses as well as the treatment itself.

SOLDIERS WHAT NEXT!

From June 15, 1915, to April 30, 1920, Roehampton alone handled 21,931 cases of limb-amputations.[1] Today it still maintains 500 beds, few of which are empty. And although it now receives any War case, medical or surgical, it does an average of 250 wound dressings every morning.

Aftermath of frostbite contracted in the trenches is the occasion of some of the work. In a stubborn fight to save affected limbs, the surgeons have been gradually forced to one operation after another, until, at the eleventh hour, complete amputation perhaps becomes necessary. Or again, and in a heavy percentage of cases, the operation is compelled by the sudden flaring-up of an old gunshot wound. Frequently this occurs with wounds that have healed, apparently soundly, over a retained foreign body such as a bullet or a bit of shell. These have gone on for varying periods of years without giving any sign of trouble, suddenly to break out into serious disorder demanding extensive surgery. An extreme instance, handled in another Ministry hospital, was that of an ex-soldier, who, ever since the Boer War, had carried a shell-splinter in his leg without suffering any annoyance therefrom until, in the summer of 1932, it suddenly flared up for the first time, requiring radical surgery.

Yet again, there are the face cases. Badly disfiguring facial mutilations have been dealt with by the Ministry with brilliance. From the start it grappled the problem with both hands, leaving no smallest room for the intervention of charity in any form. It had, in all, about six thousand Great War face cases to care for. The Queen's

[1] *Military Effort*, p. 343.

Hospital in Sidcup, Kent, where Mr. Gillies (now Sir Harold Gillies) and others, with a specially trained staff, worked their miracles of plastic surgery, was from the first devoted to this particular task. Photographic records show the long and painful but amazingly successful stages by which, little by little, leaving three to six months' intervals for healing, dental and surgical rebuilding has wiped out appalling injuries. An illuminating example of the Ministry's spirit shines in its solicitude for these outraged men.

Three years after the War, when over five thousand face cases had been returned to outer life, the Ministry undertook an inquiry, on its own initiative, to discover whether it should not provide, somewhere in the country, a refuge to which men might retire who felt that their disfigurement prevented their living and working comfortably under the gaze of the world. The Ministry was quite prepared to establish and maintain such a Home, and to make it thoroughly attractive. But, although every case was investigated and many personally visited and consulted, not one was found whom friends and neighbours considered painful to look at, not one who felt himself embarrassed or handicapped by his appearance, not one who desired special care or protection from ordinary life.

The Queen's Hospital at Sidcup finished its task some years ago; since which time the remaining face-surgery patients have been treated in Queen Mary's Hospital at Roehampton. As late as October, 1932, no fewer than twenty-two men, War cases all, were domiciled in the Roehampton Hospital for their fifteenth or twentieth facial operation. Surely an eloquent testimony, in its patience, faith, and endurance, of the good already done!

Sir Arthur Stanley testifies that when, during the War, the Queen walked through the hospital at Sidcup, stopping at each bedside, speaking to every man, and showing the while nothing but calm, friendly interest, without one trace of effort or of shock, 'her achievement, in view of the ghastly sights before her, was superb.' The worst of these cases have died. Of the rest it is stated today on authority beyond dispute that all are restored to reasonable looks, and that not one is hidden or needs to be hidden away from view in any hospital, home, or retreat.

But Roehampton's outstanding name is as a limb-fitting centre. In the United Kingdom over 35,000 men lost legs or arms or both in the Great War.[1] Of these, 13,000 residents in the southeastern counties of England that form Roehampton's sector, are listed in that one hospital as cases under its supervision and care. Each man's whole history as a patient, every move in his case, minutely kept, is here on file. Here his amputation may have been done; here his new limbs were fitted; here, mind and body, he was trained to their use, and hither he turns for all further care, whether of his 'stump' or of his artificial limbs, as need occasions.

Wherever he may be, if he wants attention he sends in a request, receives a blank, fills and returns it. If he is in physical discomfort, he is summoned in person, his fare and other expenses involved being covered; also, if he is in a job, he is compensated for lost time. If his trouble is that his artificial limb needs repair, he is sent a special col-

[1] *Fifteenth Annual Report of the Minister of Pensions*, p. 8.

lapsible carton for its return by post to the hospital; whence, after being put in order, it goes back to him; or else, a new one is fitted in its stead.

Every patient is entitled to two limbs for each amputation, these to be repaired or replaced forever. Both limbs and their repair, like all surgical care, are given free of cost.

The natural leg of a man of one hundred and fifty-four pounds weight weighs twenty-eight pounds. A modern duralumin metal leg of the Desoutter type, as used by the Ministry, weighs, with its belt, five pounds, two ounces. Some are attached to a waist-belt, some are hung by suspenders from the shoulders. The choice is dictated by the type of movement the wearer most desires — whether free play from the shoulder or from the waist. In any case the 'cushion-type' foot secures movement of toes and ankle. The patients of Roehampton dance, ride, play billiards and golf, with their man-made legs and ·arms, and do it well. One of them, at least, is earning his living as a riding-master. The life of the metal leg is indefinite. The majority last over five years. Some go on twice as long, or even longer. A great deal depends on the character of the wearer — how careless he is, how nervous he is — and also on his occupation. Fishermen and dock-hands, much in the water, are hard on their legs. Certain other classes, as miners and farm labourers, often declare against flexible feet for daily use, choosing an old-fashioned peg-leg for work days and one of the new type for Sunday wear. But where metal, as a material, was considered essential a decade ago, wood is now increasingly favoured.

Among the many matters of interest to be noted in

Roehampton hospital, not the least important is this: every leg and every arm used by its 13,000 patients is fitted on the spot, under the eyes of the hospital surgeons; and all repairs are handled in the same manner. The workshops, War-type wooden bungalows like the other buildings, lie not ten paces from the limb-fitting surgeons' offices. Here, in these shops, individual firms of contractors make the limbs, the Ministry buying their product.

But at every stage the makers are under the strictest and most constant personal supervision by the surgeons and inspectors.

To quote Major Kelham, the chief limb-fitting surgeon at Roehampton: 'No two stumps are the same, no two legs are the same. The artificial calf must match the other absolutely, in circumference, at every point. The whole fitting and making is a matter of extreme skill and delicacy. Seasoned willow is used for our wooden legs, and in the big original willow block from which the leg is carved the central hole (perhaps an inch in diameter) may be made by machine. But from that point to the finish the job is exclusively a hand job special to that one man who is to wear it.'

This practice has seemed quixotic, extravagant, or out-of-date to the advocate of mass production, of purchase by the mail-order system, or of sending your pensioner to a commercial leg-shop to get his wooden leg from off the shelf, as you might send him to a cobbler to get a pair of shoes, neither cobbler nor client knowing a good fit from a flitch of bacon. But, quixotic or not, it has given deep cause for thankfulness to the men so respectfully handled.

414

Men have been driven to the verge of suicide by a badly made, badly aligned, badly fitted artificial leg that chafes, hurts the stump, wears on the nerves. 'Yet no man,' say the Roehampton surgeons, 'need suffer discomfort from wearing an artificial leg if he will allow us time to study his case. But today that is our difficulty. In view of the unemployment in the country, any man lucky enough to have a job is afraid to jeopardize it by going on leave. So we have to combine sure fitting with the greatest feasible rapidity. Employers must not be allowed to say: "This fellow is always going back to hospital. We can't afford to bother with him. Sack him."'

The fitting of arms is a much less difficult matter, yet there is an arm for every amputation and a tool for every occupation. Only two types of mechanical hands are in use; but, after observing for a time the workmen at Roehampton's shop benches, one sees that the Ministry surgeons are speaking literal truth when they assert that the man with an amputated limb, when they have finished with him, may, if his own spirit is willing, go back to his former calling.

Thirty-seven ex-service men minus an arm or a leg are employed in these workshops, on limb construction. Most of the armless men are using a 'universal appliance' to grip the tool they hold. One is swinging a seven-pound hammer, cutting eight-inch steel. One is using an auger.

'Wait! Let me show you!' cries a third, a young tawny-haired Scot, all eagerness and pride — 'I'm a better mechanic today with one arm than I was before the War with two.' Whereupon he turned again to the delicate job he had in process, managing his instrument with a jeweller's precision and ease. 'But that's only that. See here!' and, seizing a clawhammer, he first with two blows drives an eight-penny nail into his bench up to its head, and then, with one haul, jerks it out again. Next he picks up a cricket-bat, swinging it with a great swirl. 'Cricket's my game,' says he. After that it was a hairbrush, a heavy iron shovel heaving bags of sand, a match struck, a cigarette lighted, and the tying of fine string into knots, that exhibited his powers. He wanted no one's sympathy — that one-armed enthusiast with shining eyes. All he wanted was to declare his work with rejoicing.

'All our surgeons,' says Major Kelham, 'must have psychological training. In fact, the work of itself would give it to them — and perhaps it helps that several are, themselves, ex-service men minus a limb. Just as no amputated stump is exactly like any other amputated stump, so no man's mind is exactly like any other man's mind: each new case that we get must be treated as an individual psychological problem. I see each man several times before he comes into the ward as a patient. I talk to him about whatever interests him — the sea, books, gardening, fishing, dogs, watching his mentality, getting his confidence. I let him observe, as if by accident, other men who have undergone the operation ahead of him, and who have triumphed over it, now going easily and actively about their work. Before he comes to the operating table, I must have him at the point where he already thinks of his amputation, not as a finality, an arrest, but as a transitional move into new competence.

'Then, while the wound is healing, and later, when he is beginning to try to use his new limb, his courage and

416

ambition must be kept up. The ideas that stimulate his neighbour may not serve him. His surgeon must study his mind as well as his body, lifting him through the stage of depression and nervous self-consciousness into the confident will to make good.'

Watching the Roehampton patients in their pleasant, airy, flower-decked wards and rooms, or in their gymnasium or their comfortable lounge or their theatre or on the broad verandahs or under the great yew trees of the garden; knowing their merciful deliverance from anxiety concerning their families during this their period of withdrawal,[1] and coming through cumulative observation more and more to understand the calibre and spirit of the men that have built and now direct the whole Pension Ministry Service — one cannot but feel that much may be said for a world in which these things happen.

Roehampton takes care of Ministry patients for southeastern England. Those of the other end of the island — northeastern Scotland — go to Edenhall, near Edinburgh. During the War, when wounded men were rolling in by trainloads, the great Craigleith Hospital, still closer to the city, was the Ministry's local seat. But by 1928 the Warwork had diminished sufficiently to warrant removal to smaller quarters; and so 'Pinkie Burn,' a good private house secluded in the country, became the Ministry's hospital for that wide region.

Rechristened 'Edenhall' after a previous site in England, and transformed for hospital purposes, it now receives both medical and surgical War cases. The professional quality of its work may be inferred from the fact

[1] Cf. *post*, pp. 444–45.

417

that the resident chief medical officer has on his staff an
assistant medical officer, one surgeon, one ear, nose, and
throat specialist, one physician, and one radiologist, all
of whom are also on the staff of the Royal Infirmary of
Edinburgh. In addition, the resident chief medical officer
can at any time call on any Edinburgh specialist as required. The operating theatre and the X-ray equipment
are of the most modern and complete. The wards, which
have a bed strength of one hundred and three, could not
be surpassed for pleasantness. Light, air, space, and, as
always, an abundance of flowers, make background for
details of homely comfort. And here, as in Roehampton,
when one sees the motherly, wholesome-faced nurses
going about their work with War-ribbons spread on their
breasts, one instinctively feels the steady, solid old-com-
radely understanding that exists between patient and
ministrant.

Some of the nurses here speak Gaelic — a happy thing,
since some of the patients know no other tongue. These
are men come down from north of Inverness or in from
the Hebrides, hitching along by the postman's gig or by
small boats as the storms allow, until they reach road or
rail to bring them and their troubles to this haven. And
a splendid, sturdy, man-faced lot they are.

In Edenhall as in Roehampton much of the work is
surgical, whether from break-downs of stumps or scars
— plastic operations — or from the flaring of old wounds.

Hamish MacLeod, for example, here before us in the
first cot on the right, shot in 1917, was operated upon in
a field station, under desperate pressure, by a surgeon
whose hands had scarcely laid down the instruments in

418

twenty-four hours. The wound healed perfectly and gave no trouble whatever until last month, when it flared. Hamish dropped down from his outer island eyrie, by whatever means he found. An Edenhall surgeon bored into his bad spot — and drew out a piece of flannel shirt.

Edenhall has three visiting days a week, for patients' friends. If a man is thought seriously ill, his relatives are notified by post and may come at any time. If his condition is held to be dangerous, the nearest kin is informed by telegraph and the Ministry pays the travelling costs. But one gathers the impression, in that vigorous atmosphere, that most men get well.

The ample grounds, aside from the big vegetable and flower gardens, afford tennis courts and a very popular short putting course. Some of the men do a little desultory hoeing and raking around garden paths and lawns, but are not keen about it, nor are they pressed; although, as in Germany, the surgeons wish, for the cure's sake, that they possessed the magic to make such work desired.

There is a library of a thousand books, and Ministry volunteer workers from Edinburgh appear with clocklike regularity, to find what other books the men may want, and bring them.

There is also a particularly good recreation room, with a good stage, good billiard tables, and plenty of big soft lounging-chairs and couches. And here entertainments of many sorts are frequently given by the faithful people of Scotland, whose memory is longer and stronger than time.

Two hundred patients, the Minister finds, is the smallest number that can be handled with practical economy in one hospital. Given fewer, the per capita overhead rises. Yet with only a hundred and three beds in Eden-hall, the Ministry nevertheless maintains numbers of men in peaceful little Saint Rafael's Home, a few miles distant. Saint Rafael's, like Saint David's, near London, was founded during the Great War by Lady Ann Kerr, mother of the present Lord Lothian, and entrusted to the charge of the Blue Sisters — the Little Company of Mary — in desire of surrounding slowly dying men with an atmosphere of the greatest possible solace, not only of body but of the soul.

'Praise cannot be too strong for either Home. We have the highest opinion of both,' says the Ministry. And so, discarding all consideration of practical economy, of per capita overhead, and of its own constant battle to reduce administration expenses, the Ministry again exposes its bureaucratic flintiness by continuing to maintain patients in these two little ante-chapels of heaven.

CHAPTER VIII

FOUNDATIONS ON ROCK

THE stories of America, France, Germany, and Italy differ radically, each from each. That of England differs from them all. Analyze the English performance and its root-cause emerges: the Englishman's inborn acceptance of his own personal responsibility, active and imperative, inseparable from his citizenship, regardless of his class or condition, toward the common weal.

The evidence in hand is a National Parliament, a Ministry of Pensions, a general public, and a body of ex-service organizations all co-operating in one rounded effort to one agreed end.

Unlike her Continental neighbours, who, before the War, were nations of trained soldiers, England, until 1916, had never practised conscription. She had left the land fighting of her wars to her small Regular Army, which, on August 1, 1914, numbered only 247,432 officers and men.[1]

Pensions arising from former wars, Navy and Army alike, had always been dealt with in branches of the Admiralty and the War Office. But with the progress of the Great War, and the building of a huge, new citizen army, the magnitude of the task, as has already been shown, early swamped existing means of control.

Exactly how the emergency should be met was not at once obvious. Besides the great outburst of private ef-

[1] *Military Effort*, pp. 157 and 159. Over half of the Regular Army were killed in the course of the War.

fort, there were sporadic gropings in a Parliament already overloaded with the burdens of the War. There were settings-up of measures and machines that ran for a time, only to sink, each in turn, under ever-mounting pressure. There were creakings, complainings and denunciations of the people, by the people, for the people. And finally, in December, 1916, there was the erection of a new Department of State — a Ministry of Pensions, which began to function on the fifteenth of February of the next year.[1]

But now arose a new difficulty — the available trained personnel was very limited. Nearly all experienced hands were already engaged in other War business. The Department had to be staffed mainly with women and elderly men entirely unfamiliar with governmental office work. With such untrained though devoted forces, each day became a breathless struggle against ever-mounting odds, and no little confusion unavoidably ensued.[2]

So passed another twenty-two months of War.

By the time that period was over, the United Kingdom had enlisted within itself, since the outbreak of the War, nearly 5,000,000 men. This figure relates to the land forces alone, and is exclusive of the Regular Army, Reserve and Territorial Forces, which as of August 4, 1914, numbered 733,514 men; exclusive also of all Admiralty and Air Force strength. Its enrolment was thus distributed: [3]

[1] Ministry of Pensions (Transfer of Powers) Order, 1917, S. R. & O. 1917, no. 125.

[2] For a brief account of the difficulties and efforts, within the Government, of this period, together with an appreciation of the merits of the early American War Pension System, see *War Pensions: Past and Present*, by His Honour Judge Parry and Lieutenant-General Sir A. E. Codrington, K.C.V.O., C.B., London, Nisbet and Company, Ltd., 1918.

[3] *Military Effort*, pp. 363; 740.

422

Country	Total enlistment to Nov. 11, 1918	Estimated total population in July, 1914	Estimated male population in July, 1914	Percentage of male population represented by enlistments
England	4,006,158	34,618,346	16,681,181	24.02
Wales	272,924	2,489,202	1,268,284	21.52
Scotland	557,618	4,849,500	2,351,843	23.71
Ireland	134,202	4,374,500	2,184,193	6.14
Total	4,970,902	46,331,548	22,485,501 [1]	22.11

Since these present chapters are concerned with the effort of the United Kingdom only, exclusive of the Dominions and of India, a glance at the whole Empire's Great War death-roll becomes pertinent. It also carries interest for those who recall the statement, persistently floated in the American Army in France, to the effect that the English were sheltering their home troops behind the Dominion contingents, using the latter as chief combatant forces.

Number of officers [2] and men who lost their lives in and through the World War (*Whitaker's Almanack*, 1933, p. 381):

Losses of the United Kingdom alone.................... 812,317
Combined losses of Canadian, Australian, New Zealand, South African, Newfoundland, Indian and Colonial contingents... 277,602
Empire's total loss................................1,089,919

[1] According to the statement of the Imperial War Museum, the total number of men of the British Isles who served in the Armed Forces of the Crown, by sea, land, and air, during the Great War, reached 6,554,821. Men withheld by Government in 'reserved occupations' — munitions work, rail and transport work, ship-building, agriculture, etc. — numbered as of October 31, 1918, 2,574,860. In July, 1914, 14,000,000 of the male inhabitants of the British Isles were either below or above the then service age — 18 to 40 — a period later extended to from 18 to 50 years. These figures total 23,129,681. Especially if allowance be made for the facts concerning Ireland, they appear sufficiently to account for the entire male population of the British Isles, which, as of July, 1914, numbered 22,485,501. See *Military Effort*, p. 368.

[2] The proportion of the total casualties of officers to the total casualties of non-commissioned officers and men, in the United Kingdom's entire army in France, exclusive of the Royal Air Force, was as one officer to 21 men of other ranks. This is almost exactly the proportion of officers to other ranks (excluding Royal Air Force) in the British Army in France. *Military Effort*, p. 245.

From these, the official figures, the fact appears that of the combined Great War death-losses of the entire Empire, over 75 per cent were sustained by the home forces of the British Isles.

At the close of the War, the new Ministry of Pensions found itself confronted with an enormous number of claims. And the Government, able at last to give the subject the attention it required, appointed a Select Committee of the House of Commons, drawn from all political parties, to study and to establish principles of entitlement and of rates. A second committee appointed by the Minister of Pensions fixed the organization and machinery of the Department. Legislation necessary for administration purposes followed, and by the time the Peace Treaty was signed the whole structure of the Pensions Ministry had taken final shape.

'Final shape,' indeed. In its first beginnings, as in the breaking-in of any new machine, strains showed up here and there, to be adjusted; but the original scheme itself has remained untouched in all essentials. Since the Pensions Ministry was set up, all three political parties (Labour, Conservative, Liberal) have, in turn, held control and each has contributed its part. But not one of them has interfered with the main lines of the system that, working together, they originally framed. No new general warrant — the instrument governing the grant of pensions — has been framed since 1919. *No new War-pension legislation has been enacted since 1921;* and it is to be observed that practically the whole, even of this legislation, dealt merely with administrative machinery. America, in enacting her law of October, 1917, thought she, too, was enacting a finality. Since that time she has subjected her law to some two hundred and forty changes, the great majority being 'liberalizations' effected by political interference to create new bodies of dubiously entitled favorites.

British authorities give as reason for their own law's unattacked stability the fact that the Government at the start faced its full liabilities, thus leaving no room for assault.

Happy is the land where such an explanation explains!

But from the American point of view other explanations exist. As, for example: the Minister of Pensions is a member of the House of Commons. From his seat on the Government benches he is ready to answer directly any questions concerning his Department that may arise from the floor. He, subject to the provisions of the Pensions Acts, is the sole administrator and interpreter of the Royal Warrants. No higher authority, no political interference, no persons or power can come between the Minister and his work. The Minister may say, on any private proposal put forward in the House: 'No. As a Government we cannot agree to this' — and the proposal can go no farther. For the Minister of Pensions is a member of Government, which stands or falls as one.

Nor is the British public, on its side, lax in the exercise of the advantage thus given it. Whether in complaint or inquiry, it makes itself felt by its Parliamentary representatives, showing a continuous watchfulness. For instance, on April 19, 1923, the Minister of Pensions was called upon to answer officially no fewer than forty-five questions — at that time a typical day's battery. Questions, however, have progressively diminished, until in

the present Parliament practically none have been put —
showing that Parliamentary agreement has been approxi-
mated among all concerned.

A second feature in the British system peculiarly suggestive to Americans, because it embodies the extreme
opposite of American practice, is this: no one but a
Minister, himself a member of the current Government,
can propose in Parliament an expenditure of public funds;
no Member of Parliament excepting a Minister can, for
any reason, introduce an appropriation bill. The Government thereby becomes directly, clearly, and immediately
responsible for whatever disbursements are authorized or
refused. Pressure through individual members of Parliament is ruled out, no quiet tinkering takes place, nobody's particular friends can be taken care of by reciprocal collusion called courtesy, and the taxpayer knows
the exact authorship of whatever action occurs.

A third point of much practical importance is that the
conditions and rates of pension and the classes of case
affected are determined, not by Parliament in any law of
its making, but by a Royal Warrant — an act of the
Executive authority, issued over the King's and the
Minister's signatures. This means that Parliament, again
in extremest contrast to the United States Congress, cannot wrangle over the detail of pension policy, nor can individuals or groups in Parliament secure special benefits
for particular men or bodies of men. Parliament may
criticize, and has on occasion criticized, broad features
of warrant provision and the Minister from his place in
Parliament has met that criticism. But no power of the
purse lies in Parliament's hands.

It is the duty of the Minister under the warrants to award every man suffering from a disability attributable to,[1] or aggravated by,[2] service in the Great War, and not due to his own serious neglect or misconduct, such pension, gratuity, or allowance as his case may be found to justify. Service-incurred or service-aggravated injury, and that only, constitutes entitlement. No claim can be established on any other base.

'It does not follow,' says the Ministry, 'that every disability sustained during the War was due to War-service; an applicant for disablement pension must show, not only that he is suffering from a disability which he had not, or had not in the same degree, before enlistment, but also that the impairment of his condition is due to his service in the War.'[3]

This principle has from the first been upheld, by each successive Government, and with the utmost strictness. For it constitutes, as they have all pointed out, whatever their political party, the only possible ground on which the country can hope to be as generous as it desires in providing for the real victims of the War. Every unproved case written into the pension rolls would diminish the country's power to serve claims that are certain.

[1] War Pension (Administrative Provisions) Act, 1919 [9 & 10 Geo. 5, ch. 53], Section 7, gives a statutory right to pensions awarded by the Ministry of Pensions subject to the conditions in the warrant under which awarded and subject to the provision of the necessary funds by Parliament.

[2] The legal interpretation of 'aggravated' as given with the Royal Warrant is as follows: 'An injury or disease shall not be deemed "aggravated" by military service, or by active service, as the case may be, unless it was sustained or contracted before the date of mobilization (or enlistment if later), and was and remains worsened by such service, or having been sustained or contracted during such military or active service, as the case may be, was and remains worsened thereby.' Royal Warrant of 6th December, 1919, Article 24 (12).

[3] *Notes on War Pensions*, p. 11.

The rates of the Great War pension, fixed by the all-parties Select Committee of 1919 [1] — a period when the cost of living was high — were calculated on a scale of 115 per cent in excess of pre-War living costs. The Royal Warrant provided, however, that if, after an initial period of three and a half years, the general costs of living of working-class families should change by 5 per cent or more, whether up or down, pension rates might be altered accordingly. [2]

Since 1919, these costs of living in England have dropped to 37 per cent above the pre-War figure. The National Exchequer has been continuously hard-pressed. Government outlay in many directions has suffered repeated curtailment. Every salary in the British public service and particularly in the Pensions Ministry, beginning with that of the Minister himself, has been heavily cut, and subjected to the general taxation, which has been murderous. Yet, War-pensions have never been touched.

In 1927, costs of living had already fallen about 42 per cent from the 1919 level. But the people were then paying, to meet Great War pensions, taxes in excess of those consumed by any other expenditure of Government — taxes comparing as follows with those paid by other countries for the same purpose: [3]

[1] Royal Warrant of 6th December, 1919, applying to the Army and applied to the Navy and Marines by Order-in-Council of 11th June, 1920, and to Airmen by His Majesty's Order of 11th May, 1920. Similar documents dealt with the cases of officers. All these documents operated from 3rd September, 1919.

[2] In 1925, the Government further decided, as announced by the Minister in the House of Commons on July 30 of that year, that no change should ever be made except upon a three-years' averaged change in costs of living.

[3] Memorandum No. 2 on War Pensions Administration, Ministry of Pensions, 1927. Figures are as of 1926.

	£	s.	d.	
British Isles	1	9	6	per head of population
France		18	6	per head of population
Germany		19	2	per head of population
United States		8	3	per head of population

If at this time of intense economic distress the Government had cut War-pensions as, under Royal Warrant, it had a right to do, it would have reduced taxation on that head by 12 per cent. And if the principle of granting War-pensions only for War-incurred disablements of really disabling degree had not been so consistently and rigorously honoured, a cut could scarcely have been avoided.

As it was, the main anxiety manifested by the tax-oppressed English public was one of fear lest that cut be made.

House of Commons records, in this matter, provide suggestive reading. Questions are addressed to the Minister, by members of all parties, anxiously asking for reassurance. The Minister repeatedly reassures them; War-pensions will *not* be cut. Labour Members, particularly, urge that War-pensions be stabilized at the 1919 rates; pensioned men are kept on tenterhooks, they say, for fear of reductions to come. At length, in 1928, the Minister — Major the Right Honourable G. C. Tryon, M.P., Conservative — informs them decisively that the Conservative Government, recognizing the desirability of relieving the men's minds, will stabilize existing rates, but, though it promises never to cut War-pensions, it insists on preserving its power to raise them if — 'but only *if*' — living costs should on a three years' average rise beyond the 1919 level.

The Minister then adds two statements of extreme

429

significance, whose implications must control the stabilization of rates.

First: Under the present law of entitlement, with its *sine qua non* of War-injury, 'the pension list... involves a steadily diminishing liability'; this in excuse for the Government's decision, in spite of existing public distress, to stabilize War-pensions and so forego a reduction of six and a half million pounds in the year's War-pensions costs.

But, second: So long as it remains remotely possible that the present strict entitlement might be weakened and dropped to admit cases of doubtful or no service connection — 'new classes of beneficiary, to whom the present high rates would automatically become applicable, the Government of the day must be free to review its rates of pension in the light of its aggregate liability.' [1]

In plainer words, if England should ever so far reverse her present standards of public morals as to allow her War-pensions service to become a pawn of politics, then it is England's disabled soldiers who will have to take the consequences.

[1] Memorandum (No. 3) on the present position of War-pensions, Ministry of Pensions, September, 1928. House of Commons, July 31, 1928. See also House of Commons Reports of January 22, 1924; June 11, 1925; July 30, 1925; January 28, 1931; June 9, 1932. Mr. Winston Churchill, Chancellor of the Exchequer, said in the House of Commons, March 16, 1926: 'It was open to the Government, in consequence of the fall in the cost of living, to reduce on 1st April next the pensions to the wounded soldiers in the Great War, and in this case there could have been no charge of breach of faith, because power was explicitly reserved [in the Royal Warrant] to make such a reduction should the cost of living fall. We decided, however, that our financial situation, however difficult, in no way justified such a harsh step, and the Minister of Pensions [Major the Right Honourable G. C. Tryon, P.C., M.P.] was accordingly authorized by the Cabinet to make the announcement for which he had so earnestly pressed, and which he so ardently desired.'

The decision was the decision of all parties, reaffirmed through the years. In 1931, the Committee on National Expenditure, appointed by the Labour Government shortly before it went out of office, and at a most critical time, reported on the possibility of budget savings through War-pensions cuts. Its findings were, in effect, that the statement of the Conservative Minister in 1928 must stand: War-pensions should not be cut so long as entitlement thereto unqualifiedly demands War-service injury.[1]

In 1932, an unofficial Committee of Members of Parliament, dissatisfied with the economies effected by the National Government, also undertook a study involving the point of possible War-pension cuts, only to report, in turn, that the statement of the Minister in 1928 was so sound as to preclude any reopening of the question.[2]

And on February 3, 1933, Mr. Neville Chamberlain, the present Chancellor of the Exchequer, said, of the cutting of War-pensions: 'I cannot think that any Government would dare to contemplate this unless in the case of direst need. And, much as I desire to reduce taxation, greatly as I think the country needs reduction, I should say that reduction, bought at such a price as that, was bought too dearly.'

It is a proud record. A front so solid could have been attained by one means only — unshaken and absolute loyalty to original sound principle. So long as the Nation knew that the money spent in War-pensions was going to men actually disabled in the Nation's defence, it was will-

---

[1] *Report*, paragraphs 533 and 534.

[2] *Report* of Private Members of the House of Commons Economy Committee, 1932, paragraph 229. P. S. King and Son, London.

431

ing and glad, man by man, woman by woman, to bear the costs. But, had there ever been the slightest swerving, the slightest relaxation of standard, Great War pensions, in these last years of England's sharp distress, must have plunged from their shrine of the Sacrosanct Apart.

CHAPTER IX

THE STEADY HAND

THE legal time-limit within which a man may lodge a claim to pension in respect of War-disablement is seven years from the date of his discharge — i.e., the termination of his active service; or seven years from the end of the War,[1] whichever was the earlier. This seven-year limit was set, all political parties agreeing, by Parliamentary action. Its basis was the united opinion of high medical authorities that the period named ordinarily gave ample time for the development of War-incurred injuries. It is not contended that no exception can arise to this general rule, but it is emphatically held that laws should not be framed to fit special or exceptional cases, lest there be an endless piling-up of complications and liabilities. Discretion, however, remains with the Ministry to deal with *bona-fide* exceptional cases 'by administrative action.'

The Ministry's responsibility in the matter is not a light one. War-pension rates considerably exceed — sometimes by more than double — those granted under governmental social services, such as the Unemployment or Health Insurance or Old-Age Pensions systems. The Nation must not be asked to pay War-rate pensions on account of disabilities due, not to War-injury or War-aggravation, but merely to the normal encroachment of years or to other circumstances which bring men within the proper

[1] War Pensions Act, 1921 [11 & 12 Geo. 5, ch. 49], Section 5. The end of the Great War, by England's official dictum, is August 31, 1921.

433

sphere and provisions of other established governmental
relief agencies. Yet the desire is always to give every ex-
service man his due, and liberally. And the fact remains
indisputable that, in England as in Italy and in America,
many men refused to apply for pension until years of evil
fortune had robbed them of the power to choose. To quote
one distinguished ex-officer: 'Lots of the stoutest fellows
wouldn't squeal. They cut their own throats by carrying
on in silence until twelve years or so had passed, and then,
with their remnant of health gone and no jobs to be found,
for their children's sake they had to swallow their pride and
ask for help.' So, in spite of the law no man is turned
away because of the seven-year time-limit only. And the
late applicant is given every opportunity to establish his
claim.

In cases of debatable status, eminent independent medical specialists from a list selected by the Royal College of
Physicians and Surgeons are called in to advise the Ministry; and their advice has never in any case been rejected.
All of which applies mainly in cases of disease as distinguished from wounds. Any ex-service man who can show
that he is now suffering serious disability from a wound inflicted by the enemy, even though he has kept the matter to himself until today, receives his pension without
delay.

In cases where claim was made within the seven-year
limit, and by the Ministry rejected, appeal may be taken
from the Ministry decision, as to whether the claim was
rightly refused. Such appeals are heard by 'Pensions Appeal Tribunals.' These are independent tribunals constituted under the Lord Chancellor in various parts of Eng-

land and Wales, but in Scotland appointed by the Lord President of the Court of Sessions.[1]

And their careful and regulated composition should be particularly interesting to Americans, in view of the quality of the boards that, in the summer and autumn of 1933 are being appointed to review America's dubious 'presumptive' lists. Pensions Appeal Tribunals consist of three members — one barrister or solicitor of not less than seven years' standing; one disabled officer or man who was retired or demobilized during the Great War while suffering from his injury; and one duly qualified medical practitioner; also whenever necessary a specialist in the appellants' supposed disorder is called in. The legal member sits as chairman. If the claimant is an officer, the second member of the Tribunal must be an officer; if the claimant is a ranker, then the second member must be a ranker too.[2]

As must naturally happen in a country where War-service was so widely inclusive, the Tribunal is often composed entirely of disabled ex-service men — a point that adds significance to the small proportion of Ministry decisions altered by these bodies — for decisions of the independent tribunals are legally binding, final alike to the Ministry and to the appellant.

Up to March 31, 1933, Great War pensions claims had been admitted from 1,970,000 persons — officers, men, widows, and dependants, of which claims 97.6 per cent had been admitted on the Ministry's original decision, while

[1] War Pensions (Administrative Provisions) Act, 1919 [9 & 10 Geo. 5, ch. 53], Section 8 Schedule.

[2] 'Ranker' in English usage, like 'other ranks' in official phrasing, signifies the soldier below commissioned degree.

435

only 2.4 per cent came in through Pensions Appeal Tribunals.[1]

Rare instances have, however, occurred where fresh
evidence, produced after the decision of the Tribunal, has
shown that a rejected claim ought properly to have succeeded. In such cases, Government has authorized the
Minister to rectify the position by administrative action.

Claims presented by disabled men later than seven
years after the man's discharge cannot be carried to the Appeal Tribunals. But claims in behalf of widows and other
dependants of pensioners are still heard by them, as are
also complaints from disabled men who, having received a
final award, are dissatisfied with its amount. When such
a 'rate of assessment' appeal is being considered, a second
medical man sits in place of the barrister or solicitor, thus
making a bench composed of two doctors and one ex-service man of the rank of the claimant.[2]

As early as 1920 the Ministry began to feel the desirability of making its pension awards final. Up to that time it
had called pensioners before its medical board once, twice,
or thrice a year for review of progress, thereby 'boarding'
as many as 25,000 officers and men a week.[3] But this practice embarrassed the men's time and was found to make
some of them nervous, despondent, or fearful of the future.
Also, the handling of adjustments was costly in administrative machinery. This wholesale boarding, moreover,
restricted the number of qualified medical practitioners
available to the civil population. The Government accord-

[1] Answer of the Ministry of Pensions in the House of Commons, June 1, 1933.
[2] War Pensions Act, 1921 [11 & 12 Geo. 5, ch. 49], Section 4.
[3] See *ante*, p. 403.

ingly decided that, not later than four years after the man's discharge from service or after his first award of pension, every case should be considered with a view to arriving at a permanent settlement of the basis on which compensation should issue. This was to be done by a system of 'final award' and the pensioner was to have the statutory right, for one year after the Ministry's decision in his case, of appealing to the Pensions Appeal Tribunal against the Ministry's settlement.[1]

This policy, which went into effect in January, 1922, has worked well. As of March 31, 1932, 423,000 men were assured of their life-pensions by means of final awards, leaving 56,000 still on the conditional basis, under medical observation.[2]

It is recognized, however, that in exceptional instances, despite the most expert medical advice, mistakes may be made in important medical facts, resulting in a final award based on a wrong diagnosis or forecast. Free medical and surgical treatment is continued in all cases; and where in the course of treatment serious and permanent error is eventually found to have occurred in a final award, revised grant is made by the Ministry; but no right of appeal arises beyond that conveyed under the statute's one-year limit available for the final award only.

'A final award,' says the Ministry, 'is not made (under the Regulations) in a case where the man is obviously getting worse or can be seen to be likely to get materially worse in the reasonably near future. Indeed, some of the cases still in receipt of conditional award, which are

[1] War Pensions Act, 1921.[11 & 12 Geo. 5, ch. 49], Section 4.
[2] *Whitaker's Almanack*, 1933, p. 640 (based on official information).

437

steadily deteriorating, will probably never be found suitable for a final award because it would be against the man's interest to make one. On the other hand, in a case which is obviously improving materially, a final award is not made, because to do so would involve perhaps the award of a life pension at a rate which would soon cease to be justifiable.'[1]

The following distinction is worthy of note: In the case of a man whose disablement was attributable to Great War service, and who in consequence is pensioned and under medical supervision, if his disablement disappears, his pension ceases; yet, if his disablement revives from a War-cause, the man may be given a further grant of pension by the Ministry at their discretion. But, in the case of a man whose disablement was not War-occasioned, but merely War-aggravated, if the aggravation is certified to have passed away, the pension ceases without privilege of revival.[2]

New claims still come forward on grounds of development of latent War-incurred ailments. The year 1930–31 brought forth 1212 applicants who were granted first awards, of whom 1050 were outside the seven-year statutory limit; 1931–32 produced 690 claimants, including 618 beyond the limit. Of these 426 were accepted for pension, the rest for lump-sum gratuities once for all, or for medical treatment.[3]

[1] Memorandum No. 2, Ministry of Pensions, August 27, 1925, pp. 2–3.
[2] *Handbook*, p. 8, paragraphs 14 (2) and (3). A distinction is made between 'disablement' and 'disability,' the former signifying the incapacity suffered in consequence of the injury and the disease (disability) sustained.
[3] *Fourteenth and Fifteenth Annual Reports of the Minister of Pensions*, pp. 1 and 2.

The flaring-up of old wounds, requiring operations and more radical amputations, is a frequent source of new and higher disablement percentages; but, while increased pensions keep pace with increased disabilities, the Ministry never reduces any final award, however much the disability lessens, unless fraud is proved. And attempted fraud is relatively infrequent.

Pensions or compensatory gratuities have been paid in respect of more than two men [1] out of every five who served in the Great War, the killed and disabled numbering 2,681,884.[2]

The total number of persons, including dependants, in receipt of Ministry benefits during 1931–32 was 1,181,000 as against 1,265,500 in the year previous.[3] As of March 31, 1932, the total expenditure on War-pensions, including administration, since 1914, was about £1,063,000,000.[4] The expenditure, on all heads, for 1931–32 was £49,466,537. This disbursement was £2,298,908 less than that of the previous year,[5] which, in turn, was £2,334,939 less than that of 1929–30, the year preceding.[6]

So orderly a decline, at a rate that makes it possible to

[1] See Memorandum, June, 1926, Ministry of Pensions: 'Out of the whole body of six million men of all ranks mobilised in this country during the Great War, claims have been made in respect of three out of every six and the claims have in the aggregate been *admitted in five out of every six cases.* The bulk of the claims were, of course, made during the two years following the end of the War,...'

[2] Killed, 812,317. See *Whitaker's Almanack*, 1933, p. 381 (based on information supplied by the Imperial War Graves Commission). Disabled, 1,869,567. See House of Commons Report, May 5, 1921.

[3] *Fifteenth Annual Report of the Minister of Pensions*, from 1st April, 1931, to 31st March, 1932, p. 1.

[4] *Whitaker's Almanack*, 1933, p. 640.

[5] *Fifteenth Annual Report of the Minister of Pensions*, p. 2.

[6] *Fourteenth Annual Report of the Minister of Pensions*, p. 5. For a full table of Ministry expenditures from 1918 to 1934, see British Appendix IX.

predict the date of extinction in about the year 1960, arises from six main causes:

First, absolute freedom from political interference; and this, often as it has already been said, cannot be overemphasized.

Second, the unbroken pursuit of one national policy.

Third, strict adherence to War-incurred disablement or death as necessary to entitlement.

Fourth, an exercise of economy that, together with shrinkage of work and consequent reduction of staff, has steadily reduced administrative costs. These costs today consume well under 2 per cent of the Ministry Budget, the remaining 98 per cent going straight to the benefit of the pensioner.[1]

Fifth, natural causes — deaths of pensioners, coming-of-age of pensioned children, and remarriage of pensioned widows.[2]

Sixth — and not least — a highly centralized and ably handled administration, controlled, undisturbed, by men of single purpose and distinguished character.

[1] During the confusions of War and in the early post-War years, the Ministry's costs of administration were at the maximum, in 1920 running to 15½ d. in every pound of sterling of benefit expenditure. By 1931–32, they had been lowered through gradual process to 5d. in the pound. Economies effected during the following fiscal year reduced administration expenses to 4.8d., in the pound, or 2.01 per cent of the War-pension budget, and for the year 1933–34 the administration expenses are estimated at 1.83 per cent of the cost of benefit. (*Eleventh Annual Report of the Minister of Pensions*, p. 1, *Fifteenth Annual Report of the Minister of Pensions*, p. 1, and *Memorandum by the Financial Secretary to the Treasury*, 1932, p. xxi, and 1933, p. xx.)

[2] The Ministry *Annual Reports* show figures for the last two years in round numbers as follows:

	1931–32	1930–31
Deaths of beneficiaries	24,000	22,000
Children reaching 16, the pensionable age-limit	62,000	80,000
Remarriage of widows	1,300	2,000

CHAPTER X

MAN, WIFE AND WIDOW

'THE whole secret of our scheme,' repeats Sir George Chrystal, Secretary of the Ministry, is just this: 'Be sure your man is entitled — be sure that his disability is service-incurred; *and then, nothing you can do is too good for him.*'

Three factors determine the amount of the ex-service man's pension: first, his military rank; [1] second, the degree of his disablement; [2] third, and potentially, his pre-War earning capacity. [3] His degree of disablement is fixed by comparing him with a normal, healthy man of his own age; any percentage of inferiority that is due to War-service being his percentage of compensability. The minimum degree of disablement recognized by the English law as pensionable is 20 per cent. [4]

The private soldier assessed as less than 20 per cent disabled receives, in lieu of pension, a lump sum, which may be paid by instalments, not to exceed £200, and under such

---

[1] Certain technical features differentiate the handling of the pensions of commissioned officers from those of other ranks, which latter, with few exceptions, are alone considered in this writing. For schedule of officers' pensions, however, as well as those of other ranks, see British Appendix II.

[2] For schedule of disablement with percentages and pension scale attached, see British Appendix II.

[3] Provision is made for grant of pension on a higher scale, called 'Alternative Pension,' where the man's pre-War earnings were above the average. But a pensioner must apply for this higher rate of pension within one year of the Ministry's first officially recognizing him as War-disabled. The award is then based on the proved pre-War earnings, loaded by 60 per cent because of the increased cost of living, less the money equivalent of his present earning capacity as assessed by a special board. The maximum is £5 a week. For further information see British Appendix I.

[4] Royal Warrant of 6th December, 1919, Article 1 (3).

conditions as the Ministry may determine.[1] 'Royal Warrants,' say the Ministry,[2] 'have always recognized that, for
minor ailments or injuries involving no material incapacity to the man, compensation was properly given in *final*
settlement in the form of a lump sum or a terminal allowance, and not as a life-pension.'

In other terms, if the enemy took off your little finger,
your account against the Government, if you see fit to render one, may best be settled once and for all by cash in
hand rather than that public money be spent to keep books
about it and post weekly cheques to you for the rest of your
earthly existence.

The one variation in the procedure occurs when the disablement in question can be remedied by dental treatment,
or by corresponding medical or surgical care. Such provision is then authorized following examination by a medical board of the Ministry; but no money award of any sort
is then made, though payments may be made to the men
during such treatment where treatment prevents him from
earning for the support of his family.

Under certain exceptional circumstances, *permanent*
disability pensions can be commuted, but only when, after
the strictest investigation, the Ministry is satisfied, not
only that it would be to the pensioner's distinct and lasting
advantage to give up part of his weekly pension for life in
exchange for a lump sum, but also that he would suffer
grave hardship if his application were refused.[3]

[1] *Fourteenth and Fifteenth Annual Reports of Minister of Pensions*, pp. 1, 2.

[2] Memorandum No. 2 in connection with Resolutions passed by Advisory
Councils and War Pension Committees. Ministry of Pensions, August 27, 1925,
p. 4. For full table of such gratuities, see British Appendix III.

[3] *Notes on War Pensions*, Ministry of Pensions, London, 1926, pp. 26–30.
Cf. British Legion, *Notes of War Pensions*, by A. G. Webb, London, pp. 40–41.

Applications for commutation are seldom entertained unless the sum is required for a definite and substantial purpose, such as to assist in the purchase of a house or in the setting-up of a business in which there is good prospect of success. It is never allowed for the payment of current debts, never allowed to a man who, medically examined, fails to show good health and normal expectation of life, and never allowed to compromise the allowance for wife and children. In any instance, only that portion of the pension [1] in excess of fourteen shillings a week, or twenty-one shillings per week in the case of a warrant officer, first class, may be commuted. The Ministry's experience shows that 'it is only in the rarest instances that commutation proves to be the ultimate benefit of the pensioner.'

A totally disabled private soldier is entitled to a minimum pension of two pounds a week, or, in cases of less than total disablement, to the proportionate number of tenths of this sum. If a totally disabled soldier has a pensionable wife, he gets ten shillings for her maintenance. If he has a wife and children, he draws also 7s. 6d. weekly, for the first child and 6s. for each in addition. If, living at home, he needs constant attendance because of his helpless condition, he is granted an allowance up to one pound a week to employ such services as are required. No reduction is made if the attendant is a member of his family.

The maintenance allowance for wife and children corresponds to the degree of the man's disablement. And,

It is to be noted that, though a man may have commuted part of his pension, he remains eligible for money allowances during treatment, less an appropriate deduction because of his commuted pension.

[1] Calculated at the rates provided in the Royal Warrant of 17th April, 1918, plus 20 per cent (i.e., about 33/40 of the rates of the Royal Warrant of 6th December, 1919).

within those limits, the children's allowance may be continued to the age of sixteen; or it may run up to the age of twenty-one, in case the child is earning only nominal wages or is being educated in a secondary school, a technical institution, or a university; or if it is continuously infirm.

But, in the sight of the law, the pensioned ex-service man's family claims exist only as they existed at the moment of his 'removal from duty.' The wife that he married after the receipt of his wound; or after his disablement by the infirmity for which he is pensioned; or after his discharge; or after the end of the War — that wife entitles him to no allowance on her behalf, neither is she pensionable as his widow. Nor can he draw benefits on account of any child of his that is born over nine months after the events just rehearsed.[1]

The restriction puts a definite quietus on the veteran-marrying speculators, those hardy trans-Atlantic industrialists. And, moreover, from the Ministry's point of view, it means that for pension purposes about fifty per cent of the ex-soldiers today on the Great War pension rolls rank as single men.

To the rule above cited, concerning the non-pensionable family, there is, however, one important exception: If a War-pensioned man goes to hospital because of a War-incurred illness, his regular pension is suspended for that period; but in its stead, he is entitled to two pounds a week for himself,[2] and, regardless of the date of his marriage or

[1] Royal Warrant of 6th December, 1919, Article 1a (2); Article 24 (2) and (3).
[2] From this, nineteen shillings is deducted for his hospital treatment and keep.

444

MAN, WIFE AND WIDOW

of the children's birth, he is entitled to a pound a week for his wife and a further allowance for the children. In addition he may receive during treatment any sickness benefit (15s. a week) or disablement benefit (7s. 6d. a week) to which he may be entitled as an insured person under the National Health Insurance scheme.

This practice arose from the Ministry's anxiety, in the early years after the War, to persuade men to accept treatment and thus at least to arrest their maladies when the men themselves, allured by the high wages then current, were inclined to neglect their health and cling to their jobs. It amounts, indeed, almost to bribing the disabled to mend their disablements, the inducement lying in the removal of fear lest the home suffer during the bread-winner's eclipse.

The procedure is applied only in case of men known to be, normally, workers earning for the support of themselves and their families, and prevented only by their medical treatment from doing so now. But in the course of its sixteen years of work, the Ministry has spent £36,520,000 in special [1] allowances to its patients and their families, during treatment, and in addition to their ordinary pensions.

The disabled man, if below commissioned rank, may also be granted maintenance allowance on behalf of an 'unmarried wife,' living with him as his wife, provided that she drew separation allowance on his account during the War.[2] For the 'unmarried wife' the highest weekly allowance is 7s. 6d., as against the lawful wife's ten shillings, unless the man is undergoing medical treatment away from home. In that case, if no sort of grant is being paid

[1] *Whitaker's Almanack*, 1933, p. 640.
[2] Royal Warrant of 6th December, 1919, Article 1 a (4).

445

on account of a legal wife, the unmarried wife may draw an allowance of fourteen shillings weekly.[1] The relationship is not recognized as to any commissioned officer.

If the disabled War-pensioned man goes to jail or prison, for any offence less than high treason, his entitlement to his pension is not thereby affected. That entitlement was established once and for all by his War-service. But the Government does not pay twice for his maintenance: his pension is forfeited during his imprisonment, though the Ministry may and do allow as much of it as necessary for the keep of his wife and family. After serving his term in Wormwood Scrubs, he may walk across to the Ministry's Pension Issue Office, in Acton, and get it renewed to him.

But nine ex-service pensioners out of ten give no sort of trouble, leaving the tenth to disappear into institutions, under an *alias*, to lose his books or his mind, to desert his wife, or to indulge in whatever other fandango may disturb the peace of ledger-keeping clerks. Little fraud of any sort has, however, been attempted.

In the event of the death of the pensioned ex-service man: If he dies in a Ministry hospital, the Ministry bears the funeral costs without question as to the cause of death.[2] If he dies at home, and because of the ailment for which he was pensioned, or from a development of that ailment properly so certified, the Ministry will either meet reasonable burial expenses according to contract rates agreed locally for such cases, or, if relatives prefer private arrangements, the Ministry may contribute a grant not exceeding £7.10.[3]

Every disabled ex-service man's widow in respect of whom her late husband was entitled to draw wife's main-

[1] *Handbook*, paragraph 248.　　[2] *Ibid.*, 269.　　[3] *Ibid.*, 941.

tenance has, upon one condition, a right to the maximum widow's pension, whether or not her husband himself was a pensioner. That condition is that the husband's service-incurred or service-related disablement was the cause of his death within seven years after his discharge or removal from duty; if his death occurs later, his widow's right to pension will depend on his having been himself a pensioner.

If, the husband being a pensioner, his death occurs more than seven years after his disablement, the widow's pension-rate will be affected by the degree of connection between his death and his War-service. If his death was wholly and directly due to his War-disablement, the widow's pension will again be the maximum. If his death was only partially due to his War-disablement, then the widow's pension is at the rate of one-half of her husband's disablement pension. But no widow's pension, in this case, is payable on behalf of a man whose disablement was of less than 40 per cent.[1]

The general rates of widows' pensions are determined by the husbands' rank. A private soldier's widow, either over forty years old or with children eligible for allowance, may receive 26s. 8d. weekly. Under the age of forty, without eligible children, she would receive twenty shillings a week.

But pension on the alternative scale [2] may be granted to the widow whose husband died within seven years of his discharge, under the following conditions:

---

[1] Royal Warrant of 6th December, 1919, Articles 11, 17a and 17b, and Ministry of Pensions Memorandum No. 5, 10th September, 1925, pp. 4–5.

[2] See *ante*, p. 441, note 3, and British Appendix I.

447

Where she is under forty years of age, without eligible children, thus receiving a minimum pension, and, where her present pension is less than one-half her husband's pre-War earnings loaded by 60 per cent because of increased cost of living, she may be awarded an alternative pension up to a maximum of fifty shillings a week.

Where she is over forty years old, or with eligible children, and so receiving a pension at the maximum rate, provided that her pension, with the children's allowance, is or may be less than two-thirds of her husband's pre-War earnings loaded by 60 per cent, she may be awarded an alternative pension up to 66s. 8d. a week.

Where an alternative pension is granted, no addition thereto is made for children.

A pensioned widow, remarrying, loses her pension, but may, if pensioned within seven years of her husband's discharge, receive a lump gratuity equal to one year of her pension, or a somewhat larger sum if she is above the age of forty-five.

Under no circumstances may widows or dependants commute any part of their pension.

The pension due to the lawful widow on account of each child, so long as she herself maintains the child, is, weekly, for the first child, ten shillings; for the second, seven shillings, six pence; for each child after the second, six shillings. The term 'child,' here, means any child born to the man before or within nine months of his removal from the army on account of the disability for which he was discharged or which caused his death.[1] The term also includes his step-children, or his young brothers and

[1] Cf. *ante*, p. 444, for condition.

sisters, if he was their main support at the time of his enlistment or when the War began, whichever is the later.[1]

The basic limit of the child's pensionable age is sixteen years; but, as in the already cited case of children of living pensioners, eligible orphans may be carried on the rolls for a longer period.

[1] Royal Warrant of 6th December, 1919, Article 12. But no addition is made to a widow's alternative pension for children as such, though they will entitle her to the higher (two-thirds) rate if she is under forty years of age.

CHAPTER XI

CHILDREN AND OLD FOLK

We have no record of any case in which a guardian
has misappropriated the monies belonging to a child. — Sir
George Chrystal.[1]

NOWHERE does the National Trait stand out more
clearly than in the treatment of pensioned children of ex-
service men. The whole people seem to accept their appeal, but the Ministry's performance in particular is
kindly, tireless, and minutely painstaking. The number
of children that have come under its care in consequence
of the Great War reaches 1,456,743.[2] In the year 1931-32,
126,085 still remained on its books. Yet under Ministry
handling each child is a special and individual case.

If the child is motherless and neglected, or in hands
that endanger its moral safety, or, if the mother is found
by a court of law to be an unsuitable guardian, the
Minister may assume its custody, and so, as its guardian,
becomes responsible, not merely for placing it in more
promising surroundings, but for making humanly certain
that that promise is kept.[3]

Foster-parents are always preferred to institutions.

[1] Sir George Chrystal, K.C.B., Secretary of the Ministry of Pensions since
July, 1919. The statement above quoted was given in October, 1933.

[2] *Whitaker's Almanack*, 1933, p. 640.

[3] These children are known as 'Section 9' children, from the Section of the Act
that places responsibility for them upon the Minister. War Pensions (Administrative Provisions) Act, 1918 [8 & 9 Geo. 5, ch. 57], Section 9; War Pensions
Act, 1920 [10 & 11 Geo. 5, ch. 23], Section 9; and War Pensions Act, 1921 [11
& 12 Geo. 5, ch. 49], Section 8.

450

Such obvious precautions as seeing that the child's foster-parents are of the same religion as that of the child; that the foster-mother is in every way, by leisure, by habit, by character and experience, capable of properly looking after the child; that the child is well-fed, rightly clothed, and kept clean; that its sleeping-quarters are suitable; that it is not turned into a household drudge, but goes regularly to the right school; that any ailments are at once reported and receive medical care; that the foster-parents do not insure its life — such obvious precautions as these are observed as a matter of course.

But their observance is not left to be enforced by a presumption; by stereotyped order; by outraged neighbours; by the Red Cross; by the S.P.C.C.; by the British Legion; or through someone's possible complaint to a local magistrate; nor is it entrusted to a court-appointed guardian. The Ministry, being charged with the responsibility, itself carries out that responsibility. Every six weeks at least, and frequently much oftener, the child is visited in its home by a faithful voluntary worker,[1] already described — one experienced with children and familiar with their needs and care, whose duty it is to keep careful watch over all these matters, and in general to see to the health, well-being, and happiness of that particular child.

The relationship ordinarily continues unbroken through the years between the growing child and this one intimate, keenly interested, and responsible friend.

[1] See *ante*, p. 387. The voluntary worker acts under the Local War Pensions Committee, both unpaid and both drawing their authority from the Ministry. In matters relating to care of children, their central pivot is the Ministry's Special Grants Committee, to whom power is delegated to increase pensions when need arises.

Apart from 'Section 9' children áre the 'total orphans' in the care of relatives or friends. Here the Minister exercises a general supervision through the voluntary workers or War Pensions Committees previóusly mentioned. But his powers in regard to such wards are not as extensive as they are in relation to 'Section 9' children, the main object of this supervision being to ensure that the child is satisfactorily cared for and that its pension is properly applied for its benefit.

It is, however, worthy of note, that the Ministry, up to October, 1933, had not in the full course of its history, a single record of misappropriation of orphans' funds by the guardians.[1]

Up to the age of fourteen, schooling is compulsory. But the regular pension goes on until the child is sixteen years old, in order to enable further continuance at school if that is desired.[2] And the child of a disabled or dead non-commissioned officer or man may receive the best and most extended education in the land if it can be shown that the father, but for his War-injury, would probably have provided it and that the child cannot now receive it without help; or, if it seems clearly established that the native ability of the child would warrant the outlay.

Today about two thousand children of ex-soldiers are receiving higher education at State expense.

But the majority, naturally, have had enough schooling by the end of the ordinary term; at which juncture it becomes the duty of their Ministry friends to start them

[1] For the American record, see *ante*, p. 178.
[2] Where a total orphan, between the ages of 14 and 16, becomes a wage-earner, the Ministry retains a part of its pension, to build a resource for the future.

in life — to apprentice them, to put them in suitable special training, or to find them appropriate jobs. The Ministry's financial aid does not necessarily stop with the pension-rate; each case being handled on its own merits. No attempt to squander funds could proceed very far, but if a child needs particular training to develop its individual powers, the money is found.

But this general period, the year 1933, is a time of trial for Ministry workers. Children of a difficult generation are floundering in their difficult age. Many of them dislike their first choice of study or of jobs. They want what they have not planned to get. They turn against the thing in hand, and there is no peace in them. The situations produced would often be comic were they not made beautiful by the patience and devotion of the Ministry's handling. 'It is hoped,' says the Minister, in the general instructions to his staff, 'that the personal and friendly interest which is so important a feature of this work may be maintained as far as possible after they [the children] have started in life.'[1]

Those instructions are carried out to an incredible degree. No trust is broken, here, with the soldier-father whose earthly race is run! Alas, America!

The 'unmarried wife,' at the death of the pensioned ex-soldier of non-commissioned rank upon whom she was wholly or substantially dependent,[2] and on whose account

[1] *Handbook*, paragraph 407.

[2] That is, '[Was] wholly or in part dependent... for a reasonable period immediately before the commencement of the War, or before enlistment if subsequent to the commencement of the War, and up to his death unless he was prevented from contributing by circumstances beyond his control.' *Handbook*, paragraphs 127 and 128, note; see also Royal Warrant, 6th December, 1919, Article 20.

she drew or was eligible for separation allowance as for a
wife, during the War, may be granted pension as follows:
If, and for so long as she has any of the dead man's
children in her keeping, twelve shillings weekly, plus the
same allowance for the children as that granted for legitimate offspring. If she has no children by the man, or
ceases to have them in her charge for reasons other than
her own misconduct, she may receive twelve shillings a
week for twelve months after the War; or for twelve
months after the last child leaves her keeping. If through
infirmity or years she is then wholly or partly incapable
of self-support, the pension may be extended.[1] In case
of misconduct, she loses both her pension and the custody
of the children, who are then eligible for a larger pension
as though motherless. If the woman marries, she may
receive, in gratuity, a lump sum not exceeding twenty-
six weeks' pension,[2] in lieu of further pension, and the
allowances for the children may continue.[3]

The illegitimate child of a man who died of War-incurred injury, provided that it was born not later than
nine months after the man's removal from duty on account
of his injury, may be awarded a pension not exceeding
eight shillings a week. This pension may be granted even
when the mother was not the father's 'unmarried wife,'
if satisfactory proof of his fatherhood is established.[4]

The parents [5] of a son killed in the Great War; or the

[1] Royal Warrant, 6th December, 1919, Article 20.
[2] Calculated at the rates of the Royal Warrant of 17th April, 1918.
[3] Royal Warrant, 6th December, 1919, Article 23.   [4] *Ibid.*, Article 18 (2).
[5] The term 'parent,' in the sense of the War Pension Law, 'includes a grandparent or other person who has been in the place of a parent to a man, and has
wholly or mainly supported him for not less than one year at some time before

parents of a son who died of Great War service-con-tracted or service-aggravated injury, and whose death occurred within seven years of his discharge or from his removal from duty as disabled, whichever is earlier, have been pensionable by one of three classes as follows: [1]

1. If they were dependent, wholly or in part, upon their son for a reasonable period before his enlistment, or be-fore the War, and up to the time of his death, they may be granted a 'dependency pension'; or

2. If their son was unmarried, and if no pension is being paid in respect of him to any dependant; and if he was under twenty-six years old when the War began or when he joined, if later; then, irrespective of pre-War depend-ence, age, infirmity, or pecuniary need, they may be granted a 'flat-rate pension.'

3. If at any time, through age or infirmity, and taking all sources of income into account, they become wholly or partly unable to support themselves and are in pecuni-ary need, they may be granted a 'need pension.' This third class of pension has been, since the first of April, 1922, the only class of pension awarded to new claimants.

In regard to the dependency and the flat-rate pensions, neither may be paid to a mother if she married or remarried after the date of her son's mobilization, or enlistment, if later.

In regard to the need pension, 'incapacity for self-support' is recognized solely on grounds of disablement by age or infirmity, not for causes such as preoccupation

the commencement of the War.' Royal Warrant, 6th December, 1919, Article 24 (4).

[1] Royal Warrant, 6th December, 1919, Article 21 (1).

with household duties or with the care of young children. And 'pecuniary need,' in the sense of this regulation, is officially defined as 'the existence of disproportion between a standard income and the actual income. In arriving at the actual income the amount of contributions to household expenses made by persons living in the house, and through possible assistance by children who are in a position to help, are included.'[1]

As to the amount of the award, a dependency pension may reach, but not exceed one pound a week; a flat-rate pension, five shillings a week. A need pension may not be less than five shillings or more than one pound weekly, being fixed according to the necessities of the case, under a maximum means limit of twenty-five shillings weekly for one parent, and thirty-five shillings weekly for two. But when the parent is in receipt of an old-age pension, the need award is limited to an amount that will not cause a reduction of that revenue.

The governing principle is that the State makes up what the deceased son would have been expected to give his parent had he survived.

The amount of the dependency pension or flat-rate pension is the same, whether there be one or two parents, and on the death of one, the full amount may be continued to the survivor.[2]

Where two or more sons have died from service-incurred injury, a dependency pension, or a flat-rate pension may be granted on account of each son. But the total may not exceed one pound a week for each parent. If,

[1] *Handbook*, paragraph 129.
[2] *Handbook*, paragraph 130 (4). For practice in other countries, see *ante*, pp. 45, 244, 279, 335.

however, the pre-War dependency on the sons exceeded this amount, then a gratuity may be awarded, in respect of the balance.

When the son died more than seven years after discharge (or removal from duty, if earlier), need pension as above may be granted to the parents if death was directly due to War-incurred disablement for which pension was being paid. If, however, the death, while not directly due to War-incurred disablement, was so far connected with that disablement as, in the opinion of the Minister, to justify a grant, an award of need pension may be made to the parents if pension for at least forty per cent disablement was being paid to the son at time of death. In such case the parents' need pension is not to exceed one-half of the son's pension.

The following tables [1] tell their own story:

OFFICERS AND NURSES

	Disabled officers pensioned	Officers' widows pensioned	Officers' dependants including motherless children pensioned	Nurses pensioned
August 4, 1914, to March 31, 1932	60,764	12,254	8,926	2,470
Pensions in Payment, March 31, 1932	23,613	8,374	5,267	991

OTHER RANKS [2]

	Disabled men pensioned	Widows pensioned	Motherless children pensioned	Dependants pensioned
August 4, 1914, to March 31, 1932	1,277,933	260,330	16,465	418,369
Pensions in payment, March 31, 1932	454,155	127,970	4,000	275,078

[1] *Fifteenth Annual Report*, Ministry of Pensions, pp. 1 and 7.

[2] 'Other ranks,' in British usage, means men below the rank of commissioned officer.

SOLDIERS WHAT NEXT!

The total expenditure, in pensions, gratuities, and treatment allowances, for pensioners of the first table, for the year 1931–32, was £4,908,910 ($23,857,303); £42,041,559 ($204,321,977) covered the total annual expenditure for the second table.

CHAPTER XII

A JOB AND A HOME

IT IS important to remember that in the United Kingdom the ex-service man, falling upon evil days that do not entitle him to Pension Ministry care, is not thereby left without resource. His Government then offers him, through other Ministries and in common with all other citizens, aid according to his predicament.[1]

This fact eases the task of each Ministry in sticking to its own bailiwick.

Of the War-pension itself, its purpose is achieved when the amount of the award offsets, as nearly as may be, the degree of the recipient's War-incurred sub-normality. The handicapped man being thus brought, as nearly as may be, to the level of his neighbours, the Ministry of Pensions may step aside. What happens thereafter will be due to conditions confronting the whole public; and needs, each according to its nature, will become the care of other agencies existing for ex-service and non-service men alike on grounds of equal citizenship.

Yet it is worthy of special note that on December 31, 1932, in Great Britain and North Ireland, the percentage (10.5) of unemployment among disabled ex-service men as registered at the employment exchanges was considerably less than half that among the general insured popula-

[1] For the schemes of National Health Insurance and of Unemployment Insurance, see British Appendix VII.

459

tion (27.6 per cent).[1] For this fact, which represents a continuous condition, the King's National Roll Scheme is largely accountable.

The King's Roll is a brilliant device of the Ministry of Labour, which, with the co-operation of the Ministry of Pensions, as early as August, 1919, unveiled to the public eye a plan. By this plan employers of labour were invited to pledge themselves to give to disabled ex-service men a stated minimum percentage — about five per cent — of the paid positions on their staffs. The percentage was to be assessed and from time to time revised by a local committee acting with judgment. No compulsion was imposed or implied. But the Minister of Labour, in the House of Commons in April, 1921, announced a Cabinet decision that 'save in very exceptional circumstances all firms contracting for Government contracts, to whom the conditions for membership of the King's National Roll are applicable, must be on the King's Roll.'[2] The following Resolution was passed in both Houses of Parliament on February 16, 1926:

That, in the opinion of this House, it is the duty of the Government in all Government Contracts to make provision for the employment to the fullest possible extent of disabled ex-service men, and to this end to confine such contracts save in exceptional circumstances to employers enrolled on the King's National Roll.

In other words, if, for example, the Office of Works were to issue a call for tenders to supply a thousand tables, no tenders would be considered save such as came from enrolled firms.

[1] *Report of the Ministry of Labour*, 1932, p. 26.
[2] *Ibid.*, 1923 and 1924, pp. 94 *et seq.*

A JOB AND A HOME

Whatever may have happened before, this announcement applied no brakes. Shops, clubs, hotels, manufactur-
ing firms, banks, insurance companies, public and private
business of all sorts responded, to the number, as of
December 31, 1932, of 25,108; by which means alone employment was being supplied to 346,618 disabled ex-
service men.[1]

The example has been followed by many municipal
bodies, and in Government service it obtains on the
grand scale.[2]

Also, for all temporary Government employment, as
between two applicants equally qualified, the ex-service
man, disabled or not, has been given preference; while
between two ex-service men, preference has gone to the
disabled.

As to vocational rehabilitation, this was handled
through three Ministries — their combined expenditure
on that head reaching $172,530,000.

It was the Ministry of Labour, not the Ministry of
Pensions, that administered industrial training for War-
pensioners considered unfitted for their old callings.
About 100,000 ex-service men were so retrained, while
124,000 received 'civil liabilities' grants — a maximum of
£104 to one man — to set up in trade or business. The
Ministry of Pensions, however, provided vocational

[1] *Report of the Ministry of Labour*, 1932, p. 26.
[2] The total male staff of the Ministry of Pensions, in 1930–31, numbered 3379,
of whom 95.3 per cent were ex-service men. Of the ex-service men 56.8 per cent
were War-disabled. In the year following, the male staff had fallen to 2761, of
whom 94.7 per cent were ex-service men, 56.7 per cent being War-disabled. See
Fourteenth and *Fifteenth Annual Reports of the Minister of Pensions*. The total
male staff in all Government Departments, October 1, 1932, was 238,925. Of
these 157,794 were ex-service men.

461

training for the man who still needed medical treatment, but who during treatment could begin the preliminaries of training; in the case of tuberculosis, on account of its special nature, vocational training was arranged by the Ministry of Health in conjunction with the Ministry of Pensions.

Yet a third Ministry, that of Agriculture and Fisheries, handled the Government's scheme for training ex-service men in agriculture and for settling them on the land — a scheme that, before the great achievement of Mr. Mussolini, was the most important land settlement project carried into practice as toward the ex-soldier anywhere in the world.

As to training, this scheme took four forms:

First: For ex-service officers and for educated men from the ranks, without regard to physical condition, it provided (a) practical training on farms for a maximum period of two years, with yearly maintenance allowance up to £125; (b) scholarships up to £175 yearly, for three years, tenable at university departments of agriculture and agricultural colleges, to enable holders to take degrees and diplomas in agriculture; (c) maintenance allowance to enable applicants to complete agricultural courses interrupted by the War; or, (d) grants for overseas training.

Second: Training for disabled ex-service men was provided on specially selected farms; on poultry farms; or at fifty-eight training centres offering three types of instruction — (a) in ordinary farm-labour routine; (b) in market-gardening, poultry and pig-keeping; (c) in specialized poultry-keeping. To be received for any of

462

these three courses, the candidate must show either that he had no occupation before joining the forces, presumably because of youth; or that his disablement seriously diminished his earning capacity in his original employment. If, after his course of training, he began business on his own account, he could claim a grant of tools to a maximum value of ten pounds, provided that he had not already received a civil liabilities grant.[1]

Third: A maximum of two years' training on farms at home or abroad, or in agricultural colleges or farm institutes, was made available to the disabled officer in receipt of disablement retired pay who was medically unfit to resume his pre-War occupation. But this privilege was conditional upon the possession either of a minimum five hundred pounds capital to start farming for himself when trained; or else of a definite offer of agricultural employment other than that of labourer.

Fourth: Four to eight weeks' courses for able-bodied ex-service men with little or no agricultural experience who desired to go into farm work with a view to ultimate acquisition of small holdings. These courses served in secondary purpose as sieves for the sorting-out of men never likely to be suitable for work on the land.[2]

Of the total number of applicants for holdings, about half were rejected or persuaded to withdraw. Preference was given to ex-service men, and to women who had worked on the land for at least six months during the War.[3]

[1] See above.
[2] For all four of these schemes, fuller particulars will be found in two *Reports* of the Work of the Intelligence Department of the Ministry of Agriculture and Fisheries — that for 1919-21, p. 107, and that for 1921-24, p. 92.
[3] Ex-service preference lapsed in 1926.

No account was taken of the size of the applicant's family,[1] his service record and his personal qualifications being the only points considered. No non-service applicant was accepted when a suitable ex-service man was available.

The Act of Parliament governing the scheme left, however, latitude for judgment in the hands of its administrators. It is said that statutory small holdings should be sold or let 'at the best price or sum that can reasonably be obtained.' This dictum the Ministry read as meaning that 'the holding is *not* to be let at a fancy rent to some exceptional person, and *not* at a specially low one in order to put an ex-service man in a particularly favourable position.... It was the intention of Parliament to give ex-service men preference over other applicants in the access to the holdings, but not to subsidize them annually by charging them lower rents than could be obtained from other qualified tenants.'[2]

The total number of persons so provided with farming land between the years 1919 and 1926 was 24,319. At the end of that period, when the Ministry finished its work, 18,915 men remained in occupation, of whom 16,334 were ex-service men; 4937 of their number having, for one reason or another, departed.

As of March 31, 1926, when the Ministry of Agriculture and Fisheries withdrew its administration in favour of county authorities, about half of the Government's investment of £16,000,000 had in some form to be written off.[3]

---

[1] Cf. *ante*, p. 346, for Italian practice.

[2] *Land Settlement in England and Wales*, issued by Ministry of Agriculture and Fisheries, 1925, p. 21.

[3] *Land Settlement in England and Wales*, 1925, p. 53.

The whole scheme had been operated under conditions compelling heavy outlay. The purchase price of the land, to the Government, averaged £42 10s. an acre. Market rates for labour and material ran high, and everything had to be built from the ground up — houses, barns, roads, fences, water-supply; added to which was the charge of 6½ per cent interest on borrowed money.

Yet, as a result a considerable number of growing families of ex-service men have been established in good modern houses, in healthful surroundings, with food as well as shelter safe in their hands, at a time when such blessings are by no means the common lot. Meantime, the patient and laborious Ministry has been adding through experience to the sum of its wisdom.

Here are nuggets therefrom: [1]

Only in exceptional cases have settlers with little or no agricultural experience proved a success, whereas hardworking experienced men have generally succeeded in spite of adverse seasons or falling values.

The least successful element has been the five hundred disabled ex-service men who, previous to settling on small holdings, had received a short course of instruction in some branch of agriculture.

The most successful settler on the small holding is the individualist and often the specialist. Citing a specific case: A disabled ex-service man who, before the War, had been a clerk in a large city office, on doctor's orders took up a holding of ten acres. After six years of steady work on his land, directed chiefly to the growing of bulbs for sale, he journeyed up to London to visit his old colleagues at

[1] *Land Settlement in England and Wales*, 1925, pp. 46 and 51–53.

their office desks. Having considered them carefully, he expressed these views: that he would change places with none of them, because he was now his own master, which none of them would ever be; because he was worth more money than any of them; and because both he and his family were in better health than either they or their families could equal. Says an official report:

> A small holder, in order to succeed, must, for many years after entering into the occupation of his holding 'scorn delights and live laborious days.' Every penny that can be saved must be saved and invested in his land... not only will he have to work harder than at any previous time in his life, but, should he be fortunate enough to make money in one of his early years, he must not be misled into thinking that he can increase his personal expenditure. There may be good years, but it is quite certain that there will be bad years.[1]

Also, great importance is ascribed to the type of the man's wife.

And indeed it is more than interesting to find in the pages of a Ministerial Report that same theme-note that rings through every aspect, however unrelated, of the British effort. Having discussed many elements of prosperity, whether capital to invest, congenital habit, or knowledge to fall back upon, the final verdict runs: 'Experience has taught most Small Holdings Committees to attach more importance to *personal character* than perhaps to any other factor in estimating an applicant's prospects of success.' [2]

But that cap fits other heads. Whatever the success of

[1] *Land Settlement in England and Wales*, 1925, p. 46.

[2] *Ibid.*, p. 46. Statements in this chapter rest, except where another source is cited, upon information personally given by the Ministries in question to the author in London, October, 1932.

the 'Ex-Service Man's Land Settlement Scheme,' much of it must be credited to the personal character of those same 'Small Holdings Committee' members — volunteer workers again, the substantial people of the counties, who, through the years, and without any sort of recompense, have tirelessly given their time, knowledge, and energies to public service. 'In every district of the country,' so the Minister himself bears witness, 'entirely without payment and with scarcely any thanks [they have given] endless hours to interviewing applicants, inspecting land, visiting men in their holdings after they have been settled, attending Committee meetings and even coming to London to discuss [with the Ministry] some particular difficulty that may have arisen. Looking back, it can be said without any qualification, that the work and knowledge so placed at the disposal of the scheme... [have deserved] the deep gratitude of the Nation as a whole.'

The Minister may well be grateful, for by such powerful and steady co-operation is his own work buttressed and entrenched. But 'the Nation as a whole' will entertain no such sentiment. How should it be grateful for what runs in the blood?

It was a United States Senator who said, rather sadly, in the dark winter of 1932–33:

A self-disciplined people of strong character and of firm moral standards will make a success of any form of government. Where those qualities are lacking, iron discipline imposed from above may perhaps build character and gradually create standards. But where discipline is non-existent and where character and standards are alike unsure, no form of government can fill the void nor protect the future.

CONCLUSION

'REMEMBER THIS, AND SHEW YOURSELVES MEN'

AMERICA, France, Germany, Italy, England — we have run their stories through. If, in those varied contrasts our American record gives small cause for pride, whose is the fault?

Can it be laid to any or all of the Presidents of the United States? President after President, regardless of party affiliations, has done his best to save the Nation's honour — has fought manfully to save it, and has failed.

Can it be laid to Congress? If a Congressman uses his seat for his personal interests, is he to be condemned by citizens too sunk in their personal interests to lend him any dependable support or encouragement in work for the country's good? Shall they expect him to stand alone and defy all their enemies for them, at the cost of his own future, while they sleep too heavily to give him a thought or lend him a hand?

Can it be laid to the Administrator of Veterans' Affairs? No man in America deserves more sympathy or more respect than he. A character of deep integrity, humane and just. General Hines has seen his duty as duty is seen by the best type of public servant this world over. His task has been to administer the law as given him by the law-making body; and, while defending that law, so to administer it as to bring about the greatest possible good to those for whom it is framed.

In other countries — in England, for example — the

corresponding public officer is a member of the Government itself, and as such is protected and sustained in the undeviating performance of his task by the whole Government's strength. He can fulfil his duties without fear or favour. No pressure can be brought to bear upon him from exterior sources to force him from his proper course. But the position of an American Administrator of Veterans' Affairs is as vulnerable as that of his compeer is strong. Entirely out of scale with the importance of his work, with his responsibilities, and with the huge sums of public money for which he must account, it leaves him open to attack on all sides and continuously uncertain whether the President of the day, as a measure of political convenience, may or may not reward fidelity in trust as has sometimes been done in the past. The historic precedent is not single.[1] And too often legislators who helped to make the pension laws are loudest against that Administrator of Veterans' Affairs who dares to respect the laws when made.

As to the present Administrator, while on the one hand he has offended by maintaining the purpose of the law in so far as power lay with him, on the other hand his sympathy and compassion for ex-service humanity in its difficulties have been too warm and too understanding to allow him carelessly to accept the confines of any legislative reform scheme.

In consequence, General Hines, in his ten years at the head of Veterans' Affairs, has received and borne, without swerving, as without impatience and without malice, the high tribute of general abuse.

[1] Cf. *ante*, pp. 22-23, and 32-33.

470

CONCLUSION

If not upon the Presidents, if not upon Congress, if not upon the Administrator, upon whom, then, shall the fault of our poor national showing be laid? Upon the Legion Lobby, that prides itself as author of so many towering works? But how is the Legion Lobby to be distinguished from our other great lobbies, unless by its often superior skill? Washington lobbies are established factors in our way of government.[1] Men are master lobbyists as they are master bank presidents. In either case the interest of the general public is not notably their affair. They do the thing they are paid to do, more or less faithfully and well. The Legion Lobby does it faithfully and well and has richly earned its hire. It has shown brilliant political sense in its own sphere of operations, much imagination and dramatic genius, immense industry, unlimited audacity and dash. It has advised against some of the most unwise projects laid upon its knees. Its boast is true: It 'always obtains its objectives.' And its business morals, the while, have been much of a piece with those of some of its financial and professional critics.

If, then, not among the Presidents, not in Congress, not in the Administrator, not in the Legion Lobby, where shall we find the author of our shame?

Since the Lobby's shoulders shed the curse, will it fit, perhaps, on those of the whole Legion?

The American Legion was born in France, in the sacred memories and the solemn light of the War. That light, those memories, the A.E.F. brought home in its heart, a

---

[1] See *Group Representation Before Congress*, by E. Pendleton Herring, Ph.D., The Johns Hopkins Press, Baltimore, Maryland, 1929.

471

SOLDIERS WHAT NEXT!

supreme gift to the country. But the Nation was blind to their light nor shared their memories. The Nation saw few values of any sort save the value of material gain — the thing it called Success. So, in its bigness and strength, though itself a suicide thereby, it quenched the light and it beat the memories down till they shrank into silence and hiding. As for the A.E.F., its divine gift repulsed, for a time, in despair, it gnawed its own vitals; then, steeling itself to forget its vision, it plunged down headlong into the game of Success as played by the national rules.

That part of the A.E.F. that came into the American Legion made only the nucleus of the great body presently formed. The rest had never gone overseas, had no knowledge of the War nor, for the most part, of its spiritual flowering — had, for the most part, no knowledge of any life save as governed in the main by the rules of the Game.

The Legion was young, was vigorous. Its dreamers were soon submerged in the mass. Entering the public stadium, with the pride of its power upon it, it has played the great Game of the Nation against all comers, played by the Nation's own long-accepted rules and played to win. Will the curse rest with the Legion? No.

Must it then lodge, as many say, upon our form of government, outgrown, amiss, no longer apt for the needs of the people?

Once there was a child called Samuel, whom, in the night, his Maker summoned thrice by name. And Samuel answered, 'Here am I.'

So all his life long did Samuel follow that summons, serving his God, as judge and prophet over Israel. And

472

the Lord was with him and let none of his words fall to the ground.

Now it came to pass that, when Samuel was old, and his years a burden upon him, he remained in his own city and charged his sons to ride the long circuits, from Bethel to Gilgal, from Mizpah to Ramah, judging Israel there in his stead.

But Samuel's sons, as they moved through the land, dealt not as their father dealt. They turned aside after lucre, took bribes, perverted judgment.

Yet two there must always be to any bribery — one to give as well as one to take. Where justice is sold, there surely is one who buys, as well as one who sells. And all men who look on without protest partake of the sin thereof.

But the elders in Israel, though they perceived that evil was come, saw not through to the cause thereof. They saw not the perversion of the people's minds that endured to witness bribery, and permitted the selling of judgment. Only they saw the perversion of judges, that was but the crest and emblem of the whole people's decay.

So the elders came before Samuel in trouble and sore discontent, saying: The form of our Government is amiss, and is no more apt for the needs of the people. Our judiciary is corrupt. Behold thou art old and thy sons walk not in thy ways: now make us a King to judge us, like all the other nations.

When Samuel heard the complaint of the elders, his heart sank down within him. For he feared that in his old age he had sinned, and failed in his charge toward Israel, in that Israel was turned from the paths of right-

473

eousness to go after evil, and would now cast off the law itself, by which he had taught it to live.

So Samuel humbled himself before his Maker in agony of spirit, as an unprofitable servant who had failed in his trust.

And the God of his childhood, the God of his youth and his manhood, who had heard him always, heard him now, and removed from his soul that blackness of fear.

'They have not rejected thee,' said the Lord God of Israel, comforting his old servant as a mother comforts her first-born. 'They have not rejected thee, but *they have rejected Me, that I should not reign over them.*'

THE END

APPENDICES

APPENDIX

I

RATES OF EXCHANGE

ɔse of this book the rates of exchange as to Great
America are given as they stood before both
t off the gold standard.   As to France, Italy, and
rates given are those in force since their return to
lard after post-War inflation and fluctuations.

	par 3.9170	cents per franc	(3.92)
ark	par 23.82	cents per RM.	(23.82)
	par 5.2632	cents per lira	(5.26)
	par $4.86656	per sovereign	($4.86)

ⵏ in parentheses are those used in this book in
ign currency to dollars.

II
UNITED STATES APPENDIX

I. HISTORY AND STRUCTURE OF THE UNITED STATES VETERANS' ADMINISTRATION

THE Bureau of War Risk Insurance, created by the Act of September 2, 1914, came into being to provide insurance on cargo and freight vessels of American registry exposed to the dangers of the World War.

When the United States entered the War, she determined to set up a new law, on modern lines, to care for her disabled and the dependants of the dead, and to offer insurance, at peace-time rates, against death or disablement to the armed forces.

The various parts of this undertaking were at first handled under three agencies, the Bureau of War Risk Insurance, the Rehabilitation Division of the Federal Board for Vocational Education, and the Public Health Service.

By the Act of August 9, 1921 (Public 47, 67th Congress), an independent bureau, called the Veterans' Bureau, was set up, in which were consolidated the Bureau of War Risk Insurance, the Rehabilitation Division, and as much of the Public Health Service as then related to the examination, assignment to hospitals, and welfare of World-War ex-service men who were patients of the two agencies.

At this time provision was made for decentralization of activities of the new Veterans' Bureau, at the discretion of the Director. Authority was given to establish fourteen regional offices, and sub-offices not in excess of fifty.

By the World-War Veterans' Act of June 7, 1924, Section 7, decentralization was pushed farther, this Act decreeing a central Office in Washington, and regional offices and sub-offices, 'not exceeding one hundred in number, within the territory of the United States and the outlying possessions.' These regional offices, under the Director of the Bureau, were to hear com-

479

UNITED STATES APPENDIX

plaints, examine, rate and award compensation claims, grant medical, surgical, dental, hospital and convalescent care, and vocational training.

The Director of the Veterans' Bureau was further authorized, in the same Act, Section 10, to utilize for the care of the disabled or sick, existing or future facilities of the Federal Public Health Service, of the Departments of War, the Navy, or the Interior, the National Home for Disabled Soldiers, and other Governmental facilities as authorized. The Director, subject to the limits of the appropriation, might alter, improve, or extend existing Government facilities, buy or build new properties, or contract with State, municipal, or private institutions.

Empowered by the Act of July 3, 1930, the President of the United States, on July 21, 1930, issued an Executive Order for the consolidation and co-ordination of governmental agencies affecting ex-service men of all wars into a unit to be called the Veterans' Administration. This meant the bringing under one head of the United States Veterans' Bureau, the National Home for Disabled Volunteer Soldiers, and the Bureau of Pensions; the chief of the combined agencies, entitled Administrator of Veterans' Affairs, to be appointed by the President.

General reorganization followed, under a load of work continually shifting and increasing with each upheaval occasioned by new legislation creating new classes of beneficiaries.

As of October 31, 1932, there were 39 Regional Offices and 15 combined facilities. As of this date there were 14 tuberculosis hospitals; 18 neuropsychiatric hospitals; 11 general hospitals; 9 homes and 2 diagnostic centres. As of October 31, 1933, there were 38 Regional Offices, 16 combined facilities; 14 tuberculosis hospitals; 20 neuropsychiatric hospitals; 10 general hospitals and 12 homes and 2 diagnostic centres. The establishment of 'combined facilities' has for its purpose the giving of full service to the veteran, which includes hospitalization, domiciliary care, the handling of examinations, rating and adjudication of claims. The Central Office of the Veterans' Administration is in the city of Washington. Its personnel as of October 31, 1932, numbered 5233; as of October 31, 1933, the number was 4673. The total number of employees of the whole Administration was, as of October 31, 1932, 36,201, 66.59 per cent of the male part being

480

UNITED STATES APPENDIX

ex-service men. The total administrative costs, for the fiscal year 1932, represented about 3.78 per cent of the total annual expenditure for benefits.[1]

For administrative ends, the country, before 1933's changes, was divided into four areas — the Eastern area, centring in New York, the Southern, centring in Birmingham, Alabama, the Western, centring in San Francisco, and the Central area, whose headquarters were in Chicago. This plan of organization is no longer employed under the new policy inaugurated in 1933.

CHANNELS OF APPEAL

Up to 1933's changes, in each administrative centre's area, boards of review operated — appeal boards, each comprising medical men and rating specialists. These bodies heard appeals from the decisions of the rating boards of the Regional Offices. From the decision of an Area Board, appeal could again be had to the Central Office in Washington. And after Washington had rendered verdict, a dissatisfied man who had acquired new evidence could still reopen his case and swing it again around the same circle, times without number. This privilege was largely exercised.

II. WORLD-WAR MONTHLY COMPENSATION RATES AND PERCENTAGES OF DISABILITY

As Affected by Pre-War Occupation, Current
June 7, 1924 to June 30, 1933

The following schedule illustrates, by means of a few examples, the permanent ratings of World-War compensation provided by the law current from June 7, 1924, until its super-session in 1933. Only the medium and maximum rates — those for occupational variants 5 and 9 — are here given (see *ante*, p. 106), those for the remaining seven occupational variants not being

[1] For 1932 figures see statement of Administrator of Veterans' Affairs before Joint Committee, 73rd Congress, 2nd Session, December, 1932, pp. 46 and 48–49.

481

UNITED STATES APPENDIX

included. Multiple disabilities are computed according to the
French system, for which see French Appendix I, Article 12.

	MEDIUM (per cent)	MAXIMUM (per cent)
Ankylosis of ankle:		
Favourable angle	20	38*
Unfavourable angle	35*	56
Ankylosis of wrist:		
Favourable angle		
Major	25	44
Minor	20	38
Unfavourable angle		
Major	35	56
Minor	30	50
Loss of sight of one eye	35	56
Loss of one eye	†	†
Nearly total deafness in one ear	20	38
Total deafness of one ear	30	50
Slight deafness of both ears	10	23
Severe deafness of one ear and slight of the other	30	50
Nearly total deafness of one ear and slight of the other	35	56
Total deafness of one ear and slight of the other	40	61
Severe deafness of both ears	70	85
Total deafness of one ear and severe of the other	80	91
Deafness of both ears existing in a degree nearly total	90	96
Loss of thumb, index, and middle fingers:		
Major	50	70
Minor	40	61
Loss of thumb and index finger:		
Major	35	56
Minor	27	46
Loss of thumb:		
Major	25	44
Minor	20	38
Loss of all the fingers, thumb and palm remaining:		
Major	50	70
Minor	40	61
Loss of index and middle fingers:		
Major	35	56
Minor	27	46

* Percentage=dollars; e.g., 20 per cent gives $20, 38 per cent gives $38, etc.
No additional allowance for dependants, with permanent rates. If rated on a
temporary basis, rate was based upon $80 for total disability plus additional
allowance for wife, child or children and dependent parents.

† Sixty per cent in all occupations (disfigurement included).

UNITED STATES APPENDIX

	MEDIUM (per cent)	MAXIMUM (per cent)
Loss of little and ring fingers:		
Major	15	31
Minor	10	23
Loss of index finger:		
Major	20	38
Minor	15	31
Loss of all the toes of one foot	20	38
Loss of great toe	10	23
Chopart's amputation of foot, with good results — amputation tarsometatarsal joint	30	50
Abdominal Wall, hernia:		
Truss or belt not prescribed	0	—
Well supported by truss or belt under ordinary conditions	10	23
Not well supported by truss or belt under ordinary conditions, or where such cannot be worn	25	44
Recurrent, post-operative, large hernias, not supported under ordinary conditions	50	70
Post-operative, massive, irreducible evisceration, very severe diastasis, or extensive diffuse destruction or weakening of muscular and fascial support may in extreme cases be rated permanent and total. (All occupations.)		
For bilateral hernias each ratable at 15 per cent or more, 15 per cent added by combination to the unilateral rating.		
Amputation of arm at shoulder joint:		
Major	94	98
Minor	89	96
Amputation at hip joint	85	94
Amputation of arm near shoulder joint:		
Major	89	96
Minor	80	91
Amputation of thigh near hip joint	80	91
Amputation of arm near elbow:		
Major	84	94
Minor	75	89
Amputation of thigh near knee joint	58	77
Amputation of a hand:		
Major	70	85
Minor	61	79
Amputation of a foot	44	65
Total disability of one hand:		
Major	70	85
Minor	61	79
Total disability of one foot	44	65

UNITED STATES APPENDIX

Loss of use of both eyes and one or more limbs; or double total permanent
disability.. $200
Loss of sight of both eyes.. 150
Loss of use of both feet; or hands; loss of one hand and one foot; or one
foot and one eye; or one hand and one eye; loss of hearing, both ears;
organic loss of speech; permanently helpless or permanently bedridden. 100
Additional allowance for attendant if helpless; or statutory award for arrested tuberculosis... 50
Additional compensation for loss of use of a creative organ, or of one or
more feet or hands... 25
> (This is over and above whatever compensation regularly attaches to
> the injury incurred. Cf. French Appendix IX, *note*. Amputation.)

III. CLASSIFICATION ACCORDING TO DISABILITY PERCENTAGES

DISABILITY COMPENSATIONS * IN PAYMENT AS OF JUNE 30, 1932,
FOR DISABILITIES DIRECTLY OR PRESUMPTIVELY RESULTING
FROM SERVICE IN THE WORLD WAR

DEGREE OF IMPAIRMENT	NUMBER	MONTHLY VALUE
No disability†	857	$21,425
10–19..............	73,716	1,207,646
20–29..............	102,697	3,281,278
30–39..............	32,546	1,127,506
40–49..............	21,272	919,878
50–59..............	19,321	998,631
60–69..............	10,900	693,704
70–79..............	12,616	928,604
80–89..............	5,053	434,855
90–99..............	1,478	140,984
100................	48,202	4,745,681
Total........	328,658	$14,500,192

* *Annual Report of the Administrator of Veterans' Affairs*, 1932, p. 108.
† This figure means cases of 'loss of use of a creative organ,' interpreted to
mean one testicle, to which condition was attached by statute an extra award
of $25 monthly, aside from any compensation that may have been awarded
covering the defect. Section 202 (3), World-War Veterans' Act as amended.

UNITED STATES APPENDIX

DISABILITY ALLOWANCES ‡ IN PAYMENT TO WORLD WAR EX-SERVICE
MEN FOR DISABILITIES NOT CONNECTED WITH WAR SERVICE,
JUNE 30, 1932

DEGREE OF IMPAIRMENT	NUMBER	MONTHLY VALUE
25 per cent disability	258,663	$3,103,956
50	96,484	1,736,712
75	23,525	564,600
Total disability	28,912	1,156,480
Total	407,484	$6,561,748

‡ *Annual Report of the Administrator of Veterans' Affairs*, 1932, p. 115.

IV. WORLD-WAR VETERANS

RECEIVING COMPENSATION ON JUNE 30, 1933, FOR THE FOLLOWING DISABILITIES

PRIMARY DIAGNOSES	CASES
Blindness { Total	675
Blindness { Partial	927
Deafness { Total	342
Deafness { Partial	2,446
Respiratory diseases (includes bronchitis)	25,200
Nervous diseases (including endocrines)	43,547
Insanity	22,105
Rheumatism { Arthritis, chronic	6,329
Rheumatism { Myalgia	
Rheumatism { Lumbago	
Epilepsy	3,307
Trench feet	19
Hernia	4,709
Nephritis — Bright's disease	1,329
Appendicitis	39
Curvature of spine	811
Debility, general	456
Heart disease	25,639
Frost bite	9
Amputations { leg and foot	2,935
Amputations { arm and hand	1,105
Amputations { fingers and toes	3,945
Injuries (includes wounds, fractures, and contractions)	26,952

UNITED STATES APPENDIX

V. NOTES ON THE ACTS OF MARCH 20, AND JUNE 16, 1933

Public No. 2, 73rd Congress, an Act to Maintain the Credit of the United States Government, became law on March 20, 1933, superseding previous laws. It purposed, in principle, to bring into uniformity the several and diverse pension laws hitherto appertaining to the various wars of the United States, applying particularly to service during and subsequent to the Spanish-American War. It did not, however, fully adopt the general European principle of entitlement — War-incurred or War-aggravated injury essential to War-pension. On the contrary, in certain directions the new American policy still bestows War-pensions as benefits on a limited class where the disability or death giving rise to the pension has no War connection and where European governments, if granting aid, bestow it upon all citizens alike.[1] Thus, the Acts of March 20, 1933, and of June 16, 1933, with their accompanying Veterans' Regulations, give old-age pension, at the age of sixty-two, as a War-pension, to Spanish-War veterans who sustained no War-injury; they admit as pensioners at thirty dollars a month men who enlisted at any time during the Spanish War or World War; who remained ninety days in the service; who were honourably discharged; who in after life, because of circumstances unrelated to War service, but not their own misconduct, became totally and permanently disabled; and whose annual income, if single, does not exceed $1000, or, if married or with minor children, $2500. And they grant free hospitalization in Veterans' Administration institutions to ex-service men of any war who served ninety days, and who are permanently disabled by non-service-incurred disease or injury, including tuberculous or neuropsychiatric ailments, if they have no adequate means of support and if their disability is not due to misconduct.

With the above exceptions, recognizing as compensable at War rates no disability but those contracted in or aggravated by active military or naval service in line of duty; and including ex-service men of the Spanish-American War, the Philippine Insurrection, the Boxer Rebellion, and the World War in the same

[1] Cf. British Appendix I, II, and VII.

provision, Public Number 2, 73rd Congress, established the following rating schedule, comprising five steps only:

If and while disability is rated at	Monthly compensation
10 per cent	$ 8
25	20
50	40
75	60
Total disability	80

Six higher awards, grading up to $250 monthly, were further provided, by statute, for heavy disabilities.

By reduction of the rating scale to five steps whose maximum brought $80, instead of the former $100, such changes as the following resulted: A man who had lost a thumb and two fingers in combat, who had previously been rated as 40 per cent disabled, and who therefore drew $40 a month in compensation, would now be cut to 25 per cent disability, and would be paid $20. This reduction would not take effect till the end of the fiscal year, June 30, 1933, but such prospects raised much protest. On June 6, 1933, by Public No. 78, and accompanying Regulations, the steps and rates for disabilities contracted in or aggravated by active military service as above were raised thus:

If and while the disability is rated at	Monthly compensation
10 per cent	$ 9
20	18
30	27
40	36
50	45
60	54
70	63
80	72
90	81
Total disability	90

The ten-step rating scale is stated by the Administrator of Veterans' Affairs (*New York Times*, July 30, 1933) to have produced an average reduction of ten per cent in the pensions of men whose disability was acquired in or aggravated by active War service. No reduction could have been necessary had these men not been carrying the burden of 400,000 hangers-on, draw-ing War-pension for civilian ailments.

Statutory monthly rates for specified service-incurred disabili-ties were at the same time fixed thus:

1. Loss or loss of use of only one hand, one foot, or one eye, in addition to pension as rated........................ $25
2. Loss or loss of use of both hands, or both feet, or one hand and one foot; or so helpless as to need regular aid and at-tendance... 150
3. Loss of both hands and one foot or both feet and one hand or light perception, only, in both eyes.................. 175
4. Light perception only, in both eyes, and loss or loss of use of one hand or one foot............................... 200
5. Combination of two or more injuries named under 2, 3, and 4 above, i.e. double total disability as described......... 250

NEW CHANNELS OF APPEAL AS FROM JUNE 16, 1933

By Executive Order of July 28, 1933, Veterans' Regulation No. 2 (a) Part II, a Board of Veterans' Appeals was appointed by the Administrator of Veterans' Affairs, with the approval of the President. This Board is composed of a chairman, vice-chairman, and not over 15 associate members, with, in addi-tion, the needful administrative and professional personnel, to hear appeals from decisions rendered by Rating Boards. The Board of Appeals is divisible, by its chairman, into working sec-tions of three members each. The finding of a section, when unanimous, is now in principle the final decision of the Board of Veterans' Appeal, subject, however, to change on discovery of obvious error, or on additional official information supplied by the War or Navy Departments. All claims involving bene-fits are held subject to one review by the Veterans' Administra-tion through this Board of Veterans' Appeal. But no claim, when disallowed thereby, may be reopened excepting when, subsequent to such disallowance, new and material evidence in the form of official reports from the Army or Navy Departments is secured. This Regulation should greatly reduce the volume of appeal work, hitherto both heavy and interminable.

UNITED STATES APPENDIX

Public No. 2, was modified by Public No. 78, the Act of June 16, 1933. This measure permitted extension of time for continued payment of compensation to World War ex-service men whose disabilities were rated as presumptively service connected (cf. *ante*, p. 201). By the new law such men could draw, until October 31, 1933, three-fourths of the compensation they had received under the prior law. Meantime all presumptive cases must be examined by Special Review Boards, whose decision would, when rendered, determine the status or termination of the compensation. By Presidential order, the provisional terminal date was again extended to November 30th.

The Special Review Boards were appointed by the President, under authority contained in Public 78. Five members were assigned to each Board, it being provided that three men out of the five must not have been in the employ of the Veterans' Administration at the time of the passage of the Appropriation Act. To these Boards were referred the cases of World War ex-service men who entered the service before November 11, 1918, and whose disabilities, not caused by their own misconduct, were only presumptively of service origin. That is to say, their disabilities owed their compensability to one of two arbitrary statutes. First, that which declared all men presumably sound at time of enlistment unless there and then otherwise officially recorded. Second, that provision of the World War Veterans' Act (Section 200) which ruled that any man showing a ten per cent development of certain diseases [1] before January 1, 1925, must be presumed to have acquired his disability in World War service.

These Boards were authorized to review the claims referred to them and determine whether service connection should be granted under Public No. 2, and were given broad authority under the law with reference to rendering these decisions, all reasonable doubts to be resolved in favour of the veteran and the burden of proof in such cases resting on the Government.

[1] Any neuropsychiatric disease, any active tuberculous disease, spinal meningitis, paralysis agitans, encephalitis lethargica, and amœbic dysentery.

UNITED STATES APPENDIX

Approximately 40 per cent of the total number of cases that were referred to these Boards have been continued on the rolls as service connected; this is as of November 23, 1933.

By Public No. 78' the Independent Offices Appropriation Act, reduction of compensation of directly service connected cases is limited to a maximum of 25 per cent. And although as of November 22, 1933, no definite estimate was yet available, it is officially recognized that under the Rating Schedule of June 16, 1933, many men even if cut 25 per cent, will still be insured of receipt of pension in excess of that which they formerly received. This Act also provides that the dependants of deceased World War ex-service men who were pensioned for presumptions no longer recognized, shall not be reduced in their monthly compensation.

III
FRENCH APPENDIX

I. THE GREAT-WAR PENSION LAW OF FRANCE

MARCH 31, 1919

Modifying the legislation of pensions of land and sea forces, concerning wounds received and maladies contracted or aggravated in service, as well as consequent death

TITLE I

ARTICLE 10

Maimed individuals whose infirmities render it impossible for them to move, to attend to themselves or to fulfil the essential actions of life, have a right to hospitalization if they apply for it, in which case the expenses of hospitalization are deducted from the pension granted to them.

If they do not receive or if they cease to receive that hospitalization, and if, living at home, they are obliged to have constant recourse to the assistance of a third person, they are entitled, by special allowance, to an increase equal to one-fourth of their pension.

The right to that hospitalization or to that increase of pension is approved by the Invaliding Commission on the occasion when it decides the maimed man's degree of disablement.

ARTICLE 11

In case of multiple infirmities, none of which involves total disability, the percentage of invalidity is calculated entirely upon the main infirmity, and for each of the supplementary infirmities is granted proportionally to the remaining ability. To that effect, the infirmities are classified in decreasing percentage order of invalidity.

However, when the main infirmity is considered as involving an invalidity of at least 20 per cent, the degrees of invalidity of

491

each of the supplementary infirmities are raised from one, two, or three categories, be it 5, 10, 15 per cent, and so on, according to the rank, whether second, third, or fourth, that they occupy, in the decreasing order of their importance.

ARTICLE 12

In the case of multiple infirmities, one of which involves total disability, there is granted, in addition to the maximum pension, a supplement varying from one hundred (100) to one thousand (1000) francs in multiples of one hundred francs, in order to take into account the infirmity or the supplementary infirmities estimated upon a scale from one to ten.

If two or more supplementary infirmities are added to the principal infirmity, the degree of disability is calculated by according to each of the supplementary wounds the increase indicated in the preceding article.

Article 11 being difficult to understand, even for a Frenchman, the following illustration has been furnished by the Minister of Pensions, to whose courtesy is also due the above translations of Articles 10, 11, and 12:

'In the case of a man suffering from three infirmities, the first rated at 80 per cent, the second at 30 per cent, and the third at 15 per cent:

'The first infirmity, that of 80 per cent, counts for its whole value. Then we say, "80 per cent from 100 per cent leaves 20 per cent."

'With the second infirmity, that of 30 per cent, we begin by increasing this second infirmity by 5 per cent, i.e., 30 per cent plus 5 per cent equals 35 per cent. But the man is entitled as by the preceding paragraph to only 20 per cent of this second rating. Twenty per cent of 35 per cent is 7 per cent; therefore his total infirmity is now raised from 80 per cent to 87 per cent.

'With the third infirmity, that of 15 per cent, we begin by raising this third infirmity 10 per cent. Fifteen per cent plus 10 per cent equals 25 per cent. Since his preceding infirmities total 87 per cent, we say 87 per cent from 100 per cent leaves 13 per cent. We then take 13 per cent of the 25 per cent above indicated, or 3.25 per cent. This we add to the 87 per cent, thus arriving at a total infirmity of 87 per cent plus 3.25 per cent, or 90.25 per cent.

'According to the law, rates of disablement are calculated by degrees of 5 per cent, and we take always the upper degree, consequently the rate of disablement of the individual just discussed would be fixed at 95 per cent.'

II. PENSIONS OF WIDOWS AND THEIR CHILDREN

The Law of 1919 establishes the right to pension (1) to the widows of soldiers or former soldiers dying from cause attributable to service whether the husband was pensioned or not during his lifetime, (2) to widows of former soldiers dying from a disease not attributable to service and drawing a pension at a rate representing a disablement of at least 60 per cent.

A higher pension is awarded to the widow of the man dead from service-attributable causes than to the widow of the second or reversionary category. But the first rate is always granted to the widow of the beneficiary by Article 10; i.e., a man who was incapable of performing alone the essential acts of life, whatever may be the cause of death. The rates of widow's pension vary with the *rank* of the husband.

In order to establish a widow's claim to pension, it must be shown that the husband's state of health at the date of marriage did not warrant the forecast of death within a short time. If the marriage was not contracted *before* the soldier's wound or his infirmity was incurred, the right to widow's pension is granted only where the soldier's death is attributable to service, and is subject to the condition that the marriage lasted *at least two years.* In such a case pension is granted at the reversionary rate (the lower), except as regards the widows of maimed men who are beneficiaries under Article 10.

A woman who, not fulfilling the conditions of priority indicated above, has married a man pensioned at 80 per cent at least, is admitted to reversionary pension on the sole condition that the marriage was contracted within two years of her husband's return to civil life and that it has lasted at least one year. She is admitted to pension without any condition as to duration of marriage if the cause of death was accidental. When death is attributed to service, proof must be established by a medico-legal report. Nevertheless, attributability to service is admitted by *legal presumption* if the wound, disease, or aggravation of the condition of health has been recognized and recorded during service, and if death did not occur more than one year after the man's return to his home. (Every death occurring before the 4th December, 1919, has been, in the absence of contrary proof, recognized as attributable to service.) Divorced widows cannot claim pension under this law. The same holds good with regard to legally separated widows, and to the widow who has forfeited her parental rights; and her children, if she has any, are considered as orphans (see below, paragraph 3). If the deceased man has left minor children of a previous marriage, the widow receives only one half the normal pension.

SUPPLEMENTATION OF PENSION

To the basic rates fixed by the law there is at present added, but only for widows who have not remarried, a special temporary supplement fixed at 140 per cent of the rate for a private's widow. Moreover, for each child under eighteen, or infirm, a supplement of the basic rate of 300 francs is granted whatever the rank of the father. This supplement is at present increased by various allowances which bring it actually to the total of 1028 francs.

REMARRIED WIDOWS

It has been shown above that a widow who remarries receives a rate of pension considerably lower than that awarded to widows who have not remarried. On the other hand, the rate of allowances for children is maintained unchanged. If, in the case of a widow who remarries, there are children of a previous marriage of the deceased soldier, such widow does not receive less than the pension of a remarried widow of a private; that is to say, 800 francs at present, or 500 francs if it is a question of a reversionary pension. A widow who remarries may, moreover, by final surrender of her pension, receive a lump sum equal to three years' pension.

494

FRENCH APPENDIX

When the death of a soldier occurs in circumstances entitling his widow to pension, his minor children are entitled to pension up to the age of twenty-one years or for their lifetime if they are infirm:

(1) If their mother dies or is already deceased.

(2) If she is ineligible to receive pension; for example, if she is not of French nationality or has lost such nationality.

(3) If she forfeits her right to pension. The rights which appertain or would have appertained to the mother pass then to the orphan child; if there are several children they benefit conjointly by a pension comprising:

   (a) A principal pension equal to widow's pension.

   (b) As many supplements to the basic rate of 300 francs (increased by the additions mentioned above) as there are children, *less one*, under eighteen or infirm.

If the soldier's death is not of such a nature as to entitle the widow to pension, children under eighteen years or infirm continue to receive the benefit of the supplement for children (which varies with the father's rank) to which their father was entitled during his lifetime. Children whose pensioned mother remarries become entitled to the supplements for children attached to widow's pension; moreover, half their mother's pension is allotted to them. If the mother who remarries foregoes her pension, the pension is transferred to the children's name under the same conditions as if their mother was deceased. If the widow leaves, at her death, children of a previous marriage who were maintained by the deceased soldier, these children enjoy the same advantages as if they actually were the children of the soldier. Minor children of a previous marriage of the deceased soldier share to the extent of one-half, with their step-mother and with her children, the pension to which she is entitled by the father's death. If the step-mother remarries, they keep the share which has thus been allotted to them. Whether the step-mother remarries or not, there is allotted to each child under eighteen, or infirm, a supplement of the basic rate of 300 francs increased by corresponding additions. Recognized natural children are entitled to pension under the same conditions as legitimate children on condition that they were conceived before the event which gives rise to pension and that they were recognized within two months of their birth. Following the War of 1914–18 recognition, if before the 4th March, 1920, was accepted in cases where there were reasonable grounds for delay. If, in the case of a widow or legitimate children, there are also natural children, the pension of the natural children is calculated like that of orphans who are the issue of a previous marriage of a deceased soldier.

III. PENSIONS OF *ASCENDANTS*

For the first time in France, the law of the 31st March, 1919, established pensions in favour of parents of soldiers who died for France. These pensions are granted even if a pension is already allotted to the wife and children of the deceased soldier. Persons eligible to receive *ascendants'* pension are the following:

(1) The father and the mother.

(2) Failing father and mother, then grandparents; it being understood that each grandparent or each pair of grandparents can receive only one pension.

(3) Instead and in place of father and mother, any person who can prove that he or she has brought up and maintained the soldier when a child and who has taken the place of his parents (or of one of them) until his coming of age or until his call to the colours. Pension is granted only if the circumstances of death are such as to entitle a widow to pension. *Ascendants* must be aged at least sixty years if male, or fifty-five if female. If, however, the *ascendant* (or the *ascendant's* spouse) is afflicted with an incurable infirmity, the age limit is relaxed in accordance with the degree of infirmity.

Furthermore, the widowed mother is not subject to any condition as to age if she has in her charge at least one child minor or infirm, or called to the colours. Originally it was made a condition that the income of the *ascendant* must be below income tax level, but at present the law grants a reasonable latitude in this connection.

496

FRENCH APPENDIX

Ascendants of foreign nationality were at first excluded from all entitlement to pension, but the law of the 28th July, 1921, admitted them to pension. Nationals of a state formerly at war with France are subject to the condition that they must reside in France. If one of the conditions referred to above is no longer fulfilled, the pension is suspended, but it may be ultimately restored.

There are two basic rates of *ascendant's* pension, the same for all ranks:

(1) The rate of 800 francs is granted at present to (*a*) married *ascendants*. (If, although married, they are in fact separated, pension is divided into two equal portions.) (*b*) *ascendants* of either sex, widowed, divorced, separated, or unmarried.

(2) The rate of 400 francs is granted to *ascendants* of either sex remarried and to those who did not contract marriage until after the decease of the soldier.

If the *ascendants* who are entitled to pension have lost several children in the service of France, the rate is increased by 100 francs for each child deceased after the first.

The basic rates above (800-400-100 francs) are at present increased by special temporary supplement of 140 per cent.

IV. CHANNELS OF APPEAL

The law of the 31st March, 1919, established special tribunals to deal with disputes to which its application may give rise.

(1) In the first instance, disputes are heard before a 'departmental' pensions tribunal sitting in principle in the chief town of the *département*. This tribunal is at present composed of three members: a civil judge of tribunal, a doctor, and a war pensioner.

(2) On appeal disputes are taken before a Regional Pensions Court sitting in principle in the same town as the Court of Appeal. The Court comprises three magistrates of the Court of Appeal. Finally the Council of State is competent to deal with appeals against decisions of the 'departmental' tribunals or Regional Courts when it is

alleged that such tribunals or courts have exceeded or misused their powers, or where informality or illegality is alleged.

V. THE THREE 'NATIONAL OFFICES'

The National Office for Maimed and Discharged Soldiers, *L'Office National des Mutilés et Réformés de la Guerre*, renders varied services to War-victims, such as the vocational re-education of maimed men and War-widows, the grant of allowances and loans, and the implementing of legislative measures concerning cheap dwelling-houses and Friendly Societies. The Office also grants subsidies to charitable societies which assist War-victims. This Office also issues disablement certificates by which disabled men get concessions in travel-rates by land and sea.

The National Ex-Soldiers' Office, *L'Office National du Combattant*, also affords help as to cheap housing and as to Friendly Societies.

The National Office of Wards of the Nation, *L'Office National des Pupilles de la Nation*, is charged with the special duty of protecting War-orphans and, in certain circumstances, the children of maimed men. It facilitates their education by the grant of scholarships and allowances and in general comes to their aid when necessary.

Of these three Offices, the first two are under the Ministry of Pensions; the last under the Ministry of National Education. All three constitute public establishments having financial autonomy. Their income is provided principally by State subsidies and to a certain extent by private generosity. They are administered by Councils in which the beneficiaries concerned are largely represented. The State subsidy to the National Office of Wards of the Nation came to 141,000,000 francs for the year 1932; that to the National Office of the Maimed and Discharged Men was 35,000,000 francs; and that to the National Office of Ex-Soldiers reached 50,000,000 francs.

By virtue of the Laws of the 4th August, 1923, and 30th December, 1928, the State increases by a proportion, which varies from twenty-five to sixty per cent, payments made by ex-service men and war victims to Friendly Societies with the

providing pensions up to 6000 francs per annum after
f sixty years. In the 1932 Budget, the amount of these
bsidies reaches 120 millions. The State grants subsi-
)oo to 15,000 francs in order to enable maimed men to
:heap dwelling-houses. These subsidies vary according
sability and the family expenses of the men concerned.
nated amount in this connection for the 1932 Budget
'o millions.
.mon fund, consisting of the fines incurred by indus-
)loyers who have not complied with the rules govern-
)ulsory employment of maimed men, has been set up for
onal Office for Maimed Men in order to enable it to
:abled men who are not complete invalids, but who, by
f their wounds, are nevertheless, unemployable.
:s rebates on taxes have been conceded in favour of
men.
:ate has made itself liable for one-half per cent interest
granted to military pensioners or civil victims of the
Societies of Agricultural Credit or Building Societies.
unt estimated for this purpose in the 1932 Budget comes
ooo francs.

VI. MINISTRY OF PENSIONS

CREDITS GRANTED FOR THE YEAR 1932

Finances — War-Pensions...................frs.	4,983,600,000
Pensions for Heavily Disabled..................	353,566,000
Pensions — Provisional Allowances..............	345,545,000
Allowances for the Care of the Tuberculous........	222,000,000
Retraite du Combattant [1]	1,140,000,000
Prosthetics.................................	22,000,000
Grants through Social Insurance Societies to implement free help to war-disabled members........	112,600,000
Grant to *L'Office National des Mutilés* [2]	35,000,000
Grant to *L'Office National du Combattant* [2]........	50,000,000
Grants-in-Aid toward payment of Mutual Benefit Association dues owed by war-disabled members....	120,000,000
Grants for the construction of cheap houses for the maimed...................................	70,000,000
Appropriation to reduce rate of interest..........	2,700,000
Grant to *L'Office des Pupilles de la Nation,* [2] (War Orphans).................................	141,000,000
Total...............................frs.	7,598,011,000

[1] *Retraite du Combattant.* This indicates the pension conferred by the Finance Law of April 16, 1930, in which service-incurred disability is not necessary to entitlement. See *ante,* p. 250.

[2] Independent Departments, to which Government contributes these sums by annual act. Each Department has its governing board some of whose members are appointed by Government and some elected. These Boards include representatives of Government as such, and are composed of Senators, Deputies, ex-service men, and members of ex-service men's organizations.

FRENCH APPENDIX

VII. CLASSIFICATION OF PENSIONERS

1. Classification of Pensioners according to percentages of Disability, as of October, 1932.

PERCENTAGES	NUMBER OF BENEFICIARIES
100 — Articles 10 and 12 of the Law of March 31, 1919 (See French Appendix I)	2,700
100 — Article 10	7,475
100 — Article 12	10,232
100	38,288
95	8,499
90	19,284
85	14,298
80	26,000
75	7,250
70	17,000
65	51,000
60	57,000
55	7,500
50	51,000
45	18,000
40	78,000
35	21,200
30	120,000
25	56,210
20	193,000
15	114,000
10	242,000
Total	1,159,936

2. Number of Beneficiaries classified under Heavy Disablement. 125,617

3. Number of Tuberculous pensioned at 100 per cent disablement, not hospitalized, receiving a nursing allowance of 10,000 francs annually. 24,577

4. Number of pensioned widows:
   Widows not remarried. 416,524
   Widows remarried. 275,000

5. Number of *ascendants* pensioned. 833,901

FRENCH APPENDIX

VIII. RATES OF WAR–PENSIONS FOR OFFICERS

The appended table offers an abbreviated measure of the annual allocation of pension, as increasing with rank, to commissioned officers of the French Army; it shows only the lowest, middle and highest degree of disablement. In the French service, company officers are subdivided by rank as follows: Captains and lieutenants, four degrees; sub-lieutenants, two degrees; in regard to these company officers the superior degree alone is here exhibited.

To ascertain the full pension of a disabled officer of given rank, take the pension due to a private, of the same degree of disablement (see Schedule of War-Pensions, Appendix IX) and add to it the sum indicated for that disablement as attached to the rank of the officer.

Per cent of Disability	Sub-Lieutenant two bars	Lieutenant four bars	Captain four bars	Lieutenant-Colonel	Colonel	General of Brigade	General of Division
	fr.	fr.	fr.	fr.	fr.	fr.	fr.
100	1,200	1,800	2,750	4,400	6,000	7,800	10,200
50	600	900	1,375	2,200	3,000	3,900	5,100
10	120	180	275	440	600	780	1,020

Code, pp. 222–23.

IX. SCHEDULE OF WAR-PENSIONS, 1932 — RATES FOR PRIVATE SOLDIERS

Category of Pensions	Amounts of the Pensions (in francs)				Increase for Children			
	Base Pension	Temporary Supplement 140%	Heavily Disabled Allowance	Total	Base Increase	Temporary Supplement 140%	Heavily Disabled Allowance	Total
A. Heavily Disabled								
100%, Article 10 and 12.[1] Blinded, having two limbs amputated, paraplegics entitled to double benefit of Article 10.	4,250	5,950	28,500 to 29,500	38,700 to 39,700	300	420	308	1,028
100% Article 10 and 12, apart from the three types above specified........	4,250	5,950	27,500 to 28,500	37,700 to 38,700	300	420	308	1,028
Tuberculous...........	4,250	5,950	27,500 to 28,500	37,700 to 38,700	300	420	308	1,028
100%, Articles 10 and 12 (5 degrees). Blinded, having two limbs amputated, paraplegics	3,625	5,075	18,500	27,200	300	420	308	1,028
100%, Articles 10 and 12 (5 degrees), apart from the three types above specified.........	3,625	5,075	17,500	26,200	300	420	308	1,028
Tuberculous..........	3,625	5,075	17,500	26,200	300	420	308	1,028

[1] Awards in this table are paid annually. See Appendix I for text of Articles 10, 11 and 12.

SCHEDULE OF WAR–PENSIONS, 1932 (continued)

Category of Pensions	Amounts of the Pensions (in francs)				Increase for Children			
	Base Pension	Temporary Supplement 140%	Heavily Disabled Allowance	Total	Base Increase	Temporary Supplement 140%	Heavily Disabled Allowance	Total
100%, Article 10. Blinded, two limbs amputated, paraplegics..............	3,000	4,200	16,000	23,200	300	420	308	1,028
Other 100%, Article 10, including the Tuberculous.................	3,000	4,200	15,000	22,200	300	420	308	1,028
100%, Article 12 — (5 degrees)	2,900	4,060	5,900	12,860²	300	420	308	1,028
Tuberculous²	2,900	4,060	5,900	12,860²	300	420	308	1,028
100%, by reason of multiple infirmities...	2,400	3,360	1,400 to 5,400	7,160 to 11,160	300	420	308	1,028
100%, without multiple infirmities.......	2,400	3,360	1,400	7,160	300	420	308	1,028
100% tuberculous²	2,400	3,360	1,400	7,160²	300	420	308	1,028
95% built up by multiple infirmities......	2,280	3,192	1,120 to 2,120	6,592 to 7,592	285	399	266	950
95% without multiple infirmities.........	2,280	3,192	1,120	6,592	285	399	266	950
90%.................	2,160	3,024	840	6,024	270	378	252	900
85%.................	2,040	2,856	700	5,596	255	357	238	850

Note. Amputations. The Heavily Disabled other than those 100% disabled who come under Articles 10 and 12 having right to the double benefit of Article 10 and other than the disabled of 100% or 95% built up by multiple injuries, may be granted, if they have an amputated limb, an additional allowance varying from 100 to 1,000 francs.

² To this classification of the Tuberculous a Nursing Allowance of 10,000 francs is granted and should be added to their total.

SCHEDULE OF WAR-PENSIONS, 1932 *(continued)*

CATEGORY OF PENSIONS	AMOUNTS OF THE PENSIONS (IN FRANCS)				INCREASE FOR CHILDREN			
	Base Pension	Temporary Supplement 140%	Heavily Disabled Allowance	Total	Base Increase	Temporary Supplement 140%	Heavy Disabled Allowance	Total
B. Other Disablements								
80 per cent	1,920	2,688	—	4,608	240	336	—	576
75 per cent	1,800	2,520	—	4,320	225	315	—	540
70 per cent	1,680	2,352	—	4,032	210	294	—	504
65 per cent	1,560	2,184	—	3,744	195	273	—	468
60 per cent	1,440	2,016	—	3,456	180	252	—	432
55 per cent	1,320	1,848	—	3,168	165	231	—	396
50 per cent	1,200	1,680	—	2,880	150	210	—	360
45 per cent	1,080	1,512	—	2,592	135	189	—	324
40 per cnet	960	1,344	—	2,304	120	168	—	288
35 per cent	840	1,176	—	2,016	105	147	—	252
30 per cent	720	1,008	—	1,728	90	126	—	216
25 per cent	600	840	—	1,440	75	105	—	180
20 per cent	480	672	—	1,152	60	84	—	144
15 per cent	360	504	—	864	45	63	—	108
10 per cent	240	336	—	576	30	42	—	72

Note. Amputations. Certain disabled men of from 55% to 75%, who are not beneficiaries of Article 65 of the Law of March 31, 1919, and who have lost a limb by amputation, may claim, in addition to their assigned rate, an allowance varying from 100 to 600 francs. See *Code*, pp. 323-24.

X. CHEDULE OF WAR-PENSIONS, 1932 — RATES FOR SOLDIERS' DEPENDANTS

Category of Pensions	Amounts of the Pension			Increase for Children			
	Base Pension	Temporary Supplement 140%	Total	Base Increase	Temporary Supplement 140%	Heavily Disabled Allowance Special Increase	Total
C. Widows not Remarried and Orphans having right to a Pension for reasons other than the remarriage of their Mother:							
a) of soldiers killed by the enemy..........	frs. 1,200	frs. 1,680	frs. 2,880	frs. 300	frs. 420	frs. 308	frs. 1,028
b) of those dead as result of service-incurred disablement	1,200	1,680	2,880	300	420	308	1,028
c) of soldiers drawing pension of 100%, Article 10, but who died from cause other than that for which pension was granted.........	1,200	1,680	2,880	300	420	308	1,028
d) of soldiers drawing pension of 60%, dead from cause other than that for which pension was granted...	800	1,120	1,920	300	420	308	1,028
D. Remarried Widows. Orphans having right to a pension on account of the Mother's remarriage							
a) of soldiers killed by the enemy.........	800		800	300	420	308	1,028
b) of those dead as result of service-incurred disability..	800		800	300	420	308	1,028
c) of soldiers drawing pension of 60%, dead from cause other than that for which pension was granted...	500	—	500	300	420	308	1,028

SCHEDULES OF WAR-PENSIONS, 1932 (continued)

Category of Pensions	Amounts of the Pension			Increase for Children			
	Base Pension	Temporary Supplement 140%	Total	Base Increase	Temporary Supplement 140%	Heavily Disabled Allowance Special Increase	Total
E. 'Ascendants' (Parents, etc.)							
a) Father or Mother not widowed, not divorced, not separated and not celibate.	frs. 400	frs. 560	frs. 960	frs. 100	frs. 140	—	frs. 240
b) Father widowed, divorced, separated or not married.	800	1,120	1,920	100	140	—	240
c) Wife widowed, divorced, separated, or not married..	800	1,120	1,920	100	140	—	240
d) Father and Mother, conjointly.	800	1,120	1,920	100	140	—	240
e) Grandfather or grandmother not widowed, not divorced, not separated or celibate.	400	560	960	100	140	—	240
f) Grandfather widowed, divorced, separated or not married.	800	1,120	1,920	100	140	—	240
g) Grandmother widowed, divorced, separated or not married.	800	1,120	1,920	100	140	—	240
h) Grandfather and grandmother, conjointly.	800	1,120	1,920	100	140	—	240

IV

GERMAN APPENDIX

I. THE WIDOW

The widow's pension is fifty per cent of her husband's base pension plus his compensation allowance if such he received. When she has passed her fiftieth year, or, if she is temporarily incapable of earning money to eke out her living, her pension is raised to 60 per cent of her husband's annuity. And a widow who is an incurable invalid in body or mind may be allowed, in addition, a sum equal to one-third of what a woman, given normal health and the same actual equipment of skill and training, should earn by her work in the region in question.[1]

The widow who remarries may for a dowry draw the amount of three years' pension in a lump sum, and thereby closes her claim.

The widow of a pensioned ex-service man at least 50 per cent or more disabled, but whose death was not due to his War-injury, has no title to a pension. Nevertheless, if her husband was at least 50 per cent disabled, she may be allowed a grant-in-aid.[2]

The widow's right to pension rests wholly on her husband's entitlement as a War-disabled soldier. Her own character and conduct, therefore, are not a subject of enquiry on the part of the pension authorities.

II. ORPHANS, AND CHILD-DEPENDANTS

Orphans of the War-pensioned man who died in direct consequence of his service disablement are entitled, during the lifetime of the mother, to 25 per cent of the amount of the deceased father's base pension plus his compensation allowance;

[1] *Handbuch*, Articles 36 and 37.
[2] *Handbuch*, Article 40.

509

or, to 40 per cent thereof if the mother, too, is gone. This entitlement holds until the child has completed its sixteenth year. If at that time the vocational training is not finished, the pension may be continued through the twenty-first year.[1]

When needful or expedient, a grant-in-aid may be given to orphans of heavily disabled men whose death was not in direct consequence of the War-disablement for which they were pensioned.[2] But this grant-in-aid may not exceed two-thirds of the pension due to the orphan of a man whose death directly resulted from War-injury. And in all cases each orphan is under the care of a guardian appointed by and responsible to the courts, who is charged with its proper upbringing.

By law the allowance for children may be continued to the child's twenty-first year to help forward the completion of vocational or higher education, and at discretion educational assistance may be continued still longer in cases of extraordinary promise.

For mentally or physically deficient children incapable of self-support, the allowance continues for life. These laws for education and maintenance extend their benefits to step-children; to adopted and foster-children if the disabled man was supporting them before his disablement and as long as their necessary support rests entirely upon him; and to illegitimate children who were begotten before the pensioner's War-disablement and whose paternity is not open to doubt.[3] The term 'orphan,' in the law, is therefore to be interpreted as meaning 'child-dependant.'

III. PENSIONS OF PARENTS AND OF THOSE
IN LOCO PARENTIS

The parents of an ex-service pensioner whose death was the result of his War-hurt are entitled to pension if in need, and for the duration of their need. Their pension is the same as the widow's, i.e., 50 per cent of the base pension of the dead soldier, plus his compensation allowance, if such he had.

'Need' is understood to mean that the mother is over fifty

[1] *Handbuch*, Article 41. [2] *Handbuch* Article 42. [3] *Handbuch*, Article 30.

510

years old, that the father is over sixty, that the dead man was their substantial support, that they now have no claim for support upon anyone in a position to maintain them; or that, age aside, they are unable to earn money — although a mother still burdened with the care of young children is not required to earn money under this law — and that their monthly income does not exceed from 52 to 60 Reichsmarks.[1]

But if either of the pair dies, the pension of the survivor is reduced to 30 per cent of the soldier's base pension.[2]

Parents who have lost more than one son as a result of War-injury receive an additional 20 per cent for each son, beginning with the second.[3]

The word 'parents,' as used in this law, includes grandparents; adopted parents, when the adoption took place before the pensioned man's War-disablement; or step or foster-parents whose support the dead pensioner had been.[4]

IV. PROVISION FOR REVIEW

War-pensioned ex-service men have always the right of appeal from Pension Office decisions on their status. The first court of appeals is the *Versorgungsgericht* — the 'Court of Pensions'; from whose verdict recourse may be taken to a superior bench, the *Reichsversorgungsgericht* — the State Court of Pensions. The lower of these courts consists of a judge-president, usually a major official of the civil service, supported by two assistants. Of the two assistants, one will be a member of the legal staff of the Red Cross or similar non-governmental social service, and the other a representative of some organization of service-disabled men.

The higher court consists of three men chosen as above, sitting with one judge of the common courts and one member of the *Reichsversorgungsgericht*. In a certain percentage of the cases examined, the court of appeal alters or reverses the decision of the Pension Office's doctors.

[1] *Handbuch*, Article 46.　　　　　　　　[2] *Handbuch*, Article 46.
[3] *Handbuch*, Article 46. The difference between 52 and 60 Reichsmarks represents, here, the possible range of difference in zone of residence.
[4] *Handbuch*, Article 44.

GERMAN APPENDIX

This last fact, in the opinion of some German medical authorities, arises from failure always to include a medical man in the bench, which, they believe, is thereby exposed to error in judging the condition of the applicant from impression rather than from experience.

The case of the plaintiff as against the Pension Office is generally prepared and pushed for him by that particular ex-service men's organization to which he belongs. These organizations are entirely unofficial. Nevertheless, they are recognized by the Pension Office as the ex-service man's legal advisers, in which capacity they represent him in court.

The *Reichsverband Deutcher Kriegsopfer,* for example, claiming a roster of 300,000, declares itself a mutual-aid society neutral alike in politics and religion. Its members are War-disabled soldiers and their dependants, and these only. Its dues are from 80 Pfennig ($0.19) to 1.10 Reichsmarks ($0.26), monthly. These cover all expenses and entitle the membership, without extra charge, to representation with the Ministry, in court, or before local authorities, to defend or advance their interests.[1]

Most of the service organizations, however, have now, in one direction or another, a strong political cast. Yet, whether political activity or pleasant old-comradeship over a pipe and a glass of beer be the major purpose of their existence, each declares, as a rule, an intention to guard the interests of its own people.

V. TABLE OF DISABLEMENT PERCENTAGES OF ARTICLE 25

(Decree of September 1, 1920, modified by Decree of December 21, 1927)

A heavily disabled soldier receives, without regard to the degree of diminution of his earning capacity, a minimum pension on the basis of the following rates. If the diminution of earning capacity entitles him to a higher pension, he receives that higher pension; for multiple disablements with decreased earning capacity, a more favourable pension will be granted:

[1] Statement of Herr Dietrich Lehman, chairman, to the author, Berlin, September 1, 1932.

GERMAN APPENDIX

	Per cent
Loss of a leg or an arm	50
Loss of a leg below the knee	40
Loss of a foot	30
Loss of the forearm or the entire hand of the arm used	50
Loss of the other arm	40
Loss of three or more fingers including the thumb of the hand used	35
Loss of the other hand	30
Loss of three or more fingers exclusive of the thumb of the hand used	30
Loss of the other hand	25
Loss of the thumb only of the hand used	25
Loss of the entire scalp	25
Loss of or total blinding of one eye	25
Hemianopsia	40
Loss of a jaw or more than one-third thereof	30
Loss of the palate	25
Loss of all the teeth	25
Loss of both auricles	25
Loss of considerable tissue of the tongue causing heavy impediment of speech	30
Loss of the larynx	50
Loss of the entire nose	50
Ozena	30
Facial disfigurement, making it difficult to consort with others	25 to 50
Loss of both testes or of the male organ	30
Loss of the uterus	30
Loss of the spleen or a kidney	30
Unnatural anal urinary or intestinal fistula	30
Loss of the sphincter ani; severe prolapse of rectum	30

Other physical injuries similar to the above list will be granted corresponding consideration.

The physical disability of itself will not be rated higher than a 50 per cent diminution of the earning capacity, even if there are multiple injuries.

Handbuch, Article 25.

VI. *ZUSÄTZRENTE* OR COMPENSATION PENSION

The *Zusatzrente* [1] is allotted thus, in annual payments:

50 to 60 per cent disablement .... 144 RM	or $34.30
70 80............................ 300 RM	71.30
Over 80............................ 504 RM	120.05
For a widow entitled to pension........ 408 RM	97.19
For the widow without pensioned children, and entitled to 60 per cent of her late husband's pension.............. 450 RM	107.19
For a fatherless orphan entitled to pension 120 RM	28.58
For a parentless orphan............... 180 RM	42.88
For a single parent................... 150 RM	35.73
For a parent couple.................. 240 RM	57.17
For a recipient of rent-money or transitional relief....................... 300 RM	71.46
For a widow in receipt of grant-in-aid [2] .. 240 RM	57.17
For an orphan in receipt of grant-in-aid [2] . 96 RM	22.89
In addition to the above, the heavily disabled man or the beneficiary in receipt of rent-money, may, when charged with dependent children, be granted in extra allowance for each child............ 108 RM	25.73

[1] *Handbuch*, Articles 88, 89, and 90.

[2] The grant-in-aid, whether to widow or to orphan, may not exceed two thirds of the pension.

VII. TABLE OF THE REICH'S PE

FROM JULY, 1931

TABLE I. PENSION FOR DISABLEMENT *WI1*
TORY SUPPLEMENT

MONTHLY RATES (IN REICHSMA:

Diminu- tion of Earning Capacity (Per cent)	Locality	Pension without Wife's and Children's Supplement	Wife's Supple- ment	Child's Supple- ment
30	S	13.40*	—	3.35
	A	12.75		3.20
	B	12.10		3.—
	C	11.45		2.85
	D	10.80		2.70
40	S	17.85		4.45
	A	17.00		4.25
	B	16.10		4.05
	C	15.30		3.80
	D	14.49		3.60
50	S	31.60	3.15	6.30
	A	30.10	3.—	6.—
	B	28.55	2.85	5.70
	C	27.05	2.70	5.40
	D	25.50	2.55	5.10
60	S	37.80	3.80	7.55
	A	36.—	3.60	7.20
	B	34.15	3.40	6.85
	C	32.35	3.25	6.45
	D	30.50	3.05	6.10

* The basic pension figures, in the 3rd column above, i
per cent groups represent the amounts made effective A
ing a reduction of practically 20 per cent in the rates e

GERMAN APPENDIX

Table I. Pension for Disablement (*continued*)
MONTHLY RATES (IN REICHMARKS)

Diminu- tion of Earning Capacity (Per cent)	Locality	Pension without Wife's and Children's Supplement	Wife's Supple- ment	Child's Supple- ment	Pension for Married Men Without Children	Supplement of 3/10 of Base Pen- sion to Man without Wife and Children
70	S	44.65	4.45	8.95	49.10	13.40
	A	42.50	4.25	8.50	46.75	12.75
	B	40.30	4.05	8.05	44.35	12.10
	C	38.15	3.80	7.65	41.95	11.45
	D	36.—	3.60	7.20	39.60	10.80
80	S	52.10	5.20	10.40	57.30	15.65
	A	49.55	4.95	9.90	54.50	14.85
	B	47.05	4.70	9.40	51.75	14.10
	C	44.50	4.45	8.90	48.95	13.35
	D	42.—	4.20	8.40	46.20	12.60
90	S	61.40	6.15	12.30	67.55	18.40
	A	58.40	5.85	11.70	64.25	17.50
	B	55.45	5.55	11.10	61.—	16.65
	C	52.45	5.25	10.50	57.70	15.75
	D	49.50	4.95	9.90	54.45	14.85
100	S	76.70	7.65	15.35	84.35	—
	A	73.75	7.40	14.75	81.15	—
	B	72.—	7.20	14.40	79.20	—
	C	69.60	6.95	13.90	76.55	—
	D	67.25	6.75	13.45	74.—	—
	—	59.—	5.90	11.80	64.90	—

Handbuch, p. 355.

Supplement for Nurse or Attendant: 1st, 50 RM; 2nd, 75 RM; 3rd, 100 RM; 4th, 125 RM.

Columns showing the pension inclusive of the supplement for children from 1 to 7 in number, have been omitted, as the amount given in the 5th column above represents the supplement per child.

Tables 2 and 3 are omitted. Table 2 embodies the pension for disabled men receiving an *ordinary* (single) Compensatory-Supplement which means an increase of 35 per cent over figures appearing in the 6th column above.

Table 3 covers pensions for disabled men receiving the *higher* (increased) Compensatory-Supplement which means an increase of 70 per cent over figures appearing in the 6th column above.

516

VIII. NUMBER OF EX-SERVICE MEN CARRIED ON THE PENSION ROLLS IN 1924-32

With the Degrees of Their Disablement

Diminution of Earning Capacity (Per cent)	October 1924	October 1926	May 1928	May 1930	May 1931	May 1932
	Number of Disabled					
30.............	291,985	294,318	305,213	357,398	357,560	346,355
40.............	116,694	118,787	121,354	128,563	128,107	124,676
50.............	127,846	130,338	132,915	138,908	138,709	137,161
60.............	65,276	66,308	67,050	68,734	68,311	67,611
70.............	56,204	55,393	56,839	59,071	58,910	58,299
80.............	25,516	27,293	28,758	30,660	30,705	30,604
90.............	4,905	5,407	5,840	6,332	6,568	6,373
More than 90....	32,493	38,793	42,761	49,287	49,490	49,324
Lack of data....	12	230	564	443	——	——
Total.......	720,931	736,867	761,294	839,396	838,360	820,403

Die Zahl

IX. NUMBER OF DEPENDANTS CARRIED ON THE PENSION ROLLS FROM 1924 TO 1932

	October 1924	October 1926	May 1928	May 1930	May 1931	May 1932
Total number of Widows.......	364,950	361,024	359,560	362,190	360,930	360,164
Those receiving 50% of full pension......	305,367	273,070	247,404	217,192	201,939	185,116
Those receiving 60%........	59,583	87,954	112,156	144,998	158,991	175,048
Half Orphans...	962,486	849,087	731,781	562,700	456,637	332,528
Orphans.......	65,486	62,070	56,623	46,000	38,768	28,884
One Parent.....	131,187	141,064	148,230	155,131	145,699	138,733
Parent Couple..	62,734	67,230	73,852	77,746	66,664	58,702
Widows receiving a grant-in-aid..........	6,845	9,957	12,441	15,817	15,561	14,513
Half Orphans' grant-in-aid..	3,268	6,337	8,590	11,550		
Orphans' grant-in-aid.......	169	396	537	774	9,800	8,143
Parents' grant-in-aid (single).	—	6,631	16,375	57,853	71,634	71,534
Parents' grant-in-aid (couple).	—	10,354	22,772	75,732	87,178	79,308

Die Zahl

518

X. POST–WAR SHIFTS IN INDUSTRIAL STATUS OF EX–SERVICE MEN WHO HAVE LOST ONE ARM [1]

	Per cent
1. Brain Workers (*Kopfarbeiter*):	
Improved in position since War	25.5
Same in position as before War	69.
Fallen in position since War	5.5
2. Agriculturists:	
Improved in position since War	34.1
Same in position as before War	36.6
Fallen in position since War	29.3
3. Artisans:	
Improved in position since War	42.3
Same in position as before War	13.1
Fallen in position since War	44.6
4. Unskilled Labour:	
Improved in position since War	13.6
Same in position as before War	13.6
Fallen in position since War	72.8

Of the Brain Workers, the 69 per cent who have maintained their pre-War status are, in general, teachers, clerks and minor officials.

Of the Agriculturalists, the 34.1 per cent who have bettered themselves have become farm overseers or have acquired better holdings.

Of the Artisans, the 44.6 per cent who have lost ground are now letter-carriers, hotel door-men, station porters, etc.

Of the Unskilled Labourers, the 72.8 per cent, who have deteriorated have become street vendors of small nothings, street sweepers, idlers, beggars.

[1] From a table in the Museum of the Ministry of Labour, Berlin.

V

ITALIAN APPENDIX

I. EXCERPTS FROM THE WAR–PENSION LAW OF ITALY

(Royal Decree of July 12, 1923, n. 1491) *

TITLE II

ARTICLE 13

[Entitlement of the Disabled]

The soldier disabled by wounds, injuries or sickness incurred or aggravated in War-service, as described under any one of the Categories of Table A, is entitled to a life-pension if his disablement is permanent; or, to a renewable allowance if his disablement is susceptible to improvement.

When the disablement comes under one of the Categories in Table B, a lump-sum indemnity is granted at the time of discharge, provided that the service given does not entitle to rest-dues or to rejection-dues.

Disablement not named in Tables A and B will come under that category which is equivalent to the degree of the soldier's disability.

ARTICLE 15

[Direct Privileged War-Pension, Article 15, 1st paragraph; Direct Ordinary War-Pension, Article 15, 2nd paragraph]

When wounds, injuries or sickness have been incurred from enemy weapons... in actual warfare or even outside the combat-zone whilst belonging to a mobilized unit, provided that the soldier shall have already rendered effective service in the combat-zone, he is entitled to a... Privileged War-Pension, of an amount determined by his rank and by his degree of disablement as found under the Categories of Table C. [For Tables A to L see pages following.]

521

ITALIAN APPENDIX

In the cases not falling under Table C, the claim to a Pension or War-Allowance will be established under the provisions of Table D.

ARTICLE 17
[Allowances for super-disability and for nursing]

Besides the pension or the renewable allowance, an allowance for super-disability and supplementary assistance is granted to the heavily-disabled who are listed under Table E, in accordance with their classification under that Table if they are in receipt of a direct *privileged* War-pension. If they are drawing a direct *ordinary* War-pension, the extra allowance under Table E will be decreased by one-quarter.

To the tuberculous who are not entitled to super-disability-allowance, a supplementary nursing-allowance of 720 lire per year is granted if the disabled soldier is drawing a direct *privileged* War-pension. If he is drawing a direct *ordinary* War-pension, the supplementary nursing allowance will be decreased by one-quarter.

When other infirmities co-exist with a disability of the first category under Table A, a supplementary-allowance for multiple disability is granted, in the proportion indicated in Table F.

TITLE III
ARTICLE 23
The Claims of the Widows and of the Orphans

The widow of a soldier who died through War-service or through causes attributable to the War, and against whom no separation judgment has been passed, is entitled to a *privileged* War-pension in the proportion established under Table G if the death was caused by wounds, injuries, or disablements inflicted by enemy weapons or else was incurred in actual warfare or even outside the combat-zone while belonging to a mobilized unit, provided the soldier shall have already rendered effective service in the combat-zone, as determined by Article 15.

When the soldier's death is caused by War-service or through causes attributable to the War, but under other circumstances, the widow is entitled to an *ordinary* War-pension, in the proportion established under Table H.

ARTICLE 26

When there are orphans of soldiers who died because of War-service or through causes attributable to the War, of less than 14 years for boys, or 16 years for girls, and until completion of said age on the part of the last orphan, then the widow who of herself, if childless, would be eligible to a pension under Table G, is granted the pension corresponding under Table I, and the widow so eligible under Table H is granted the pension corresponding under Table L.

The sons who have attained the age of 14 years and the unmarried daughters who have attained the age of 16 years are reckoned as being under said age, even after having attained majority, provided they have become, before the death of their father, totally unable to perform any remunerative work through an infirmity included under Category One of Table A. They are also reckoned as such if they have become totally unable to perform any remunerative work after the death of their father but before having attained majority.

Even if there are no orphans as described in the present Article, the pension is still granted according to Tables I and L should the widow of the soldier, through an infirmity included under Category One of Table A, be unable to perform any remunerative work; and provided also that she is proved to be without the necessary means of subsistence.

[The translation of the above Articles, from the Italian legal text was kindly made by H. I. M. Consulate-General, in New York.]

ITALIAN APPENDIX

II. STRUCTURE OF THE FASCIST GOVERNMENT'S SCHEME FOR THE AID OF WAR-DISABLED, WAR-ORPHANS AND EX-SERVICE COMBATANTS

The Fascist Government's scheme for the assistance of ex-service men falls into three parts:

(1) *L'Opera Nazionale per la protezione e l'assistenza degli Invalidi di guerra* — 'The National Institute for the Protection and Aid of the Maimed and Disabled of the War.'

(2) *L'Opera Nazionale per gli orfani di guerra* — 'The National Institute for the Protection and Assistance of War Orphans.'

(3) *L'Opera Nazionale per i Combattenti* — 'The National Institute for Fighting Men.'

These *Opere* or 'Institutes' derive their power from the delegated authority of the State and are financed from the national Treasury. Each *Opera* has as its counterpart an *Association* of the same name. The *Opera* represents the Government. The Association represents the beneficiary body. And to co-ordinate the work of the two, delegates from each Association sit in each meeting of its corresponding *Opera* directorate. It is the business of the Association to present the needs of the beneficiaries, whether men or War-orphans, and the business of the *Opera* to decide how Government is to meet those needs.

All three pairs — *Opere* and Associations — are under the control of a special bureau of Government, called *L'Assistenza Reduci e Famiglie caduti in guerra.*

WAR-ORPHANS

The Fascist Government's organization for the care of War-orphans, *L'Opera Nazionale per gli orfani di guerra,* operates under a central direction placed in Rome. This direction has its commission in each province; and in each commune of each province, under the chairmanship of the *podestà*, the municipal judge, is a working committee whose duty it is to keep in close touch with the individual child.

For children who are ailing, the *Opera* has its own children's colonies, both in the mountains and by the sea. For those who need special hospital treatment, special children's hospitals are provided; or sometimes the patient is sent to a general hospital having children's wards for such cases.

Children who are physical defectives are cared for in two Homes, one in Leghorn, the other in Rome.

Children who are ill, but who can be cared for at home, are looked after by the visiting nurse and supplied with medicine and food.

.As far as possible, the child is left with its relatives. But if such are lacking, or if for any reason they are unable or unsuitable to have the care of a child, excellent orphanages have been established by the *Opera*, where the child may remain until its eighteenth year, and where it is given an education and a trade or calling, chosen in accordance with the aptitude and intelligence developed in the individual case. The child of an agriculturist, however, must follow agricultural lines. Otherwise the question of birth and parentage affects nothing.

Great importance is attached to the development of agricultural proficiency, and the *Opera* maintains no fewer than fortynine agricultural school colonies for War-orphans, both boys and girls, where they are given a good home and where, with a common education, they are taught practical farming in all branches.

Upon marriage, the *Opera* gives the War-orphan a little dowry, as a nest-egg for the new household.

All this work is done at the expense of the State.

III. CLASSIFICATION OF DISABILITIES ESTABLISHING ENTITLEMENT

Injuries and Infirmities Constituting Entitlement to Life Pension or to a Renewable Allowance

Table A. First Category [1]

(Title 11, Article 13, 1st paragraph)

(1) Total loss of both hands and feet, above the wrists and the ankles.
(2) Loss of both hands above the wrists, and the loss of one foot above the ankle.

[1] The Law sets forth eight categories of injuries and infirmities which give claim to life-pension or to a renewable allowance. It has seemed sufficient to give, here, only the first and the eighth category, thus indicating their embrace.

(3) Organic and irreparable change of both eyes, having produced absolute and permanent bilateral blindness.

(4) Organic and irreparable changes in both eyes, entailing such reduction of sight as scarcely to permit the counting of the fingers at a distance of ordinary near vision.

(5) Loss of both hands.

(6) Permanent insanity rendering the individual totally incapable of any kind of profitable work and dangerous to himself and others.

(7) Permanent and serious injuries to the central nervous system [as inflammation or softening of the brain], necessitating isolation or causing profound and irreparable disturbance of the most necessary functions of organic and social life.

(8) Loss of both legs by disarticulation or by amputation.

(9) Loss of two members, upper and lower, on the same side [disarticulation or amputation of the arm and of the leg].

(10) Loss of an arm and of a leg not on the same side [disarticulation or amputation of the arm and of the leg].

(11) Total loss of one hand and two feet.

(12) Total loss of one hand and one foot.

(13) Total loss of all fingers on both hands; or, the total loss of the two thumbs and of seven or six other fingers.

(14) Total loss of one thumb and of eight fingers.

(15) Total loss of five fingers on one hand and of the first two on the other hand.

(16) Total loss of both feet.

(17) Cachexy and marasmus refusing cure.

(18) Pulmonary and extra-pulmonary disturbance of a tubercular nature; and all other permanent organic and functional infirmities and injuries serious to the point of producing absolute incapacity for profitable work.

TABLE A. EIGHTH CATEGORY

COMPRISING THE LOWEST DEGREE OF DISABLEMENT RECOGNIZED AS PENSIONABLE, BY LAW

(1) Organic and irreparable change of one eye, the other being sound, which reduces the accuracy of vision from one twelfth to one quarter of the normal.

(2) Organic and irreparable change of peripheric vision of one eye (the other eye having a normal central and peripheric vision), in the form of a concentric restriction in the field of vision to a degree leaving free only the central zone;... or else a defect of

such proportion as to occupy a half of the field of vision, or equivalent sector.

(3) Extensive scars on the face or elsewhere on the body which are painful, or which adhere or contract or are inclined to ulcerate, but which, in their gravity, are not to be classed with the infirmities named in the preceding categories.

(4) Mouth injuries which produce disturbances of mastication, of deglutition and of speech, together or separately, without reaching the degree of number 3 in the second category or of number 4 or number 5 of the third category.

(5) Complete anchylosis of articulation of the left hand.

(6) Total loss of three fingers of both hands, other than thumbs and forefingers.

(7) Total loss of a forefinger and of another finger of the same hand, exclusive of the thumb.

(8) Total loss of the left thumb.

(9) Loss of the last two phalanges of the forefinger and of the last two phalanges of the other fingers, all on the same hand exclusive of the thumb.

(10) Total loss of five or four toes of both feet, including one great toe; or of the last four toes on one foot.

(11) Total loss of six or five toes, from both feet, exclusive of great toes.

(12) Loss of one great toe, or of the nail phalange, in addition to the loss of the nail phalanges of eight or six other toes from both feet.

(13) Complete anchyloses of tibio-tarsica of one foot, without distortion and without noticeable disturbance to walking.

(14) Considerable shortening or contraction (not less than four centimetres) of a leg.

IV. INJURIES AND INFIRMITIES

WHICH GIVE ENTITLEMENT TO A LUMP SUM INDEMNITY SETTLED BY A SINGLE PAYMENT

TABLE B

(Article 13, 2nd paragraph)

(1) Organic and irreparable changes in both eyes which reduce the acuteness of vision from one quarter to two thirds of normal.

(2) Loss of one of the testes.

(3) Absolute, permanent, and unilateral deafness.

527

(4) Total loss of two of the last three fingers of one hand, or between the two hands.

(5) The permanent scar-contracted orifice of the exterior of the auditory channel, bilateral or unilateral, or the entire loss on one side or both sides, of the auricle with other permanent injuries... constituting a noticeable deformity.

(6) Total loss of a forefinger, accompanied or not by the loss of one of the last three fingers of the other hand.

(7) Loss of the last two phalanges of one of the forefingers and those of two other fingers, between the two hands, excluding those of the thumbs and of the other forefinger; or, the loss of the last two phalanges of the three last fingers of one hand, or of four between the two hands.

(8) Loss of the two last phalanges of the two forefingers.

(9) Loss of the nail phalange of the two thumbs.

(10) Loss of the nail phalange of one of the two thumbs, together with the nail phalange of another finger.

(11) Loss of the nail phalange of six or five fingers, between the two hands, exclusive of thumbs; or, of the nail phalange of four fingers, between the two hands, including one forefinger.

(12) Loss of a great toe and of the corresponding metatarsus.

(13) Loss of three or two toes of one or both feet, including a great toe (with the integrity of the corresponding metatarsus); or, the total loss of four toes excepting the great toes, between the two feet.

(14) Loss of the two great toes, accompanied, or not, by the nail phalange of two or of one single toe of one foot.

(15) Loss of one great toe, or of the nail phalanges of both great toes, together with the complete loss of the nail phalanges of another four or three toes between the two feet.

(16) Loss of the nail phalange of eight or seven toes, exclusive of great toes, between the two feet.

(17) Neurotics rebellious against treatment, whose infirmity is not sufficiently serious to come under the preceding categories.

	1	2	3	4	5	6	7	8
Lieutenant General	15,000	15,000	15,000	15,000	12,855	10,702	8,550	6,397
Major General	15,000	15,000	14,190	13,212	11,316	9,420	7,524	5,628
Brigadier General	15,000	12,900	12,064	11,227	9,615	8,002	6,390	4,777
Colonel	15,000	11,820	11,051	10,282	8,805	7,327	5,850	4,372
Lieutenant Colonel	14,070	11,064	10,342	9,621	8,238	6,855	5,472	4,089
Major	13,530	10,632	9,937	9,243	7,914	6,585	5,256	3,927
Captain	10,965	8,580	8,014	7,448	6,375	5,302	4,230	3,157
Lieutenant	8,805	6,852	6,394	5,935	5,079	4,222	3,366	2,509
2nd Lieutenant	7,725	5,988	5,584	5,180	4,431	3,682	2,934	2,185

[1] *Direct* Ordinary Pension is that pension granted to the Combatant himself, as distinguished from the Indirect Pension, granted to his dependant on his death.

Privileged Pension is a pension granted on account of injuries received *within* the Zone of Combat.

TABLE C. DIRECT PRIVILEGED WAR-PENSIONS (*continued*)

(Article 15, 1st paragraph)

Ranks in the Royal Army	Pensions by Category of Disablement (Annual award in lire)							
	1	2	3	4	5	6	7	8
Battalion Adjutant, Marshal & Master of Arms, Pilot of 1st & 2nd class and other military of equal rank..	6,180	4,560	4,190	3,870	3,600	3,180	2,510	1,840
Chief Quarter-Master, Q-M, Sergeant-Major, Sergeant, Non-Com. Officer of the RR.CC, Vice N.CO., 2nd Pilot & other military of equal rank..	4,980	3,960	3,790	3,470	2,950	2,430	1,910	1,440
Chief Corporal, Corporal & Carabiniere, sub-Pilots and other Military of equal rank..	4,560	3,264	3,000	2,736	2,328	1,920	1,512	1,104
...Privates & Cadet Carabiniere, Seamen of super grade, ordinary Seamen of 1st & 2nd class..	4,080	2,880	2,640	2,400	2,040	1,680	1,320	960

For service-acquired disablements duly established before July 1, 1923, the pension or temporary allowance is awarded as follows:

For Lieutenant General assigned to class 6, 7, and 8, L.10,930, 8,810, 6,490.
For Major General assigned to class 5, 6, 7, and 8, L.11,600, 9,680, 7,710, 5,740.
For Brigadier General assigned to class 3, 4, 5, 6, 7, 8, L.12,490, 11,570, 9,900, 8,230, 6,560, 4,890.
For Colonel assigned to class 3, 4, 5, 6, 7, 8, L.11,490, 10,620, 9,100, 7,530, 6,010, 4,490.
For Captain assigned to class 8, L.3,240.
For Sub-Lieutenant assigned to class 7 and 8, L.3,110, L.2,290.

VI. TABLE D. DIRECT ¹ ORDINARY WAR–PENSIONS

SERVICE-INCURRED DISABLEMENTS SUSTAINED OUTSIDE COMBAT ZONE

(Article 15, 2nd paragraph)

RANKS IN THE ROYAL ARMY	PENSIONS BY CATEGORY OF DISABLEMENT (ANNUAL AWARD IN LIRE)							
	1	2	3	4	5	6	7	8
Lieutenant General........	15,000	15,000	15,000	14,647	12,555	10,462	8,370	6,277
Major General........	15,000	14,688	13,770	12,852	11,016	9,180	7,344	5,508
Brigadier General........	15,000	12,420	11,644	10,867	9,315	7,762	6,210	4,657
Colonel........	14,175	11,340	10,631	9,922	8,505	7,087	5,670	4,252
Lieutenant Colonel........	13,230	10,584	9,922	9,261	7,938	6,615	5,292	3,969
Major........	12,690	10,152	9,517	8,883	7,614	6,345	5,076	3,807
Captain........	10,125	8,100	7,594	7,088	6,075	5,062	4,050	3,037
Lieutenant........	7,965	6,372	5,974	5,575	4,779	3,982	3,186	2,389
2nd Lieutenant........	6,885	5,508	5,164	4,820	4,131	3,442	2,754	2,065

¹ *Direct* Ordinary Pension is that pension granted to the combatant himself.

TABLE D. DIRECT ORDINARY WAR-PENSIONS (*continued*)

SERVICE-INCURRED DISABLEMENTS SUSTAINED OUTSIDE COMBAT ZONE

(Article 15, 2nd paragraph)

RANKS IN THE ROYAL ARMY	PENSIONS BY CATEGORY OF DISABLEMENT (ANNUAL AWARD IN LIRE)							
	1	2	3	4	5	6	7	8
Battalion Adjutant, Marshal & Master of Arms, Pilot of 1st & 2nd Class and other military of equal rank....	5,340	4,080	3,770	3,510	3,300	2,940	2,330	1,720
Chief Quarter-Master, Q-M, Sergeant-Major, Sergeant, N.C.O. of the RR.CC, Vice-N.C.O. of the RR.CC, 2nd Pilot and other military of equal rank..........	4,140	3,480	3,370	3,110	2,650	2,190	1,730	1,320
Chief Corporal, Corporal & Carabiniere, sub-Pilots & other military of equal rank................	3,720	2,784	2,580	2,376	2,028	1,680	1,332	984
...Privates & Cadet Carabiniere, Seamen of super grade, ordinary Seamen of 1st & 2nd Class........	3,240	2,400	2,220	2,040	1,740	1,440	1,140	840

For service-incurred disablements duly established before July 1, 1923, the pension or temporary allowance is awarded as follows:

For Lieutenant General assigned to class 6, 7, and 8, L.10,690, 8,630, 6,370.
For Major General assigned to class 5, 6, 7, and 8, L.11,300, 9,440, 7,530, 5,620.
For Brigadier General assigned to class 3, 4, 5, 6, 7, 8, L.12,070, 11,210, 9,100, 7,930, 6,380, 4,770.
For Colonel assigned to class 3, 4, 5, 6, 7, 8, L.11,070, 10,260, 8,880, 7,290, 5,830, 4,370.
For Captain assigned to class 8, L.3,120.
For 2nd Lieutenant assigned to class 7, 8, L.2,930, 2,170.

ITALIAN APPENDIX

VII. TABLE E. ALLOWANCES FOR SUPER-INVALIDITY

(Article 17, 1st paragraph)

A

(1) Complete loss of both hands and both feet.
(2) Organic and irreparable change in both eyes, which has produced complete bilateral blindness, and which is accompanied by another infirmity attributable to one of the first five categories of Table A.
(3) Injuries to the central nervous system (brain and spine) producing total paralysis of both legs and the paralysis of the bladder and of the rectum (*paraplegici retto-vescicali*).

Annually, L. 14,400.

B

(1) Organic and irreparable change of both eyes, which has produced absolute and permanent bilateral blindness.
(2) Permanent and incurable change in mental faculties causing profound disturbances of the organic and social life, necessitating confinement in an insane asylum or similar institution.
(3) Serious and permanent injuries of the central nervous system (brain and spine) necessitating isolation or causing profound and irreparable disturbance to the organic and social life.
(4) Tuberculosis producing absolute and permanent incapacity for any kind of physical activity, and necessitating continuous or almost continuous confinement to bed.

Annually, L.12,000.

C

(1) The loss of two hands and one foot.
(2) Loss of both arms, of which one is amputated at the upper third, and the other above the hand.
(3) Amputation at the joint of both thighs; or amputation in the upper third, making it impossible to apply any prosthesis.

Annually, L.9,600.

D

(1) Loss of both hands.
(2) Loss of both legs, one in the upper third of the thigh, the other in the lower third.

Annually, L.8,400.

ITALIAN APPENDIX

E

(1) Organic and irreparable change of both eyes with such a reduction of vision as barely to permit the counting of the fingers at the distance of ordinary close vision.

(2) Loss of both legs in the lower third of the thigh.

(3) Loss of an arm and of a leg in the upper third respectively of the arm and of the thigh.

(4) Loss of ten or nine fingers, thumbs included.

Annually, L.7,200.

F

(1) Total loss of one hand and of both feet.

(2) Loss of two limbs, one upper, one lower. Of these one limb, if an arm, amputated in the upper third; or, if a leg, amputated in the upper third of the thigh. The other limb, if an arm, amputated in the middle third of the forearm; if a leg, amputated below the knee.

(3) Change in mental faculties causing disturbance of the organic and social life.

(4) Tuberculous or other infirmity of such seriousness as to involve absolute and permanent incapacity for any physical activity whatsoever, though not necessitating a continuous or almost continuous confinement to bed.

Annually, L.4,800.

G

(1) Tuberculosis so advanced as to produce absolute incapacity for any profitable work.

Annually, L.2,100.

ITALIAN APPENDIX

VIII. TABLE F. SUPPLEMENTARY ALLOWANCE FOR MULTIPLE DISABILITIES

(Article 17, 2nd paragraph)

	Annual Allowance Lire
For two Heavy-Disablements, as named in Table E	3,000
For a second disablement of the first category of Table A	2,000
second	1,200
third	1,000
fourth	800
fifth	600
sixth	500
seventh	400
eighth	300

IX. TABLE G. INDIRECT [1] PRIVILEGED WAR–PENSIONS

GRANTED TO WIDOWS WITHOUT CHILDREN, TO PARENTS AND TO COLLATERALS OF SOLDIERS WHO DIED FROM WOUNDS RECEIVED IN THE COMBAT ZONE

(Article 23, 1st paragraph)

Ranks in the Royal Army	Lire
Lieutenant General	7,155
Major General	6,300
Brigadier General	5,355
Colonel	4,905
Lieutenant Colonel	4,590
Major	4,410
Captain	3,555
Lieutenant	2,835
2nd Lieutenant	2,475
Battalion Adjutant, Marshal and Master of Arms, Pilot of 1st and 2nd Class and other military of equal rank	1,860

[1] The *Indirect* Pension is that pension granted on behalf of the combatant to his dependants.

535

ITALIAN APPENDIX

Ranks in the Royal Army	Lire

Chief Quarter-Master, Quarter-Master, Sergeant-Major, Sergeant, Non-Commissioned Officers of the RR.CC, Vice N–C.O. of the RR.CC., 2nd Pilot and other military of equal rank... 1,480

Chief Corporal,... Corporal and Carabiniere, sub-Pilots, and other military of equal rank............................. 1,200

...Privates and Cadet Carabiniere, Seamen of super grade ordinary Seamen of 1st and 2nd Class................... 990

X. TABLE H. INDIRECT ORDINARY WAR-PENSIONS

GRANTED TO WIDOWS WITHOUT CHILDREN, TO PARENTS AND COLLATERALS OF SOLDIERS WHO DIED FROM WOUNDS RECEIVED OUTSIDE THE COMBAT ZONE

(Article 23, paragraph 2)

Ranks in the Royal Army	Lire
Lieutenant General	6,975
Major General	6,120
Brigadier General	5,175
Colonel	4,725
Lieutenant Colonel	4,410
Major	4,230
Captain	3,375
Lieutenant	2,655
2nd Lieutenant	2,295

Battalion Adjutant, Marshal and Master of Arms, Pilot of 1st and 2nd Class, and other Military of equal rank.......... 1,680

Chief Quarter-Master, Quarter-Master, Sergeant-Major, Sergeant, Non-Commissioned Officers of the RR.CC, Vice N–C.O. of the RR.CC, 2nd Pilot, and other Military of equal rank... 1,300

Chief Corporal,... Corporal and Carabiniere, sub-Pilots, and other Military of equal rank............................. 1,020

... Privates and Cadet Carabiniere, Seamen of higher rating, and ordinary Seamen of 1st and 2nd Class................... 810

ITALIAN APPENDIX

XI. TABLE I. INDIRECT PRIVILEGED WAR-PENSIONS [1]

(Article 26)

Ranks in the Royal Army	Lire
Battalion Adjutant, Marshal and Master of Arms, Pilot of 1st and 2nd Class, and other Military of equal rank	2,060
Chief Quarter-Master, Quarter-Master, Sergeant-Major, Sergeant, Non-Commissioned Officers of the RR.CC, Vice N–C.O. of the RR.CC, 2nd Pilot, and other Military of equal rank	1,860
Chief Corporal,... Corporals and Carabiniere, sub-Pilots, and other Military of equal rank	1,800
... Privates and Carabiniere Cadets, Seamen of higher rating and ordinary Seamen of 1st and 2nd Class	1,560

[1] Granted to dependants of soldiers dead from wounds, injuries, or infirmities sustained or contracted *within* the Zone of Combat; such dependants being the widow with dependent children, or, incapacitated for work; or parents and collaterals incapacitated for work.

XII. TABLE L. INDIRECT ORDINARY WAR-PENSIONS

GRANTED TO CHILDREN

(Article 26)

Ranks in the Royal Army	Lire
Battalion Adjutant, Marshal and Master of Arms, Pilot of 1st and 2nd Class, and other Military of equal rank	1,880
Chief Quarter-Master, Quarter-Master, Sergeant-Major, Sergeant, Non-Commissioned Officers of the RR.CC, Vice N–C.O. of the RR.CC, 2nd Pilot, and other Military of equal rank	1,680
Chief Corporal... Corporals and Carabiniere, sub-Pilots, and other Military of equal rank	1,620
... Privates and Carabiniere Cadets, Seamen of higher rating and ordinary Seamen of 1st and 2nd Class	1,380

[1] Granted to dependants of soldiers dead from wounds, injuries, or infirmities sustained or contracted *outside* the Zone of Combat; such dependants being the widow with dependent children, or, incapacitated for work; or parents and collaterals incapacitated for work.

ITALIAN APPENDIX

XIII. THE FASCIST GOVERNMENT'S ANTI-TUBERCULOSIS CAMPAIGN

In 1926, Italy's death-rate from tuberculosis was 14.6 to each thousand inhabitants. In 1927, Il Duce declared war to the finish against the White Death. By 1930, the rate had already fallen about 25 per cent.

Il Duce's campaign, like all his campaigns, was thought through to its end before it opened. Its first step was the enactment of two laws — that of June 23, 1927 (n. 1276), creating the 'Provincial Anti-Tuberculosis Societies'; that of October 27, 1927 (n. 2055), creating the 'National Fund for Social Insurance.'

The second law set up compulsory anti-tuberculosis insurance for all labourers and employees whose wage is less than 800 lire a month. Half the premium is paid by the insured, half by his employer. The man who has paid a premium for six months or longer is entitled to free care for himself or for any member of his family, if stricken by the disease, without time limit.

This measure almost at once became popular, particularly amongst industrial workers.

To meet the immediate necessity born of the law, and to do it without handicap of old methods, a set of temporary sanatoria was built. These have now given or are giving place to permanent structure, some on the plains, some in the high mountains, as follows: eleven sanatoria finished, thirty-one in construction, seven in project. Ten thousand beds are now ready, twenty-two thousand will be available when the scheme is complete.

Il Duce's plan rested on the fact that tuberculosis is most easily cured in its early and less easily recognizable stages. Therefore he must have an army of specialists capable of identifying and dealing with the disease; to produce which he is building in Rome a large research institute, with every adjunct of laboratories and hospitals.

Meantime, the work of finding out the sick, all over the country, is carried on by the Provincial Anti-Tuberculosis Societies (created by the Law of June 23, 1927, above mentioned) working in conjunction with the doctors. As identified, sufferers are at once removed to special local hospitals, built for their immediate shelter, where they remain briefly until it is determined which of the great main Sanatoria will best suit their case, or until they are in condition to travel. If the case is arrested, through treatment in the major Sanatorium, the man is then sent to a Post-Sanatorium Colony, where his physical resistance to work is tested. Not until he has there proved his ability to work six consecutive hours without producing fever is he allowed to return to his family and a social life. With a view to avoiding friction with the general labour market, production in the Post-Sanatorium Colonies is confined to articles used in the various Sanatoria.

All costs, aside from the Insurance receipts, are borne by the Fascist Government, and the control rests absolutely in Il Duce's hands.

VI
BRITISH APPENDIX

I. ROYAL WARRANT OF 6TH DECEMBER, 1919

PART III

PRE-WAR EARNINGS

[Alternative Pension]

24. (6) (*a*) 'Pre-war earnings' means, in the case of a man who was in employment under a contract of service, the average weekly earnings during the twelve months immediately preceding the outbreak of the war. Average weekly earnings shall be computed generally in accordance with the provisions of the Workmen's Compensation Act, 1906: Provided that where in the course of such twelve months there was a change in the man's rate of remuneration, and such change was not of a temporary but of a reasonably permanent nature, then the average weekly earnings shall be calculated on the man's earnings during the period since such change in his remuneration, or since the last of such changes if there were more than one. In the case of a man in a trade, business, or profession the average profits of the last three years preceding the commencement of the war shall be taken, or of such lesser period as he engaged therein.

(*b*) In the calculation of the pension payable to or on account of a (*man*) who at the commencement of the war was serving and had served not less than one year as an apprentice in any recognised trade, the standard rate of wages of that trade in the district at the time of the commencement of the war may be substituted for pre-war earnings, provided enlistment took place before the age of 26, and the man is by reason of his disablement incapable of completing or has completed his apprenticeship.

(c) In computing the average weekly earnings or average profits of a man or the standard rate of wages of his trade, as the case may be, an addition of 60 per cent may be made to any such earnings, profits, or rate of wages.

(d) In the calculation of the pension payable to or on account of a (*man*) who, for the purpose of qualifying for any profession or employment, had, after the age of 16, attended regularly any school, college, university, or hospital, or had been articled in accordance with the recognised practice of any profession an amount equivalent to what would have been the (*man's*) disablement pension for the highest degree of disablement, with an addition of 8*s*. for each completed year of such attendance or 'articles' before the age of 23, may be substituted for pre-war earnings, up to a maximum of 80*s*. a week: provided enlistment took place before the age of 26 and the man is by reason of his disablement incapable of qualifying or has qualified for such profession or employment.

BRITISH APPENDIX

II. SOLDIERS AND AIRMEN

Pensions that may be Granted for Specific Injuries

[Below rank of officer]

Degree of Disablement	Specific Injury	Proportion Corresponding to Degree of Disablement Per cent	Disablement Pensions according to Rank.	
			From N.C. Officer to Warrant Officer s. d. s. d.	Private, etc. s. d.
I	Loss of two or more limbs Loss of an arm and an eye Loss of a leg and an eye Loss of both hands or of all fingers and thumbs Loss of both feet Loss of a hand and a foot Total loss of sight Total paralysis Lunacy Wounds, injuries, or disease resulting in disabled man being permanently bedridden Wounds of or injuries to internal, thoracic, or abdominal organs, involving total permanent disabling effects Wounds of or injuries to head or brain involving total permanent disabling effects, or Jacksonian epilepsy Very severe facial disfigurement Advanced cases of incurable disease	100	43 4 to 60 0	40 0

Note. [In the case of left-handed men, certified to be such, the compensation in respect of the left arm, hand, etc., will be the same as for a right arm, hand, etc., and *vice versa*.]

Compiled from *Notes on War Pensions*, pp. 75–77.

BRITISH APPENDIX

Pensions that may be Granted for Specific Injuries
(continued)

Degree of Disablement	Specific Injury	Proportion Corresponding to Degree of Disablement Per cent	Disablement Pensions according to Rank.	
			From N.C. Officer to Warrant Officer s. d. s. d.	Private, etc. s. d.
2	Amputation of right arm through shoulder	90	39 0 to 54 0	36 0
3	Amputation of leg at hip or below hip with stump not exceeding 5 inches in length measured from tip of great trochanter; of right arm below shoulder with stump not exceeding 6 inches measured from tip of acromion; or of left arm through shoulder Severe facial disfigurement Total loss of speech Lisfranc operation, both feet	80	34 8 to 48 0	32 0
4	Amputation of leg below hip with stump exceeding 5 inches in length, measured from tip of great trochanter, but not below middle thigh; of left arm below shoulder with stump not exceeding 6 inches measured from tip of acromion; or of right arm below shoulder with stump exceeding 6 inches measured from tip of acromion, through elbow; or below elbow with stump not exceeding 5 inches measured from tip of olecranon			
	Total deafness	70	30 4 to 42 0	28 0

BRITISH APPENDIX

PENSIONS THAT MAY BE GRANTED FOR SPECIFIC INJURIES
(continued)

Degree of Disablement	Specific Injury	Proportion Corresponding to Degree of Disablement Per cent	Disablement Pensions according to Rank From N.C. Officer to Warrant Officer s. d. s. d.	Private, etc. s. d.
5	Amputation of leg below middle thigh through knee, or below knee with stump not exceeding 4 inches; of left arm below shoulder with stump exceeding 6 inches measured from tip of acromion, through elbow, or below elbow with stump not exceeding 5 inches measured from tip of olecranon; or of right arm below elbow with stump exceeding 5 inches measured from tip of olecranon	60	26 0 to 36 0	24 0
6	Amputation of leg below knee with stump exceeding 4 inches; or of left arm below elbow with stump exceeding 5 inches measured from tip of olecranon Loss of vision of one eye	50	21 8 to 30 0	20 0
7	Loss of thumb or of four fingers of right hand Lisfranc operation, one foot Loss of all toes of both feet above knuckle	40	17 4 to 24 0	16 0
8	Loss of thumb or of four fingers of left hand, or of three fingers of right hand	30	13 0 to 18 0	12 0
9	Loss of two fingers of either hand Loss of all toes of one foot above knuckle Loss of all toes of both feet at or below knuckle	20	8 8 to 12 0	8 0

BRITISH APPENDIX

III. TABLE B

(Regulation 8 (2) (A))

Part I — Petty Officers and Seamen in the Navy; Warrant Officers, Class II, and Non-commissioned Officers and Men of the Marines; Warrant and Non-commissioned Officers and Men in the Army and Air Force.

This scale is to be applied to cases only in which the disability has been assessed at less than 20 per cent and the disability is permanent and has reached its final and stationary condition.

(1) Loss of terminal phalanx of left thumb, £75.

(2) Loss of finger	Loss of whole finger	Loss of two phalanges	Loss of one phalanx	Loss of tip, including nail, but not bone
	£	£	£	£
Index finger of right hand.......	75	60	50	30
Index finger of left hand.........	50	40	30	25
Middle finger of either hand.....	40	30	25	20
Ring or little finger............	25	20	15	10

(3) Loss of toe	Loss of whole toe	Loss of one joint of toe
	£	£ s.
Great toe of either foot..............	50	20 0
One other toe of either foot..........	20	10 0
Two toes, excluding great toe........	30	15 0
Three toes, excluding great toe.......	35	17 10
Four toes, excluding great toe.......	50	20 0

(4) Loss of ear (hearing not affected), £40.
(5) Fixed finger unable to be flexed or extended. Scale as under (2) for loss of finger of part of finger affected.

Notes on War Pensions, pp. 100–01.

BRITISH APPENDIX

IV. NAVY, ARMY, AIR FORCE AND MARINES

RETURN OF OFFICERS AND OTHER RANKS [I.E. NON-COMS.
AND PRIVATES] PENSIONED FOR DISABILITY FROM THE
BEGINNING OF THE GREAT WAR TO 31ST MARCH, 1932, SO
FAR AS CLASSIFIED ACCORDING TO NATURE OF DISABILITY

Disability	Number	Percentage of Gross Total
Eyesight cases..............................	31,592	2.4
Wounds and injuries to legs (necessitating amputation).....................................	24,357	1.8
Wounds and injuries to arms (necessitating amputation).....................................	10,947	0.8
Wounds and injuries to legs (not necessitating amputation).....................................	171,433	12.8
Wounds and injuries to arms (not necessitating amputation).....................................	99,056	7.4
Wounds and injuries to hands (not necessitating amputation of whole hand)......................	52,803	4.0
Wounds and injuries to head...................	46,228	3.5
Hernia..	20,596	1.5
Miscellaneous wounds and injuries..............	97,699	7.3
Chest complaints, including bronchitis, tuberculosis	121,800	9.1
Rheumatism...................................	84,734	6.3
Heart disease.................................	118,789	8.9
Epilepsy......................................	8,408	0.6
Nervous diseases (including neurasthenia)........	74,898	5.6
Insanity......................................	9,595	0.7
Deafness......................................	33,822	2.5
Frostbite (including cases of amputation of feet and legs)......................................	6,663	0.5
Miscellaneous diseases:		
Nephritis and Bright's disease...............		
Debility.................................		
Ulcer of stomach..........................		
Varicocele................................		
Enteric and malaria........................	325,277	24.3
Spinal...................................		
Appendicitis..............................		
Gas poisoning.............................		
Other diseases............................		
Total.................................	1,338,697	100.0

Fifteenth Annual Report, Ministry of Pensions, p. 8.

BRITISH APPENDIX

V. EXTENT OF HOSPITAL IN-PATIENT ACCOMMODATION PROVIDED BY THE MINISTRY OF PENSIONS, 1919–1929

Year ending 31st March	Hospitals directly controlled by the Ministry of Pensions		Hospitals reserving beds for the Ministry of Pensions		Total no. of beds available
	No.	Beds	No.	Beds	
1919.....	9	374	32	1,786	2,160
1920.....	46	9,845	26	2,461	12,306
1921.....	67	13,225	46	5,378	18,603
1922.....	55	13,396	40	2,630	16,026
1923.....	37	10,047	36	2,672	12,719
1924.....	33	7,843	46	3,024	10,867
1925.....	29	6,919	40	2,566	9,485
1926.....	22	5,038	33	2,715	7,753
1927.....	19	4,138	27	2,497	6,635
1928.....	19	3,686	25	2,363	6,049
1929.....	17	3,093	22	2,005	5,098
1930.....	16	2,775	21	1,663	4,438
1931.....	14	2,349	19	1,592	3,941
1932.....	11	1,876	20	1,706	3,582

Casualties Dealt with by the Ministry of Pensions, p. 314.

VI. NEUROSIS AND PSYCHOSIS

As Handled by the Ministry of Pensions

Of this part of the Ministry work, the following excerpts are drawn from the *Medical History of the War-Casualties and Medical Statistics* (p. 341): 'The diagnosis and treatment of cases of neurosis and psychosis needed much time, skill and patience. In their more acute forms these conditions presented many novel features and amidst the various theories and therapeutic suggestions it was difficult at the outset to decide on the most effective form of treatment. Indeed treatment had often to be largely empirical. A relatively small group soon emerged, in which the existing neurosis was shown to be but a reflection from a generalised or local organic condition, such as heart disease or

548

a gunshot wound and for these the treatment was directed to the underlying organic cause.

'For most of the cases comprised in the general group "neurasthenia" it was clear that the prognosis and the nature of the treatment required would mainly depend on the inherent predisposition to neurosis, apart from the factor of war stress.

'In cases of true "war" neuroses — i.e., those manifested in men with a minimal predisposition — the symptoms rapidly disappeared on the cessation of exposure to war conditions. In cases of neurosis occurring in men with a fairly well-marked predisposition, the subsequent progress depended largely on the environment and conditions to which the men were afterwards subjected. If the circumstances were favourable, and the men were able to obtain suitable employment, they lost all their symptoms; but if the circumstances were not favourable the condition was perpetuated and the men remained amongst those for whom the Ministry had to provide facilities for special treatment. In the more severe cases of neurosis, occurring in men with a pronounced predisposition, improvement only occurred when the environment was made exceptionally favourable. For the most part these men could not in any case have made successful adaptation to the conditions of post-War life, and there can be little doubt that, even if there had been no war, these men would sooner or later, and from one cause or another, have been likely to break down under the stress of everyday life.[1]

In the Ministry's early scheme for the care of mental cases, out-patient clinics played a considerable part. The first purpose of the clinic was to conduct examinations for determination of treatment; but the treatment itself — whether by psychotherapy or by gymnasium work, was often given on the spot. This proved specially advantageous because the patient, if in employment, could pursue his treatment while holding his job; and regularly normal work, taken together with the clinic's care, tended to restore the wavering mind. As psychotherapy wore away its own usefulness, curing those susceptible to its benefits, out-patient clinics gradually disappeared.

[1] For the German theory, *see ante*, p. 287.

BRITISH APPENDIX

Meantime the Ministry's own neurological hospitals were placing more and more confidence in occupational therapy — keeping men steadily employed at some interesting work, to take their attention from themselves and to encourage regrowth of concentration, application and self-reliance. But a margin had always to be left for men subject to sudden breakdowns of self-control; for relapses into violence, sometimes suicidal, sometimes homicidal; for erratic or associal outbursts, in which, if the patient could be quickly removed to a hospital specially adapted to such extreme cases, certification of lunacy might still be escaped. For neurological patients the Ministry has still its special institutions — one, with approximately 350 beds, for the less severe cases, and one, with nearly 300 beds, for cases more severe — and in this way the Ministry now cares for all non-certified war pensioned neurasthenic men. Its remaining epileptic patients, numbering some 250, are distributed among three institutions.[1]

VII. THE NATIONAL INSURANCE SCHEME OF HEALTH AND UNEMPLOYMENT

I

NATIONAL HEALTH INSURANCE

The National Health Insurance scheme, which is administered by the Ministry of Labour, was adapted by Mr. Lloyd George from the German model, was enacted as law on December 16, 1911 and later amended. Popularized under the motto — 'Nine-pence for Four-pence,' it works today as follows:

Every employer, weekly, for each person in his employ, affixes to that person's insurance card a stamp of a certain value, the stamp being paid for in part by the employer, in part by the employee. This is obligatory for all employees in manual work and for everyone drawing up to £250 a year in other kinds of employment. The total value of the stamp, for a man, is 1s. 6d.; for a woman 1s. 1d. Out of this, 9d. in the case of the man, 8½d. in the case of the woman, is allotted to health insurance, the rest

[1] *Medical History of the War — Casualties and Medical Statistics*, pp. 341-43.

going toward old age, widows' and orphans' pensions. Of the health insurance allotment, the male employee pays 4½d., the woman 4d., which sum the employer may deduct from wages.

The money brought in by the sale of stamps is paid into a central Health Insurance Fund under the control of the Ministry of Health and this Fund is drawn upon by various Approved Societies, to one or another of which the employee belongs. Each Society establishes its credit in the Fund by surrendering to the Ministry of Health at the end of each half-year, stamped contribution cards collected from its members. Upon this credit it draws for the payment of statutory benefits and for expenses of administration. One-seventh of the cost of such benefits in the case of men, and one-fifth in the case of women, is met by the National Exchequer.

If the person thus insured falls ill, he turns to his Approved Society and 'claims sickness benefit.' If his illness lasts more than twenty-six weeks, he then claims 'disablement benefit.' Every insured person is free to choose his doctor from a list of 'panel doctors' in his neighbourhood; the panel doctor takes care of the patient and is paid, by the Society, a certain fixed annual sum for every insured person on his list. Every qualified medical practitioner is entitled to be enrolled as a panel doctor.

During the War, the State kept up the soldier's health insurance, paying for each man's stamps. And today, if the insured ex-service man falls ill of a malady not due to War service and therefore not accepted for care by the Ministry of Pensions, he, in company with every other citizen so insured, civilian and ex-service alike, receives free medical treatment from the Ministry of Health.

II

National Unemployment Insurance

This scheme is administered by the Ministry of Labour. Generally speaking it covers the same classes of workers as those served by the Health Insurance, the main exceptions being persons employed in agriculture and in domestic service. The Contributor's Unemployment Insurance card is stamped each week by the employer, with stamps of the value of 1s. 8d. and 1s. 6d.

respectively, in the case of men and women over 21. The employer deducts half the cost of the stamp from the employee's wages and the National Exchequer pays into the Unemployment Fund an amount equal to the worker's contribution. The scheme is compulsory on persons within its scope and there is no provision for voluntary contribution. The first condition for the receipt of benefit is that the contributor must have paid thirty weekly contributions, during the previous two years. If however, he is an ex-service man in receipt of disability pension, he has only to show payment of ten weekly contributions during the two year period, or even during four years, if illness has occasioned his failure to meet this regular condition. The insured man, if he loses his job, can then enjoy unemployment benefit for 156 days in the benefit year, provided the other conditions are satisfied and though he be a disabled ex-service man drawing a useful pension, or though he inherit a million gold doubloons from his uncle, his personal resources in no wise effect his receipt of his unemployment insurance money. The weekly rates of benefit for adults are, men 15s. 3d., and women 13s. 6d. In certain circumstances, additional allowances are payable in respect of dependants.

After 156 days, if he is still unemployed and in need of relief he can turn to the second part of the Labour Ministry's scheme, and apply for 'Transitional Payments.'

Eligibility to this benefit is established by having at any time paid thirty contributions to the Unemployment Insurance scheme; or, by having paid eight contributions within the last two years. This condition is waived for the disabled ex-service man who has been in receipt of war-pension for the two preceding years and who can show that his failure to meet the condition was due to war-disablement. The applicant must also show that he is normally employed and will normally seek to obtain his livelihood by means of insurable employment. But, in the matter of Transitional Payments, all the applicant's personal and household resources, including one-half of the war-disabled pension, come under review, in what is known as 'the Needs Test.'

The amount of the Transitional Payments is assessed in each individual case by the Public Assistance Committee of the elected

County Council or County Borough Council. And these committees give particular consideration to the disabled ex-service man, weighing against his pension any special expense to which his disability puts him. In any event one-half of his disability pension must be completely ignored by the committee.

Finally, the point may come at which the man on transitional payments is considered no longer eligible to receive that aid — usually because he is no longer in the insurance field — no longer likely, whether now or later, to obtain insurable employment. And here, at the door of this third stage, stands 'Public Assistance' — formerly called Poor Law Relief — which so operates that no one in the United Kingdom need starve or go without necessary lodging and clothes. In proof of which, if it can be shown that a man has died of want after having stated his need to the local relief official, the law lays the full guilt of his death upon that official's head. With these and other social provisions of Government, such as the Old Age Pension, such as the Widows' and Orphans' Contributory Pensions, caring for ordinary emergencies; and with a great number of schemes semi-public or private caring for cases outside the law, it has been the easier for the Ministry of Pensions to stick to its proper charges, the actually War-disabled.

BRITISH APPENDIX
VIII. MINISTERS OF PENSIONS

The Rt. Hon. G. N. Barnes, M. P.   (Labour)
February 15, 1917, to August 13, 1917.

The Rt. Hon. John Hodge, M.P.,   (Labour)
August 20, 1917, to January, 1919.

The Rt. Hon. Sir Laming Worthington Evans,
Bt., C.B.E., M.P.,   (Conservative)
January 16, 1919, to March 25, 1920.

The Rt. Hon. Ian Macpherson, K.C., M.P.,   (Liberal)
April 3, 1920, to October 24, 1922.

Major The Rt. Hon. G. C. Tryon, M.P.,   (Conservative)
November 2, 1922, to January 23, 1924.

The Rt. Hon. F. O. Roberts, M. P.,   (Labour)
January 24, 1924, to November 6, 1924.

Major The Rt. Hon. G. C. Tryon, M.P.,   (Conservative)
November 13, 1924, to June 4, 1929.

The Rt. Hon. F. O. Roberts, J. P., M.P.,   (Labour)
June 10, 1929, to August 26, 1931.

Major The Rt. Hon. G. C. Tryon, M. P.,   (Conservative)
September 4, 1931, to date.

IX. EXPENDITURE OF MINISTRY OF PENSIONS, 1917-1933

1 Year ending 31st March	2 No. of disabled officers and men in receipt of pension	3 No. of pensions in payment to widows and dependants of deceased officers and men	4 Total No. of pensioners	5 Benefit Expenditure £	6 Cost of Administration £	7 Total net Expenditure ‡ £
1918	308,012	253,179	561,191	22,174,562	501,653	22,676,215
9	610,812	420,167	1,030,979	45,159,929	1,403,903	46,563,832
1920	1,151,799	562,291	1,714,090	94,041,436	4,879,227	98,919,663
1	1,198,262	544,241	1,742,503	100,085,631	6,280,869	106,365,500
2	923,180	538,230	1,461,410	89,780,657	5,524,100	95,304,757
3	752,430	528,030	1,280,460	75,885,092	4,241,602	80,126,694
4	673,275	517,685	1,190,960	68,648,303	3,461,387	72,109,690
5	560,575	509,985	1,070,560	66,431,200	2,995,456	69,426,656
6	536,710	498,240	1,034,950	64,399,242	2,396,246	66,795,488
7	516,000	482,120	998,120	61,263,055	1,854,407	63,117,462
8	514,565	469,315	983,880	58,236,564	1,507,748	59,744,312
9	503,250	453,700	956,950	55,400,486	1,289,864	56,690,350
1930	494,460	441,860	936,320	52,770,523	1,295,244	54,065,767
1	487,875	430,675	918,550	50,506,828	1,220,651	51,727,479
2	480,840	416,475	897,315	48,395,130	1,041,233	49,436,363
3	472,597 †	403,480 †	876,077	46,314,300	929,500	47,243,800 *
4 *	465,000	390,000	855,000	44,389,500	810,500	45,200,000

* Estimated.   † Provisional.

‡ In arriving at the figures of net expenditure the total appropriations-in-aid realized are set off against gross expenditure.

INDEX

INDEX

Administrator of Veterans' Affairs (United States), 469, 470

American Army in France, 4; composition of, 5; character of, 5–10; official name of, 7 *n*.

American Expeditionary Force (A.E.F.), official name of the Overseas Army, 7 *n*.; returns home, 9, 10, 53; demobilization of, 11; men of, after demobilization, 11–15, 53–57, 67, 68; becomes Bonus Army, 16; disliked officers, 68, 69; and the Legion, 471, 472

American Legion, 16, 64; attitude toward Army officers, 69; plans for organization of, 69; first National Convention (Nov. 11, 1919), 69, 70, 72; Constitution of, 70, 109, 124; National Legislative Committee (Washington Lobby), 70–72, 73, 81, 82; second National Convention (Sept. 1920), 71, 73–77, 79; National Executive Committee, 73; National Commander, 73, 158; demands cash tribute, 73, 78, 79; resentment felt in, at demand for bonus, 79–81; eligibility to, 88, 88 *n*.; publicity directed by, 88, 89; Americanization work stressed by, 88, 89; answer of Lobby to Secretary Mellon's letter on the Bonus, 89, 90; Lobby's diatribe against the office of the Secretary of War, 90; third Annual Convention, 90; diatribes of leaders of, 90–93; pushes Bonus Bill by mass meetings, 95; dwindling numbers of, 99; Lobby and 'Misconduct Clause,' 104, 105; demands of, for disabled ex-service officers, 109; glories in its victories, 111; Lobby stigmatizes needs clause as pauper clause, 112;

Lobby and Civil Service, 113–1 review of its performances, 124, 12 repudiates Disability Allowance Bi 138; its publicity on insurance, 14 its bond with the present-d; 'Lemons,' 154; further history of t Bonus and, 156–63; National Cor mander dictates to Senate and Hous 158; Detroit Convention of (Sep 1931), 159; the Virtue and the fau of, 179; Convention of 1931, 18 membership of, 187, 188; and t Economy Bill (1932), 188–92; Lobl rejects economy considerations, 19 its reception of Pres. Roosevel talk (March 5, 1933) and of tl Credit Act, 203–10; Chicago Co vention (1933), 211–18; the spii of its activity, America's deadlie enemy, 219; the Lobby's boast, 47 the curse rests not with, 472

American Legion Weekly, official she of Legion, 82, 88

American Regular Army, base-pay 49 *n*.

Americanism, 88, 90

Andrew, A. Piatt, quoted, 223

Appeal, channels of (United State 481, 488; (France), 497

Arditi, 302–04

Armistice, the, after, 9, 10, 53

Arosio, Milan, 319

Arrears Pension Act (United State 30–33, 36, 37, 39

Ascendants (forebears), 244, 245, 4 497

Ashtead Pottery, 395

Ashurst, Henry F., Senator, speaks Bonus, 93; speaks for Spanish-V Veterans, 120, 121

Associations, Italian, 317, 351

INDEX

INDEX

insurance schemes of health and unemployment, 550–53; Ministers of Pensions, 554; expenditure of Ministry of Pensions, 1917–33, 555

English, great national trait of, 381, 384, 388, 450

Eté, Bernard d', quoted, 226

European countries, the pension roll in, is an honour roll, 168. *See also* England; France; Germany; Italy

Evans, Henry Clay, Pension Commissioner, 22, 23

Evans, Sir Laming Worthington, Minister of Pensions, 386

Ex-Service Man's Land Settlement Scheme (England), 467

Ex-service men's benefits, expenditure on, in different countries, 128, 129

Ex-service officers, Legion demands for, 109–14

Ex-service organizations, European, 17

Fascism, growth of, 304–09; what it means, 350

Fascist Revolution, 309–14; tenth anniversary of, 351

Fascists, enter Rome, 312; become 'Volunteer Militia for National Safety,' 315

Federal Board for Vocational Education, 58; Director of, 64

Federal Soldiers' Homes, 146

Fish, Hamilton, Jr., Representative, on the Bonus, 160, 161

Fitzgerald, Mother, 7

Florence, Villa Demidoff, 319

Franc, value of, at outbreak of the War, 228 *n.*

France, treatment of War-disabled in, 129, 130, 135, 168; expenditure for World-War Ex-Service Men, 167, 194; number of disabled men, 167; her War dead, 223; her War-dependants, 223; her disabled, 223; the wreckage of her Front, 224, 225; edict of April 6, 1919, 225; pensions in, by Law of 1831, 228, 229; pension law of March 31, 1919 ('Great Pension

Law'), 230–39, 491–98; coloured troops, 231 *n.*; right of appeal, 232, 497; re-education, 235–37; students, 237; War-incurred injuries, 237; War-disabled ex-service men, 237, 238; hospitalization, 238, 239; widows of ex-soldiers, 240, 493, 494; *compagnes* (unmarried wives), 242, 243 (*see also* 230); War-orphans, 243, 244, 495, 496; illegitimate children, 244; forebears (*ascendants*), 244, 245, 496, 497; numbers of Great-War pensioners, 246, 247; changes in Pension Law, 247–49; *La Retraite du Combattant*, 250; character of Ministry of Pensions, 251; original concept of War-pension, 251, 252; the three 'National Offices,' 498, 499; Ministry of Pensions, 500; classification of pensioners, 501; rates of War-pensions for officers, 502; rates for private soldiers, 503–05; rates for soldiers' dependants, 506, 507

Fraser, Capt. Ian, quoted, 378, 398, 401

Frederick the Great, 284–86

French, the, their love for the family hearth, 226, 227

Gallipoli Peninsula, 357, 359

Garfield, James A., 33

German Revolution, 257–62

Germans, the sufferings of, 255, 256

Germany, sentiment toward pensions in, 130, 131, 168; hospitals, 144, 145; expenditure for World-War Ex-Service Men, 167, 194; number of disabled men, 167; suffering in, 255, 256; Revolution in, 257–59, 261, 262; Stahlhelm, 263–68; condition of, at end of War, 269; old pension law (1906–07), 270; new pension law (May, 1920), 270–81; hospitalization, 276; dependants, 279, 509–11; 'unmarried wife,' 279; Hindenburg Fund, 282–84; *Invalidenhaus*, 284–86; blinded soldiers and dog 'leaders,' 287–90; provision for review, 511, 512; compensation pension,

INDEX

before the War, 295; in the War, 295–303; the Arditi, 302–04; Fascist Revolution, 305–14; National Institutes, 316–22; House of the War-Blinded in Rome, 322–24; *Casa Madre dei Mutilati* ('Mother House'), 324, 325, 353; War-Pension Law (1923), 326–38; widows, 332; *campagnes*, 333; children, 333, 334; redemption of marshes, 339–48; grain production, 348; the soul of, 351–53; excerpts from the War-pension law of, 521–23; structure of the Fascist Government's scheme for the War-disabled, War-orphans, and Ex-service combatants, 524, 525; classification of disabilities establishing entitlement to life pension or renewable allowance, 525–27; injuries and infirmities entitling to lump sum indemnity, 527, 528; direct privileged War-pensions, 529, 530; direct ordinary War-pensions, 531, 532; allowances for superinvalidity, 533, 534; supplementary allowance for multiple disabilities, 535; indirect privileged War-pensions, 535–37; indirect ordinary War-pensions, 536, 537; anti-tuberculosis campaign, 538, 539

Jacob, Field Marshal Sir Claud, 380
'Jaic Ginger Cases,' 142 *n.*
Jamaica ginger, 142 *n.*
Jellicoe, Earl, and the British Legion, 379
Johnson, Royal C., Representative, 151 *n.*, 153, 164, 189
Junior Stahlhelm, 265–67

Karstedt, Dr., 283, 284
Kelham, Major, surgeon at Roehampton, 414, 416
Kerr, Lady Ann, 420
Kiel, mutiny at, 257
King's Fund, 396
King's Roll, 460
Kitchener, Lord, memorial of, 396

La Guardia, Fiorello H., Representative, on the Bonus, 161
League of Blinded Soldiers (Germany), 290, 291
'Legal presumption of origin,' 233
Lemon, George E., pension claims agent, 29–40
Les Invalides, 238, 286
Lest We Forget Association (England), 396
Liebnecht, Karl, 257
Lister, Corp. Thomas Frederick, 366
Littoria, 342, 344, 345 *n.*, 347, 348
Long, Huey P., Senator, on the Credit Act, 207
Lord Roberts Memorial Workshops, 395, 396
Lothian, Lord, 420
Ludendorff, Erich von, 300
Luxemburg, Rosa, 257

McAdoo, W. G., Secretary of the Treasury, on Judge Mack's pension system, 43, 99
McCall, John, of Tennessee, at Detroit Convention of Legion, 160
McDougall, Dr. J. B., Medical Director and Superintendent of Preston Hall Enterprise, 373–75
Mack, Judge Julian W., his pension system, 42–49
McKinley, William, his pension policy, 22, 23, 25
Magdeburg, 259, 261, 262
Malaria, control of, 343 *n.*
Marshes, Italian, conversion of, into healthful, productive land, 339–48
Maurice, Major-Gen. Sir Frederick, 363; President of British Legion, quoted, 366, 368, 378, 379
Mellon, Andrew W., Secretary of the Treasury, opposed payment of bonus, 85, 89; Legion's attacks on, 89–92; on the Bonus, 159
Mental defectives in the War, 60–62
Mexican War soldiers' widows, 175 *n.*
Ministry of Pensions (England), methods of, 382–90, 421–29; (France), 500

564

INDEX

INDEX

United Kingdom, expenditure for World-War Ex-Service men, 167, 168, 194; number of disabled men, 167; enlisted men of, 422, 423. *See also* England

United Services Fund (England), 369, 373, 396

United States, war declared by (1917), 5, 41

United States Public Health Hospitals, 59

United States Public Health Service, 58

United States Veterans' hospitals, 104

United States World War Army, size of, 41 *n.*|

'Unmarried wives,' 174 *n.*; French, 230, 242, 243; German, 279; Italian, 333; English, 445, 446, 453, 454

Varrier-Jones, Sir Pendrill, 372 *n.*

Venereal diseases, 103, 104, 120, 121, 201; French, Italian, and British procedure in regard to, 122, 123. *See also* Social disease

Versailles, Treaty of, 229, 292

'Veteran,' the title, 126

Veteran-marrying speculators, 444

'Veterans' Adjusted Compensation Bill,' 83. *See also* Bonus Bill

Veterans' Administration (United States), history and structure of, 479-81

Veterans' Administration Guardianship service, 179

Veterans' Administration Hospitals, 103, 143, 146, 480

Veterans' Administration's Medical Department, 179

Veterans' Bureau (United States), 479, 480

Vittorio Veneto, 300

Vocational rehabilitation, 165, 166. *See also* Vocational training

Vocational Rehabilitation Act, 106

Vocational training, 48, 58, 62-66, 176, 177; in England, 461-67

'Volunteer Militia for National Safety,' 315

Vulci, Marchesa Anna Guglielmi di, 323

Walsh, David I., Senator, in colloquy with Senator Cutting, 206

'War-disabled Comrades' and 'disabled War Comrades,' 192, 193

War-disabled veterans, without a lobby, 164; numbers, 165, 169, 170; payments to, 165-68; in danger of being considered pretenders, 169; dependants of, 170-75

War of 1812, pension legislation in connection with, 29, 30; ex-service men of, 30 *n.*

War Risk Insurance Act, 47, 50-53, 62, 66, 124, 148, 149, 151, 156, 165, 171, 177; amendments to 52, 98, 142

War Seals Flats, 395

War Service Canteens (England), 369

Ward and guardian, 178

Wards of the Nation, 243, 498

Warner, Adoniram J., Representative, on the *National Tribune*, 36, 37

Watson, Thomas E., Senator, on the Bonus Bill, 87

Weaver, Sir Lawrence, 395

Widow's preference, in Civil Service appointments, 177, 177 *n.*

Widows, of veterans of World War, 171-75; of Mexican War soldiers, 175 *n.*; in the 1933 Credit Bill, 202; of French ex-soldiers, 240, 493-94; German, 279, 509; Italian, 332, 333; English, 446-49

'Wilful-misconduct' clause. *See* 'Misconduct clause'

Williams, John Sharp, Senator, 94

Williams, Wally, of Maryland, at Detroit Convention of Legion, 160

Wilson, Woodrow, refuses to visit battle-fields, 13; private pension measures signed by, 26; opposed to preparation, 41; on Judge Mack's pension system, 43

Women, in the World War, 4-6

INDEX

Wood, Major-Gen. Leonard, at Convention of American Legion (Sept. 1920), 74–77, 79

Workmen and Soldiers' Councils, 257

World War, American Army in, 3–10

'World War Adjusted Compensation,' 95. *See also* Bonus Bill

World-War dead, mothers of, 170, 171; widows of, 171–75; children of, 176–82. *See also* England; France; Germany; Italy

World War veterans, record of Governmental favours to, 125, 126

World-War Veterans' Act, 99–108, 176 *n.*; Presumptive Clause, 101

Jun 14 '34	May 23 '34		
Jul 22 '34	May 22 '46		
Aug 27			
31 '34			
Nov 17 '34			
Dec 10 '34			
Feb 31 '35			
May 2 '35			
Jun 12 1936			
Jan 15			

Lightning Source UK Ltd.
Milton Keynes UK
UKHW021916180219
337529UK00011B/1117/P